# Business and Professional Women of Colonial America

## Also by Mary Ellen Snodgrass and from McFarland

*Ken Follett: A Literary Companion* (2025)

*Witch Trials: A Worldwide Chronology* (2024)

*Women Warriors in History: 1,622 Biographies Worldwide from the Bronze Age to the Present* (2023)

*Octavia E. Butler: A Literary Companion* (2022)

*Edwidge Danticat: A Companion to the Young Adult Literature* (2022)

*Asian Women Artists: A Biographical Dictionary, 2700 BCE to Today* (2022)

*Television's* Outlander: *A Companion, Seasons 1–5* (2021)

*Rachel Carson: A Literary Companion* (2021)

*Marion Zimmer Bradley: A Companion to the Young Adult Literature* (2020)

*Lee Smith: A Literary Companion* (2019)

*Coins and Currency: An Historical Encyclopedia, 2d ed.* (2019)

*Gary Paulsen: A Companion to the Young Adult Literature* (2018)

*World Epidemics: A Cultural Chronology of Disease from Prehistory to the Era of Zika, 2d ed.* (2017)

*Brian Friel: A Literary Companion* (2017)

*Settlers of the American West: The Lives of 231 Notable Pioneers* (2015)

*Isabel Allende: A Literary Companion* (2013)

*Leslie Marmon Silko: A Literary Companion* (2011)

*Peter Carey: A Literary Companion* (2010)

*Jamaica Kincaid: A Literary Companion* (2008)

*Kaye Gibbons: A Literary Companion* (2007)

*Walter Dean Myers: A Literary Companion* (2006)

*World Shores and Beaches: A Descriptive and Historical Guide to 50 Coastal Treasures* (2005)

*Barbara Kingsolver: A Literary Companion* (2004)

*August Wilson: A Literary Companion* (2004)

*Amy Tan: A Literary Companion* (2004)

*Who's Who in the Middle Ages* (2001; paperback 2013)

*Encyclopedia of World Scriptures* (2001; paperback 2011)

*A Multicultural Dictionary of Literary Terms* by Gary Carey and Mary Ellen Snodgrass (1999; paperback 2006)

# Business and Professional Women of Colonial America

## *146 Biographies, 1585–1781*

Mary Ellen Snodgrass

McFarland & Company, Inc., Publishers
*Jefferson, North Carolina*

**ISBN (print) 978-1-4766-9773-4**
**ISBN (ebook) 978-1-4766-5543-7**

Library of Congress cataloging data are available

Library of Congress Control Number 2025024912



Front cover image: Anne Catharine Hoof Green, circa 1769,
artist Charles Willson Peale, painting oil on canvas, 91.4 × 71.1 × 2.5 cm (36 × 28 × 1")
(National Portrait Gallery, Smithsonian Institution; partial gift with funding
from the Smithsonian Collections Acquisitions Program
and the Governor's Mansion Foundation of Maryland;
frame conserved with funds from the Smithsonian Women's Committee, CCO).

Printed in the United States of America

*McFarland & Company, Inc., Publishers*
*Box 611, Jefferson, North Carolina 28640*
*www.mcfarlandpub.com*

# Acknowledgments

Appalachian State University, Boone, North Carolina
Atkins Library, University of North Carolina at Charlotte
Bert Lippincott, reference librarian and genealogist, Newport Historical Society, Rhode Island
Beth Saunders, Quaker Archives, Guilford College, Greensboro, North Carolina
Dan Rogelio, reference, Newport Public Library, Rhode Island
Davidson College Library, Davidson, North Carolina
Davis Library, University of North Carolina at Chapel Hill
Duke University Library, Durham, North Carolina
Elivia Edge, reference clerk, Quincy Public Library, Quincy, Massachusetts
Elizabeth Hayden, reference, State Library of North Carolina, Raleigh
Gardner-Webb University Library, Boiling Springs, North Carolina
Gaston County Library, North Carolina
Hilde Perrin, Librarian, Massachusetts Historical Society, Boston
Hulst Library, Dordt University, Sioux Center, Iowa
Jackson Library, University of North Carolina at Greensboro
Joyner Library, East Carolina University, Greenville, North Carolina
Julie Burrey, archivist, Plymouth Public Library, Plymouth, Massachusetts
Kerri Donnelly, archivist, Thomas Crane Public Library, Quincy, Massachusetts
Leigh Schoberth, reference librarian, Robinson Research Center, Rhode Island Historical Society, Providence
Linda Bridges, reference librarian, Bull Street Library, Savannah, Georgia
Linda Christensen, Preston Historical Society, Preston, Connecticut

Sarah Hisnanick-Murphy, South Carolina Room reference, Charleston County Public Library, Charleston, South Carolina
Sierra Dixon, Connecticut Museum of Culture and History, Hartford, Connecticut
Smith Library, High Point University, High Point, North Carolina
State Library of Louisiana, Baton Rouge
State University Library, Raleigh, North Carolina
Stephen Luce, director, Portsmouth Historical Society, Portsmouth, Rhode Island
Victoria Do, reference, Georgia Historical Society, Savannah

I owe special thanks to the State Library of North Carolina for use of the "Early American Newspaper" series, a source that places details and exact words in media pages. Multiple thanks to publicist Mary Canrobert, an ever-ready consultant, and to Steve Baker, who tames my hooligan computer. Bless you all.

# Table of Contents

*Acknowledgments* v
*Preface* 1
*Introduction* 5

I—Founding a Nation, 1585–1680 11
II—The Shot Heard Round the World, 1681–1701 85
III—The Treaty of Paris, 1701–1755 110
IV—A Constitutional Democracy, 1760–1781 215

*Chronology* 225
*A Guide to Business and Professional Women by Career* 231
*A Guide to Business and Professional Women by Place* 238
*Glossary* 241
*Bibliography* 249
*Index* 259

"Whatsoever thy hand findeth to do, do it with thy might."
—Ecclesiastes 9:10

"I shall be quite a Farmeress another year."
—Abigail Adams, 1776

# Preface

McFarland's women's history compendium *Business and Professional Women of Colonial America* plumbs two centuries of androcentric culture to disclose the females who defied convention as they built a career and earned a living. The one hundred forty-six subjects acknowledge female entrepreneurs during two major conflicts, the French and Indian War and the American Revolution. Personal details place women in a wide range of commercial endeavors, from sorting fish, vending brooms and baskets, and marketing plum cake and West Indian fruit to publishing poetry and surveying the shells, fishbones, birds, and seaweed of the American East Coast. In the list of pathfinders, familiar names stand out—first lady Abigail Smith Adams, satirist and political historian Mercy Otis Warren, poets Anne Bradstreet and Phillis Wheatley, agronomist Eliza Lucas Pinckney, negotiator Nancy Ward, evangelists Anne Hutchinson and Mary Dyer, publisher Anna Catharina Zenger, and frontier trader Rebecca "Mrs. Daniel" Boone. More valuable to women's past, the obscure profit-makers qualify as models of industry in a milieu unsupportive of female ambition.

*Business and Professional Women of Colonial America* injects the difference between keeping house and wresting profits from the basics of domestic science. Innkeeping, catering, weaving, and tailoring drew on familiar home experience at bargaining for rations to stocking a pantry, serving meals, and stitching garments from homemade textiles. The addition of tending patients and birthing expanded on household first aid and basic mint, cherry and willow bark, and other herbal remedies. The overview of pioneering employment details the commercial possibilities of operating a ferry, fitting spectacles, translating languages, inventing, landscaping, teaching dance and keyboard music, bookbinding, litigating lawsuits, and distributing mail.

The text follows shifts in the settlement of an American frontier dominated by Indians and bearing indigenous names, such as Nahant (modern

Charlestown) and Naumkeag and Massachusetts (modern Salem). For accurate locations, descriptions name rivers and mountains rather than precolonial borders. While the Hudson Valley took shape as the future New York, female entrepreneurs avoided arson and murderous raids by deracinated Indians while attending to families in New Amsterdam's forts and stockades. Genealogies link generations of such exceptional families as the Boones, van Rensselaers, Kittamaquund, and Adams.

When European newcomers gradually seized property, internal clashes between whites focused less on ethnicity and more on religious strictures and boundary squabbles. The end of the French and Indian War and King Philip's War found the British dominant over the Narragansett, Nashaway, Nipmuck, Ponduck, and Wampanoag and the New York Dutch. While patriots swore allegiance to liberty and an end to the Stamp Act, the British military breached battle lines of the American Revolution on land and sea to scuttle rebellion. In the grand upheaval, women maintained a nonmilitary presence that profited from a growing list of commercial opportunities. In the post-war era, female ingenuity dominated fashion, food, travel, healing, the media, and the arts.

A chronology notes key dates in American history, especially combat, the arrival of English pilgrims of the Great Puritan Migration to eastern North America in 1620 and 1628, and the flourishing interaction of the British navy with smugglers, pirates, and privateers in shipping lanes. The tight cluster of events between 1773 and 1783 outlines familiar advances on independence as patriots vindicated liberty and no taxation without representation. Names identify influential people—John Adams, Anne Bradstreet, General James Edward Oglethorpe, Charles II, Muskogee Creek, Crispus Attucks, Abigail Adams, Thomas Jefferson, George III, Clara Barton, Benedict Arnold, the Sons of Liberty, Mercy Otis Warren, and Thomas Paine.

"A Guide to Business and Professional Women by Career" and "A Guide to Business and Professional Women by Place" enable students, teachers, researchers, feminists, and history buffs to gauge the amount of commercial activity in each colony. The list of careers places some workers in multiple areas—for example, Sarah Kemble Knight as shopkeeper and teacher, Martha Ballard and Jane Golden in herbalism and cheesemaking, Molly Ockett in healing and storytelling, and Deborah Dunch Moody in cartography and town management. Placement varies with business and professional woman who moved around, as with Margaret Brent in Maryland and Tennessee, Esther Pinheiro in Massachusetts and New York, and Anne Hutchinson in Massachusetts and Rhode Island.

Following the text of individual doers and earners, a glossary introduces the reader to terms from biology, equipment, fashions, food, literature, marine life, music, religion, substances, and textiles:

*biology*—rhizome, loam, myopic, leveret, genera, creole, Linnaean system
*equipment*—fulling mill, matchlock rifle, limbeck, fomentation, magazine, pillory
*fashions*—patch, brolio, stomacher, ferret, chip hat, polanese, tippet, beaver hat
*food*—rusk, chine, syllabub, pluck, head sauce, bolted, sackposset, emptins
*literature*—closet drama, picaresque, pastiche, broadsheet, hornbook, psalter
*marine life*—pinnace, scow, naval impressment, ketch, caracoa, trammel
*music*—coloratura, rigadoon, libretto, jig, minuet, bourrée, carillonneur
*religion*—Ursuline, Sephardic, Awakening, homily, nonconformist, Huguenot
*substances*—musk, salvolatile, balm, tincture, terroir, amber, mastic
*textiles*—chenille, mechlin, cambric, osnaburg, kersey, crepe, russel, lawn

Definitions clarify particulars, e.g., the endangerment of nonconformist Huguenots and Sephardic Jews and the purpose of the Linnaean classification system to organize types of living things.

Sixty-nine titles identify primary sources, including a letterbook; journals and diaries; genealogy; biography; verse collections; a cookbook; and urban histories of Nantucket, Savannah, New York City, Plymouth Plantation, Greenwich, Charleston, New London (Connecticut) and Newport (Rhode Island). Period spelling and punctuation replicate the state of standardized language from the seventeenth to early nineteenth centuries among the poorly educated. Overviews of women's history cover Linda Sturtz's *Within Her Power: Propertied Women in Colonial Virginia*, William H. Guthman's *The Correspondence of Captain Nathan and Lois Peters*, Eleanor Kelley Cabell's *Women Merchants and Milliners in Eighteenth Century Williamsburg*, Geraldine Brooks' *Dames and Daughters of Colonial Days*, and A.J.F. Van Laer's *Correspondence of Maria van Rensselaer 1669–1689*.

General topics range from J. Bunker Clark's *American Keyboard Music Through 1865* and Helen Walker-Hill's *From Spirituals to Symphonies: African-American Women Composers and Their Music* to Henry

Sweetser Burrage's *The Beginnings of Colonial Maine, 1602–1658* and Deborah Dash Moore's *City of Promises: A History of the Jews of New York.* In addition to academic texts, internet sources, and journals, groundwork incorporates media reports from *Historical Magazine; Journalism History; Early American Studies; Pilgrim Hall Museum; Digital Maryland; Journal of the American Indian Archaeological Institute; Scientific American;* and original media pages from the *Maryland Gazette, Portland Press Herald, Boston Gazette, American Weekly Mercury,* and *New Amsterdam Gazette.* Thorough indexing lists specifics, particularly broad topics (food, newspapers, botany, dysentery), events (Great Puritan Migration, Winthrop Fleet, Great Savannah Fire), legal terms (indenturing, Committee of Safety, *gens de couleur libre*), places (Jamaica, Hudson Valley, Great Wagon Road), prominent leaders (Hannah Callowhill Penn, Roger Williams, patroons, Benjamin Franklin), religion (Quakers, Calvinism, Puritans), and tribes (Wampanoag, Mohegan, Seminole, Abenaki).

# Introduction

Retire the spinning wheel. Pack the churn off to the attic. There was more spunk and initiative in colonial women than pictured in history books. A feminist view of New World pioneering requires a survey of outback pragmatism in both genders. The wartime economy during the French and Indian War, King Philip's War, and American Revolution cost families mates and sons, leaving widows to cope, not spin. For Lois Crary Peters of Preston, Connecticut, operating a saddlery after her husband's enlistment under General George Washington in the Continental Army paralleled a cash-flow shutdown. In a period of limited currency and leather shortages, her persistent letter writing informed Captain Nathan Peters that she struggled to keep up trade in cartridge cases, water bags, dispatch pouches, and pistol buckets. Bitterly, she blamed volunteer militiamen for signing up and leaving behind unpaid debts for women to redeem.

Gaps in information and romanticized retellings omit the details of hands-on labor and the citizen's intent to transform a colony into a sovereign state. In an era of high conception, cyclical pregnancy and postpartum recovery occupied females such as Anne Bradstreet at the height of their creativity. By reducing Elizabeth "Betsy" Ross, mother of seven, to a stitcher of five-pointed stars on George Washington's flag, career accounts overlooked her labor potential—upholstering furniture and the grueling handwork that readied and repaired uniforms, boots, tents, sails, and banners for an eight-and-a-half-year war. A similar survey of publisher Anna Catharina Zenger, mother of eight, and her mental labors for the *New York Weekly Journal* glosses over the winnowing of opinions and weighing of options for editorials during her husband Peter's nine-month imprisonment for libel and sedition. A legendary widow, she later badgered debtors in the hopes of keeping the paper afloat.

Identifying less legendary colonial businesswomen by name and location is an iffy proposition. Some, like Wampanoag land dealers

Wunnatuckquannum of Nunepog, Askamapoo of Nantucket, and Hepsibah Cogenew of Chappaquiddick, exercised considerable sway over native negotiations with early Massachusetts Bay pioneers, but left little detail of their business practices. From the margins of women's history, data on Margaret Hardenbroeck Philipse's role as a Dutch New York trader and shipping agent vary greatly in multiple sources. More examples slip through the historical crevices—the immigrant Salzburg women who wound silk threads from cocoons in Georgia, efforts of Henrietta Dering Johnston to support a Charleston minister's household by painting miniature portraits on ivory, and the operation of a dock and outpost on the Kentucky River by Rebecca Bryan Boone, provider for a household of eighteen.

## *A Female-Powered Economy*

Contrasting the minimal incomes of these isolated pioneers, the matrilineages of New Amsterdam generated a steady labor supply of brokers, shippers, and merchants from the wealthy van Rensselaer, Schuyler, de Peyster and Livingston dynasties. Mary Spratt Provoost Alexander profited from the wisdom of her maternal grandmother, Cornelia "Neeltje" Lubberts De Peyster, a New Amsterdam trader with the Virginia Colony. In widowhood, Mary built on investments in realty and transatlantic dry goods a net worth of £100,000 (approx. $28,608,435.23). The pinnacle of female ambition, Maria van Cortlandt van Rensselaer managed ten children and a million-acre manor in eastern New York that fused two phenomenally rich Dutch American clans. The fifth patroon of Rensselaerswyck estate, she grappled from Dutch family members' ownership of a Hudson Valley tract twenty-four miles long by forty-eight miles wide. At retirement in August 1687, she allotted the massive plat to her American heirs. Researcher Patricia Cleary pursued a Scots parallel to the Dutch hegemony through her biography of Boston businesswoman Elizabeth Murray Inman, a mentor to nieces from Scotland. The matriarchy grew into a female network of Boston she-merchants who included Jane Eustis and sisters Ame and Elizabeth "Betsy" Cuming, two loyalists who endured intimidation by belligerent patriots before relocating their shop to Halifax. To the chagrin of their persecutors, the Cuming duo made even more money in Nova Scotia.

A surge of patriotism brought out the moxie of female professionals. In colonial Savannah, merchant and planter Abigail Minis gained respect as a founding mother of the coastal settlement and backer of the Continental Army. Multi-talented Boston musician and composer Elizabeth

Johanetta Catherine von Hagen performed patriotic ballads and marches on piano and organ with husband Peter Sr., son Peter Jr., and daughter Catherina. Printer and editor Clementina Grierson Rind of Williamsburg distributed the *Virginia Gazette* with a nationalistic edge and supported Thomas Jefferson's concept of liberty. Jane Vobe and Christiana Campbell entertained top brass at their Williamsburg taverns, where the military and political leaders retreated to private rooms to play cards, eat, and discuss the demand for independence. In Savannah, Lucy Mouse Tondee risked hanging by collaborating with the Sons of Liberty, local rowdies who plotted the Revolutionary War while she served them pie and ale. Boston gunsmith Elizabeth "Betsy" Hager added to her weaponry skills the variolation of neighbors who feared smallpox more than minié balls.

Key to research into colonial womanhood, women's biographies by Marla Miller, Laurel Thatcher Ulrich, Charlotte Alice Baker, Lee Agger, Melissa A. McEuen, Adrienne Rich, and Ann Little recovered the essential labors of frontierswomen. The studies of Christina J. Hodge, a Harvard lecturer, yielded a microcosm of Newport, Rhode Island, and the mercantile competitors of Rhode Island merchant Elizabeth Woodberry Pratt. Kristi Rutz-Robbins's research found that, of Boston's forty-three shopkeepers in 1713, 39 percent were widows. For the multi-racial background of Louisiana rancher and apothecary Coincoin, scholar Elizabeth Shown Mills published a maze of documents that contested spurious legends. A consummate scholar, Hannah Humphreys outlined the career path of pomologist Ann Jessop, a North Carolina Quaker who impacted American foodways by grafting multiple apple species to augment the uses of a humble fruit.

Some entrepreneurial women partnered well with husbands and sons and bore the brunt of war when males died in battle or disappeared into British prison galleys. The number of remarriages indicates the necessity of men in the lives of some survivors, notably Virginia milliner Lucy Carter Harrison Randolph Necks; Maine midwife and undertaker Martha Moore Ballard; and Connecticut apothecary Elizabeth "Bess" Fones Winthrop Feake Hallett, mother of seven. In *Albion's Seed: Four British Folkways in America*, historian David Hackett Fischer summarized colonial gender inequalities: "Whenever a culture exists for many generations in conditions of chronic insecurity, it develops an ethic that exalts war above work, force above reason, and men above women" (McEuen and Appleton, 2015, 27). The pragmatism and determination of dynamic female capitalists set them apart as strivers willing to compete with the opposite gender, even when society impugned their choices.

## *From Pioneering to Combat*

The first military charge at Lexington, Massachusetts, on April 19, 1775, jolted working women into advantageous capacities, beginning with a boycott of British imports. At Boston, blacksmith Elizabeth "Betsy" Hager retooled six brass cannons from the battle of Concord and hauled them to patriot arsenals. Connecticut seamstress Elizabeth "Betty" Foote Huntington supplied domestic needs for shirts, bed rugs, quilts, and knitted goods, essentials during the privations of a winter at Valley Forge. Creole rancher and mother of seven Ana Gallum "Nansi" Wiggins of Palatka, Florida, fed the growing demand for beef. The prime wartime career woman, Abigail Smith Adams, supplied ammunition to troops and turned the family acreage into a depot of salable commodities—grain, hay, firewood, dray animals, potatoes, and cider, all in short supply during a home-front war. To nourish tired soil, she raked forty loads of seaweed from the Braintree seashore to enrich cropland. The sources of ready cash enabled her to invest in bits of Massachusetts farmland, newer equipment, and laborers and to steady President John Adams after his failure to win re-election.

By war's end, opportunities for female entrepreneurs increased with the outlook for American commerce, equality in marriage, and access to political, commercial, media, and educational venues. Amelia Simmons saturated colonial recipes with New World commodities in *American Cookery,* which she published in Hartford, Connecticut. In Philadelphia, Elizabeth Marshall shored up finances of the Marshall Drugstore, a woman-owned profession and training center for apothecaries. At the Escambia River delta in Pensacola, Florida, Mariana Bonifay competed with Eufrosina Hinard for the expanding brick market. The use of natural clays enabled both women to provide for fatherless children. In Piedmont North Carolina, herbalist Rachel Stout Allen, mother of twelve, recorded directions for mixing tooth cleaner, salves, medicines, poultices, emetics, syrups, cordials, and purgatives. Director Margaretta Sully West took on competition from the Old American Company by touring Virginia's colonial theaters while Philadelphia mime Anna Gardie relaxed urbanites with Creole drama, melodrama, dance, and ethnic masking. Well into the nineteenth and twentieth centuries, the spirit and savvy of American females helped to set the direction and tone of national accomplishments and to press feminists to demand full citizenship and human rights for minorities.

### *Sources*

Cleary, Patricia. *Elizabeth Murray: A Woman's Pursuit of Independence in Eighteenth-Century America.* Amherst, MA: University of Massachusetts Press, 2000.

Hodge, Christina J. *Consumerism and the Emergence of the Middle Class in Colonial America*. New York: Cambridge University Press, 2014.
Humphreys, Hannah. *The Ghost Orchard*. Toronto: HarperCollins, 2017.
McEuen, Melissa A., and Thomas H. Appleton, Jr. *Kentucky Women, Their Lives and Times*. Athens: University of Georgia Press, 2015.
Mills, Elizabeth Shown. "Marie Therese Coincoin," *KnowLA Digital Encyclopedia of Louisiana*, https://web.archive.org/web/20110612024433/http://www.knowla.org/entry.php?rec=799.
Rutz-Robbins, Kristi. "'Divers Debts': Women's Participation in the Local Economy," *Early American Studies* 4:2 (2006): 425–441.

# I

# Founding a Nation, 1585–1680

From the first arrivals on North American shores in 1620 and 1628, women have dedicated their labors to family first and personal aspirations second. Lacking in power over children, property, and earnings, female settlers persisted in business management and professions as integral to community as trade and shipping, taverns and ferry management, midwifery, and herbal medicine. Native American women saw an opportunity for betterment by selling tracts of land to European arrivals. Deborah Dunch Moody set a standard for founding mothers by plotting and raising the town of Gravesend, New York. Her example predated womanly society building at Plymouth, Boston, Savannah, Philadelphia, Charleston, Newport, and Albany.

**Deborah Dunch Moody (April 3, 1585–May 1659)**
**Town Manager, Cartographer**
**Gravesend, New York**

A nonconformist refugee and the first female American landholder, Deborah Dunch Moody founded the first colonial town and offered freedom of religion. An aristocrat born at Gray's Inn to radical Protestant Deborah Pilkington Mervyn and attorney Walter Dunch, she came from prestigious monarchist stock and attended school in London during an outbreak of plague. Her maternal grandfather, James Pilkington, was a progressive author, Cambridge professor of divinity, and bishop of Durham. Her paternal grandfather, William Dunch, the sheriff and justice of the peace of Berkshire and esquire of Elizabeth I, audited the Royal Mint for Henry VIII and Edward IV. Deborah's grandmother, Mary Cromwell Dunch, was the aunt of Oliver Cromwell.

At age twenty-one, Deborah wed Henry Moody, a member of the

House of Commons and the sheriff of Wiltshire, and bore Henry Jr. in 1607 and Catherina in 1608. She learned city planning by designing several villages. After Charles I dissolved parliament, Henry returned home to Garsdon Manor and died at age forty-five. In widowhood at Wiltshire Manor, she faced aspersions for her faith in civil liberties and risked excommunication from the Church of England. Under the law of Charles I, she weathered persecution for her Anabaptist belief that infants should not be baptized. In April 1635, the Star Chamber forced her out of a London residence at Fetter Lane within sight of a gallows at the corner of Fleet Street. During the Great Puritan Migration in 1636, she and son Henry Jr. settled on a hundred-acre plot at Saugus in greater Boston before establishing a four-hundred-acre tenant farm in April 1640 near Salem one mile from the ocean at Swampscott.

## Persona Non Grata

John Endecott, the Puritan governor of Massachusetts Bay Colony, declared Deborah an evil danger to unity. Because of her banishment as a dissenter from the Church of Salem by a court trial in December 1642, she and other religious refugees chartered the migrant ship *James*. The company relocated to southwestern Long Island, New York, a tolerant patroonship of thirty-eight settlers founded by the Dutch West India Company. In October 1643, the Canarsie, a Lenape tribe of fishers, hunter-gatherers, and traders, forced the newcomers to abandon their crops. The refugees sought protection by the Dutch militia at Nieuw Amersfoort (modern Flatlands), a fifteen thousand-acre agrarian community northeast of Coney Island.

On December 19, 1645, at age seventy-two, Deborah received a land patent and town charter from the Dutch governor Willem Kieft to "all the havens, harbors, rivers, creeks, woodland, marshes, and all other appurtenances" of southwestern Long Island (Quick, 2022). She mulled over the possibility of returning to Swampscott, but chose to sell the farm and accept the New Netherlands offer, the first ever made to a female. Surrounded by five Dutch towns, she founded Gravensande (Grafes Ende or Grove's End, now called Gravesend), a seven thousand-acre area of Long Island plus Coney Island, named for its population of wild coneys (rabbits).

Two years after Boston midwife Anne Hutchinson's murder by Siwanoy Indians of Pelham Bay, Deborah repaid the Algonquian-speaking Canarsie for their ancestral acreage with guns, gunpowder, and seashells worth $15 (approx. $1,122.24). Under freedom of self-rule, she laid out forty plots by a grid system of square blocks emulating the design of Gravesend, Kent. Her plan called for intersection of Gravesend Road and Gravesend Neck Road, twenty-eight plantation lots, hundred-acre triangular boweries (farms), and a one-acre commons. The planner chose the town hall system of government and, in 1655, became the first female registered to vote. English citizens honored her by naming the civic center Lady Moody Square.

### City Manager

On the Atlantic Seaboard, Deborah and Henry Jr. took possession of three plots and two plantations on the corner of the stockade at Johnson's Lane and built a residence northeast of town center. Deborah grazed pigs on Coney Island and accessed Gravesend Avenue for travel and trade of farm produce. Gravesend citizens paid a tax of one guilder (approx. 56¢) and received three more if they shot predatory wolves. When the English pirate vessel *Seven Stars* approached the island, the name "Lady Deborah Moody" frightened the brigands away. She completed a church and school that espoused religious pluralism and separation of church and state and welcomed Quakers to hold their first New World meeting in her house. She converted to Quakerism in 1657.

Deborah's plotting and supervision of the community won the praise of Dutch Director-General Peter Stuyvesant, whom she entertained at her home. He appointed her a mediator of tax disputes. Her powers included appointing Gravesend magistrates and designing Bensonhurst, Brighton Beach, Coney Island, Midwood, and Sheepshead Bay. Her son's library became the largest research source in the New World. The shore offered the historic landing site of flat-bottomed boats carrying twenty thousand British and Hessian troops on August 21, 1776. Their arrival at Gravesend preceded the battle of Long Island and the capture of New York City from General George Washington's ten thousand-man Continental Army.

*Sources*

Ditmas, Charles Andrew. *Long Island Bulletin*. Brooklyn, NY: Ditmas, 1913.
Quick, Sarah. "The Lady of Gravesend," https://www.bklynlibrary.org/blog/2022/10/25/lady-gravesend-0.

## Jane Angell Hawkins (1587–after July 30, 1656)
**Midwife, Herbalist**
**Boston, Massachusetts; Portsmouth, Rhode Island**

A separatist prophet turned healer, Jane Angell Hawkins joined the Great Puritan Migration at perilous times for female settlers in New England. While living in her native St. Ives in Cornwall, she wed Richard Hawkins at Bluntisham-cum-Earith on July 11, 1602, and bore four daughters and five sons. Four of her children—Elizabeth, Ruth, John, and Sarah—died at birth or early childhood. For income, Jane traveled the roads peddling small goods. In 1629, she drew crowds to hear her spiel of Latin doggerel, a performance that prompted suspicion of sorcery.

After son Job's two-month migration from London to colonial Boston on April 2, 1635, aboard the two-masted *Planter*, the family built a house on thirty acres. Jane became a follower of radical religious leader Anne Hutchinson and set up a practice in medical care and midwifery. Among her treatments, she relied on plasters, emollients, potions, herbal teas, and surgery and dispensed oil of mandrake to encourage conception in barren women.

At age fifty, Jane joined a communal birthing for Quaker midwife Mary Barrett Dyer. Because the premature infant arrived dead and malformed, Jane followed the advice of the Rev. John Cotton and aided Anne in hiding the corpse in a secret burial. Discovery of the anomalous breech birth in October 1637 brought a charge of demonism and exile from Massachusetts Bay Colony. Governor John Winthrop maligned Jane as satanic. Local authorities impugned her medical treatments. They convicted her of practicing medicine illegally and exiled the "dangerous person" to the woods.

The religio-legal uproar occurred late in Anne's pregnancy with a sixteenth child, who was stillborn in May 1638. Conveyed by three sons—brick mason James, carpenter Job, and taverner Thomas Hawkins—in June 1638, Jane relocated with Anne to Portsmouth, Rhode Island, a state that accepted political dissenters and religious and social exiles. The Hutchinsons lived on a sheltered shore of the Pocasset River. Mary Dyer chose Aquidneck in Narragansett Bay for practicing medicine and delivering infants. Jane attempted a return to Boston in 1641 but again fled to Portsmouth.

In the early months of Jane's widowhood, son Job liquidated twenty acres of her land. She died at age sixty-nine. Her colleagues suffered horrendous deaths—Anne and five of her family and two servants slain by Siwanoy chief Wampage and his warriors in August 1643 and Mary hanged on June 1, 1660, for spreading Quakerism in the strict Puritan colony. In 1676, Samuel Groome's exposé *A Glass for the People of New England* blamed Puritans for the persecution of Boston's martyred healers.

## *Sources*

Beal, Jane. "'The Sainted Anne Hutchinson': Midwife of Grace (1591–1643)" *Midwifery Today* 122 (Summer 2017): 29–31.

Hall, David D., ed. *Witch-hunting in Seventeenth-Century New England*. Boston: Northeastern University Press, 1991.

Traister, Bryce. "Anne Hutchinson's 'Monstrous Birth' and the Feminization of Antinomianism," *Canadian Review of American Studies* 27:2 (1997): 133–158.

## Squaw Sachem (1590–1667)
**Real Estate Broker**
**Mystic, Massachusetts**

An Algonquian-speaking widow and leader of three thousand Pawtucket, Squaw Sachem (or Saunkskwa), Queen of the Massachusetts, began selling Native American land to white settlers in 1619. Pictured in sculpture by Utah-born artist Cyrus Edwin Dallin in braids, beads, and fringed dress, she appeared alert, but humble. Around 1608, she married Nanepashemet (New Moon), the Sachem of the Pawtucket Confederation of Indian tribes, and made their home at Mystic Lakes northwest of Cambridge. By 1618, she had a daughter, Yawata or Abigail, and sons Wonohaquaham (Sagamore John of Mystic River), Montowampate (Sagamore James of Saugus), and Wenepoykin (Sagamore George No Nose of Naumkeag, modern Salem) and Nahant (modern Charlestown). In a time of warfare against the Pawtucket, Nanepashemet dispatched the family to a wetu (wigwam) in central Massachusetts. He died in battle at Medford in 1617 against the Abenaki.

Left in charge in widowhood, Squaw Sachem abandoned her hidden residence. In the name of her young sons, she assumed authority of the Pawtucket from Marblehead to Concord and Charlestown. She developed an amicable relationship with the English and attended gatherings at Merrymount (modern Quincy). Out of reverence for her position, natives called her by the title Squaw Sachem and refused to speak her birth name. In 1622, she negotiated peaceful relations with the Plymouth settlers at Wessagusset (modern Weymouth), but raided outsiders infringing on ancestral lands. She instructed Europeans on how to plant corn in hills and cultivate it with hoes.

### The Realty Business

During an epidemic, in December 1633, smallpox reduced the native population by 90 percent to three hundred, killing Squaw Sachem's two eldest sons in their twenties. The pestilence scarred the face of her youngest son, who survived. At age forty-five, on September 12, 1635, she sold Massachusetts Bay leader, militiaman, and fur trader Simon Willard the beginnings of Concord on six square miles of land. She continued bartering real estate to colonists with the sale of Winchester in 1637. For land between the Charleston and Menotomy rivers, she accepted thirty-six shillings (approx. $480.12) along with lifetime tribal access for planting, hunting, and fishing.

After union with Webcowet, a priest-healer, on February 15, 1639,

Squaw Sachem advanced in prestige after she negotiated the sale of Cambridge, Charlestown, and Watertown (modern Boston). In a pact of mutual defense, she offered a special parcel in Boston to Governor John Winthrop. When she and Webcowet signed in April 1639 with an X, the colonists paid her a greatcoat, twenty-one Redcoats, cotton and linen fabric, hatchets and knives, hoes, shoes and stockings, a hat, three bushels of corn, wampum (shell money), and five shillings (approx. $68.22).

### Acculturation

Squaw Sachem adapted to life among whites. She accepted from Cambridge residents a tribute of thirty-five bushels of corn and four coats annually for two years. At age fifty-three, she received from the colonial court powder and shot and repair on her rifle by a gunsmith. On March 8, 1644, she capitulated native powers to the colony and sought instruction in Christianity. She retired to Medford, west of Mystic Lake, Massachusetts, and placed her dwelling by a spring.

After blindness and deafness limited Squaw Sachem in 1662, she died sometime in her midseventies of paralytic stroke. Her youngest son Wenepoykin followed her career as tribal authority over the environs of the Charles River. During King Philip's War on June 20, 1675, English troops seized Wenepoykin and sent him to Barbados as a slave. In his absence, Montowampate's widow Wenuchus followed her mother-in-law's example and served the tribe as squaw sachem and proprietor of land at Naankege (modern Salem).

### *Sources*

Hurd, Duane Hamilton, ed. *History of Middlesex County, Massachusetts.* Cambridge, MA: Harvard University, 1890.

Shattuck, Lemuel. *History of the Town of Concord.* Boston, MA: Russell, Odiorne & Co., 1835.

## Margaret Cammock Josselyn (after 1590–after May 2, 1680)
**Business Manager**
**Black Point, Maine**

A frontierswoman and inheritor of property, Margaret Cammock Josselyn appears to have parlayed profits from her first and second marriages into a fortune. In early 1630, she married a Maldon-born mariner, Captain Thomas Cammock, master of the ship *Robert,* who sailed between the Bahamas and Bermuda to Central America. The couple resided at Piscataqua on the Maine–New Hampshire boundary. Thomas served John

Mason and Ferdinando Gorges as agent for a land patent between the Kennebec and Merrimack rivers. The couple relocated to a house on the headland of Black Point (modern Scarborough, Maine), the shore location of vessels receiving and shipping goods.

Historians identify the site at Ferry Rock on a fifteen hundred-acre tract on Prouts Neck between the Black Point and Spurwink rivers as fronting wilderness where Saco Indians came to trade with the English. After Thomas's death en route to Barbados around October 14, 1643, Margaret probated his will and acquired title to five hundred acres of the original estate along with its timber, wildlife, and metals. Thomas left the care of his wife to settler and family friend Henry Josselyn. An Englishman educated at Cambridge, Henry had arrived in New England in summer 1634. After Henry married Margaret, the couple assumed ownership of the entire parcel.

Henry Josselyn sired son Henry Jr. and hosted his brother, historian John Josselyn. At Pemaquid, the trading center and fishing station to the northeast, Henry served as justice of the peace and deputy governor of Maine. The town grew with fifty houses, a garrison, and magazine plus herds of cattle, sheep, and horses. Part of Margaret's inheritance was a corn mill, of which no details survive. In lieu of currency, settlers used flour and corn like cash for barter and commerce. On July 3, 1676, she proved the will of William Smith. Two months later, Indians captured Henry, who fled west to Plymouth colony to avoid King Philip's War. The attackers destroyed the Josselyn house and garrison.

### *Sources*

Agger, Lee. *Women of Maine*. Portland, ME: Guy Gannett, 1982.

Burrage, Henry Sweetser. *The Beginnings of Colonial Maine, 1602–1658*. Portland, ME: Printed for the state, 1914.

## Bridget Lee Fuller (1597–after May 2, 1667)
**Teacher, Midwife**
**Plymouth, Massachusetts**

A self-supporting widow, Bridget Mary Lee Fuller avoided a second marriage in favor of independence as colonial America's first midwife. An Englishwoman from Somerset, she, younger brother William, and older brother Samuel were born to Josephine "Joos" Lee at Vest near Leiden's Marepoort, Holland. Shortly before Josephine's death, at age seventeen, Bridget wed Dr. Samuel Fuller, Sr., a thirty-seven-year-old physician and surgeon widowed after the death of second wife Annis Carpenter Fuller with their newborn son in July 1615. A *Mayflower* passenger, Samuel took on board with him an underage servant, William Butten, who died on November 6, 1620, within sight of Massachusetts Bay Colony. Samuel's older brother Edward, wife, and eight-year-old son Samuel also traveled aboard the *Mayflower.* Because of the couple's death during the disastrous first year at Plymouth, Samuel took responsibility for his nephew.

In April 1623, on the supply ship *Anne,* Bridget followed husband Samuel to New Plymouth, Massachusetts, leaving in Holland four-year-old daughter Bridget Jr. Already skilled in midwifery, Bridget Sr. delivered three babies born on the voyage. She ended the three-month crossing in July 1623 to Samuel's two acres of land, which stretched toward Massachusetts Bay south of Town Brook. The family resided at Smelt River; her portion of acreage lay by a pond. After the May 1627 allotment of livestock, the Fullers raised thirty pigs, a donkey, ten goats, and five cattle. Samuel Sr. owned substantial kitchen and dairying equipment as well as carpentry tools.

During a period of lethal smallpox, scurvy, and a chill winter, at Naumkeag (modern Salem) in 1627 and 1629, Bridget suffered a stillbirth and produced two more children, Mercy and Samuel Jr. Samuel Sr. served the pilgrims as church deacon and tax assessor. Bridget was the matriarch of the four-member family, which shared housing with nephew Samuel, two servants, and foster children Sarah Converse, Elizabeth Cowles, and George Foster, whom Samuel educated. During treatment of plague victims in Charlestown on August 2, 1630, the doctor informed Governor William Bradford that he wished to be home with his family and regretted the lack of pharmaceuticals and supplies.

While Samuel made peripatetic calls in Salem, where pilgrims suffered from fever and malnutrition, Bridget managed the family alone. When he succumbed to contagion—possibly smallpox—in early fall 1633, his will left two acres south of town, two upland acres at Strawberry Hill, and one at Reed Pond to son Samuel Jr. Additional bequests included a library of thirty volumes, surgical equipment, a country house worth £10 (approx. $2,931.73), and corn valued at £25 (approx. $7,329.33).

Apparently well provisioned by her husband's will, Bridget established a private school and taught a fatherless boy, Benjamin Eaton, until 1637. She distributed physic to ailing pilgrims and received an invitation from Rehoboth to the northwest on the West Branch Palmer River to work as town midwife and trainer of apprentices. Her donation of ground on Leyden Street preceded construction of a parsonage for the Plymouth Congregational Church on Town Square. Her losses mounted with the demise of daughter Bridget Jr. in 1641 and Mercy in 1650. Bridget Sr. died in New London, Connecticut, at age seventy. Her son, the Rev. Samuel Fuller, Jr., ministered to the Church of Christ at Middleborough and fathered her seven grandchildren.

### *Sources*

Beal, Jane. "Bridget Lee Fuller," *Midwifery Today* (Autumn 2015): 50–52.
Bradford, William. *The History of Plymouth Plantation*. Boston: Massachusetts Historical Society, 1856.
Fuller, Samuel. "The Last Will & Testament of Samuel Fuller," *Pilgrim Hall Museum*, https://pilgrimhall.org/pdf/Samuel_Fullers_Will_Inventory.pdf.

## Joan Barton Smith (1599–1644)
**Cheese Maker**
**Portsmouth, Rhode Island**

An importer of British foodways, Joan Elizabeth Barton Smith introduced Rhode Island pioneers to Gloucestershire cheese. Born northwest of London near the Welsh border, she was the first of the five children of Ellioner Burnell and William Barton. At Thornbury near England's River Severn at age twenty-two, she married Richard Smith, Sr., a widower from Halmore, Berkeley, on May 28, 1621. Her children included Joan Newton, Elizabeth Viall of Rehoboth, Katherine Op den Dyke, and stepsons James and Richard Smith, Jr.

Richard, Joan, and two children reached Taunton, Plymouth Colony, Massachusetts, in April 1637 during the Great Puritan Migration. They lived at Newport, Rhode Island, in 1638 and Portsmouth in 1640 before establishing Smith's Castle, a fortified two-story trading nexus with Narragansett Indians at Wickford on the Annaquatucket River. Identified as the first settler of Narragansett County, Richard purchased thirty thousand acres at Cocumscussuc from Narragansett Indian sachems, Canonicus and Miantonomi. Richard became a wealthy landholder in frontier Kingston, where he raised goats, sheep, pigs, and horses.

Although lacking in historical backstory in Wickford, Rhode Island, Joan Smith gained fame for her high-quality cheese, a savory daily comestible in homes, saddle packs, and inns. Her recipe, one of Great Britain's oldest, gained popularity with the Royal Navy and with Newport exporters on Thames Street for its crumbly, semi-hard texture and rich buttery flavor. Cheddar and nutty Gloucester cheese added to the colonial economy along with butter, corn, sheep, and Narragansett pacers, an American original breed. Transported through Newport, cheese exchanges for slaves, sugar, and molasses completed commerce with West Indian planters of Barbados.

At Joan's death in 1644, Richard relocated to Manhattan and bought thirteen thousand acres at Mespath, Long Island. In 1676 during King Philip's War, Narragansett attackers burned Smith's Castle, which Richard Jr. rebuilt. A religious and political center, it became America's oldest extant plantation house.

### *Sources*

Kindstedt, Paul. *Cheese and Culture*. London: Chelsea Green, 2012.
Peterson, Edward. *History of Rhode Island. New York*: John S. Taylor, 1853.

## Margaret Brent (1601–May 19, 1671)
### Real Estate Broker, Trader, Attorney
### St. Mary's City, Maryland; Stafford County, Virginia

A colonial original, Margaret Brent developed a land grant into a source of realty trading and tobacco and livestock commerce. A prestigious Catholic from Gloucestershire northwest of London, she was one of thirteen children born to Elizabeth Reed and Richard Brent, the sheriff of Stoke-Admington, England. A descendant of knights of Glastonbury dating to the twelfth century, she claimed kinship with Henry I and the Bassett and Montague clans. She may have been a celibate member of Mary Ward's sisterhood, which aided Jesuits in protecting persecuted Catholics in the New World.

With siblings Fulke, Giles, and Mary, Margaret immigrated to Baltimore on November 22, 1638, and became Maryland colony's only female landowner by acquiring one hundred twenty acres at Brent Point, Virginia. The Brent women named their residence Sisters' Freehold. Subsequent dealings awarded Margaret eight hundred acres plus one thousand acres from her brother Giles of Kent Island on the Chesapeake Bay. Unmarried and ambitious, she applied her education to mercantile interests, usury, and the trading of indentured servants. Financial savvy and female assertiveness made her prominent and respected in court, where she sued debtors as America's first female lawyer. Tobacco planters trusted her to serve as agent in one hundred twenty-four court cases.

### Mediator in Court

Because brother Giles Brent married Margaret's ten-year-old foster daughter Mary Kittamaquund, a Piscataway native, and claimed her ancestral properties, dissension with Cecilius Calvert during the English Civil War resulted in an anti–Catholic raid on February 14, 1645. Acts of violence and arson forced Margaret to sue for damage to her home and mill, for recovery of rent corn, and for theft of farm equipment and cattle. Being a friend and distant relative of Governor Leonard Calvert introduced her to inheritance law as executor of his will and to negotiations with colonial militia.

To ease a dangerous religious power shift, in June 1647, Margaret petitioned the Maryland assembly for the right to liquidate Calvert's estate. To prevent a mutiny, she sold Cecilius' cattle to free funds for soldiers' pay. A subsequent petition for voting rights in the assembly failed, making Margaret the first suffrage activist in North America and a prime voice for religious tolerance and colonial independence. With the appointment of William Stone, the first Protestant governor, Margaret and Mary were forced to relocate to the south, where they founded a manor called Peace at Aquia, Stafford County, Virginia's first Roman Catholic settlement.

## Enjoying the Profits

Margaret's wealth increased with investment in ten thousand acres at Great Hunting Creek in present-day Alexandria, Virginia, on the Potomac River and to the south of the Rappahannock in modern Fredericksburg. She bolstered the community with the importation and protection of Catholic immigrants to the colony. Her nephew, George Brent, Jr., served as the attorney general under Charles II and established a sandstone quarry on Aquia Creek that remained operational for a century. The stone supplied builders of the U.S. Capitol.

**Brent-Calvert-Kittamaquund Genealogy**

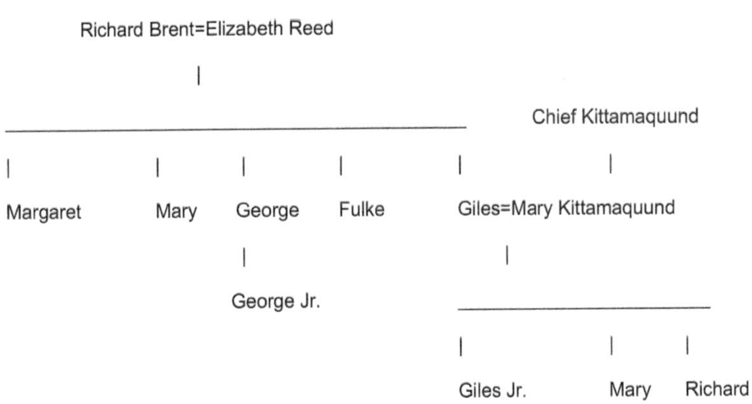


## *Source*

Chilton, W.B. "The Brents in Maryland and Virginia," *Virginia Magazine of History and Biography* 15:3 (January 1908): 324–329.

## Elizabeth Harris Glover (1602–June 23, 1643)
**Printer, Publisher**
**Cambridge, Massachusetts**

The first printer in the Thirteen Colonies, English immigrant Elizabeth Harris Glover set up shop in Cambridge, Massachusetts. The daughter of the Rev. Nathaniel Harris and Mary Greene Harris, she and siblings Richard, Edward, John, Mary, Alice, and Jane were natives of Sutton, Surrey, England. Only Richard joined Elizabeth in emigrating to North America. After marrying a widower, the Rev. Joseph "Jose" Glover, rector of St. Nicholas Church, Sutton, in 1630, she reared four-year-old Elizabeth, two-year-old Sarah, and seven-year-old Roger, the stepchildren borne by the late Sarah Owfield. Elizabeth and Joseph produced Priscilla and John, who trained in medicine at the University of Aberdeen, Scotland, and died of plague in London the next year.

Because Joseph ministered to religious non-conformists, Church of England conservatives forced his emigration to North America. In retirement, he intended to democratize learning and education in New England. Before traveling to Cambridge, he had acquired two hundred acres in Boston and built a home. With donations from seven friends in England and Holland, he purchased used fonts and office supplies for his press to supply the colony with scriptural books, catechisms, broadsides, and religious tracts.

To avoid interference by the British Parliament, Elizabeth joined Joseph in establishing Cambridge Press. He indentured the semiliterate British locksmith Stephen Daye as pressman on June 7, 1638, for a two-year term at an annual salary of £50 (approx. $11,714.49). The Glover family, Rebecca Wright Daye, and Stephen Daye with sons Matthew and Stephen Jr., stepson William Bordman, and three technicians departed Hull, Yorkshire, on the three-masted ship *John of London*. Two weeks before completing the Atlantic crossing, Joseph sickened and died, possibly from smallpox, which killed eighty-two at Monmouthshire in southeastern Wales.

### The Lady Pressman

By autumn 1638, Elizabeth took possession of her husband's investment. Rather than live in Boston, she chose to reside near her printshop at Harvard College, Cambridge, the prospective capital of Massachusetts Bay Colony. The family occupied a stylishly furnished two-and-a-half-story house kept by nine servants. The staff set up the hand-press in a downstairs room in the Daye house on Holyoke Street three blocks north of the

Charles River. Their first publication, the broadsheet *Oath of a Freeman,* a pledge of loyalty and duty to Massachusetts Bay Colony, was the composition of the colony's governor John Winthrop in 1631. The freeman's vow legalized citizenship and guaranteed allegiance and obedience to the colony.

The printshop's second issue, *An Almenack for the Year 1639,* compiled the words of Captain William Pierce, shipmaster of three vessels carrying New England's first pioneers. Beginning the year with March, it became the colony's first almanac and guide to farming. No copies have survived. Because of their popularity with mariners and farmers, Stephen Daye continued issuing almanacs until 1646.

With the labor of eighteen-year-old Matthew Daye, a printer trained in England, Elizabeth's firm began publishing seventeen hundred copies of *The Whole Booke of Psalmes Faithfully Translated into English Metre*, their third project and the first book printed in British North America, in October 1638. The one hundred forty-eight page sacred text bound in calfskin velum contained one hundred fifty Hebrew psalms. Typography conformed to the period standard:

**Psalm XXIII:1–4**

Hee in the folds of tendr-graffe,
both cause men down to lie:
To waters came me gently leads
Restore my foule doth hee:
hc doth in paths of righteousfness:
For his names fake leade mee
Yea though in valley of deaths fhade
I walk, none ill I'le feare:
becaufe thou art with mee, thy rock,
and ftaffe my comfort are.

Set in English ballad meter with frequent inversions of subject and verb, the text took the form of rhyming quatrains of alternating iambic tetrameter and trimeter lines.

The psalter recorded the translation of scripture by John Eliot, Richard Mather, Thomas Weld, and thirty colonial Puritan ministers known as the Roxbury poets. They added no new verbiage and avoided paraphrasing the psalmist David's verse. The translators fitted it to verse stanzas for communal singing as liturgy, lesson, and prayers of distress and approved no other hymnal for their services. The style contained forced rhymes and such period spelling inconsistencies, misreadings, and typographical faults as owce (house) Gounr (Governor), alwaies (always), vehemtly (vehemently), euy (every), pmise (promise), and constitucons (constitutions). The thirteen-page preface was the work of either John Cotton or Richard Mather and aimed for a plain text agreeable to most worshippers.

## New England's Metrical Psalmody

Popularly known as the Bay Psalm Book, some eighteen years after the arrival of English newcomers to Plymouth Rock, the compilation replaced the Sternhold-Hopkins metrical psalter that exiles brought from England for use in most New England pews. Production overhead for the psalter cost Elizabeth £29 (approx. $6,794.40) for paper for a total of £33 (approx. $7,731.56). During Elizabeth's three years in the colonial printing business, her book earned £141 (approx. $39,856.04), from which she netted £79 (approx. $22,330.69) in profit. Based on the King James Bible, Elizabeth's work promoted the ideals of estheticism, Puritan zeal, unlimited religious choice, and freedom of the press.

The volumes passed to a shop in 1640 for sale at twenty pence (approx. $60.68) by artilleryman and real estate investor Hezckiah Usher, New England's first bookseller. He initiated commerce in the first floor of his house at the corner of Dunster and Winthrop streets in Harvard Square and added the psalter to stocks of catechisms, lumber, grain, fish, fur, and Caribbean goods. The hymnal made Usher wealthy. It remained in demand for a century and anticipated the need for printed essays, homilies, and sermons.

Despite the book's discrepancies and errors, Elizabeth rewarded the Daye family with three hundred acres of land. On June 22, 1641, she wed the Rev. Henry Dunster of Bury, Lancaster, the president of Harvard University, and relocated the press across Massachusetts Avenue from the twenty-two-acre Harvard Yard. After Elizabeth's death two years later at age forty-one, Stephen Daye continued operating her printing business with the aid of pressman Samuel Green. Subsequent years showed a slowing of demand for publishing after Henry fired Stephen and named Matthew Daye the new manager.

Henry dedicated himself to educating Elizabeth's five children and, in 1651, issued a refinement of the *Bay Psalm Book*. It reformed vernacular to contrast the cadencing of the Catholic Mass. He donated Elizabeth's original equipment and supplies to Harvard, which established Harvard University Press. All-time selling prices for first editions of the psalter outpaced the value of other printed works.

**Genealogy of the Glover-Harris Family**

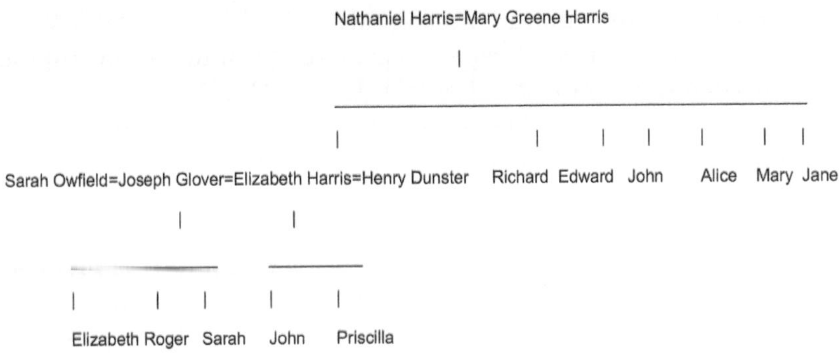


## *Sources*

Barnstone, Willis. "Misalliance of Theory and Practice or Parable of the Bay Psalm Book," *Translation Review* 32:1 (1990): 22–26.
Dorenkamp, J.H. "The Bay Psalm Book and the Ainsworth Psalter," *Early American Literature* 7:1 (1972): 3–16.
Morris, Amy. "The Art of Purifying: The Bay Psalm Book and Colonial Puritanism," *Early American Literature* 4:1 (2007): 107 130.
*Stephen Daye and His Successors*. Cambridge, MA: Cambridge Press, 1921.

## Elizabeth Fones Hallett (January 21, 1610–c. 1673)
### Apothecary
### Greenwich, Connecticut

During the Puritan Great Migration, Elizabeth "Bess" Fones Winthrop Feake Hallett brought valuable medical skills to the pioneers of Massachusetts Bay Colony and Connecticut. A native of Suffolk, England, and granddaughter of a wealthy clothworker and the auditor of Trinity College, Cambridge, she claimed ancestry dating to eleventh-century Normandy. She grew up at Groton Manor, Suffolk, with two brothers, three sisters, and their parents, Anne Winthrop and Thomas Fones II (or Ffownes).

While helping out in their father's apothecary shop, Martha and Elizabeth Fones gained an introit to pharmaceuticals. With mortar and pestle, they mixed *materia medica* such as ambergris, cherry bark, cloves, mint, nutmeg, and rosewater. Elizabeth's successful apprenticeship preceded her father's death in April 1629 and a teen marriage in London to her cousin, Henry Winthrop, a failed tobacco planter in Barbados. On his first day in the New World, he drowned in the North River, leaving fatherless Martha Johanna Winthrop, his six-week-old daughter.

## New World Bound

Under the protection of a maternal uncle, Governor John Winthrop, an earnest Puritan, Elizabeth embarked from Bristol aboard the three-masted immigrant ship *Lyon* on August 23, 1631, and arrived in Nantasket (modern Hull, Massachusetts) on November 2, 1631. At the urging of Uncle John, her father-in-law, a month later, she married widowed landowner Robert Feake, a goldsmith and militia officer. From their eighty acres at Watertown and the addition of sixty-four acres, they moved southeast to reside among Dutch and English settlers. East of Manhattan Island, they founded Horseneck (modern Greenwich, Connecticut) on July 18, 1640. Elizabeth used inherited money to complete the purchase, which overlooked a whirlpool known as Hellgate. Robert signed a boundary settlement negotiated in November 1641 with founders of Stamford.

The Feakes' post-and-beam clapboard home on Elizabeth's Neck (modern Greenwich Point) occupied marshland bought for twenty-five coats from Amogerone and Owenoke, the Siwanoy sachems of Asamuck River. Robert's mental illness caused Elizabeth to sign another agreement with the Dutch on April 1642 giving her control of Greenwich Manor. By 1647, the family grew to include daughters Elizabeth "Lisbet," Hannah, and Sarah and sons John and Robert Jr.

## Career and Crises

To local needs, Elizabeth applied her skill at medical treatment and production of simples, oils, and home-brews. At the same time, she trained daughter Hannah Feake Bowne in growing medicinal herbs and compounding colonial nostrums, such as calamine for skin lesions and rashes, chalk for reflux, vinegar for headache, spearmint tea for anxiety, horehound toddy for cough, ginger root and blackberry cordial for queasy stomachs, and cinchona bark for malaria and fever. The couple's domestic anguish precipitated Robert's abandonment of his family and return to England, perhaps to seek psychological counsel. Under Dutch law in New Amsterdam, Elizabeth arranged an annulment in 1647 and, in 1653, the sale of their property, which she owned.

Elizabeth's third marriage to William Hallett, Robert's business manager, aroused hostility in March 1648 that threatened hanging for Elizabeth and exile for William. To avoid Puritan backlash, the Halletts settled in New Netherlands at Hallett's Cove (modern Astoria, Queens) on the East River. Authorities issued warrants for the couple's arrest, which they avoided in July 1648 by sheltering with brother-in-law John Winthrop, Jr. in Naumeag (New London, Connecticut). The couple's union in August

1649 preceded the birth of William Jr. and Samuel, a scandalous progeny for a divorced woman.

During the Esopus War, the family witnessed arson by the Hackensack Lenape, who leveled house and farm in September 1655. Elizabeth bought property in Flushing, Long Island, where William served as *schout* (sheriff). From Nyack sachems Erramorhar and Shawestcont of Sunswick Creek (modern Astoria), on August 1, 1664, they purchased Riker's and Berrien's islands for seven coats, four kettles, a blanket, and fifty-eight fathom (348 feet or 116 yards) of wampum worth more than a laborer's annual income. From Canarsie members Pomwaukon and Roweroenesteo, on July 9, 1666, the Halletts amassed two thousand two hundred acres at Bowery Bay and raised tobacco, flax, and corn. To promote religious tolerance, they abandoned strict Puritanism and became Quakers.

*See also* Hannah Feake Bowne.

**Fones-Winthrop Genealogy**

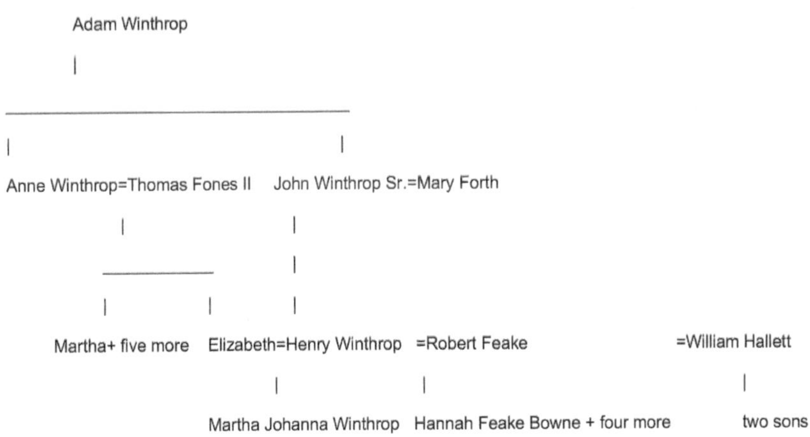


## *Sources*

Mead, Spencer Percival, and Daniel M. Mead. *Ye Historie of Ye Town of Greenwich*. New York: Knickerbocker Press, 1911.
Whitmire, William H. *Notes on the Winthrop Family*. Albany, NY: J. Munsell, 1864.
Wolfe, Missy. *Insubordinate Spirit*. Guilford, CT: Globe Pequot, 2012.

## Anne Bradstreet (March 20, 1612–September 16, 1672)
### Poet
### Salem, Massachusetts

A self-starter and pioneer of North American verse, Anne Dudley Bradstreet began a poetry career in her teens. She claimed kinship with a sheriff, knights, an heiress, a forester, and seneschals as well as William the Conqueror. She was born to Dorothy Yorke Dudley at Far Cotton, Northampton, in central England, on March 20, 1612, and incurred physical weakness from a bout of rheumatic fever and smallpox. From home-schooling at age seven by her father, Sempringham land manager Thomas Dudley, she learned history, theology, music and dance, literature, and four languages—Hebrew, Greek, Latin, and French. With free reading in the estate library of Theophilus Clinton, the Earl of Lincoln, she educated herself in Homer, Hesiod, Xenophon, Aristotle, and Thucydides and the Roman classics by Virgil, Ovid, Livy, Suetonius, Seneca, Pliny, and Plutarch. Her knowledge of English masters included the Geneva Bible and the verse of epicist John Milton, Sir Walter Raleigh, Philip Sidney, and Edmund Spenser.

After marriage at age sixteen to widower Simon Bradstreet, Thomas's deputy manager, Anne lived a pious womanhood and fought the scourge of Catholicism and the anti–Puritanism of Charles I. Immigration in June 1630 with her parents and husband brought her to Naumkeak (modern Salem, Massachusetts) aboard the 350-ton, three-masted *Arbella*. The flagship of the Winthrop Fleet of eleven ships and seven hundred passengers, it carried her along with Puritan leaders and Massachusetts Bay Colony Governor John Winthrop and his son. The convoy included the *Ambrose, Jewell,* and *Talbot,* transports of the Great Puritan Migration, which took eighty thousand citizens from England.

## An Unfulfilling Home

Anne suffered homesickness and disapproved of male primacy that enabled male pilgrims to ridicule, exile, or hang self-empowered females, particularly midwives Mary Dyer and her friend Anne Hutchinson. In the first year, two hundred immigrants or 29 percent died. The four Dudley-Bradstreet adults lodged in one house and hovered at the only fireplace. At a nadir of colonial prospects, Anne epitomized Christian piety among nonconformist settlers racked with scurvy, contagion, hunger, and perpetual terror of the Massachusetts tribe. To stave off misery, in July, the family relocated to Charlestown before moving at Braintree and Wood streets near Harvard Square in Newtowne (modern Cambridge), where she suffered paralysis to her joints.

Motherhood in 1633 confined Anne for the birth of son Samuel, the first of eight children her poem "In Reference to Her Children" called "eight birds hatcht in one nest" (Bradstreet, 2010). At home on the Boston and Haverhill road a mile from the Merrimac River, she undertook domestic duties, which were often complicated by Simon's travels as colony magistrate, shipper, and owner of five hundred acres and a sawmill. She commented on his absence "southward" in "A Letter to Her Husband, Absent upon Public Employment." Fear of fevers and disappointment in New World amenities filled her writings, beginning in 1632 with "Upon a Fit of Sickness" and continuing with "For Deliverance from a Fever" and "Upon Some Distemper of Body," which left her lame. Her despair at the ephemeral nature of earth's joys concluded with a dutiful yielding to the divine scheme of human life.

## The Lyrical Stylist

Written in ballad style, the poem "Upon a Fit of Sickness" reveals a skill at alternating rhyme scheme and imagery comparing mortality to a bubble, which she links by medieval-style alliteration to "blast." A more sophisticated musing on worldly pleasures, "Contemplations" compared her delight in sunshine to the sun worship of ancient pagans. To draw the seven lines into one tight apotheosis, she rhymed the iambic pentameter lines ababbbb, further compacting the sense of wonder with assonance of the long e sound in "leavie tree" and "thee a Deity." The noble quality of her poems earned her the title "Empress Consort of Massachusetts."

In 1635, after the household moved to High Street in Ipswich, Anne compiled *The Tenth Muse Lately Sprung Up in America,* a collection of poems published by brother-in-law John Woodbridge and dedicated to her father, a co-founder of Harvard University. As an exercise in consistency, she opened on a series of fours—the elements fire, earth, air, and water; the humors blood, choler, phlegm, and melancholy; the ages childhood, youth, middle age, old age; and seasons spring, summer, fall, and winter, based on the governing concepts of Renaissance science. Her well governed choice of subjects extended to four ancient civilizations of world history, Assyria, Persia, Greece, and Rome.

Anne portended the feminism of American women. She charged, "Masculines, you have thus taxt us long" with "carping tongue" to satisfy themselves with needlework, the chosen occupation for females in "The Prologue." An encomium to Queen Elizabeth I in 1643, "In Honor of That High and Might Princess Queen Elizabeth" thrust at the male hierarchy and men's refusal to praise a woman so preeminent as England's last Tudor monarch. Anne's epitaph for her mother stressed the typical virtues of Puritan females—worthiness, love, obedience, wisdom, spirituality, and generosity to the poor.

## The Lingering Shadow of Death

Anne's outlook improved with a final move to North Andover's Academy Road in 1648. On a one-acre lot, the co-founding family occupied a roomy three-story farmhouse. Simon acquired more property in Rhode Island. At Stephen Bowtell's London shop at the sign of the Bible in Pope's Head Alley, her uniquely personal verse sold well to the English at the price of one shilling (approx. $3.95). By 1650, she could look back on England and compare its internal upheavals under leader Oliver Cromwell to the vicissitudes of the Massachusetts Bay Colony.

The conflict of Elizabethan refinement and Puritan evangelism dominated the poet's mature thoughts, a constant mental skirmish noted in the spiritual autobiography, "To My Dear Children." On March 20, 1664, she dedicated *Meditations* to son Simon. Still mourning the death of infant grandchild Elizabeth, the Dudley-Bradstreet family survived a careless servant's fire on July 10, 1666. The flames devoured Anne's eight hundred books and the conclusion to "The Roman Monarchy" and lost the family £900 (approx. $224,515.90) worth of possessions. In "Verses upon the Burning of Our House," she scolded herself for worldly grief over loss of "my pleasant things."

At the family's new home, Anne continued developing *The Tenth Muse* for the posthumous 1678 edition of modest, but self-confident lyrics entitled *Several Poems Compiled with Great Variety of Wit and Learning*. Among her most praised works, "To My Dear and Loving Husband" took the form of the Elizabethan sonnet rhyming aabbccdddeeeff. Elegiac tone in "Before the Birth of One of Her Children" revealed her stages of sorrow in adulthood at the possibility of dying in labor and at the loss of her parents, daughter Dorothy, sons Simon and Samuel, grandson Simon, granddaughters Annis and Elizabeth, and sister-in-law Mercy Dudley Woodbridge. Anne's struggles with Puritanic certainties disclosed personal doubts and distractions from godliness. Preacher Cotton Mather's *Magnalia* extolled her wit and intelligence. She died of tuberculosis at age sixty.

### *Sources*

Bacon, Edwin Monroe. *Literary Pilgrimages in New England.* New York: Silver Burdett, 1902.

Bradstreet, Anne. *The Works of Anne Bradstreet.* Cambridge, MA: Belknap Press, 2010.

Mawer, Randall R. "'Farewel Dear Babe': Bradstreet's Elegy for Elizabeth," *Early American Literature* 15:1 (Spring 1980): 29–41.

## Margery Hoar Flynt (1614–March 10, 1686)
**Music Teacher**
**Braintree, Massachusetts**

A pious, gentle Englishwoman from St. Mary de Crypt, Gloucestershire, Margery Hoar Matthews Flynt taught music to proper Boston girls. The oldest child of Joanna Hincksman and brewer Charles Hoar, Jr., an alderman and sheriff of Gloucester, she claimed ancestry with an Anglo-Irish clan dating to 1216 and bore the name of her paternal grandmother. In her twenties, Margery left home with the Great Puritan Migration to New England accompanied by her widowed mother and four siblings.

Margery wed John Matthews, father of son Charles, who died in 1641. In widowhood at age twenty-five, she married the Rev. Henry Flynt, minister of the First Congregational Church of Braintree (modern Quincy) Massachusetts, and bore eleven more children, the last a set of twins who died in infancy. Henry's will left Margery eighty acres in Boston and a home and two lots in Braintree.

Margery was one of the first known music instructors in the New World. According to her tombstone, her lessons added to the refinement of the girls of Massachusetts Bay Colony. Her scholarly brother, Leonard Hoar, president of Harvard College, offered a left-handed compliment to music pupils. He acknowledged the importance of instrumental training for girls "for whom 'tis more proper and they also have more leisure to look after it" (Ammer, 2001, 13).

### *Sources*

Ammer, Christine. *Unsung: A History of Women in American Music.* Portland, OR: Amadeus, 2001.

Snodgrass, Mary Ellen. *American Colonial Women and Their Art.* Jefferson, NC: McFarland, 2017.

Wilson, Daniel Munro. *Where American Independence Began.* Boston: Houghton, Mifflin, 1902.

## Shaumpishuh (ca. 1618–February 1686)
**Real Estate Broker, Cartographer**
**Guilford, Connecticut**

An Algonquian-speaking sunk squaw sachem, Shaumpishuh sold aboriginal land at the future town of Guilford in south central Connecticut. She gained prestige as the niece of Sachem Qussuckquansh of the Kuttawo River and Totoket (modern East River and Branford) and sister of Momauguin, sachem of the widespread Quinnipiac residing from New Haven to Meriden. She led forty-seven natives of the Narragansett band at Menunkatuck (modern Guilford), a village named for menhaden, common food fish of the herring species. On three hundred square miles extending twenty miles inland, tribal subsistence fishers and farmers hunted deer, and gathered fruit and nuts.

After marriage to Nashump, Shaumpishuh bore daughter

Shambisqua, future leader of the New Haven Quinnipiac, and sons Nausup and James Keyhow. The family endured war and enslavement by the Pequot from 1636 to 1638. During the Beaver Wars in the St. Lawrence Valley and the Great Lakes, which peaked in the late 1630s, the Quinnipiac gained wealth by trading beaver pelts(*Castor canadensis*) with the Dutch for sale in western Europe. The agencies shipped more than fifty-two thousand pelts annually in trade for needles, glasses, kettles, axes, guns, and duffel wool, a coarse fabric with a thick nap.

## Trading in Land

On May 26, 1637, English colonists allied with Shaumpishuh's people to defy the Pequot at Mistick Fort (Mystic, Connecticut). In the wake of the Great Dying from devastating outbreaks of plague and smallpox, on April 24, 1638, she allied with two English settlers, Puritan minister John Davenport and Theophilus Eaton, a London merchant. The newcomers welcomed instruction in native style eel spearing, deer hunting, and meat preparation. The Quinnipiac illustrated drying acorns and chestnuts for winter, digging for clams, navigation in canoes, and the building of fish weirs (dams) to catch menhaden. Native watchmen slew wolves to save domestic herds and volunteered to guide explorers and deliver messages.

Before the Pequot War spread southwest to New York and east to Rhode Island, on September 29, 1639, nineteen-year-old Shaumpishuh completed the sale of ten square miles of property between Stony Creek and the East River to the Rev. Henry Whitfield and five other Puritan colonists. The deal included Faulkner Island in the Long Island Sound, which offered ideal pasturage for ruminants. For tribal use, she retained acreage east of the Kuttawo River and local planting and hunting rights in exchange for a dozen coats, wampum (shell money), a dozen magnifying glasses, a dozen pairs of shoes and stockings, a dozen each of hatchets and knives, scissors, a dozen hats, a dozen each of spoons and porringers, and two English Redcoats. She signed the deed with a large D crossed by an arrow.

## Losing Ground

Although illiterate, Shaumpishuh and her elderly uncle received from Whitfield paper, quill pen, and ink on August 23, 1639, for outlining terrain covered by the deed. For a month, they sketched a minimal map of Guilford between Clinton and East Haven on the Connecticut shore, a rare example of Indian communication with whites. Scribe John Higgenson labeled land, place names, and waterways that served as tribal boundary markers.

Endangerment by Uncas and his Mohegans caused Shaumpishuh to relocate the Quinnipiac westward adjacent to English settlements at Branford, East Haven, and New Haven. Because of turmoil in England after Puritans beheaded Charles I on January 30, 1649, Whitfield repatriated to London in 1650. In 1657, some tribe members attempted to buy back Oyster Point. Because the English demanded that they kill their watchdogs, the Indians refused the deal. During King Philip's War in 1675, Shaumpishuh's braves fought alongside the English against Metacomet and lost six hundred or 67 percent of their fighting force.

On return to heritage land, the Narragansett discovered that the English had encircled their homeland with a fort that allowed no Indians. In the exile known as the Algonquian migrations, some of the Quinnipiac journeyed to Farmington to join the Tunix tribe, leaving behind the aged and infirm. When Shaumpishuh died around age sixty-eight, her son Nausup took her place as sachem and sold land north of Guilford to settlers. Her daughter Shambisqua advanced to leader of New Haven. By 1774, only twenty-three Quinnipiac Indians survived at Guilford.

### *Sources*

Braccio, Nathan. "Quassaquanch's and Shaumpishuh's 1639 Map of the Connecticut Coast," web.sas.upenn.edu/earlyamericanstudies/2022/03/13/quassaquanchs-and-shaumpishuhs-1639-map-of-the-connecticut-coast/ (13 March 2022).

*A Handbook of New England*. Boston, MA: Porter E. Sargent, 1916.

Menta, John. "Shaumpishuh, 'Squaw Sachem' of the Quinnipiac Indians," *Artifacts. Journal of the American Indian Archaeological Institute* 16 (1988): 3–4.

Nietering, Kristen, and Jordan Sorensen. "Historic and Architectural Resources Inventory for the Town of Guilford, Connecticut," guilfordpreservation.org/wp-content/uploads/2016/02/GPA-Context-Statement-Final.pdf (December 2015).

## Ann Devorix (1620–April 26, 1708)
**Farmer, Fish Processor**
**Marblehead, Massachusetts**

A fisherman's wife from Brockley, Suffolk, "Goody" Ann Humphrey Devorix (Devereaux) farmed, sorted and sold fish, and represented her husband John in shore dealings while he was at sea. John, a merchant mariner from Stoke-by-Nyland, Warwickshire, England, arrived in Salem, Massachusetts, from Yarmouth, Isle of Wight. His passage aboard the Winthrop Fleet in summer 1630 had historical significance as part of the Great Puritan Migration. John Winthrop's seventeen ship convoy sailed from Yarmouth on April 8, 1629, and increased Massachusetts Bay Colony by one thousand newcomers.

The couple built their property piecemeal. In November 1637, John secured ten and a half acres in Salem, from Old Squaw Sachem of Mistick, a widow of the Nahumkege nation. The next month, he added to the property a half-acre of marshland. After the couple married around 1645, he served as a selectman of town authority of Marblehead in 1648, 1666–1667, and 1674.

## Domestic Manager

A core family of Massachusetts Bay Colony, the Devorixes possessed acreage on both sides of the Marblehead stone wall and along the Forrest River. The land included a pond, mercantile fish houses, fish flakes (racks) for air drying, and four fishing vessels. According to scholar Daniel Frederick Vickers at Princeton, heads of household like John tended to direct "the labor of their wives, children, servants, and the occasional hired hand" (Vickers, 1984, 10). While living adjacent to the town commons, Ann reared their seven children—Hannah, Ann, Bethia, Robert, John Jr., Humphry, and Emme—and readied fields for the spring corn planting.

Because of the labor shortage in seaboard Massachusetts, on John's return from a successful voyage, Ann superintended sorting of the catch by size and species and delivered mackerel to purchasers. Serving as a town notable and constable, John frequently settled debts and business claims in court and came to blows with belligerent customers and neighbors. A respected authority on her own, in 1658, Ann settled issues of the accurate weight of pork. During a 1661 lawsuit, she testified to her hand delivery of receipts.

The family prospered on July 1, 1659, with the purchase from Charles Gott of three hundred fifty acres of meadow at Devorix Beach opposite Tinkers Island in Marblehead for £100 (approx. $23,663.26). In spring 1660, John built a house. After ruffians pulled up a fence along the shore at Throgmorton's cove, Ann petitioned the clerk of court for permission to erect another boundary. The destruction of the second fence cost the family a bull and horse drowned in the mire and required a night watch to keep animals out of cornfields. The tract increased in value in 1670 with the construction of a highway to the Neck, a rocky promontory in Massachusetts Bay.

## Taking Charge

The couple pastured two cows on the town commons in 1671 and sold a quarter acre to Vinson Stilson in 1678. John invested in 20 percent of a Marblehead windmill that he helped construct on Training Field Hill, where customers ground corn into meal. Anchorsmith John Waldron purchased one and a quarter acres from the family in November 1692. Within months of John Jr.'s death, Ann was widowed in December 1695.

Ann executed John's will, which declared her his dearly beloved. She took possession of household goods and occupied for life the family land, worth £25 (approx. $6,420.27). Son Robert, a tanner, inherited three hundred acres plus residence and barn. He led a family meeting to discuss caring for their mother in old age.

*See also* Squaw Sachem.

### *Sources*

Perley, Sidney. "Marblehead in the Year 1700. No. 3," https://marbleheadmuseum.org/wp-content/uploads/2014/03/Perley-Final-1.pdf.

Vickers, Daniel Frederick. "Maritime Labor in Colonial Massachusetts," www.proquest.com/openview/d44a0d4271fd1a658356e6efa8338563/1?pq-origsite=gscholar&cbl=18750&diss=y, 1981.

## Anna Hack Boot (November 28, 1622–July 8, 1685)
**Trader, Slave Dealer, Realtor**
**Accomack, Virginia**

One of the New World's first female traders, Anna Varlett Hack Boot brought Dutch training to New Amsterdam and became the first businesswoman to press a lawsuit in America. The youngest child of Judith Tentenier and Caspar Varlett, a silk merchant at Cologne with the Dutch West Indies Company, she was a native of Utrecht. She reached New York aboard the New Netherland Company sloop *Fortuyn* in her late twenties and, in 1665, gave birth to daughter Judith. With her physician husband Joris "George" Hack, her first cousin and father of sons George Nicholas and Peter, she bought the nine-hundred-acre Hack's Point, Maryland, plantation on the Bohemia River and Pungoteague Creek.

Anna extended Chesapeake Bay investments with two islands and four hundred acres to the southwest of Pocomoke Sound at Matchotank Creek, for which her father and brother Nicholas signed securities. After petitioning unsuccessfully for citizenship in Accomack, Virginia, in widowhood, she settled in Maryland in 1666 but kept her land and livestock holdings in Virginia. She married sea captain Nicolas Boot, a tobacco shipper who died within a year. A flair for commerce involved her in inherited livestock and land grant sales, grain contracts, and trading of furs, West Indian slaves, indentured servants, and imported textiles and furniture through the Bestevaer shippers in Graft, Holland.

Furthering her success, Anna contracted with shipwright James Fookes to build a pinnace, *The Fortune,* which exported thirty-five hogsheads of tobacco per voyage. She pledged to provide the boatwright with tar and planking. Mooring on Chesapeake Bay saved shipping costs and enabled her to load the most recent, freshest crops. For outfitting, she purchased a sail from the *Daniell of Dublin* in September 1666 and, in winter 1667, negotiated for ropes, bolts, and rigging. In June 1668, she contracted for fifty-four pieces of furniture crafted in Virginia by indentured turner and joiner John Rickards. At her direction, he built six spinning wheels, four chests, five cupboards, eight bed frames, and an armoire of oak, pine, and walnut. One of the cupboards became a family heirloom.

By allying with her brother-in-law, Bohemian surveyor and privateer Augustine Herman, and Dutch entrepreneur Cornelius Vanhoofe, Anna secured investments in Maryland, New York, and Virginia. When Cornelius welched on the deal, she sued him in Virginia's colonial court. After her death at age sixty-three, she was probably buried at Pungoteague Creek. Her son George Nicholas Hack inherited eleven hundred acres in Northern Neck, Virginia, the home of Mount Vernon, the future plantation of President George and Martha Custis Washington.

*Sources*

Hatfield, April Lee. *From Strangers to Citizens*. London: Sussex Academic Press, 2001.
Johnston, George. *History of Cecil County, Maryland*. Elkton, MD: self-published, 1881.
Snabel, Cor, and Elizabeth Johnson. *The Varlet Family of Amsterdam*. San Mateo, CA: PB Works, 2008.

## Sara Jans Kierstede (April 5, 1627–October 21, 1693)
**Linguist, Healer**
**Manhattan, New York**

## Anneke Jans (1605–February 23, 1663)
**Midwife**
**Albany, New York**

## Trijn Catherine Jonas (1582–1644)
**Midwife**
**New York City**

From a matriarchal lineage of community servants, Sara Roeloffs Jans Kierstede contributed to New Amsterdam's stability by learning the Lenni Lenape language and promoting interracial harmony. She was born in Amsterdam in 1627 to Anneke Webber Jans, a Norwegian emigrant and descendant of Dutch king William I, and Swedish mariner Roeloff Jansz van Marstrand from the Meuse valley. Aboard the small Spanish bark *Unity-Concord,* on March 21, 1630, Sara left Texel, Holland, and arrived in the New Netherlands at age three with younger sister Trijntje (Catrina).

The girls lived with two widows—their maternal aunt Marritje Jans and maternal grandmother Trijn Jonas of Vastra, Sweden, the official Dutch West India Company nurse-midwife—and may have acquired language skills from Mahican playmates. While Anneke reared another son and daughter at Broadway and Hudson River, Sara's father worked as foreman at Rensselaerswyck plantation for Dutch West India Company director Kiliaen van Rensselaer. He earned an annual wage of $72 (approx. $2,675.42) for each of four years. The family resettled in Manhattan on sixty-five acres about the time that Roeloff died.

### Female Resilience

Sara was eight when her widowed mother married the Rev. Everardus Bogardus, a Dutch Reformed evangelist who owned one hundred sixty-two acres on the Hudson River. A dissolute citizen and stepfather, he bore a reputation for swearing, arguing, and public drunkenness. At his disappearance at sea in 1647, Anneke relocated the family to 23 Whitehall Street, Beverwyck (modern Albany), a fur trading nexus, and served the community as midwife.

In June 1642, Sara wed a Saxon refugee and Dutch West Indies Company surgeon, William Hans Kierstede of Magdeburg, Prussia, the father of their ten children and the first physician in New Amsterdam. Among the elite Dutch, the couple settled on the Upper Bay shore at the corner of Pearl and Whitehall streets, where Sara bargained with Indians opposite Market Square. Hans built a surgery at back of their kitchen and planted a garden of medicinal herbs. One son, Jacobus Johannes Kierstede, became a New York surgeon like his father.

### Becoming an Insider

During Sara's residence at New Amsterdam near the dock, she lived opposite an Indian trading depot during bargaining for furs, food, and firewood, which Indians transported by canoe. In collaboration with translator Pieter van Couwenhoven, she worded the discontent of Rompsicka and Tapausagh of Long Island with the greedy English in Long Island. She interpreted the Munsee language for Chief Oratam of Hackensack, a Lenni Lenape tribe at Esopus village on the Black and Swartekill creeks. Oratam viewed the arrival of the first white Europeans to Manhattan.

Usually the only woman present at parlays, Sara easily conveyed Native American events to the Dutch because she bore neither rank nor government authority. On July 10, 1663, she facilitated the Lenape treaty with Governor Peter Stuyvesant to end the six-year Esopus Wars in the upper Hudson Valley and prevented the Munsee from forming a mass Indian alliance. On September 10, 1663, the New Amsterdam militia successfully attacked the Esopus.

## Sara's Triumph

Shortly after the death of fifth son Jacobus, Sara was nursing her infant Jacobus Johannes when she translated a crucial element of local relations. At the insistence of Sauwenaare, a Wiechquaeskeck sachem, and Metsewackos, a sachem of the Kichtawangh, from November 1663 to July 1664 she spoke for Oratam, the prime peacemaker, and completed negotiations with Esopus sachem Seweckenamo. She promoted sobriety by discouraging the sale of alcohol to tribes. After natives identified alcohol dealers by name, the governor offered to pay in cloth anyone who captured a whiskey trader. Sara's adept language knowledge and her mediation of the return of the captive Aeltje Sybrants, a Dutch bootlegger, on April 16, 1664, earned from Oratam two thousand acres along the east side of the Hackensack River. In 1663, the lengthy negotiation added to her land holdings a building lot in Manhattan on the Klatchook Road near a windmill. Six years later, Oratam died at age ninety-two.

As an aid to the practice of husband Hans, Sara translated names and uses of native medicinal plants. Two—goosefoot (*Chenopodium album*) for treating joint pain and dysentery and wormseed (*Artemisia cina*) to ease constipation and quell intestinal parasites—she grew in a home herb bed. At Hans's death in 1667, she wed a Dutch-Prussian, Cornelis Van Borsum, a Long Island ferryman. A third marriage to widower Elbert Elbertsz Stouthoff, a justice of the peace, brought four stepchildren into Sara's household.

Before Sara's widowhood in 1688, she shared a home and bakehouse with thirty-one-year-old son Luycase. Her death on October 21, 1693, preceded the distribution of six African slaves, Andries, Jan, Maria, Pieter, Susanna, and their mother Sara. In 1853, H.T. Kierstede & Son of Broadway and Spring Street advertised an herbal ointment to treat inflamed breasts. The curative references the medical collaboration of Hans, Sara, and Sara's grandmother.

### *Sources*

Huston, Geraldine. *Oratam of the Hackensacks*. Paramus, NJ: Highway Printing, 1950.

Romney, Susanah Shaw. *New Netherland Connections: Intimate Networks and Atlantic Ties in Seventeenth-Century America*. Chapel Hill: University of North Carolina Press, 2014.

## Margaret Hardenbroeck Philipse (October 14, 1630–November 30, 1690)
**Shipping Agent, Trader**
**New Amsterdam, New York**

An exemplar of female Dutch commodity agents in the Hudson Valley, Margaret Hardenbroeck DeVries Philipse thrived at bicoastal shipping and realty. One of eight children, she and siblings Andries, Johannes, and Abel were born in the Rhine Valley at Elderfield, Holland, to Marritje Katernberg and Adolph Hardenbruk, a subsequent resident of Bergen, New Jersey. In an influx of single Dutchwomen, she arrived at age twenty two from Dusseldorf, Prussia, to Winebridge Pier in the Dutch settlement of New Amsterdam.

As she-merchant and factor or broker, Margaret clerked in Manhattan at Winkelstraet (Shop Street) in the debt collection division of a shipping office owned by her Amsterdam-based cousin, Wouter Valck. In September 1659, she reported the default of Hendrick Janszen Van de Vin and promised that he would acquit his debt on Wouter's return plus interest. Addition of Dutch client Daniel des Messieres enlarged her job as trader in textiles and bear, beaver, raccoon, and wildcat furs from the Hudson Valley Indians in exchange for pins, vinegar, and vegetable oil.

In October 1659, at age twenty-nine, Margaret wed widowed merchant Pieter Rudolphus DeVries. An egalitarian acting as his full partner, she purchased three hundred acres, the beginning of Philipse Manor. She recorded an ante-nuptial agreement to secure the *usus* or property of her husband, who was twenty-eight years her senior. According to the terms, she purchased ocean-going clipper ships—the flagship *King Charles, Beaver,* two-masted brig *Morgenster* (*Morning Star*), the slave ship from Curaçao *De Nieuw Nederlantse Indiaen* (*New Netherland Indian*), and *Pearl*—and invested in River Indian property in Bergen, New Jersey, and Manhattan, New York. Margaret's mercantile in oak logs, wheat berries, and tobacco expanded from Albany, New York, to the English islands of Barbados and Jamaica. When Pieter died in late spring 1661 shortly after the birth of daughter Eva, the Orphanmasters representing the Reformed Church demanded an inventory of the child's inheritance. Margaret, who was six months pregnant, signed an agreement that Eva would receive a fair share.

### A Propitious Wedlock

In October 1662, Margaret's aptitude for merchandising Dutch liquors, pottery, glassware, and household goods contributed to marriage to Bohemian carpenter and mason Frederick Philipse of Friesland, Holland. The couple resided on the East River opposite Long Island. In the employ of Governor Peter Stuyvesant and the Dutch West India Company, Frederick became a global shipper to England and Iberia, a promoter of piracy, and a trader of wheat, spices, textiles, paper, Virginia tobacco, and slaves from Barbados. Their union flourished from her control of finances and personal property and from the birth of son Philip in March 1663. They produced ten more children; Anna, Adolphus, and Rombout did not survive infancy.

The couple's merchandising made them wealthy from trading beaver, bear, fox, mink, wildcat, otter, and muskrat fur, cowhide, buckskin, and grain and the purchase of riverfront property from Sintsink and Wiechquaeskeck Indians at Yonkers on the Pocantico River and from the Tappan (Lenape) on the Hudson. Their fleet—*Charles, Charity, Delaware Merchant, Dolphin, Fortune, Francis & Thomas, Hopewell, Jacob, John & Rebecca, Katherine, Ketch Royal, New York Merchant, Pembroke, Philip, Unity,* and *Vine*—returned to North America with musket barrels, tobacco pipes, tools, swords, and wool nightcaps. From their Tarrytown warehouse and Dock Street wharf on the Hudson River, they made deals with pirates Adam Baldridge and Edward Welch for alcohol and guns and accessed shipping lanes of the *King Charles,* which offered a master suite below the quarter deck and meals at the captain's table. Margaret made business trips in January 1664 and a one-month journey in December 1668.

Because of British usurpation of New Amsterdam for James II on August 27, 1664, and the renaming of the colony "New York," Margaret lost financial independence under strict paternalistic laws. She continued backing her husband's businesses and, in 1665, petitioned the king for a more liberal trading schedule for the ship *King Charles.* With daughter Annetje, she sailed on trans-Atlantic voyages as supercargo, which combined the jobs of purchasing agent and loadmaster. As prime slave importers from Angola and Madagascar to North America, she had her pick of the most promising laborers.

## A Mercantile Dynasty

During Lower Manhattan's building boom, Margaret rivaled the English in shrewd financial management. She owned fifty-two thousand acres (eighty-one square miles) at the stone two-story Philipse Manor which extended from the Croton and Bronx Rivers to Spuyten Duyvil Creek in Westchester County north of New York City and the Getty Square residence in Yonkers. Property management enriched her family from the productivity of tenant farmers. At Sleepy Hollow gristmill, slaves processed and ground grain; in the manor cellar, they churned milk into butter. Additional revenue from the Nepperhan sawmill in Yonkers secured their prestige. Because of her wealth, she gained a reputation for greed and selfishness. New York's richest woman, she retired in 1679 and died a decade later, the first New World entrepreneur to build a fortune.

Margaret's sons Adolphus and Philip continued shipping and trade with Europe and the West Indies in sugar, wine, rum, molasses, salt meat, cacao, iron, and slaves. The couple's loyalty to George III cost the family confiscation of two hundred fifty square miles of land in 1783 and imprisonment of their grandson Frederick Philipse III in Connecticut on the orders of General George Washington. The manor sold to a consortium of tenant farmers for £250,000 (approx. $476,532,900).

**DeVries-Hardenbroeck-Philipse Genealogy**

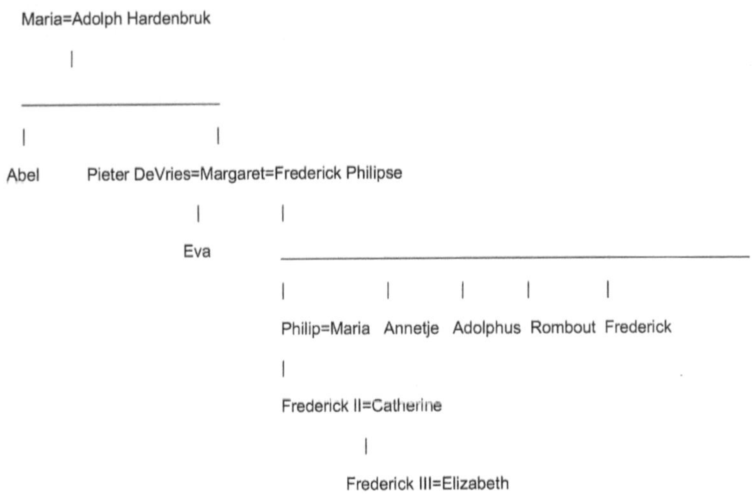


### *Sources*

Kim, Sung Bok. "A New Look at the Great Landlords of Eighteenth-Century New York," *William and Mary Quarterly* 27:4 (1970): 581–614.
Waldrup, Carole Chandler. *Colonial Women: 23 Europeans Who Helped Build a Nation.* Jefferson, NC: McFarland, 1999.
Zimmerman, Jean. *The Women of the House. New York*: Harcourt, 2006.

## Ann Marwood Durant (April 1, 1635–January 22, 1694)
**Seamstress, Coffin Designer, Attorney, Innkeeper**
**Roanoke, North Carolina**

A pioneer of coastal North Carolina, Ann Marwood Durant thrived as an independent plantation manager and the state's first female attorney.

A colonist on Chesapeake Bay, she and older sister Elizabeth Marwood Blake were the daughters of indentured servant Joseph Marwood and Alice Pell Marwood, who died shortly after Ann's birth. A refugee of the English Civil War, she wed Norman-Cornish mariner-attorney George Durant, Jr., of Blockley, England, on January 4, 1658, in Northumberland County, Virginia. He explored the colonial coastline with Captain Richard Batts, a Barbados merchant, and his brother, fur trader Nathaniel Batts of Chowan, North Carolina's first English resident.

The Durants settled on three hundred acres on the Virginia–North Carolina border near Suffolk. Three years later, they and their first two children moved to Roanoke (modern Albemarle, North Carolina) as freeholders on the Albemarle Sound at Durants Neck, a fertile land for growing corn and wheat and raising cattle and pigs and ample forests for harvesting tar and pitch. In August 1661 and March 1662 east of Edenton between the Little and Perquimans rivers, they purchased the two thousand-acre Wicocombe Plantation from Cisketando and Kilcocanen, chiefs of the Yeopim Menape, on the Great Dismal Swamp, a vast natural wetland rich in fish, fowl, and deer. The deeds, the earliest in North Carolina history, were clouded by the connivance of assemblyman George Catchmaid, who added the claims to his own property.

After selling investments in Virginia Colony, George Durant earned respect as North Carolina attorney general and speaker of the assembly of burgesses. In London, he protested the rigors of English control under Charles II. During his absences from home, Ann operated their plantation, commercial outpost, and inn, where she served to elite politicians cider, rum, and quince shrub, a vinegar syrup rich in fruit, sugar, and aromatics. Her business and the confinement of prisoners at Wicocombe required the stocking of corn, planks, and nails. Officials used the Durant property to locate pillories and stocks, the colony's first public structures, which Colonial authorities equipped to punish smugglers and pirates. While bearing and raising seven more children, Ann developed legal skills and represented the Durants and their neighbors in court.

The Durant residence became an informal courthouse and jail as well as a meeting hall for political conferences. At the home of councilman Francis Godfrey, on May 25, 1673, she sued the owners of the sloop *Two Brothers* from Barbados for the back wages of mariner Andrew Ball. Two years later, in one of twenty lawsuits, she reclaimed property and satisfied debts owed to her family from patrons of their inn. In addition to sewing leather pants and shirts for guests, she constructed coffins and scheduled funerals.

During Culpeper's Rebellion against the Navigation Act, on December 1, 1677, George was jailed for protesting a law limiting trade to English shippers. In summer 1686, Lords Proprietor Seth Sothel confiscated two thousand acres of Wicocombe, but lost his authority to rebel colonists who supported the Durants. Ann bore her last child at age forty-six and fostered two granddaughters after the death of their parents, Elizabeth and Thomas Waller, in 1687. She survived George, who died in February 1692. Their sons John and Thomas pursued ownership of their inheritance by refuting Catchmaid's fraudulent deed.

*Sources*

Hathaway, J.R.B., ed. *North Carolina Historical and Genealogical Register.* Edenton, NC: Clearfield, 1900.
McIlvenna, Noeleen. *A Very Mutinous People.* Chapel Hill: University of North Carolina Press, 2009.
Smith, Margaret Supplee, and Emily Herring Wilson. North Carolina Women Making History. Chapel Hill: University of North Carolina Press, 1999.

## Esther Pinheiro (ca. 1636–?)
**Trader, Shipper**
**New York City**

A successful Jewish merchant, Esther Pinheiro survived widowhood by profiting from New World trade. She and her mother Rachel originated among the Sephardic residents of Madrid, Spain. After marrying Isaac Pinheiro in Amsterdam, Holland, at age twenty, she began wedded life in New Amsterdam and produced three girls and two boys. The couple built a mercantile business at Charlestown, Nevis, a naval base and port in the Leeward Islands of the British Caribbean. For a growing Jewish community, a Sephardic cemetery received the dead between 1679 and 1730; congregation members built a stone-walled path and synagogue in 1684.

After the introduction of sugar production in 1648, Nevis became a profitable trade nexus and slave exchange where blacks outnumbered whites four to one. A French attack and the burning of Charlestown in 1706 and the September 9–11, 1707, hurricane devastated the island as well as St. Kitts, Antigua, Montserrat, and St. Thomas. During the disruption, she purchased from New York governor Edward Cornbury a Nevis slave named Bastiana.

After Isaac's death in New York, on February 17, 1710, his will named Esther executor and heir to his investments in a cane mill and eighteen slaves. Business demands took her to Boston in Massachusetts Bay Colony and to the Caribbean. She built a second home at Charlestown, Nevis, and sailed her twenty-ton sloop *Neptune* and its five-man crew between the Leeward Islands and New England. As supercargo, she marketed salt, sugar, and molasses before filling the hold with lumber, flour, fish, soap, and European luxuries.

*Sources*

Hershkowitz, Leo. "Colonial Entrepreneurs: A Quartet of Jewish Women," https://jwa.org/encyclopedia/article/colonial-entrepreneurs-quartet-of-jewish-women.
Levine, Yitzchok. "Glimpses into American Jewish History," https://personal.stevens.edu/~llevine/colonial_jewish_bussinesswomen.pdf.
Marcus, Jacob R. *The Colonial American Jew, 1492–176*. Detroit: Wayne State University Press, 1970.

## Hannah Feake Bowne (August 1637–November 31, 1677)
**Minister**
**Watertown, Massachusetts**

## Dinah Underhill Bowne (July 20, 1705–February 1, 1770)
**Minister**
**Flushing, New York**

Minister Hannah Feake Bowne, the great-niece of adamant Puritan John Winthrop, governor of Massachusetts, crusaded for Quakerism through preaching tours to England, Ireland, Holland, and Friesland. The daughter of Connecticut apothecary Elizabeth "Bess" Fones Hallett and Lieutenant Robert Feake, a soldier and goldsmith, Hannah was born at Watertown and grew up at Greenwich Manor, Connecticut, and lived on Elizabeth's Neck (modern Greenwich Point). After her father abandoned the family, her mother wed his business manager, William Hallett. At age twelve, Hannah moved to Hallett's Cove (modern Astoria, Queens) on the East River in New Netherlands. Attack by Hackensack Indians in September 1655 cost the family the burning of their house and farm and forced the Quakers to hold meetings in the woods.

The Halletts relocated ten miles from Manhattan to one hundred twelve acres on the Long Island Sound at Vlissengen (modern Flushing), where Hannah married vintner John Bowne, Sr., on May 7, 1656. Freed of the uncertainty of the Hallett household, the Bownes produced five daughters and two sons, who occupied a one-room farmhouse. Hannah's interest in the Society of Friends resulted in the couple's conversion from Puritanism. John advanced the Friends' cause by selling Quaker books and pamphlets. During Hannah's promotional mission tour of Maryland, England, and Holland, she furthered founder George Fox's plan for Women's Meetings. In the pulpit, she made use of a childhood bilingualism and delivered sermons in Dutch and English.

### Quaker Trials

Hannah's cousin, Tobias Feake, issued the "Flushing Remonstrance" of December 27, 1657, accusing Puritans of jealousy and suspicion. The document asserted the right of conscience and pledged Quakers to nonviolence. In 1661, the couple bought a farm and residence at the corner of Broadway and Bowne Avenue two blocks from the meeting house. Hannah welcomed the congregation to her kitchen and served as facilitator. The setting hosted the meeting twice weekly for forty years.

Governor Peter Stuyvesant issued a hostile religious backlash toward Quakers, declaring "It is forbidden to bring the strolling people called Quakers into the province without obtaining the consent of the Government" (Yarnall, 1908, 46). On September 1, 1662, John began serving four months in solitary confinement on bread and water at a Manhattan jail. He refused to pay the £50 (approx. $10,770.02) fine or to escape from the cell that guards left open. His defeat of Dutch prejudice endorsed religious tolerance in Long Island.

On John's release and exile to Ireland, he protested religious persecution to the Dutch West India Company in Rotterdam, Holland. To secure secret information, he shipped home his hat containing a bundle of papers in the crown. Following John's routing through Barbados and Maryland, the couple reunited in March 1664 after nineteen months apart. Governor Stuyvesant met John in the street and apologized for his transgressions against Quakers.

## The Committed Life

On return to England, Ireland, Holland, and Germany on March 24, 1675, Hannah sailed from Staten Island on Andrew Bowne's ship bound for London and left daughter Elizabeth to tend five children and her elderly paternal grandfather. In May 1676, Hannah suffered a stillbirth in Dublin, Ireland. She summarized her devotion to the faith in a letter to Long Island Friends on August 2, 1676. She urged them to "press on to this mark: here we shall lye down and none to make us afraid" (Jackson, 1986). She stayed at the Sign of the Peel, a Quaker clearing house at St. John Street in Clerkenwell, the residence of carpenter John and Mary Elson, a founder of London's Women's Meeting. After John joined Hannah in November 1676, she died unexpectedly at age thirty-nine.

Still devoted to his faith, John donated three acres for a Friends cemetery and meeting house site. His influence ignited Quaker enthusiasm for abolition of slavery. Their son Samuel became a minister like his mother and returned to the Bowne homeplace to serve the Friends community. The third generation involved grandson John Bowne III and wife Dinah Underhill Bowne in Christian endeavors. Dinah maintained the family home, which eventually became a station of the Underground Railroad, national shrine, and museum.

*See also* Elizabeth Fones Hallett.

### *Sources*

Jackson, Charlotte. "A Lost Letter of Hannah (Feake) Bowne (1637–1678)," https://*www.bownehouse.org/letter-from-hannah-bowne* (24 May 1986).
"Treasures of New York: Bowne House" (film), www.treasures-of-new-york/treasures-of-new-york-bowne-house-z4qsbw/ (29 November 2023).
Yarnall, Charles. "John Bowne of Flushing, 1627–1695," *Bulletin of Friends' Historical Society of Philadelphia* 2:2 (June 1908): 44–67.

## Diana Harris Foster (1641–after 1706)
## Innkeeper
## Perquimans, North Carolina

One of North Carolina colony's first businesswomen, Diana Manners Harris Foster struggled to profit from four marriages. At her arrival in Albemarle in 1665, she, husband Thomas Harris, and toddler sons John and Thomas occupied six hundred acres on Muddy Creek. Diana kept pigs and registered an ear crop mark to secure the herd. She signed legal documents with an X attesting to her sale of shoes, barrels of pork, and other goods. By November, Thomas advanced to clerk of the precinct council and added the post of public registrar.

At age thirty, Diana was co-manager of an inn and one of the state's first taverns. In widowhood in October 1677, she executed her husband's will and lived on the proceeds of cattle, pigs, and saloon customers. She passed through a second marriage to neighbor William Foster, a county court justice and innkeeper with two daughters, Elizabeth and Frances. Foster died in October 1687, leaving Diana dependent on her son John as co-manager of the inn.

In 1691, the county and general courts met at Diana's establishment, thus providing her a steady income. Citizens of all social classes came to collect local debts, thus building clientele for the inn. Author Craig Muldrew stated, "Thus, in social and economic terms, credit was a leveling force within the community" (Muldrew, 1993, 34). While she hosted court in her home, her income allowed for a bookkeeper, Thomas Hassold, who also transported supplies and tended her grain fields.

The investment soured in May 1694 during Diana's marriage to Thomas White, a poor money manager who battled fifty lawsuits to collect from debtors. On the edge of bankruptcy, in 1695, she sued Robert Kitching for £2 (approx. $513.62) in pork. The Whites parted in 1695 after Thomas sold her domestic furnishings and personal goods and ousted her from his Albemarle home. After White's death, in 1697, she regained her residence and rented rooms to boarders.

Diana inherited a relative's money that kept her financially afloat and allowed her to profit once more by testifying for defendants and witnessing sales and transfers of property. In 1698, she fell into debt for £15 (approx. $3,239.43). The last marriage to Thomas Mercer on February 17, 1703, brought more lawsuits when Diana attempted to reclaim acreage belonging to Thomas Harris. The example of female taverns expanded into the late 1700s, when 10 percent of licenses listed female owners.

### *Sources*

Muldrew, Craig. "Credit and the Courts: Debt Litigation in a Seventeenth Century Urban Community," *Economic History Review* 46:1 (1993): 23–38.
Rutz-Robbins, Kristi. "'Divers Debts': Women's Participation in the Local Economy," *Early American Studies* 4:2 (2006): 425–441.
Smith, Margaret Supplee, and Emily Herring Wilson. *North Carolina Women Making History.* Chapel Hill: University of North Carolina Press, 1999.

## Anne Toft Jenifer (1643–February 15, 1687)
**Trader**
**Accomack County, Virginia**

A property owner in Maryland and Virginia colonies and Jamaica, Anne Toft Scarburgh Jenifer turned real estate and commerce into remarkable wealth. She appears to have lived in Godalming, Surrey, southwest of London with nine siblings and parents Mary and Humphrey Toft. During a migration boom fueled by the tobacco economy, she sailed to Virginia around 1659. Following a short marriage or pretended wedlock, on November 3, 1660, as an independent widow, she received an eight-hundred-acre land grant on Chicanessecks Creek in Gloucester and Westmoreland counties from Governor William Berkeley. The property derived from headrights, an allotment of fifty acres per person for transporting sixteen immigrants to the colony to work as tenant farmers.

Known as Mrs. Anne Toft in her late teens, she became the mistress of Colonel Edmund Scarburgh II, an entrepreneur and Indian fighter. The amoral English attorney twenty-six years her senior owned thirty-four thousand acres on both shores of Chesapeake Bay. He attained prominence as shipper, surveyor, sheriff, cattleman, firearms dealer, and speaker of the House of Burgesses. While residing at Hedra Cottage at Craddockville on Occohannock Creek, he sired Annabella, Arcadia, and Attalanta Toft.

### The Female Entrepreneur

With the aid of Randall Revell, Edmund's brother-in-law, Anne bought three thousand acres at Double Purchase on Revell's Neck, Virginia, on the Manokin River between Hearns and Parramore creeks. She continued investing in slaves and acreage on August 28, 1662, with property purchased from Tapatiapan, an Accomack Indian of Onancock on Chesapeake Bay. Another boon to the colony, transporting twenty-four more colonists to work tenant farms won Anne headrights to twelve hundred acres on April 21, 1663. While she was a "privileged guest" in Edmund's Pungotege home, he remunerated her in November 1664 with Gargaphia Plantation, a coastal tract on Gargathy Neck. As mate and business partner, he continued to use the land for his cobblery, livestock breeding, tannery, and salt production.

Anne earned more grants totaling twenty-five thousand five hundred fifty acres and made propitious acquaintance with powerful men. Through an alliance with mariner and agent Robert Risdon of Devonshire in 1666, she prospered from merchandising fish in the West Indies and trading tobacco with Dutch and English shippers on the Chesapeake Bay. Additional investment in the cargo of the ship *Virginia Merchant,* which sank on March 26, 1661, at what is now Sonesta Beach, Bermuda, required circumvention from her attorney, Connecticut governor John Winthrop, Jr. She bought three thousand acres from Edmund in 1668 for some seven hundred pounds of indigo and ninety-one hundred pounds of sugar. Ambition led her to buy four thousand acres in St. Elizabeth's Parish, Jamaica. Another financial venture demanded the advice of Lieutenant Governor James Russell to settle a bungled business deal on Nevis.

## Public Infamy

Anne's household grew to forty-five people; her total land possession may have reached thirty thousand acres. When her scandalous lifestyle reached civil court by the testimony of servant Martin Moore and his wife on May 10, 1670, the record put her at risk of public shaming for fornication. The court could exact public lashing and a fine of five hundred pounds of tobacco. Punishment posed a judgment of bastardy for Anne's three daughters and a possible death sentence for Scarburgh for adultery. None of the outcomes touched her or her lover.

Still a viable merchant, in April 1671, Anne posted to Galway, Ireland, fifty-six containers of tobacco on the ship *St. Nicholas,* owned by Jan Cornelisse van Cleef, a Dutch merchant at Gravesent, Long Island, New Amsterdam. Two months later, she joined one hundred fifty Virginians in a scheme to relocate to the southern coast of Jamaica during a financial boom. In anticipation of departure, she dispatched slaves to the island, where she may have planned a single life after Edmund's death as a Caribbean planter.

### Managing Alone

After Edmund died of smallpox at Hedra Cottage, in July 1671, Anne may have needed a shield against charges of fornication and bastardy. For whatever reason, she wed London attorney and militia colonel Daniel Jenifer, father of Daniel of St. Thomas and eventual justice of the peace and sheriff of Accomack. Within months, the liquidation of slaves and property in Jamaica earned the couple a profit of £1,000 (approx. $278,391.33). With the aid of pioneer Maryland planter Randall Revell, the Jenifers acquired mining rights on eleven thousand three hundred acres in Accomack County and amassed three thousand six hundred more in Maryland. Their multiple land sales from 1675 to 1687 coincided with arrangements for Anne's teenaged daughters' inheritance.

At Anne's death at age forty-five, she owned the ship *St. Nicholas* and remained one of the wealthiest settlers of the American colonies. Daniel survived her by five years and passed to his three stepdaughters equal shares of a five-thousand-acre tract. Anne's grandson Daniel became a doctor. Her great-grandson Daniel represented Maryland on May 26, 1787, in Philadelphia as a delegate at the Constitutional Convention.

*Sources*

Kolp, John G. "'Mrs. Ann' and 'The Colonel,'" *Virginia Magazine of History and Biography* 130:3 (2022): 218–252.

Wise, Jennings Cropper. *Ye Kingdome of Accawmacke*. Richmond, VA: Bell, Book and Stationery, 1911.

## Hannah English Williams (ca. 1645–December 16, 1722)
**Naturalist**
**Charleston, South Carolina**

The New World's first female collector of flora and fauna, Hannah English Williams contributed early research data on the biota of the Carolina coast. No details survive of her parentage or childhood. She married Matthew English, who sailed on the ship *Carolina* from Downs, England, in August 1669 on South Carolina's first immigrant fleet. On a laborious route from Ireland to Nevis and Barbados, on March 21, 1670, he reached Albemarle Point at Charlestown, a six hundred sixty-five-acre expanse on the Ashley River.

The couple raised son Henroyda English and daughter Mary English Spragg. Widowed in late November 1692, Hannah owned five hundred acres at Stony Point. Upon marriage to planter William Williams in 1695, she acquired five hundred acres north of the Ashley River at present-day

Archdale, South Carolina. An exploration of the outdoors satisfied her curiosity about fossils, plants, shells, birds, reptiles, and insects. Over time, she intensified and varied her scavenging in the wild. On May 18, 1705, she posted to a London scholar "Some of Our Vipers and Severall Sorts of Snakes Scorpions and Lizzards in a Bottle and a few Other Insex" (Smith, 1986, 86).

## A Group Effort

Like Hannah Williams and Rachel Chapman of Antigua, local collectors formed an Atlantic network of scientists identifying indigenous flora and fauna. From May 22, 1701, to December 12, 1713, Hannah entrusted specimens to South Carolina shipman William Halstead for transfer to James Petiver and the Royal Society, which relayed instructions from London to eighty American collectors. For preservation, she fixed each sample on a pin or placed it in a vial of brandy or rum. James requested flies, moths, bees, wasps, beetles, and grasshoppers. In reciprocation, she asked for newspapers, brown paper, and medicines to treat problems with her "splene."

The report "Animals and Shells Sent from Carolina to Mr. James Petiver," an apothecary at the sign of the White Cross in London Aldersgate Street, began with Hannah's meticulous inspection of crustaceans. She isolated twenty-five bivalves—"Schollops, Cockles, Oysters, Muscles"—and continued with single seashells and fossils of fishbone, conches, and teeth (*Ibid.*, 90). In the next report to James, she anticipated adding butterflies and other insects and reptiles scavenged from her coastal Carolina property. The data appeared in Petiver's serial pamphlets *Musei Petiveriani Centuria Prima Rariora Naturae Continens* (The First Century Containing Nature's Rarities from Petiver's Collection).

## Contributions to Science

James informed Hannah of the specifics of his collections and sent her via Captain John Newton on the *Providence* "Hysterick pills," an anti-epileptic mix of fossilized amber in oil, oleous salt (Epsom salt), tartar salt (potassium bitartrate), and powdered human skull. In February 1704 and November 1706, he specified his need for a small fish, beehive, vipers, scorpions, lizards, salamanders, frogs, coral, crabs, moss, seaweed, and more insects. She replied that she would locate redbirds and mockingbirds in spring and send them alive after cold weather passed. Her curious finds included native herbs and medicines "with the Westo Kings Tobacco pipe and a Queens Petticoatt made off Moss" (*Ibid.*, 87). A miscommunication led her to believe James had died. She asked her son to check on his welfare and learned that the collaboration was still viable.

Petiver immortalized Hannah in the six-part 1767 compendium *Gazophylacium Naturae et Artis* (Thesaurus of Nature and Art) with commentary on a "5 holed Carolina sea Urchin or Fritter … a very singular Animal" and a "white Campeachy Spoon-Muscle (Campeacheana alba)" (*Ibid.*, 90).

The Latin treatise "An Account of Animals and Shells Sent from Carolina" also credited to the North American coast:

- double-toothed clam (*Pholas Carolinus*)
- flask-shaped Carolina sea snail (*Buccinum Campeachianum ampullaceum)*
- narrow Carolina mussel (*Musculus Carolinus angustus)*
- red-blotted Carolina crab (*Cancer Carolinus literis eleganter rubis*)
- striped blue Carolina scallop (*Mytulus Carolinus Latis striis rugosis*)
- thorny-edged Carolina crab (*Cancer Carolinus marginibus spinosus)*
- white Carolina mussel (*Musculus Carolinus albus*)

James sent illustrations of three eponymous butterflies honoring Hannah:

- Williams's orange-girdled Carolina or Viceroy
- Williams's selvedge-eyed Carolina or creole pearly eye
- Williams's yellow-tipped Carolina or dog's head.

He named the swallowtail (*Papillionidae lepidoptera)* the "Royal Williams."

Alongside biota from East India, the Caribbean, and South Africa, Hannah's Carolina collection remains in London's Natural History Museum.

### Sources

Petiver, James. "An Account of Animals and Shells Sent from Carolina," *Philosophical Transactions* (Royal Society of London) 24:299 (May 1705): 1952–1960.
Smith, Beatrice Scheer. "Hannah English Williams: America's First Woman Natural History Collector," *South Carolina Historical Magazine* 87 (April 1986): 83–92.

## Mary Baldwin Turfrey (1645–1718)
**Needlework Teacher**
**Boston, Massachusetts**

The New World's first needlework teacher, Mary Baldwin Turfrey, turned to instruction to earn a living in old age. In 1685, she married

Captain George Turfrey, a merchant and attorney who served York County, Maine, as assemblyman and as a warden of King's Chapel on Tremont Street, Boston. On July 27, 1688, the couple occupied a six-hundred-acre tract on Casco Bay at Salisbury.

George bought half of Bonython and Cow islands northeast of Portland, Maine, in 1691 and invested in a sawmill. At Saco on September 24, 1700, he managed the sixteen-man defense at Fort Mary during Queen Anne's War and the August 1703 negotiation of peace with the Wabanaki Confederacy at Pemaquid (modern Bristol, Maine). George's command lasted eight years.

The couple produced two children. Katherine Turfrey married John Briggs of Taunton, Massachusetts, and her brother, Edward Turfrey, the secretary of Samuel Sewall, Jr., died in Boston on January 8, 1702, from smallpox. After George's death in 1714, Mary opened a boarding academy for young ladies in Boston's South End. She taught the fine points of crewel embroidery and advertised classes in wool needlework in the *Boston News-letter.* Her pupils specialized in stitching false pocket slits and in covering their work with birds and flowers. Mary lived to age seventy-three.

### *Source*

Folsom, George. *History of Saco and Biddeford.* Saco, ME: self-published, 1830.

## Mary Coffin Starbuck (February 20, 1645–November 13, 1717)
**Trader, Bookkeeper**
**Nantucket, Massachusetts**

Operator of a trading post on Nantucket Island, Mary "Miriam" Coffin Starbuck partnered with husband Nathaniel Starbuck, Sr., in satisfying the material needs of cod fishers and whalers. She was born the seventh child of a Quaker household in Haverhill, Massachusetts, three years after the 1642 immigration of two aunts, her paternal grandmother Joanna Kemper Coffin, and parents Dionis Stevens and investor Tristan Coffin from Brixton, England. After abandoning comfortable estates, he acquired one quarter of Nantucket and the nine-hundred-acre Tuckernuck Island, a whaling concourse. He advanced to chief magistrate.

Tristan's generosity provided Mary with land and a model of the New World entrepreneur. At the area's first wedding, in 1662, she united with Nathaniel Starbuck, the illiterate son of the area's pioneers. At Cambridge Farm, she bore the colony's first European child, the first of six daughters and four sons. In the early years of adjusting to the New World, the family operated a ferry and tavern on Main Street north of Hummock Pond. They maintained a warehouse at the corner of Main and Union streets.

During business hours, from 1662, Mary recorded barter with the Wampanoag, who exchanged cured bluefish, wheat, rye, and bird feathers for cotton and linen textiles, thread, knitting needles, buttons, and ribbon. For clothing needs, they asked for shoes, hats, leather, and gloves. Some sought candles, pipes, powder and shot, flint, soap, kitchenware, nails, boards, beef, wine, cider, molasses, and fishing gear for use at the Squam and Sasacacha cod stations. Mary accepted in trade manual labor, mowing, plowing, carting, threshing, and spinning and carding wool. In 1685, Edward Starbuck deeded more land to Nathaniel.

A respected minister from the age of fifty-six, Mary abandoned traditional Protestant liturgy and spread the Quaker faith on Nantucket. At Parliament House, town leaders of the faith scheduled meetings in the great room overlooking Main Street until the Nantucket meeting house opened in 1708. She carefully deferred decisions to her husband but clearly dominated their business and religious matters. Every four months, she composed the Quarterly Epistles.

Mary's record book retained historical dealings with the Wampanoag from 1662 to 1715. Quakers treasured the sheepskin-covered account log along with a silver teaspoon she once owned. In a 1715 letter to a granddaughter who survived a house fire, Mary described a gift trunk filled with cloth, blankets, mutton, corn, wool, and £17 (approx. $4,359.02). At her death on November 13, 1717, Nathanial Jr. continued the ledger. Mary's exemplary superintendence of Nantucket business and religion foretold the feminism of a descendant, Lucretia Coffin Mott, who championed full citizenship for women.

### *Sources*

Macy, Obed. *The History of Nantucket*. Oxford, UK: Oxford University, 1835.
Philbrick, Nathaniel. *Away Off Shore: Nantucket Island and Its People, 1602–1890*. New York: Penguin, 2011.
*Proceedings of the Nantucket Historical Association*. Waltham, MA: Waltham Publishing Company, 1908.

## Maria van Cortlandt van Rensselaer (July 20, 1645–January 29, 1689)
**Beer Distributor, Estate Treasurer**
**Albany, New York**

The scion of a wealthy Dutch emigrant trader on the New World frontier, for thirteen years, Marritje "Maria" van Cortlandt van Rensselaer managed a million-acre manor in eastern New Amsterdam that allied two dominant Dutch-American dynasties. The maternal granddaughter of fur trader Pieter Loockerman, she was born in Holland to Anetje "Annette" Loockerman van Cortlandt and landholder Oloff Stevenszen van Cortlandt, the Dutch West India Company commissioner of cargoes. An emigrant from Amsterdam, Holland, Oloff arrived in America via Bermuda on the ship *Den Harrinck* (the Herring) on March 28, 1638, and settled on Marckvelt Street. Maria was reared among the elite with the elder sibling of Catherine van Cortlandt Philipse and Jacobus and Stephanus van Cortlandt, who were each elected twice to mayor of New York City.

Maria began clerking for her father as agent and distributor for his brewery in the stone double house on Brouwerstraat (modern Stone Street between Broad and Marckvelt), New Amsterdam's first cobblestoned thoroughfare. Precise laws governed the manufacture, export, smuggling, and marketing of beer and prohibited sale to Indians. On July 12, 1662, at age seventeen, she married Jeremias van Rensselaer, who was thirteen years her senior, and made their home in the wilderness town of Albany. Five months later, she survived a bout of smallpox during pregnancy with son Kiliaen. When infection left her tremulous and housebound after hip surgery for osteomyelitis, she accepted the aid of her twelve-year-old sister, Catherine von Cortlandt. Maria's mother-in-law, Anna Van Wely van Rensselaer, sent medicines.

Throughout the Algonquin-Mohawk wars, Jeremias ran the Hudson River brewery, promoted accord with Indians, and negotiated with Governor Peter Stuyvesant on boundary disputes and defense against British aggressors. In 1664, Maria's father Oloff aided Stuyvesant in determining terms of surrender to the British. During her pregnancy with Hendrick, on April 7, 1666, flooding of the Hudson River during an ice melt swept away the van Rensselaer's house, barn, and brewery. While Jeremias built Watervliet farm and a brewery north of Albany, in 1669, Maria suffered a stillbirth. Widowed during pregnancy with daughter Maria on October 12, 1674, the elder Maria mothered Jeremias, Johannes, and Maria Jr. on the central eastern border of New York. Meanwhile, her parents fostered Anna and Hendrick while Kiliaen studied silversmithing in Boston.

## A Promotion

At the death in 1678 of Jeremias's replacement, his uncle Nicolaus van Rensselaer, Maria became the fifth patroon of Rensselaerswyck at a salary of one hundred fifty bushels of wheat. She managed the farm in English manor style, settled estates for herself and children, and, by letter, oversaw family property in Holland. During her term as administrator, the Dutch family members harassed her to produce greater profits to relieve shortfalls in Europe. For advice, Maria wrote frequently to brother Stephanus van Cortlandt in New York, who sent her tender good wishes. In contrast, brother Richard posted to his recently widowed sister by the ship *Nieu Jorck* (New York) letters bristling with an all-business tone.

At the death of Oloff on April 5, 1684, and his wife on May 14, 1684, until son Kiliaen came of age on October 17, 1685, Maria administered the treasury of Rensselaerswyck Manor, the most profitable patroonship of the West India Company and a meeting place for Mohawk and Mahican. She feared loss of the patent on Rensselaerswyck and ruin of grain harvests by high water. During dynastic infighting, she wrested ownership from Dutch family members and allotted it to her American household. Her duties involved shipping beans and grain, setting prices for four hundred thirty-four boards, buying millstones for gristmills, transporting beaver (*Castor* canadensis) pelts to Amsterdam on the *De Beever*, leasing tenant farms, inventorying herds, and hiring laborers, whose pay and tithes she authorized.

## Buying and Selling

Minor matters that brothers Stephen and Richard left up to Maria ranged from marketing lumber from Watervliet, selling an island in the Hudson to Jurrejan Thunissen, receiving candles and oysters, transporting horses and mackerel, collecting back rent from Barent the miller, and locating four pounds of alum for niece Anna to use in dyeing. On May 20,1683, Stephen ceded to Maria the contract of farmer Gerrit Gysbertsz of Beverwyck, who violated a relocation agreement. Mixed in the correspondence, Stephen and Maria debated family losses, matters of health, the colony's two-year tax assessment of £5,500 (approx. $1,552,019.80), and attrition to the gristmill, which her brother Richard wanted to keep as a family property. She also kept Oloff informed of land sales and pondered purchasing a share of New Amsterdam colony.

Maria's estate, at twenty-four miles long by forty-eight miles wide, grew into one of the nation's largest economic enterprises. On July 22, 1686, the chartering of Albany removed from the manor the fur trading village of Beverwyck near old Fort Orange on a mile-long strip of Hudson River frontage extending inland for sixteen miles. On son Kiliaen's twenty-fourth birthday in August 1687, she relinquished accounts and bookkeeping to him. Son Hendrick distinguished himself as Indian agent and five-time member of the New York General Assembly. Hendrick's son Colonel Kiliaen van Rensselaer and grandsons Hendrick Kiliaen and Philip Kiliaen van Rensselaer fought in Revolutionary War conflicts.

**Van Cortlandt-van Rensselaer Genealogy**

Pieter Loockerman

Annette Loockermans=Oloff Stevenszen van Cortlandt

Anna Van Wely=Kiliaen Nicholaus

Catherine van Cortlandt Philipse Jacobus Stephanus Richard Maria van Cortlandt=Jeremias van Rensselaer

Kiliaen Jeremias Johannes Maria Jr. Anna Hendrick

Kiliaen

Hendrick Kiliaen Philip Kiliaen

## *Sources*


"The Ancient Brewers of New York," *Scientific American* (25 February 1871): 129.

Haxtun, Annie Arnoux. *Early Settlers of New Amsterdam*. New York: Mail & Express, 1903.

Spooner, W.W. "The Van Rensselaer Family," *American Historical Magazine* 2:10 (January 1907): 1–212.

Van Laer, A.J.F. *Correspondence of Maria van Rensselaer 1669–1689*. Albany: University of New York, 1935.


## Bridget Cutt Graffort (1651–May 29, 1701)
### Merchant, Philanthropist
### Portsmouth, New Hampshire

Bridget Cutt Daniel Graffort built a long and profitable career and bequeathed benefits to her hometown. She and older sister Margaret, the daughters of Eleanor Aldersley and Welshman Richard Cutt (or Cutts), grew up on the Piscataqua River at Strawberry Banke (modern Portsmouth, New Hampshire). They claimed a grandsire, John Cutte, who served as mayor of Bristol and member of England's House of Commons.

Bridget's parents, by migrating from Bath, England, in 1647, avoided England's Civil War and the rise of radical Puritan Oliver Cromwell, who engineered the execution of Charles II. The family resided at a fortified house at the corner of Marcy and State streets before relocating to North Mill Pond, where the girls received an education. With older brother John Thorton Cutt, Richard began shipping to Virginia sun-dried cod and mackerel from the Isles of Shoals seven miles southeast of Portsmouth. The brothers became Portsmouth's richest landowners and possessors of a tannery, grain mill, windmill, warehouses, and eight slaves. By living near their widowed mother and Uncle John at North Mill Pond, Bridget and Margaret enjoyed the company of John's two sons and three daughters.

## Two Marriages

In 1671, Bridget married Captain Thomas Daniel, an investor in fishing, keeper of a tavern, and member of the Royal Council. At her father's death in 1675, at age twenty-four, she acquired Richard's original tract plus the busy fishing port of Star Island in the Isles of Shoals, originally owned by the Abenaki. Margaret received a stone warehouse, farm animals, and a woodlot. Bridget's property encompassed a barn, warehouse, brewery, bakehouse, tannery, and wharf, all operated by five slaves. Her grist mill processed corn, wheat, rye, and oats.

Widowed on November 13, 1682, Bridget united a year later with a local merchant, Thomas Graffort, a justice of the peace and Royal Councilman. Her mother's death in July 1684 made her an heiress a second time. Bridget's uncle John, the first president of New Hampshire, died before wife Ursula Cutt. At a fearful pass for Portsmouth, on July 21, 1694, Abenaki Indians shot and scalped her and amputated her ring fingers while she reaped hay near Boiling Rock. The losses stripped the Cutt family of its older generation.

## A She-Merchant

From a second widowhood in August 1697, Bridget prospered from the government's £4.5 rent (approx. $1,075.60) on Thomas Graffort's fortification for use as a prison and a defense from Indians. The widow inherited her second husband's wood tools, fishing gear, and salt, a valuable coastal commodity that he secured in a coastal warehouse for preserving fish. In addition to a one-sixth share in the merchantman *Barbadoes Merchant,* which carried cargo over the Guinea and Madras trade routes, Bridget probably continued selling fabric from her mercantile and imported rum, sugar, and molasses from the Caribbean.

Bridget lived comfortably in a two-story residence near the family orchard with a pen for a cow and pig. At death at age fifty, she bestowed on the city Graffort's Lane (renamed Daniel Street) to the river, a fenced plot at the corner of Chapel and State streets, and a fenced tract beyond Market Square to build a school. The remaining parts of Bridget's £1,300 (approx. $367,467.05) estate passed to nieces Elinor, Elizabeth, Bridget, Margaret, Abigail, and Mary Vaughan.

### *Sources*

Howard, Cecil. *Genealogy of the Cutts Family in America.* Albany, NY: Joel Munsell's Sons, 1892.

Pope, Laura. *Portsmouth Women.* Charleston, SC: Arcadia, 2013.

## Alida Schuyler Livingston (February 28, 1656–March 27, 1727)
**Business Manager, Trader**
**Fort Orange, New York**

## Margaretha Brants van Slichtenhorst Schuyler (1628–June 27, 1711)
**Business Manager, Merchant**
**Fort Orange, New Amsterdam**

## Margaret Livingston Vetch (December 5, 1681–June 1, 1758)
**Trader, Shipper**
**Boston, New York City, Annapolis, Maryland**

A prominent Dutch colonial businesswoman, Alida Schuyler van Rensselaer Livingston anchored family shipping, trading, and land acquisition and trained her children in wise monetary standards. Her maternal grandfather Brant Arentse Van Schlectenhorst exemplified Dutch patroonship as an initial director of Rensselaerswyck, an Albany estate in east central New York. The scion of butler and baker Pieter Tjercks Schuyler of Emden, Holland, Alida was third of the ten children of Dutch German immigrants–carpenter and fur trader Philip Pierterse Schuyler and Grietje (Margaretha) Brants van Schlichtenhorst of Nykerk, an apt financier. Alida's mother, in widowhood in 1683, managed the Schuyler estate with a determination that influenced the financial acumen of her daughter and granddaughter. Alida's brother Philip became Albany's first mayor. Her brother Pieter co-financed the career of Scots pirate Captain William Kidd.

At age nineteen Alida married the Rev. Nicholaus Kiliaens van Rensselaer of Ancrum in the Scots borderland, a preacher in Albany and patroon of Rensselaerswyck estate. Widowhood three years later forced her into litigation against in-laws for her inherited property across from the van Rensselaer mansion. In 1679, she married Nicholaus's secretary, Scots accountant Robert Livingston the Elder, newly arrived from Ancrum in 1674. He spent eight thousand guilders (approx. $119,600) for a three-story brick residence called *De Vlachte* (the Flatts) that included a bowery, island, and farm named Winter's Plantation near Port Hudson, a former Mahican territory. The family occupied a three-story home on Parelstraat (Pearl Street) and Yonker Street (modern State Street) in Beverwyck (modern Albany), New Amsterdam, where a shell midden identified a former Mohican canoe landing.

## The Deputy Wife

In 1680, Robert left Albany civic affairs to Alida while he began a Manhattan trading firm featuring global shipping southward down the Hudson River to the estuary. In October 1682, she sent him three barrels of meal and reported successful herding of three hundred plump sows and purchase of nine hundred fifty pounds of flour for £50 (approx. $13,803.57). With mounting profits, she bought more land, a common aim of Dutch immigrants. While advising Robert on debt and investment, she scolded him for political ventures and ordered him to mind his own business and avoid debt.

Through Governor Edmund Andros, Robert acquired river frontage from local Mohicans on July 12, 1683, at a price of three hundred guilders (approx. $4,485), ten blankets, twenty-five duffels, shirts and stockings, six coats, twenty knives, and six guns with powder, lead, and caps. Additional items included fourteen kettles, ten each of axes and adzes, twenty each scissors and mirrors, two pounds of paint, and one hundred each of fish hooks, awls, and nails. The deal concluded with tobacco and pipes, kegs of rum, and a barrel of beer. His land patents brought him Saratoga north of Albany and Taghkanick west of the Massachusetts border.

After 1690, Robert's frequent absences on business journeys and as New York State assemblyman left Alida in a tense milieu of Algonquian, Iroquois, and Mohican attacks and storehouse theft that caused a meat shortage. For management of a sawmill, brewery, bakery, and gristmill, she took direction from Robert's correspondence dispatched from New York, Boston, and London. She reported events of the French and Indian War, when the arrival of a French army under Comte Louis de Frontenac implied that the Europeans intended to profit on the fur trade.

To raise funds for frontier defense, Robert empowered his wife to represent the family's trading and shipping empire during his 1694–1696 voyage to Portugal on the brigantine *Orange*. His hiring of Captain Kidd in 1695 increased public suspicions that Robert profited from piracy by the crew of his ship *Adventure Galley*. By March 1698, Alida's letter from Albany listed the shipping of deerskins, beaver furs, and grain, but alerted him of the shortage of linen and lace in the storeroom. By March, during a business slump, she was still curious about big city fashions. News worsened in August with a wheat crop ruined by rain; however, she was able to send furs and bearskin to Holland aboard the cargo ship *Berketeyn*.

## The Livingston Dynasty

In 1700, Robert became lord of Livingston Manor, a one-hundred-and-sixty-thousand-acre fortified estate at Upper State Street on the Roelof Jansen Kil (creek). The couple produced nine children, of whom Johanna Philippine, William, and Catharine did not survive to adulthood. The property, incorporating a twelve-by-nineteen-mile territory from Massachusetts to the Hudson River, required an updated survey. The resulting plat of 1715 accorded Robert ownership of fish and game, timber, minerals, and precious metals. While he advanced to secretary of Rensselaerswyck, Albany town clerk, Indian agent, and tax collector, his wife took charge of the trading post, meeting house, and bakery.

Alida purchased and sold slaves, bartered with Mohawk, negotiated wheat pricing, scheduled shipping, and superintended baking, milling, and brewing malted beer. Against summer heat, she postponed baking into the night. In addition to paying twenty-eight shillings in quit-rent (fees), she conducted the owner's duties of holding a court-leet or lower court to issue writs, levy and collect fines, and seize the booty of felons. Out of family accord, Robert allied with brother-in-law Pieter Schuyler in spring 1700 to negotiate a French Iroquois settlement with two hundred natives, a task that Alida co-sponsored.

## The Palatine Venture

An agreement to aid two thousand eight hundred Palatine immigrants in September 1710 allowed Governor Robert Hunter, a fellow Scot, to purchase six thousand riverfront acres for £400 (approx. $83,028.99). The contract stipulated that Alida must bake bread and provide nine hundred gallons of dark, heavily hopped ships beer daily for the immigrants. Increasing debt and pilfering from flour and beer barrels left her short on food, beer, and milk. She agreed to employ immigrant children at producing tar from pine knots by layering them with soil and heaping them with hot coals to render the tar.

Alida commented that controlling so large an estate weakened her physically. In 1711, she requested additional trading stores of sugar, tobacco, rum, molasses, pepper and ginger, soap, gloves and stockings, and scouring sand. Robert sent more merchandise for her to sell at Claverack, the Flats, and Kinderhook and ordered her not to give customers credit. She wrote about the heavy duties of overseeing slaves and providing clothing, housing, and health care that involved purging, bleeding, and sweating the sick. She recycled family shoes and marketed slaves for £50 ($10,378.62) each. For messages to Robert, she relied on the slave Lego to travel the route to New York City. Another servant named Ben carried goods to Taghkanick but hesitated out of terror of attack by marauding Cayuga and Seneca.

## Failing Business

The public humiliation of Robert in 1701 by negative rumors of illegal trading and the destruction of his mills from the 1712 flood cost the family income from outsourcing their milling upriver by canoe. During a shortage of hops and coals for brewing, flour for baking, and salt for meat preservation, Alida declared herself weary of the struggle. From 1716, husband and wife incurred ill health. While Alida struggled with postpartum fever, headache, insufficient breast milk, and edema, kidney stones impaired Robert from his role as speaker of the house. The following year, he complained that Joe the miller did a poor job processing corn meal, which the family fed to pigs.

Dutiful in business matters, Alida repaired the mill to increase the efficiency of flour, which she used as currency at home and for trade in Europe, Jamaica, and Curaçao. She improved the decor of Livingston Manor and prepared thirty-year-old son Philip to conduct family business. In May 1726, Philip added to his mother's concerns over unsaleable goods—low quality deer and bear skins. At the parents' death, daughter Margaret Livingston Vetch extended the pattern of energetic trader and shipper at her residences in Boston, Annapolis Royal, and New York. She named her only child Alida. Philip inherited the Saratoga trust and became second lord of Livingston Manor and a vigorous marketer of slaves.

### The Livingston-Schuyler Genealogy

Pieter Tjercks Schuyler — Brant Arentse Van Schlectenhorst

Philip Pierterse Schuyler=Grietje Brants van Slichtenhorst

Philip | Pieter | Nicholaus Kiliaens van Rensselaer=Alida= Robert Livingston

Philip | Margaret Vetch

Alida

## *Sources*


Lamb, Martha Joanna, and Mrs. Burton Harrison. *History of the City of New York. New York*: A.S. Barnes, 1877.

Livingston, Edwin B. *The Livingstons of Livingston Manor. New York*: Knickerbocker Press, 1910.

Schuyler, George W. *Colonial New York: Philip Schuyler and His Family. New York*: Charles Scribner's Sons, 1885.


## Dinah Nuthead (1662–1707)
### Printer, Publisher
### St. Mary's, Maryland

The first licensed female printer in the Thirteen Colonies, Dinah Nuthead thrived at official business even though she couldn't sign her name. A native Marylander from Anne Arundel County on the Chesapeake Bay, she learned the alphabet, but could only sign documents with a capital D. At age twenty, she married an experienced printer, twenty-eight-year-old William Nuthead of London, a migrant to Jamestown, Virginia, who taught her the rudiments of typesetting, inking, and copying. The couple produced children Susan and William, named for their paternal grandparents.

In November 1682, Lord Thomas Culpeper and merchant John Buckner instituted printing at Jamestown of legislative acts and hired William as royal printer. To prevent issuance of radical broadsides, on December 14, 1683, King Charles II rescinded freedom of the press in the colonies. The last evidence of William's work, an IOU dated August 31, 1685, recorded a debt of one thousand, one hundred, twenty pounds of leaf tobacco worth a penny a pound (approx. $2,849.77).

To secure liberty, the Nutheads opened a printshop in 1686 in the town center of St. Mary's on a bluff overlooking St. Mary's River, Maryland, and served governmental and mercantile customers. In October 1686, state legislature reimbursed William five thousand, five hundred, and fifty pounds of tobacco, worth approx. $13,994.40. Leaf tobacco served as legal tender before the creation of coins and paper money. By November, William was able to purchase Nuthead's Choice, a plot of three hundred acres among Quaker activists on the Tuckahoe River in Talbot County. He sold one-third of his investment on April 4, 1687.

## Maryland's Official Printer

For nine years, the printshop supplied tobacco notes, contracts, and bureaucratic forms for the government from a cache of alphabet blocks. On July 25, 1689, Colonel John Goode, a Protestant revolutionary, hired the couple to publish a manifesto, "The Declaration of the Reasons and Motives for the Present Appearing in Arms of Their Majesties Protestant Subjects in the Province of Maryland." The three-paragraph document sought "deliverance of your Suffering People … under a Proteftant Government" (Wroth, 1922, 6). To raise colonial support for the institution of Protestant monarchs William and Mary, the document passed to the new king and Lords of Trade and circulated among governors of the Thirteen Colonies. A London publisher reprinted the Protestant Declaration, which merchant Randal Taylor sold near Stationers Hall near St. Paul's Cathedral.

For customers in Cecil, Kent, and Talbot counties, the printshop apparently remained busy satisfying the need for more broadsheets composed by warring sides, Protestant rebels and monarchists. William Nuthead represented Governor Thomas Lawrence in April 1693 in the search and seizure of documents at his residence in the few weeks of his term. A rush order on October 14, 1693, for five hundred broadsides expressed Colonel Henry Darnall's anger at the replacement of Lord Baltimore by a royal Protestant appointee, Nehemiah Blakiston. Darnall and Richard Smith conducted their business at the Nuthead residence but found William unwilling to print the warrant without official permission.

### Dinah as Printer

Widowed on February 7, 1694, Dinah probated her husband's will and claimed for herself and two children his horse and business property worth six pounds and nineteen shillings (approx. $1,422.19). On his account ledger remained unpaid bills by sixty customers. Dinah continued in the same line of work—raising and lowering the lever to settle a platen on a metal frame of letters inked on the press board atop the composing stone. At the establishment of Annapolis on the Severn River as state capital in 1696, she relocated her equipment from St. Mary's to Anne Arundel County east of Washington, D.C.

From Francis Nicholson, the royal governor, Dinah requested to continue the company's work. The petition cost her £100 (approx. $23,765.11) for a bond. On May 5, 1696, the state assembly awarded her a license to produce bills, bonds, law blanks, writs, letters, and land warrants. Her first jobs included a fast-day sermon to the assembly by the Rev. Peregrine Coney. In December 1700, she married Manus Devoran, a widower who died the same year. Dinah took responsibility for stepdaughter Catherine Devoran and executed Manus's will leaving an estate of £65.05 (approx. $16,058.22), more than ten times what William left her. In 1702, she wed taverner Sebastian Oley (or Owley), a German immigrant. Little remains of Dinah's work after the state house fire of 1704 destroyed files.

*Sources*

Andes, Laurie. "Literacy's Role in Revolution and Independence," *Information, Medium and Society* 6:3 (2009): 9–16.
Marzolf, Marion. "The Woman Journalist: Colonial Printer to City Desk." *Journalism History* 1:4 (1974): 100–146.
Wroth, Lawrence C. *A History of Printing in Colonial Maryland, 1686–1776*. Baltimore, MD: Typothetae of Baltimore, 1922.

## Elizabeth Sowle Bradford (1663–July 8, 1731)
**Printer**
**Philadelphia, Pennsylvania**

A London poet introduced to New Amsterdam at age nineteen, Elizabeth Sowle Bradford made a contribution to colonial and women's history that her husband's fame overshadowed. The daughter of Andrew and Jane Sowle, she and younger sister Tace learned the printing trade in Middlesex, England, from their parents. Elizabeth wed Leicestershire native William Bradford, Sr., Andrew Sowle's apprentice in Devonshire. While aiding Andrew with Quaker print jobs in England, he published Governor

William Penn's 1682 tract *The Frame of the Government of the Province of Pennsilvania in America.*

Probably impressed by Elizabeth's stanch Quakerism, William followed her lead. The couple married on April 28, 1685, and departed along with his press on the ship *William Penn.* When they arrived in Philadelphia, they secured a New Jersey tract at Elizabethtown, followed by investments in the Hudson Valley and Perth Amboy. William at age twenty-two served the New World as its first pressman and publisher and as royal printer for Great Britain's William and Mary, Queen Anne, George I, and George II. The couple settled at Oxford outside Philadelphia and produced sons Andrew and William Jr. William Sr. originated paper milling on a thirty-six-acre Wissahickon Creek tract at Roxboro, Pennsylvania, and introduced printing in Pennsylvania and New York. At a height of ambition, he completed *Temple of Wisdom*, a compendium of essays by Francis Bacon, and proposed printing an annotated Bible to sell for twenty shillings.

## The Book Market

For a half century, William Sr. and Elizabeth issued official documents in English type for the colonies in Philadelphia, New York, and Perth Amboy, New Jersey. Their shop sold the twenty-page 1686 *Kalendarium Pennsilvaniense*, the 1688 *Leeds Almanac*, and the 1689 Pennsylvania Charter. Under the influence of radical theologist George Keith, Bradford risked issuing in 1689 *The Presbyterian and Independent Visible Churches in New England* and in 1690 *The Pretended Antidote Proved Poyson* and *A Refutation of the Three Opposers of Truth.*

For championing freedom of thought in George Keith's philosophy, in July 1692, the Bradfords distributed the broadside *An Appeal from the Twenty-eight Judges to the Spirit of Truth & true Judgment in All Faithful Friends, called Quakers.* In the first demand for freedom of the press in the American colonies, on August 24, 1692, William and distributor John McComb were arrested for malice and sedition, one of numerous controversies and lawsuits in the printer's career. Before his release after a vacated suit, in December 1692, authorities suppressed the business, seized the broadsides, and confiscated the Bradfords' type and equipment. In 1693, William canceled the company's contract with the Quakers and launched four controversial pamphlets: *A Challenge to Caleb Pusey, The Judgement against George Keith, With Answers to the Said Judgment,* and *New England's Spirit of Persecution Transmitted to Pennsilvania.*

## The Colony's Business

A short repatriation to London in 1689 sent Elizabeth and sons out of colonial printing angst to the site of Tace's success as compositor and bookseller of Quaker literature, particularly women's writings. After relocating to the Sign of the Bible at New York's Hanover Square, Elizabeth wrote a fifteen-couplet rhymed preface to Baptist preacher Benjamin Keach's "War with the Devil," a dialogue on youthful temptations. At a salary of £60 (approx. $18,576.77), she and William edited the state's first law compendium in 1694 and New York legislative acts the next year as well as contract work for Connecticut, Maryland, Rhode Island, and Barbados. With a raise to £75 (approx. $22,546.67), they produced New Jersey documents in 1703, a city map, and, in 1709, New York state currency. His company suffered from unpaid salary of £540 (approx. $128,331.61), which Governor Edward Hyrd, Lord Cornbury issued. Subsequent activities of Bradford Printing included the 1710 edition of the Book of Common Prayer and imprints under his and son Andrew's names. William followed with New Jersey laws in 1723, the Monday *New York Gazette*, the state's first newspaper in 1725, the Dutch/English text of *The Two Interests of the Country Reconciled* in 1727, and the 1739 *American Almanac*.

At Elizabeth's death in New York on July 8, 1731, William labored as an Anglican missionary until retirement in 1744 to a residence at Hanover Square and Stone Street. He claimed that his reputation depended on antipathies toward Quakers. Before he died at age eighty-nine, he aided son Andrew to restore Bradford Printing in Philadelphia at Front and Market streets. Elizabeth's grandson, militiaman William Bradford of New York, partnered with Uncle Andrew Bradford in a four-generation dynasty of printing. In Philadelphia, Andrew and wife Cornelia Smith Bradford founded the *American Weekly Mercury*. On December 2, 1742, Andrew debuted the *Pennsylvania Journal* and printed the *American Magazine*.

*See also* Cornelia Smith Bradford, Anna Catherine Zenger.

### Sources

Keith, George, and Peter Boss. *The Trials of Peter Boss, George Keith, Thomas Budd, and William Bradford*. London: Richard Baldwin, 1693.

McGuire, John P. "William Bradford: Printer to Their Majesties," *American Bar Association Journal* 42:4 (April 1956): 344–347.

Reese, William S. "Works of George Keith Printed in America," *Princeton University Library Chronicle* 39:2 (Winter 1978): 98–124.

"Substance of the Address of J.W. Wallace," *Historical Magazine* 7:7 (July 1863): 201–218.

## Sarah Kemble Knight (April 19, 1666–September 25, 1727)
### Teacher, Shopkeeper, Innkeeper, Court Recorder, Real Estate Broker
### New London, Connecticut; Boston, Massachusetts

Diarist Sarah Kemble Knight particularized the business and professional woman's travel experience in colonial Connecticut and New York. A Bostonian and the granddaughter of Nicolas "Nico" Trerice of Cornwall, England, sea captain of the *Chapman, Planter*, and *Rebecca,* she was born the last of six children to Elizabeth Trerice and merchant Thomas Kemble. He was the agent for a London company, owner of a tract in Maine, and worker of indentured Scots servants.

At age twenty-three, Sarah united with a thirty-six-year-old widower, sea captain Richard Knight, in New London, Connecticut. At her father's death in 1689, she followed the family trades of managing a stationery shop, innkeeping, real estate broker, and serving the colonial courts as scrivener and witness. She resided on Moon Street near Boston's New North Square with her mother and teenaged daughter Elizabeth and welcomed relatives to her boarding house.

### Independence

A year after Richard's death, Sarah journeyed on horseback to New Haven, Connecticut, on October 2, 1704, to mediate the estate of a cousin, Caleb Trowbridge. Her commentary in *The Journal of Mme Knight* typified hard traveling through backcountry in a riding mask and scarlet and green outfit. In eastern Connecticut, she crossed the Thames River tidal estuary by ferry. To traverse Indian territory and forests endangered by wild animals, she relied on the company of post riders and guides and lodged with a Congregationalist minister. Graphic summaries of bargaining with guides depict Sarah as cautious with expenses.

Sarah detailed nighttime wilderness conditions, rainy weather, a hard bed in a lean-to, three cent tolls, and food service among tobacco chewers and men drunk on "bare-legged punch." Before reaching Dedham, Massachusetts, she risked high water at the Charles River causeway that raised fears of drowning. In Norwalk, she enjoyed fried venison. At Saybrook ferry, she declined a cook's dinner of pickled mutton, head sauce, and corn meal and pumpkin bread costing sixpence a plate (approx. $16.93). Breakfast was equally unappealing. Dinner the next night at Killingsworth suited her better. At Groton, she enjoyed roast beef with pumpkin sauce. At Haven's, she crossed a surging river by canoe. Her six-day route ended with dinner with Governor John Winthrop and a three-day jaunt to New York, where she spent two weeks with relatives and friends.

### Mid-life Investments

At return two hundred twenty miles to Boston's north end from January 6 to March 3, 1705, Sarah operated businesses in realty, guest accommodations, and merchandise and copied legal documents. The writing school she opened on Moon Street in 1706 earned fame for her lessons in composition, which she allegedly taught to clergyman Samuel Mather and statesman Benjamin Franklin. Under an elm tree at Elm Avenue on the Norwichtown Green overlooking the Boston post road, Sarah established a boarding house and two-story saloon, the Knight Peck Tavern. A platform in the boughs became a pulpit for local orators. She set outdoor tables, served food, and disputed a court fine for dispensing liquor to Indians, which was the fault of her maid Ann Clark.

Sarah's example of the American woman testified to energy and pluck as well as a flair for snide and supercilious humor. Her business savvy influenced purchase of ten reams of paper from Holland. At age forty-eight, she settled in New London with her daughter, Elizabeth Knight Livingston. Sarah donated a silver chalice for First Congregational Church. Her sizable estate of £1,800 (approx. $500,263.61) included an inn and farms in New London and a Norwich residence, which passed to Elizabeth. Sarah's travel ledger remained unpublished until 1825.

### *Sources*

Brooks, Geraldine. *Dames and Daughters of Colonial Days. New York*: Thomas Y. Crowell, 1900.

Stern, Julia. "To Relish and To Spew: Disgust as Cultural Critique in The Journal of Madam Knight," *Legacy* 14:4 (1997): 1–12.

## Esther Brown (1672–May 28, 1708)
**Importer, Merchant**
**New York City**

Esther (or Hester) Morteira Brown of Amsterdam, Holland, spent six years of widowhood selling general merchandise. Her husband Saul de Josiau Pardo (Brown) of Rotterdam, New York's first Hazan, a lay reader at Shearit Israel on Beaver Street, the New World's only synagogue, was refused a sales license. Before his death on April 17, 1702, she lost Joseph, Sara Haim, and Isaac to disease and reared their three surviving children, Simha, Hanna, and eight-year-old Josiau. Josiau was a future rabbi like his paternal great grandsire David Pardo of Venice, maternal grandfather Saul Levi Morteira, and paternal grandsire Josiah ben David Pardo, yeshiva teacher and rabbi of Willemstad, Curaçao, and Port Royal, Jamaica's pirate haven.

Specializing in fabrics and women's stockings, Esther ran a commercial venture in Manhattan. On March 22, 1708, she chartered from Captain Samuel Chadwell the sloop *Flying Horse* for a run to St. Thomas to import twenty-five gallons of rum. At her death on May 28, 1708, at age forty, she left a draper's inventory—flannel, silk crape, damask, sheepskin gloves, women's hose, and twenty gallons of aniseed water, a healthful beverage. Her twelve-year-old daughter Abigail administered Esther's will.

*Source*

Hershkowitz, Leo. "Colonial Entrepreneurs: A Quartet of Jewish Women," https://jwa.org/encyclopedia/article/colonial-entrepreneurs-quartet-of-jewish-women.

## Alice Jones Mackelfresh Lewis (ca. 1669–1738)
**Ferrymaster, Innkeeper**
**London Town, Maryland**

An established businesswoman at a tobacco passage port in Anne Arundel County, Maryland, Alice Jones Mackelfresh Lewis survived widowhood twice and continued operating the family ferry north of Mayo Road on the South River, a ten-mile tributary of Chesapeake Bay. In the late 1660s and early 1670s, she and brother Richard Jr. were born to Mary and Richard Jones, Sr., in All Hallows Parish. At age twenty-four, she married a Scot, thirty-two-year-old David Mackelfresh of South Leith. The couple produced four sons and four daughters, of whom only Jane, Mary, and David Jr. survived.

After David's election to mayor of London Town in 1693, Alice shared the public ferry operation at Ferry Point, a critical segment of road travel five miles south of Annapolis near merchant vessels moored offshore. At David's death on January 3, 1711, she petitioned authorities for a license to continue the crossing service in a thirty-foot flat-bottomed rowboat. Government officials controlled prices and hours of operation and relicensed the ferry master annually to serve the mid–Chesapeake.

### Transportation Facilitator

In addition to transporting passengers, slaves, horses, wagons, tobacco, and trade goods, Alice conveyed essential news to the town's three hundred residents of one hundred one-acre lots, most of them English, Scot, Irish, or French. From the 1680s, steady north–south traffic to Williamsburg, Philadelphia, Boston, New York, Charleston, and the Caribbean promoted tavern business for passengers awaiting the tide to enable the ferry's return. Alice accepted wheat and produce as pay.

Around age forty-two, Alice married Richard Dixon on January 5, 1712, and shared river crossing duties with him several times daily. Because Richard quit the job and abandoned the family in August 1713, Captain Thomas Gassaway, a prominent planter on Love's Neck, complained of Richard's inattention to waterfront commerce and petitioned authorities to allow the Widow Dixon full management. By 1715, a private ferry at the main thoroughfare, Scott Street, run by taverner Edward Rummy, competed with Alice's operation. Customers paid six pounds of tobacco or six pence (approx. $15.38) at his inn to eat dinner and spend the night.

### Business Complexities

During the competition of shipwright Edward Rumney, Sr., and merchant and taverner Stephen West for ferry keeper, the judge agreed to Alice's petition under the bond of ferry keeper Benjamin Freeman, husband of Mary Mackelfresh and father of William, Alice's grandson. Alice pledged the use of two boats at a contract price of six thousand five hundred pounds of tobacco (approx. $16,666.85). Court records from November 1717 indicate her employment of three oarsmen, possibly slaves or indentured servants. To the ferry license, renewed in November 1718, at age fifty, she added an innkeeper's license in August 1719.

In 1720, Elinor McCubbins Rumney, Edward's widow, managed the South River ferry, but lost the contract to Stephen West. After daughter Jane left home to marry in 1720, Alice remained single until September 16, 1724, when she united with ferryman John Lewis. Following son David Jr.'s sale of inherited land on April 9, 1726, Alice and John settled south of Church Street at the South River shore.

### *Source*

"London Town and Gardens Collection," *Digital Maryland*, https://collections.digitalmaryland.org/digital/collection/p17340coll24.

## Sybilla Righton Masters (1670–June 23, 1720)
**Inventor**
**Philadelphia, Pennsylvania**

In a patriarchal society, Isabella Sybilla Righton Masters patented two inventions under her husband's name. A Hamilton Tribe, Bermuda, native, she and her parents Sarah Murrell and seaman William Righton were part of the influx of Friends among tobacco planters on the Caribbean. Persecution and deportation of Quakers resulted from sabbath offenses and refusal to fight with the militia. In 1676, a civil court charged

William £9 17s (approx. $2,329.67) and sent him to jail. At age eleven with five sisters, Sybilla sailed to a family plantation called Bermuda on the Delaware River in Burlington, West Jersey.

Sybilla was seventeen when she married Thomas Masters, a wealthy Quaker merchant from Philadelphia. Five years later, her widowed mother sold for £275 (approx. $92,397.12) twenty-five acres on Bermuda that she inherited from her father, Thomas Murrell. At the departure of Quakers from the island, the Masters bought land in Philadelphia for £290 (approx. $97,436.96). The couple settled in a mansion at Front and Market streets two blocks from the river and produced Mary, Sarah, Thomas, and William. Thomas Masters, Sr., invested his wealth in six hundred acres at Northern Liberties on Germantown Road and in Green Spring, a country summer house. He served on the state supreme court and tax commission and, in 1707, began the first of two consecutive terms as Philadelphia mayor.

## Colonial Technology

In her midforties, Sybilla altered the technology for grinding corn into "Tuscarora Rice" by inventing a stamping, cleaning, shelling, and curing process powered by horses or donkeys or a water wheel. In place of millstones and gears, the device rotated a wood cylinder by cogwheels like the workings of a music box. The mechanism dropped two rows of hammers onto maize kernels in mortars to pulverize corn into grits or hominy meal. The grain fell into shallow bins for drying. She intended to process American grain as well as imported produce from England, Wales, and Berwick on Tweed on the Scottish border.

Sybilla spent three years in London waiting for a royal license from George I, who issued the first patent—#401—to a New World colonist on November 25, 1715. Thomas stated on official documents that the device was his wife's design. False advertisement claimed that pulverized corn was a treatment for tuberculosis. During her absence, Thomas bought Governor William Penn's flour mill at £250 (approx. $64,103.27) on twenty-four acres at Cohocksink Creek near Green Spring. The venture proved unprofitable.

## Domestic Goods

Sybilla continued seeking patents with a weaving and staining process that turned palmetto leaves, chips, and straw into hats and bonnets. The machine adapted to the weaving of mats, market and baby baskets, and chair and stool seats. She received patent #403 from the king. With a monopoly on palmetto leaf imports from the Caribbean, for one shilling, she sold her woven goods in London under the sign of "the West India Hat & Bonnet, against Catherine-Street in the Strand" opposite Covent Garden.

The couple repatriated to Pennsylvania on May 5, 1716, to manufacture equipment for the water mill. During Sybilla's absence, Hannah Penn, wife of Governor William Penn, raised concerns for her long separation from her family. Four years after Sybilla's patents were reissued in Pennsylvania, she died at age fifty. The mill burned in 1740. In January 1787, Abigail Adams ordered a peck of Tuscarora Rice.

*See also* Abigail Smith Adams.

### *Sources*

Brown, Andrew Benson. "Domestic Arts Inventor: Sybilla Masters," *Epoch Times* (24 November 2023).

Gribble, T. Graham. "Fossil Patents," *Scientific American* 65:5 (1 August 1891): 71–72.

Jarvis, Michael J. *In the Eye of All Trade.* Chapel Hill: University of North Carolina Press, 2010.

Needles, Samuel H. "The Governor's Mill, and the Globe Mills, Philadelphia," *Pennsylvania Magazine of History and Biography* 8:3 (October 1884): 279–299.

## Hannah Callowhill Penn (February 11, 1671–December 20, 1726)
**Brewer, Trader, Politician**
**Pennsbury, Pennsylvania**

A mild-mannered, but remarkably able Quaker, Hanna Margaret Callowhill Penn excelled at domestic and colonial administration. A native of Bristol, England, she was the only surviving child of Anna "Hannah" Hollister and button maker and linen draper Thomas Callowhill, who taught her the ways of business. In her mother's style, she emulated practical aid for the poor and unemployed. Among her ancestors, she admired the combative, determined pro–Quaker stance of maternal grandfather, grocer Dennis Hollister, a member of Parliament. Her academic background awarded her the basics of math and language plus knowledge of bookkeeping.

Hannah united with Oxford graduate William Penn, the son of an admiral, after his emergence from self-exile during the Glorious Revolution of 1688, a time of religious intolerance toward Quakers. They shared the Quaker affirmation of "liberty of conscience" and rejected calls for a state church. Three years after the Penns' wedding and the death of stepson Springett, they set sail from the Isle of Wight on September 3, 1699, on the *Canterbury Merchant,* which survived a pirate attack. After a pregnancy at sea, Hannah bore John Penn in America on January 28, 1700, in Philadelphia. Three daughters of Hannah's nine children died in childhood.

## A Pennsylvania Home

In December, the family boarded William's personal six-oared and masted barge and departed to the land he bought in 1682 from Chief Tamanend of the Lenni Lenape at Shackamaxon for £7,000 (approx. $1,728,017.70). Oarsmen rowed to Pennsbury, William's isolated country home, which served as an office and colonial nerve center. The family crest pictured farm equipment, harvested produce, and netted fish, emblems of abundance. He imported from England hawthorn, hazel, flower seeds, grain, grapevines, and orchard trees to grow on a terraced lawn. Along with pippin and parmain apples, cherry, plum, and quince, he planted native ash, beech, black walnut, cedar, chestnut, cyprus, gumwood, hickory, sassafrax, and fragrant wild myrtle. He ordered a stable for twelve horses and planned a dairy as a treat for Hannah.

Hannah was again pregnant on a journey from their rented townhouse, Slate Roof House, on Philadelphia's Second Street near Walnut to England in November 1701. The couple spent the icy months in town before returning to the rural governor's mansion, where they sometimes held Quaker meetings and welcomed dignitaries, diplomats, and conferences of Indian sachems. She birthed six more children in England in the next eight years. In a formal colloquy with William III in London, William sought a stronger hold on his colonial proprietorship.

Hannah, like Eliza Lucas Pinckney in South Carolina and Maria Van Rensselaer in New Amsterdam, operated a massive property—an eight-thousand-acre estate four miles north of Bristol on the Delaware River. Under the command of steward James Harrison, William's personal agent, the great hall provided dining and entertaining space for state guests, to whom he served hot chocolate. A special chamber accommodated Letitia Penn, Hannah's stepdaughter, the owner of Philadelphia's London Coffee House at Front and High streets. A withdrawing closet offered Hannah a daybed for private moments, when she composed letters about her relationship with Amish, Catholics, German Reformed, Jews, Lutherans, Mennonites, and Presbyterians.

## Taking Charge

Hannah's jobs of spinning, weaving, brewing beer and ale, and bottling mead and marigold wine expanded to pickling and drying fruit and vegetables and airing herbs overhead in the old kitchen ell from her garden. Her cellar and larder made room for bacon, coffee berries, and madeira wine. Out the back door, she drew water from a kitchen well. Health care was her special task for staff, slaves, and visiting Indians. In addition to violet syrup for cough and sore throat, black cherry water to relieve gout and arthritic inflammation, and convulsion water for seizures and epilepsy, she powdered coral to strengthen bones. In 1709, the couple resided in Bristol and frequently lived apart while he conducted business in London.

William's faith in Hannah's humility, learning, and sound judgment took graphic shape in a will granting her the governorship of Pennsylvania province. In 1712, a stroke began his six-year decline, leaving Hannah as a Pennsylvania proprietor as well as executor of her parents' estates. For support, she received £300 (approx. $77,888.48) per year. Much anguish derived from settling the Maryland-Pennsylvania border crisis and from ending stepson William Jr.'s protests of his father's liberal will. In 1722, her father's purchase of Pennsylvania acreage on Pennipack Creek and one thousand acres in Southampton gave her additional management concerns.

During Hannah's residence at Ruscombe in south central England, she changed direction and chose to spend her last years on rental property in Hammersmith. For economy, she sold the slave Sue and her children. She maintained constant correspondence with the colony. She kept the colonial books and shared decision-making with deputy William Keith, a proponent of the Stamp Act. To raise cash, in 1724, she sold the Pennsbury furnishings, inherited land in Barryroe and Ibaune at Cork, Ireland, and Bristol acreage. After an eight-year struggle, she finished the mediation on December 13, 1726. A stroke made her mute before killing her on December 20.

### *Sources*


Dunn, Richard, and Mary Maples Dunn, Ed. *The Papers of William Penn*. Philadelphia, University of Pennsylvania Press, 1982.

Hirsch, Alison Duncan. "A Tale of Two Wives," *Pennsylvania History* 61:4 (1994): 429–456.

Hunt, Rachel McMasters Miller. "William Penn and Pennsbury Manor," *Western Pennsylvania Historical Magazine* 28:1–2 (spring-summer, 1955): 5–20.


## Elizabeth Woodberry Pratt (February 12, 1671–ca. 1749)
**Merchant**
**Newport, Rhode Island**

One of Rhode Island's coastal she-merchants, Elizabeth Woodberry Pratt held a reputation for ladylike behavior that cloaked shrewd bargaining. A native of Beverly, Massachusetts, she was born to Mary Dixon and Hugh Woodberry, a sailor and farmer who died in 1702. After marrying saddler Joseph Pratt, in 1710, Elizabeth inherited £12 (approx., $3,415.32) from her father's Bristol estate. She relocated her family to Newport, a mercantile center south of Providence, Rhode Island, and allied with the Congregational Church of Christ.

An entrepreneur at age fifty-one, Elizabeth ventured into selling domestic and culinary supplies. She reared daughters Elizabeth, Mary, and Sarah and lived in refined style, as proven by her socializing with porcelain teacups and plates and the remains of suckling pig and veal fillet. Household finery extended to silver, wine and stemware, a punch bowl, and plates adorned with blue and white chinoiserie.

In widowhood from 1721, Elizabeth occupied a two-story residence on Spring Street and rented a waterfront store a block west at Thames Street, the city's commercial thoroughfare. She invested £600 (approx. $64,545.87) in stock and hired part-time help for stitchery and quilting. In 1724, she bought fabric from Rhode Island treasurer Thomas Richardson, a wealthy Quaker merchant during the French and Indian War, and from privateer John Freebody, who sold her £77 (approx. $21,651.50) in wholesale goods imported on the sloop *Revenge of the Burthen*. She appears to have relocated her mercantile in March 1732, when daughter Mary Pratt Lawrence bought Elizabeth's shop. In September, she relocated stock to Thames Street to son-in-law John Morris's site rented from Sarah Clarke, the governor's widow.

Archaeological Christina J. Hodge proposes that the constant absence of seamen on voyages raised the demand for womanly merchandise. For customers, Elizabeth stocked twenty types of fabric, including silks and cheaper cambrics, as well as shirts, girdles, accessories, paper, and indigo. For more exotic needs, she imported flax or jute osnaburg from London and sousae, a hand loomed cloth in checks and stripes from Sind, India. Her food offerings covered standard kitchen needs: butter, cheese, sugar, nutmeg, pepper, solid chocolate in cakes and rolls, mutton, and coffee from the Indies. Domestic goods included ceramics, glassware, andirons, trammels, tongs, copper kettles, skillets, and pewter ware.

The litigious nature of the milieu placed Elizabeth frequently in claims court to pay or recover money owed, even from her sons-in-law. She relied on a slave named Dinah, a cook and seamstress. At a period of monetary shortfall, Elizabeth sold Dinah in August 1728 for £70 (approx. $17,865.95). Elizabeth appears to have shared her home with her daughter, Sarah Pratt Morris, and eleven-year-old granddaughter Elizabeth Morris after the death in 1738 of husband John Morris, a merchant who left considerable debt. Elizabeth Pratt may have lived alone until 1749. Peers remembered her hard work and dignified manner and believed her energetic and conscientious.

### *Source*

Hodge, Christina J. *Consumerism and the Emergence of the Middle Class in Colonial America. New York*: Cambridge University Press, 2014.

## Mehetabel Chandler Coit (August 24, 1673–August 1, 1763)
**Food Writer, Herbalist**

## Martha Coit Hubbard Greene (April 1, 1706–1784)
**Storekeeper, Needlework Teacher**
**Woodstock, Connecticut**

The keeper of America's earliest female diary, Mehetabel Chandler Coit filled her personal writings with verse, wit, Puritan ramblings, historical events, and recipes and folk curatives, two staples of women's field of knowledge. Born in New Roxbury, Massachusetts, to distiller John and Elizabeth Douglas Chandler, she was the scion of fifteenth-century candle maker Thomas Chandler and Yorkshire sheriff Robert Tate, the Lord Mayor of London. After education at a dame school, she began writing a leather-bound journal at age fifteen when her family relocated to Wossaquassett (modern Woodstock, Connecticut). Until her midseventies, she continued making diary observations.

On February 16, 1658, at age twenty-two, Mehetabel married shipwright John Coit of the harbor town New London, grandson of Welshman John Coit, a Cape Ann pioneer in 1632. The shipbuilding industry connected John Sr., John Jr., and grandson Samuel Coit with European and Caribbean traders and sloop captains. During King Phillip's War, the Coits resided next door to Mehetabel's mother-in-law, Annis Bayford Chandler Dane Parmenter, who lost son-in-law William Cleaves at the battle of Sudbury. During the conflict, five hundred Narragansett, Nipmuc, and Wampanoag braves under Metacomet raided Sudbury, Massachusetts, and slew a Concord militia.

### Family Threats

Perhaps to avoid danger of Indian attack, in 1686, the Coits relocated to former Massachusetts land at New Roxbury. In 1690, Mehetabel suffered illness. Four years later, she traveled to New London with her brother John and his wife and son, Mary and John Chandler, Jr. At a rate of every two years, the Coits produced sons John, Samuel, Thomas, and Joseph Coit, a surveyor for the Mohegan Indian agent, and daughters Elizabeth "Betty" Coit Gardiner and Martha Coit Hubbard Greene, a storekeeper and needlework teacher.

Three Coit sons—John Jr., Joseph, and Samuel—died young. Fear of stillbirth inspired Mehetabel's entries on threats from labor and delivery. She recorded Joseph's demise as the result of "longfever" (typhus). John Sr. inherited his father's shipbuilding facility, which he relocated to Point of Rocks, Maryland, in 1699. After thirty years in the trade, he built a new dock. John died on October 22, 1744.

## Broad Knowledge

In musings and letters, Mehetabel varied journal content from Mohegan leaders, slave purchase, and ship launchings to epidemics, treatment for illness, and the births of grandchildren. She studied nurse care for ailments—reducing fever, treating earache with limewater, soothing scaly skin with chamomile cream, distilling balm water for restoring memory, and easing toothache with powdered earthworm, mastic, or plantain water. She identifies wormwood (*Artemisia absinthium*) juice as a cure for vomiting. A plaster of soap and deer suet relieved a leg sore. Lacking chronology, the viewpoints shifted from Benedict Arnold's raid and burning of New London to retrospects on the shipyard economy and the Salem witch trials.

Mehetabel's recommendations named boiled mullein and yarrow as purges and a burn ointment prepared from millet, john's wort (*Hypericum perforatum*), sorrel (*Rumex acetosa*), leeks, and columbine leaves in cream. From hot milk spiced with nutmeg, peppercorn, clove, cinnamon, and oak bark she treated flux (diarrhea or dysentery). More specific curatives required deer's foot marrow for sore nipples, aniseed (*Pimpinella anisum*) in rosewater for insomnia, liverwort (*Marchantiophyta*) in cream for acne, and honey and egg white mixed with sage and rue for nail bed infection.

Travel lore about Boston depicted the diarist during her rehabilitation from smallpox. Diary food references mentioned curing a cough with brandied figs and serving wine, syllabub, and sack posset, easily digested restoratives based on a creamy custard. Additional kitchen instructions explain how to make French bread, rusk (twice-baked biscuit) and gingerbread, plum and rosewater cake, and quince preserved in small beer. For meats, she chose boiled trout and roasted eel, a protector of circulatory and cardiac health and a treatment for diabetes and arthritis. She made a separate list of beverages—limeade with cloves and balsam and currant wines. In 1895, the three Gilman sisters, Mehetabel's great-great-granddaughters, published *Mehetabel Chandler Coit: Her Book, 1714*. Another volume included letters to Mehetabel by daughter Martha and friend Elisabeth

Bradstreet Slaughter Wass Adams in the 1895 biography *Martha, Daughter of Mehetabel Chandler Coit, 1706–1784*.

### *Sources*

Coughlin, Michelle Marchetti. *One Colonial Woman's World: The Life and Writings of Mehetabel Chandler Coit*. Amherst: University of Massachusetts Press, 2012.
*Mehetabel Chandler Coit Her Book, 1714*. Cambridge, MA: Harvard University, 1714.

## Henrietta Dering Johnston (1674–March 9, 1729)
**Portraitist**
**Charleston, South Carolina**

The first professional female artist in colonial America, Henriette de Beaulieu Dering Johnston made a living with pastels. A French Huguenot from Rennes in northern France, she spent her childhood in London. Her parents, refugees Francis and Suzanna de Beaulieu, fled continental persecution. At marriage to Anglo-Irishman Robert Dering of Castlemore at age twenty, she left St. Martin-in-the-Fields, settled in Dublin, and bore daughters Helena and Mary. Helena died in 1704 at age eight.

Henrietta's art suggests that she studied under Irish miniaturists and developed the use of graphite, cross-hatching, and color shading, especially for hair. The softly muted tresses contrasted distinctive oval eyes and lips, the focus of her 1725 portraits of importer John Moore, his Huguenot wife Frances Lambert Moore, son Thomas, and ten-year-old daughter Frances Moore Bayard. In 1704, about the time of her husband's death, Henrietta began mastering the fresh, bright medium of French pastels, sticks of powdered pigment solidified with gum tragacanth.

At remarriage to Anglican minister Gideon Johnston, a widower with four children, Henrietta journeyed through the Madeira Islands to Charleston, South Carolina, where the Bishop of London named Gideon administrator of St. Philip's Episcopal Church, the colony's first congregation. The irregular salary and supplies forced Henrietta to work as Gideon's secretary and to support the family with commissions from portrait painting. Recurrent malaria and two destructive hurricanes slowed her work. A mission to London in April 1711 and a gift of crayons enabled her to refill art supplies during a year away from home and to petition for her husband's salary. Along the way, she survived an assault by pirates.

In a second widowhood in 1716, Henrietta received no widow's pension and found employment in New York City painting portraits of Elizabeth Colden de Lancey and the Cuyler-Van Schaick family of Albany. On laid paper 9" × 12" atop wood backboards, Henrietta applied precious imported materials to colonial head-and-shoulders depictions of elite subjects. Some, such as Earl John Perceval and Colonel William Rhett, she drew in armor.

Henrietta's colonial commissions favored Carolina low country planters and Huguenots of the Bacot, duBose, and Prioleau families. Poses featured faces slightly turned with serious expressions and large oval eyes. She signed on the back "Henrietta Dering Fecit (made this)" or "Henrietta Daring Pinxit (painted this)." Her career produced forty works from 1703 to 1725. Her daughter Mary achieved a post as lady-in-waiting at the court of George II.

### *Sources*

Jeffares, Neil. *Dictionary of Pastellists before 1800.* http://www.pastellists.com/Articles/Johnston.pdf.
Middleton, Margaret Simons. *Henrietta Johnston of Charles Town, South Carolina: America's First Pastellist.* Columbia: University of South Carolina Press, 1966.
Saunders, Richard H., and Ellen Gross Miles. *American Colonial Portraits.* Washington, D.C.: Smithsonian, 1987.

## Patience Rogers Marston (May 13, 1676–May 22, 1731)
**Accountant**
**Salem, Massachusetts**

In the standard role of shipman's wife, Patience Denison Rogers Marston kept family accounts and managed business during her husband's absences at sea. Her grandfather, the Rev. Nathaniel Rogers, fled religious persecution in England and repatriated with wife Margaret Crane Rogers in mid–November 1636 to Boston, Massachusetts Bay Colony. The last of six children, Patience was the daughter of Elizabeth Denison Rogers and the Rev. John Rogers, who practiced medicine in Ipswich. When Patience was six years old, her father advanced to president of Harvard. In Ipswich on March 15, 1696, she married a twenty-six-year-old Salem widower, Benjamin Marston, a wealthy merchant and owner of two warehouses on two wharves and the *Brigantine Essex,* a bicoastal trader named for Essex County.

In addition to becoming stepmother of twenty-year-old Abigail and nineteen-year-old Joseph, Patience cared for her mother-in-law, Mary Chichester Marston. From the couple's brick home, one of Salem's first, in 1700 at Crombie and Essex streets, she served her husband as business manager. His investments included five hundred acres and a thousand-acre island in Casco Bay, Maine, plus thirty-five acres at Northfields, three in Salem, and a sawmill, orchard, and House Island in the Manchester shipping lanes. She kept accounts during his long trade voyages to Halifax, Nova Scotia, and Barbados in the West Indies. In 1710, she recorded details of a financial matter conducted with Elizabeth Holmes, wife of Bostonian Robert Holmes, captain of the *Brigantine Essex.* Because of losses at sea to shipwrecks, pirates, and privateers and the death of son John and stepson Joseph at age nineteen, Benjamin Marston mortgaged his residence, islands, farms, and sawmill.

In poor health, Marston was unable to finance a Harvard education for his elder son Benjamin Jr., who apparently learned thrift from his parents. The two men sailed to Newfoundland in summer 1719. The son composed an overview of family finances and the cost of fifteen tons of white oak at £12 (approx. $3,263.90) after the ship left Falmouth for loading docks in Casco Bay, Maine. With pride in his profits, he mailed the data to Patience for adding to the family books. Before the *Brigantine Essex's* return, she acquired a notarized document and sent it to the captain. When father and son reached the port of Dublin, Ireland, on September 17, 1719, the elder died within ten days of smallpox, leaving his property to his children and wife. His will encouraged Patience to sell any and all that seemed suitable.

Benjamin Jr. reported recovery from smallpox without scars and cited plans to return home in May 1720, perhaps with thirty paying passengers coming aboard at Londonderry, Ireland. With a son's respect for careful accounting, he informed Patience that the ship carried a cargo worth £300 (approx. $78,256.46). He settled his father's debts and named his second daughter after his mother.

## Marston-Rogers Genealogy

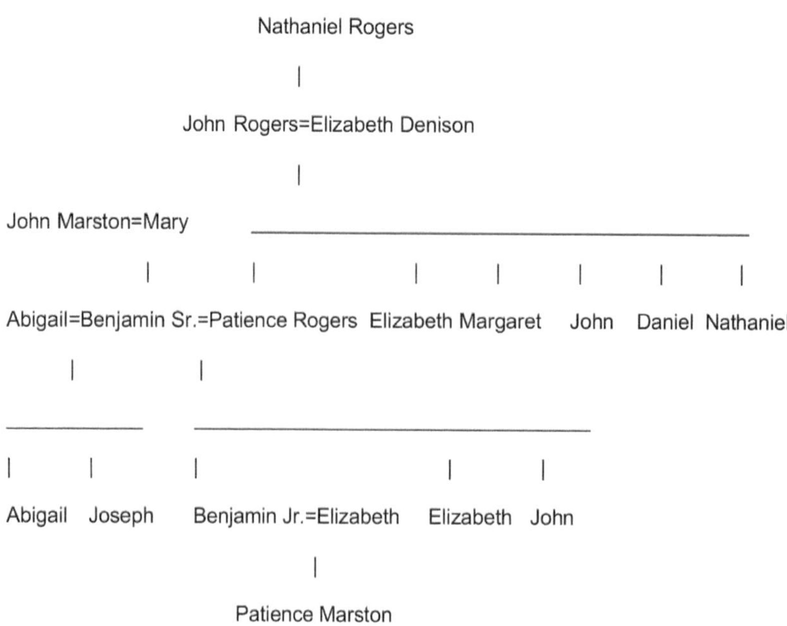

*Source*

Watson, John L. *Memoirs of the Marstons of Salem*. Boston: David Clapp & Son, 1873.

**Simja de Torres (1677–October 23, 1746)**
**Slave Trader**
**New York City**

An illiterate West Indian, Simja (also Sinya or Simha) de Silva de Torres Gomez enriched her household on the flesh trade begun by her husband. The daughter of Jewish Amsterdam merchant Moses de Silva of Kingston, she came to New York and married Brazilian merchant sea captain Joseph De Torres. Joseph bore a reputation for smuggling gold and tobacco from Brazil and, in 1721, for dealing with the Royal African Company. He constructed the Fortress of São João Baptista de Ajudá, a moated protection of Portuguese profiteering at Whydah (modern Ouidah, Benin).

With funds from a tax on bondsmen, the fort shored up the Portuguese monopoly of the slave trade. The route to the New World began with habitation in the Zomai Cabin and a walk around the Tree of Forgetting nine times for men, seven for women. Slave processing began with branding and auctioning at Place Chacha. For farewells, King Agaja planted the Tree of Return at the Place de Zoungbodji.

Left to manage the family trade for twenty-two years after Joseph's death in Jamaica in 1724, Simja sufficed as a single mother of daughter Ritzel (Rebecca), who wed Daniel Gomez on February 10. She bore Moses Gomez before dying at age twenty-seven. For fourteen years, Simja continued buying and selling African and Afro-Caribbean slaves during a decline in flesh marketing from Dahomey, the warehouse at São Tomé, and the Elmina Coast in Ghana. On March 19, 1728, she bought four slaves from the three-deck ship *Duke of Portland*. She intended a four-year-old boy as a personal servant. On July 19, 1742, she imported three more blacks.

In the particulars of a will composed in 1744, Simja awarded one slave girl to niece Rebecca Da Silva worth £15 (approx. $4,796.61) and another of equal value to Rachel Da Silva, daughter of Simja's brother Joshua. A third bondswoman passed to Rachel's sister Simja Da Silva. Her grandson, Moses Gomez, received the bulk of her estate minus three gifts of £5 (approx. $1,598.87) each to her brother Samuel, to charity and to She'erit Israel on Beaver Street, the New World's first synagogue.

*Sources*

Kaplan, Yosef. *The Posen Library of Jewish Culture and Civilization*. New Haven, CT: Yale University Press, 2023.

Moore, Deborah Dash, ed. *City of Promises: A History of the Jews of New York*. New York: New York University Press, 2012.

## Elizabeth Haddon Estaugh (May 25, 1680–March 30, 1762)
### Healer, Pharmacist, Brewer, Business Planner
### Haddonfield, New Jersey

The founder of Haddonfield, a West Jersey commercial hub in the Delaware Valley, Elizabeth Haddon Estaugh led an independent life marked by her retention of the maiden name Haddon. A Quaker born third of eight to Elizabeth Clarke and anchorsmith John Haddon, she was a native of Southwark, England. To elude religious persecution, she departed London in her early twenties in 1701 and reached Philadelphia in June. She settled south of Cooper's Creek in Newton, West Jersey, to open a wayside stop for traveling Quaker ministers.

Elizabeth received her father's power of attorney to conduct business and composed legal documents and official correspondence for the Pennsylvania Land Company, a Quaker realty consortium. On the Haddon family's five-hundred-acre plantation purchased from William Penn, she occupied a frontier house opposite Philadelphia on the Cooper River with husband John Estaugh, whom she married in 1702. Her association with the Unalachtigo Lenape and mastery of the Unami language taught her ethnobotany and the uses of medicinal plants from the thickly forested wilderness of South Jersey.

### Tending the Sick

Among standard *materia medica*, the Lenape ground these local biota in a stone mortar for poulticing or boiled them for tea:

| | |
|---|---|
| birch bark | cough, cold, liver tonic |
| blackberry | diarrhea, dysentery |
| black walnut | ringworm |
| bloodroot | stomachache, cramp, vomiting |
| box elder | nausea, laxative |
| cattail | wound antiseptic, anti-itch poultice, diarrhea, blisters |
| cherry bark | chest cold, pneumonia, cough |
| cottonwood | joint liniment |
| dandelion | blood and liver tonic, laxative |
| jimson weed | burns |
| locust bark | bronchial congestion |
| mint | bladder ulcers |

| | |
|---|---|
| muletail | acne |
| peach bark | colds |
| redbud | fever, vomiting |
| red cedar | skin irritation, repel insects |
| red oak | hoarseness |
| rosemary | headache, poor circulation, epilepsy |
| sassafras | diuretic, pain relief, wound antiseptic, blood pressure |
| slippery elm | chills |
| spurge | warts |
| staghorn sumac | sore throat, pyorrhea, arthritis, canker sores, childbirth |
| sweet grass | cough, sore eyes |
| wild grape | heart strength, anti-inflammation, laxative, breast milk |
| wild tobacco | toothache, earache, indigestion, hunger |
| yarrow | menstrual flooding |

While rearing niece Sarah Hopkins and five-year-old nephew Ebenezer Hopkins, the couple bought more land. They enlarged their living space in 1713 with construction of Haddon Hall, a three-story brick manse opposite the King's Highway (modern Main Street). In the adjacent two-story brewery and still house, the compounding of simples, tonics, and medicinal whiskey at a brick fireplace equipped with swinging crane and limbeck distillery earned Elizabeth the name of New Jersey's first female brewer and pharmacist. The Haddon Township took shape on 2.8 square miles of Camden County, where Elizabeth built a Society of Friends meeting house and graveyard in 1724. For a half century, Elizabeth served the local Friends women's society as clerk and recorder.

## Social Work and Nursing

From personal experience, diarist Esther Palmer acknowledged Elizabeth's skill as a healer of the poor and sick. Elizabeth and John volunteered to treat Sarah Ellis Woolman, a tailor in Mount Holly, during a bout of smallpox. During twenty years of widowhood after John's death in 1742, Elizabeth continued working as colonial doctor, estate management adviser, and champion of the Delaware Valley Lenape. She networked with esteemed female Quakers, including minister Hannah Dent Cooper, a missionary to Barbados and Rhode Island.

Much of Elizabeth's biography perished in the house fire of 1842. In 1845, Lydia Maria Child published "The Youthful Emigrant," the love story of John and Elizabeth Estaugh, in the *New York Daily Tribune* and included it in the compendium *Fact and Fiction*. Poet Henry Wadsworth Longfellow memorialized Hannah in the 1874 collection *Tales of a Wayside Inn*.

## *Sources*

Burstyn, Joan N. *Past and Promise: Lives of New Jersey Women.* Syracuse, NY: Syracuse University Press, 1997.

Dorwart, Jeffery M. *Elizabeth Haddon Estaugh 1680–1762: Building the Quaker Community of Haddonfield, New Jersey, 1701–1762.* Haddonfield, NJ: Historical Society of Haddonfield, 2013.

# II

# The Shot Heard Round the World, 1681–1701

Colonial patriots affirmed their unity on April 19, 1775, when militias faced down British forces at Lexington, Massachusetts, and destroyed artillery some seven miles away at Concord. The massing of sixteen hundred New England provincials ended the disastrous siege of Boston with guerrilla warfare and caused the British to recognize the extent of anti-monarchic fervor against George III. Women's contributions included the drug supplies of Elizabeth Gooking Greenleaf, whose Boston pharmacy proved valuable to George Washington's fleet and privateers. For mundane necessities, Ann Battson Wishart made and marketed candles and soap and taught the next generation of chandlers. To inform patriots of colonial happenings as far away as New Jersey, Rhode Island, and Delaware and shipping details as far south as the Caribbean, Philadelphia printer Cornelia Smith Bradford issued the *American Weekly Mercury*.

**Elizabeth Gooking Greenleaf (November 11, 1681–November 11, 1762)**
**Apothecary**
**Boston, Massachusetts**

Colonial America's first female pharmacist, Elizabeth Gooking Greenleaf established a profession that aided the Continental Army during the American Revolution. She was a native of Cambridge, Massachusetts, born the second of four to Mary Larkin and Sheriff Samuel Gooking, a militia captain. In a family dating to the fifteenth century, she claimed as paternal grandsires Daniel Gookin of Kent, England, a pioneer to Virginia in 1621, and General Daniel Gooking, leader of the Massachusetts colonial military. The Gooking family pioneered tracts in Chelmsford, Dunstable, and Groton. The wife of Harvard-trained apothecary, the Rev. Daniel Greenleaf, she married at age eighteen and bore thirteen children, one of whom died at birth in 1721. The youngest, William Greenleaf, served Suffolk County as sheriff and announcer of American independence from the Massachusetts state house on July 25, 1776.

During her husband's struggle to obtain his salary in Yarmouth, Elizabeth began her career in 1727 with a woman-owned medicine shop in Boston on Washington Street between Cornhill and Court streets. In addition to attending career matters, she nursed twelve of her children through smallpox. Her husband gave up the ministry at Yarmouth's Congregational church on Cape Cod and partnered with her in Boston until her death in 1762 at age eighty-one.

Daniel survived dire injury from a fall and remained bedfast for two years until his death in 1763. Elizabeth spent her last months caring for him. His estate was reduced to £162 (approx. $40,968.15). Despite a household torn between Tory and Whig, throughout the American Revolution, their pharmacy proved valuable to George Washington's fleet and privateers. Her eldest child, Dr. Daniel Greenleaf, served as a regimental surgeon. Son Stephen Greenleaf co-founded Brattleboro, Vermont, a trading and mill center.

## The Greenleaf Heritage

According to the Greenleaf company ledger, the subsequent staff attended the Continental Army from April 4, 1775, before its first engagement on April 19 at Lexington and Concord. Greenleaf Pharmacy supplied the field hospitals of Surgeon General Benjamin Church and patriot physician Joseph Warren with five crates of medicines worth £247 (approx. $50,200.96). Dr. Warren paid £51 (approx. $10,365.38), with the outstanding £196 (approx. $39,835.58) not reimbursed until August 10, 1775. As needs exceeded supply, on April 30, the military hired Andrew Craigie as drug deliverer on horseback. Before importation blockades, the medicaments imported from Antigua, Barbados, Bermuda, and Jamaica sufficed for three years at Concord, Groton, Lancaster, Mendon, Stow, Sudbury, and Worcester.

Before the Battle of Bunker Hill on June 17, 1775, field doctors drew up a list of medical necessities, especially jalap (*Radix Jalapa*), Epsom salts (*magnesium sulfate*), rhubarb (*Radix rhaei*), nitre (*potassium nitrate*), Peruvian or Jesuit's bark (*cortex Peruvianum*), ipecac (*Radix ipecacuanhae*), cream of tartar (*potassium bitartrate*), gum camphor (*Cinnemomum camphor*), red mercury (*mercury sulfide*), gum opium (*Papaver somniferum*), and lint for bandaging. By June 10, purchasing agents redirected drug orders through Philadelphia to supply depots during the New York campaign at Fort Ticonderoga. Pharmacies continued receiving fresh supplies from London in February 1776.

### Business Fluctuations

Rumors proved true of British sabotage at the Boston almshouse of drugs tainted with arsenic. The military confiscated twenty-five wagonloads from loyalist druggists. Only Cambridge hospital stores offered pure substances. The Greenleaf shop resumed supplying the patriot army on May 25, 1776, with £4 (approx. $831.33) worth of sponges, compresses, flannel, tape, and wound wrapping. By June, the Greenleaf firm received a £50 (approx. $10,391.65) advance to restock the shelves.

Brisk business continued at the Greenleaf shop until November 1776 with a total sale of £68 (approx. $14,132.64) in pharmaceuticals before New York supply lines dwindled, particularly antiseptic hyssop (*Hyssopus officinalis*), wormwood (*Sal absinthii*), tartar emetic (antimony and potassium tartrate), and mallow (*Malva neglecta*) for baths and for fomentation with hot moist poultices to ease pain. Prices rose on snakeroot (*Ageratina altissima*), Cantharides (Spanish flies), anti-inflammatory colchina bark, and opium. Privateers relieved Boston's dearth of medical supplies with one thousand captures of British ships.

By December 14, 1776, the Greenleaf pharmacy acquired £62 (approx. $12,885.64) in drugs from the ship *Julius Caesar* and £170 (approx. $35,331.60) in March 1777 from the brig *Three Friends*. Between September 3, 1776, and May 28, 1777, the company stocked Continental navy vessels. Shippers concealed drugs in unmarked packing cases and transported them in covered wagons at night. By October 1777, Boston pharmacists could offer sufficient jalap, gum camphor, rhubarb, Peruvian bark, salts, and gum opium for hospital needs.

### *Sources*

Brewster, Charles W. *Rambles about Portsmouth*. Portsmouth, MA: Lewis W. Brewster, 1859.

Griffenhagen, George Bernard. *Drug Supplies in the American Revolution*. Boston, MA: Hassell Street Press, 2021.

## Elizabeth Phillips (1685–May 5, 1761)
**Midwife**
**Charlestown, Massachusetts**

One of colonial America's dedicated healers, Elizabeth Meakes Langdon Phillips delivered three thousand babies. Trained in her hometown of Westminster, England, she received a medical commission at age thirty-five from Bishop John Robinson of London. The license enabled her to baptize stillborn and endangered babies in the absence of a priest. In 1721, Elizabeth emigrated to Massachusetts Bay Colony and began a forty-year career attending seventy-five births each year. She may have been the widow of Henry Langdon, who died in Boston during the 1723 smallpox epidemic.

Still employed in 1736, Elizabeth inherited the gifts of an estate and live-in care from her companion, local teacher Rebeckah Anderson in 1743. In 1751 at the Congregational Church, the midwife married widowed bookbinder Eleazer Phillips, Jr., and lived on Main Street in Charlestown. He offered a sound income from ownership of the town's wharf and warehouse and a Boston rental house on Black Rose Lane. When Elizabeth died at age seventy-six, the respected stone worker Nathaniel Lamson carved her grave marker.

### *Sources*

Beal, Jane. "Bridget Lee Fuller," *Midwifery Today* (Autumn 2015): 50–52.
Frothingham, R. History of Charlestown. Boston: Little & Brown, 1845.
Sawyer, T.T. *Old Charlestown: Historical and Biographical Reminiscences*. Boston: James H. West Company, 1902.

## Elizabeth Ann Sanford Noyes (1685–October 23, 1762)
**Merchant**
**Newport, Rhode Island**

A Newport competitor of she-merchant Elizabeth Woodberry Pratt, retailer Elizabeth Ann Sanford stocked merchandise similar to Pratt's stock in her store. The granddaughter of governors John Sanford and William Coddington, Ann was a scion of the Magna Carta barons. She was born in Newport, Rhode Island, to Mary Coddington and Governor Peleg Sanford, Sr., a former cavalry captain in 1777 during King Philip's War. The family lived at Black Point on Narragansett Bay and owned land at Elizabeth Islands, Saco, Winnegquot, and Pettaquamscutt. She was eight when Mary died, leaving motherless seven daughters and three sons.

From her father's will, at age sixteen, Ann inherited a house and fifty acres. At age twenty, she married militia captain Thomas Noyes, a New Haven County justice of the peace. Over twenty-one years, she bore seven daughters and five sons, three of whom died in childhood. Like her father, a trader of sugar, wool, and horses to England and Barbados, she became a merchant. In 1719, she wed Captain John Mason III, a teacher of Mohegans in Stonington, Connecticut, and bore two more sons.

Like Elizabeth Pratt, Ann excelled at retail. Both shopkeepers appealed to female buyers with a full range of calico, cambric, damask, silk, indigo, sewing notions, and whalebone to line corsets. Over four years, Ann bought from wholesaler William Vernon, a Triangle Trade privateer from his store on Clarke Street and at Bannister's Wharf. A slave dealer in Barbados, William carried one hundred thirty-three Gold Coast captives per voyage, which he offloaded at Taylor's Wharf and Charleston, South Carolina. He transported by the armed private sloop *Olive Branch* some £160 (approx. $48,451.29) worth of English stores—cookware, scissors, gloves, and handkerchiefs. Ann's shelves of edibles included tea and coffee, veal, sugar, pepper, raisins, mustard seed, and chocolate.

*Sources*

"Genealogical Notes," *Rhode Island Historical Magazine* 5 (1884–1885): 63.
Hodge, Christina J. *Consumerism and the Emergence of the Middle Class in Colonial America*. New York: Cambridge University Press, 2014.

## Elizabeth Penrose (1686–ca. 1740)

## Mary Hodges Townsend (1690–after 1740)
**Taverner**
**Savannah, Georgia**

A Georgia pioneer and saloon keeper, Elizabeth "Mother" Penrose gained a reputation for serving a mixed clientele. Original settlers from Gravesend, England, on the ship *Anne* on November 17, 1732, shipwright John and Elizabeth reached Georgia Colony on February 1, 1733, and made a home at 30 East Street in Savannah's Jekyll district. The couple divided their jobs to accommodate his absences from home for commercial work in New York. His reputation suffered from rowdy behavior, slander, and bootlegging. He left the saloon and shop to Elizabeth.

With an illegal servant, Elizabeth catered to the military and seamen, day workers, and travelers at an unlicensed facility. She sold rum, liquor, and punch, which carried an illicit savor. In 1735, she ventured into catering a public feast. On May 26, 1736, authorities convicted and fined her for keeping a brothel. Constable Samuel Mercer and competitor Mary Hodges echoed public distaste at Elizabeth's record for dispensing illegal rum. Elizabeth's mild punishment derived from Chief Magistrate Thomas Causton, a customer who frequented her saloon and who faced a similar charge of illicit liquor sales on April 24, 1735.

Both Elizabeth and Mary answered formal indictments for violating liquor laws. In fear of a Spanish invasion, Elizabeth fled to Carolina in September 1740. At her demise, John followed in August 1742 and died in Savannah in October 1754. Mary Hodges, who already bore a reputation for selling illegal drink from summer 1733, was a close neighbor at 36 East Street in Savannah's Jekyll district. At the death of husband Richard Hodges, a basketmaker, Mary lost her license but continued to serve the public. The single mother of Elizabeth and Sarah Hodges, on February 22, 1734, she married Edward Townsend, who managed a pub that appealed to rebels. Her public behavior generated scorn for swearing and libeling King George II. A year after Edward abandoned her, she left the colony for Carolina on July 29, 1740.

### *Sources*

Coleman, Kennedy, ed. *Colonial Records of the State of Georgia*. https://ugapress.manifoldapp.org/projects/colonial-records-of-the-state-of-georgia-07b79a80-769c-4b38-aa48-d967dd62b00b.

Jones, Charles C. *History of Savannah, Ga*. Syracuse, NY: D. Mason & Co., 1890.

## Barbara Needham de Graffenried (June 25, 1688–June 26, 1744)
**Dance Teacher**

## Mary Stagg (ca. 1690–1740s)
**Actor, Dance Teacher**
**Williamsburg, Virginia**

A multi-talented musician and dancer, "Madame La Baronne" Barbara Tempest Needham de Graffenried and her husband brought European culture to the Virginia colony. The daughter of Anne Wingate and Sir Arthur Thomas Needham, "Barbra" was an Englishwoman from Wymondsley, Hertfordshire, and wife of Robert Tempest, who died in 1744. In Charleston, South Carolina, at age twenty-six, she remarried a German-Swiss aristocrat, Christopher VI "Kit" de Graffenried, the son of New Bern's founder and bearer of a twelfth-century Swiss name and coat of arms. Because of his birth in America, he lost rights to Swiss estates and the three-spired de Graffenried castle in Worb east of Bern, Switzerland. In November 1722, she bore Baron Anton (or Anthony) Tscharner de Graffenried in Williamsburg, Virginia.

Barbara and Christopher moved from Philadelphia to Maryland and Virginia and opened an Inn. In 1721, they taught dance lessons in the homes of colonial planters William Byrd II, Judge Francis Hardyman, and Nathaniel Harrison of Berkeley Plantation, Anton's godfather. In addition to managing investment property in Brunswick County, they paid £130 (approx. $38,869.26) for the two-story Pitt-Dixon House, a Williamsburg town home on Duke of Gloucester Street, and a plantation on the James

River. Barbara was known as a gracious hostess at stylish entertainments held on their ground floor from 1722 to 1728 in the ample living and dining rooms. In 1723, they invested in a second lot on Nicholson Street for £22 (approx. $6,941.22).

To enhance Williamsburg refinement, the couple competed with fiddler Charles and dancer Mary Stagg, indentured servants to William Levingston, the builder of America's first theater. After attending classes in New Kent County, the couple tutored the Robert Carter family and promoted musicales, drama, and social dance as exercise and art. In 1735, family friend Governor Byrd recommended Barbara for her conscientious lessons and ladylike behavior.

The *Virginia Gazette* announced Barbara's sale of tickets for five shillings to a ball and assembly on April 16–17, 1736. The house parties continued on May 2, 1739, after her recovery from illness and offered music, candlelight, and liquor. After two years of widowhood, she left ample wealth and property to Anton Tscharner, the father of her sixteen grandchildren. Anton Jr. distinguished the family as a county judge and wounded veteran of the battle of Guilford Courthouse.

### *Sources*

Bell, Landon C. *The Old Free State*. Richmond, VA: William Byrd Press, 1927.
"A Corner in Ancestors," *Washington Progress* (11 February 1915): 4.
de Graffenried, Thomas P. *History of the de Graffenried Family from 1191 A.D. to 1925*. New York: self-published, 1925.

## Ann Battson Wishart (ca. 1690–1770)
**Chandler**
**Philadelphia, Pennsylvania**

In the pioneer tradition, Ann Battson (also Bateson or Betson) Wishart made and sold tallow candles to her Pennsylvania neighbors. At age twenty she wed an Orkney cooper, Peter Wishart from Sandwick. A testimony to his reliability derives from his signatures as a witness to Henry Bockholtz's deed in December 1708, John Palmer and Timothy Hanson's wills in February 1710, and William Delwyn's will in 1711. An heir of merchant Hugh Lowdon in 1723, Peter purchased medicine worth £2 (approx. $631.02) from Dr. Francis Notf for Hugh's use. Two years later, in October 1725, he witnessed the will of Abraham Bickley of Burlington, New Jersey.

In May 1717, Philadelphia's Common Council bought candles from the Wisharts for five shillings and six pence. In July 1730, the couple sold candles and soap to the New London sloop *Tryall* for Commander Samuel Bicknell, who had just refitted his merchantman with cannon for a voyage to Barbados. In 1738, the Wisharts bought paper, ledger, newspapers, and an account book from Benjamin Franklin's printshop on Market Street between Third and Fourth streets.

From the mid-1750s, the Wisharts lived in Philadelphia near several single working women—dram shop owner and landlady Rachel Draper, business manager Deborah Read Franklin, upholsterer Elizabeth Lawrence, optician Hannah Breintnall, and taverner Susannah Harditch. A widow at age sixty-six, Ann Wishart continued providing for her household by selling candles and soap at home in High Street Ward on the Delaware River. She taught chandlery to daughter Ann and son Thomas as well as apprentices. In retirement, Ann Sr. and Ann Jr. worked at increasing stock. The mother turned over the tallow craft to Thomas, who also served as neighborhood tax assessor in 1772 and 1774.

### *Sources*

Hinshaw, William Wade. *Encyclopedia of American Quaker Genealogy*. Washington, D.C.: n.p., 1938.

Wulf, Karin. *Not All Wives: Women of Colonial Philadelphia*. Ithaca, NY: Cornell University Press, 2000.

## Cornelia Smith Bradford (ca. 1690–August 1755)
**Printer, Publisher, Editor, Shopkeeper, Bookbinder**
**Philadelphia, Pennsylvania**

The owner of a printshop and newspaper, Cornelia Smith Bradford, like other colonial widows, inherited property and a career from her husband's will and competed for business against Benjamin Franklin. An heiress from the moneyed class in New York City, she married into a family of wordsmiths who included father-in-law William Bradford, a Royal Printer and initiator of paper milling and printing in Pennsylvania and New York, mother-in-law Elizabeth Sowle Bradford, and husband Andrew Sowle Bradford, a prominent newsman and Royal Printer of the Province. William Sr. trained Andrew, who, in his midtwenties, shared business for Quakers with his father. For originating the *American Weekly Mercury* and the *Pennsylvania Gazette*, Andrew earned the name of father of the newspaper and magazine and champion of tolerance and freedom of the press.

A rich widower and associate from June 1720 with nephew and adopted son and heir, William Bradford III, Andrew wed Cornelia in 1739. Their union influenced her to propose her niece as a wife for William. Wedlock would make the girl the potential owner of the bookshop, called Sign of the Bible on Second Street and Black-Horse Alley near the Great Meeting

House. Two blocks west of the Delaware River between Chestnut and High streets, the store stocked dividers, scales, mezzotint prints, English stationery, writing parchment, Dutch quills, blank journals, paper, slates, lamp black, glue, sealing wax, letter cases, ink powder, ink horns, and inkstands. Book stock included primers, William Penn's works, Bibles, prayer books, Nahum Tate and Nicholas Brady's psalter, and the popular picaresque novel *Moll Flanders* by English journalist Daniel Defoe.

Connected to the business, the Bradford bindery had a reputation for quality renewal of worn or damaged volumes. William's spat with Cornelia raised a rift between partners, causing him to relocate to his aunt's house and to underwrite marine insurance. He sold his uncle's magazine to bankers and businessmen at the London Coffeehouse on Front and High streets, Philadelphia.

## A Female Printer

At Andrew's death on November 24, 1742, the "Widow Bradford" apologized to readers for the mourning period during which she omitted the issue of December 13, 1739. She inherited five hundred acres in Dublin, Pennsylvania, the Durham Ironworks, press, bookshop, and newspaper issued at 8 Front Street with the aid of printer Isaiah Warner. Isaiah ran his own shop in Chestnut Street, where Benjamin Franklin did his printing. From December 1743, her masthead featured a woodcut of a post rider blowing his trumpet to alert citizens of delivery. In late fall and winter 1743, she sold popular agricultural and astrology manuals:

- reference compiler William Birkett's *Poor Will's Almanack*, advertised in the *American Weekly Mercury* the week of October 13–20, 1743, the seventh year of its issuance and published by Cornelia Bradford and Isaiah Warner
- astronomer and poet Jacob Taylor's *almanac Pensilvania 1743*, issued under Isaiah Warner's name
- *Bekanntmachung*, a public announcement from the Reformed Dutch Church in 1742 endorsing the Rev. Jacob Lischy, minister to twelve congregations, distributed under the names of Cornelia Bradford and Isaiah Warner
- Jacob Taylor's *almanac Pensilvania 1744*, advertised the week of November 10–17, 1743, five years after Taylor's death by Isaiah Warner and Cornelia Bradford
- *American Almanack for the Year of Christian Account 1744*, compiled by Titan Leeds, a friend and rival of Benjamin Franklin, and issued by Cornelia Bradford and Isaiah Warner

- William Ball's *The New-Jersey Almanack for the Year of Christian Account 1744*, advertised on November 24, 1743, by an anti-Catholic writer and rival of Jacob Taylor for Cornelia Bradford and Isaiah Warner
- *American Almanack for the Year of Christian Account 1744*, compiled by Titan Leeds and published by Cornelia Bradford
- *American Almanack for the Year of Christian Account 1745*, compiled by Titan Leeds and published by Cornelia Bradford
- John Jerman's *Almanack for 1744*, published by Isaiah Warner and Cornelia Bradford, the last publication of their partnership
- John Jerman's *American Almanack for the Year of Christian Account 1745*, advertised for the week of September 27–October 4, 1744, as the publication of Cornelia Bradford and later mocked by Benjamin Franklin for basing its compilation on the occult
- William Birkett's *Poor Will's Almanack for 1745*, issued by Cornelia Bradford
- Matthew Boucher's *Pennsylvania Almanack for the Year of Christ, 1745*, advertised on October 4, 1744, as Cornelia Bradford's publication
- John Jerman's *American Almanack for the Year of Christian Account 1746*, printed by Cornelia Bradford
- *American Almanack for the Year of Christian Account 1746*, compiled by Titan Leeds and published by Cornelia Bradford
- William Birkett's *Poor Will's Almanack for 1746*, published by Cornelia Bradford
- William Birkett's *Poor Will's Almanack for 1747*, issued by Cornelia Bradford
- William Birkett's *Poor Will's Almanack for 1748*, published by Cornelia Bradford as competition from Benjamin Franklin became more heated and John Jerman moved his business from the Bradford printshop
- William Birkett's *Poor Will's Almanack for 1750*, issued by Cornelia Bradford
- William Birkett's *Poor Will's Almanack for 1751*, printed by Cornelia Bradford
- William Birkett's *Poor Will's Almanack for 1752*, the last almanac published in Cornelia Bradford's name

In addition, Cornelia advertised spectacles, compasses, dictionaries, arithmetic and geography books and spellers, hornbooks, dance manuals, French and Latin grammars, and foreign currency manuals. For music, essays, and poetry, she offered:

- *A Choice Collection of Hymns from the Hymn-Book of the Moravian Brethren*, printed in 1743 and featuring multiple translations of German works
- *New-Year Verses of the Carriers of the American Weekly Mercury*, issued in 1744 in competition with a similar collection printed by Benjamin Franklin
- Tailor Krishtian Crasshold's *The Modern Poemander; Or the Wise Honest and Moral Krishtian Crasshold's Dissertation on the Deity.*

## Building an Estate

From October 1744, Cornelia relied on business manager George Brintal to honor the printshop's guarantees: "Advertisements are taken in and all persons in Town and County may be supply'd with this Paper." Size ranged from the standard two pages to four and sometimes six or eight. Coverage included European and New England events, family connections, and colonial happenings as far away as New Jersey, Rhode Island, and Delaware and shipping details as far south as the Caribbean. Chief among items were marriages, deaths, accidents, missing indentured servants, and runaway Indians and slaves along with details of height, color, teeth and hair, brands, clothes, and late whereabouts.

Until the final issue of the Mercury on May 22, 1746, Cornelia edited and printed the news in her own name. The Mercury merged with the *Pennsylvania Journal and Weekly Advertiser*, owned by William Bradford III. She invested in property in Germantown and Philadelphia, Pennsylvania, and in New York City and operated the bookshop and bindery into her sixties. One of the late additions to the shelves was a reprint of Stephen Crisp's 1691 Quaker allegory *A Short History of a Long Travel from Babylon to Bethel*. Her papers and pamphlets gained a reputation for quality fonts and inking.

### Sources


De Armond, Anna Janney. "Andrew Bradford," https://journals.psu.edu, 1983, 463–487.

Jones, Horatio Gates. *An Address Delivered at the Annual Meeting of the Historical Society of Pennsylvania*. Philadelphia: King & Baird, 1869.

Morrison, Hugh Alexander. *A Preliminary Check List of American Almanacs 1639–1800*. Washington, D.C.: Library of Congress, 1907.

Phillips, Henry, Jr. "Certain Almanacs Published in Philadelphia between 1705 and 1744" (speech), *American Philosophical Society* (18 February 1881).

Purple, Samuel S. "Genealogy of the First Printer in the Middle Colonies of British America, William Bradford," *New York Genealogical and Biographical Record* 4:4 (October 1873): 183.

## Catherine Kaidyee Blaikley (1695–October 24, 1771)
**Midwife**
**Williamsburg, Virginia**

Midwife Catherine Kaidyee Blaikley spent three decades of her career in devotion to parturient women and the unborn. A native of York County, Virginia, she and brother John were the only children of Martha Bryan and William Kaidyee of James City. Soon after William Kaidyee's death, Catherine united with widowed merchant and watchmaker William Blaikley, Sr., on September 11, 1718. Their first son named James died in infancy. Before age thirty-seven, she bore sons James II and Benjamin Sadler and daughters Mary, Elizabeth, and Jeanette Carson. Benjamin also died in infancy.

Catherine's husband expired shortly after the birth of James II. At age forty-one, she inventoried William's possessions for a York County Court hearing. She inherited slaves, household goods, a fifty-acre tract in Henrico County, a half story house with kitchen loft in Williamsburg on the fashionable Duke of Gloucester Street, and a Brunswick County mill on one hundred acres at Pohatten (Powhatan), Bentley Springs, left to stepson William "Will" Jr. by his maternal grandmother, Sarah Efford Weldon.

For thirty-five years, Catherine remained alone at the same address, preserving for posterity a *Book of Common Prayer*. She survived handily as keeper of a boarding house lodging businessmen and politicians passing through Williamsburg. Three years later, she initiated home health care for women and the eventual delivery of three thousand newborns.

Catherine's altruism extended to a son-in-law, Colonel Griffith Stith, whom she aided financially. Her epitaph in the *Virginia Gazette* idealized her as "eminent." Mary Blaikley Stith of her children lived to produce six granddaughters and four grandsons. Catherine's fifth great-granddaughter, Virginia Belle Sholar, followed the matriarchal career and, at age fifteen, delivered an infant.

### *Sources*

Grant DePauw, Linda. *Founding Mothers: Women of America in the Revolutionary Era*. Boston: Houghton Mifflin, 1975.

Sturz, Linda. *Within Her Power: Propertied Women in Colonial Virginia*. New York: Routledge, 2002.

## Ann Smith Franklin (October 2, 1696–April 16, 1763)
**Printer, Publisher, Editor**
**Boston, Massachusetts, Newport, Rhode Island**

The Puritan wife and partner of journalist James Franklin, Sr., Ann Smith Franklin, New England's first female printer, inherited a typography business in widowhood and advanced to editing and compiling an almanac. A Bostonian, she was born on October 2, 1696, to Anna and Samuel Smith and wed James on February 4, 1723. On August 7, 1721, the couple published the wry and witty biweekly *New England Courant* in their Boston office, a broadsheet that profited from their experiment in freedom of the press. On a wood press, they began colonial parody with gibes at Puritan theocracy and ridicule of Cotton Mather, a proponent of smallpox variolation, a crude form of introducing microbes into a slit in the arm to generate antibodies and boost immunity.

James's jailing for libel from June 12–July 1722, for sneering at government and Puritan authorities and for airing his brother Benjamin's anonymous taunts at commonwealth hypocrites forced the couple to leave Boston. They relocated to Newport near his brother, chandler John Franklin, to found Rhode Island's first printshop on Tillinghast's Wharf. The staff debuted the Rhode Island Gazette on September 27, 1732, which Ann sold along with fabric, books, broadsides of quarrels and scandals, and newspapers, until the Gazette's demise on May 24, 1733. After the birth of five children, her twelve-year marriage ended in widowhood in 1735.

## The Presswoman

To support James Jr. and daughters Elizabeth and Mary, the "Widow Franklin" secured a contract from the Rhode Island legislature with a petition dated October 1736. The printing of money, ballots, legal forms, and law books sustained the household for more than a quarter century. She set up the press in Washington Square in the cellar of Newport's school. Her accomplishments included printing pamphlets, commercial ads, sermons, and novels and selling brother-in-law Benjamin Franklin's *Poor Richard's Almanack*. Her daughters aided the business by typesetting the weekly *Newport Mercury* newspaper. Stepson James Jr. continued the *Rhode Island Gazette.*

In addition to typesetting a primer and an original work, *A Brief Essay on the Number Seven in 1735*, and the state charter by Charles II, in 1737, Ann began distributing the *Rhode Island Almanack*, an original compendium that remained viable for five years for its weather predictions, calendar, and citations. She profited in 1745 from inking five hundred copies of Rhode Island's *Acts and Laws*. Two years later, on February 26, 1747, she billed the colony for printing twenty-four copies of the *Acts of Assembly* at £5 each (approx. $1,442.88), which two co-signers verified. A second receipt stated the cost of a ream of paper at £5 and 40 shillings.

## A Growing Business

At Queen Street on June 12, 1758, the company launched the first state newspaper, the *Newport Mercury*, the first to publish West African poet Phillis Wheatley and comment on burgeoning prewar shipping of local paints and other New England goods to the Caribbean. In addition to Samuel Johnson's *Elements Philosophical* and Lew Evans's map of the British colonies of America in *Geographical Essays*, articles alerted readers to increasing petitions for debt relief because of currency reform and slow repayment of debt. On August 11, 1761, David Douglass's new dramatic production of William Shakespeare's *Othello* earned the recommendation of Governor Francis Fauquier, who reported the comic troupe prudent and discreet. Ann's alliance with printer Samuel Hall in 1761 and production of a folio of sixteen state schedules from August 1748 to May 1763 continued to her death at age sixty-seven. Her voluminous stock included these publications sold from the town school:

- Joseph Stafford's *The Rhode Island Almanac for the Year 1737*
- John Aplin's *John Walton's Religion, Proved Not to Be the Religion of Jesus*, issued in 1737
- Joseph Stafford's *The Rhode Island Almanac for the Year 1738*
- the sixteen-page *The Rhode-Island Almanack for the Year, 1739*
- Ann Franklin's *The Rhode-Island Almanack for the Year, 1740*
- *The Chronicle of the Kings of England*, compiled in 1741 by Nathan ben Saddi, Robert Dodsley, and Philip Dormer Stanhope Chesterfield, which Dodsley reissued in London in 1745
- the sixteen-page *The Rhode-Island Almanack for the Year, 1741*
- *The Charter Granted by His Majesty, King Charles II to the Governor and Company of the English Colony of Rhode-Island and Providence-Plantations, in New-England in America*, which Ann sold in 1744 and Samuel marketed in 1767
- Acts and Laws of His Majesty's Colony of Rhode Island and Providence–Plantations, in New-England, in America, compiled for March 1, 1663, to May 27, 1745, Ann's largest project at five hundred copies, which she sold in 1744
- Rhode Island ballots, currency, mortgages, and ship registrations, completed in 1744
- Thomas Deloney's *Fair Rosamond*, sold in 1746 covering Queen Eleanor of Aquitaine's murder of the mistress of her husband, Henry II, at Woodstock
- Charles Bowler and James and Ann Franklin's *Reflections on the Conduct and Principles of the Quakers in North-America*, sold in 1758

- *At the General Assembly of the governor and Company of the English colony of Rhode-Island, and Providence Plantations, in New-England, in America*, an explanation of changes to Rhode Island tax law with tabulations of assessments for twenty-seven towns, printed in 1762 by Samuel Hall and Ann Franklin
- Samuel Hall and Ann Franklin's *Remarks on a Late Performance, Sign'd, a Freeman of the Colony, in Answer to a Dialogue between the Governor of the Colony of Rhode-Island, and a Freeman of the Same Colony*, on the subject of the sugar trade and smuggling, sold in 1762.

**Franklin-Smith Genealogy**

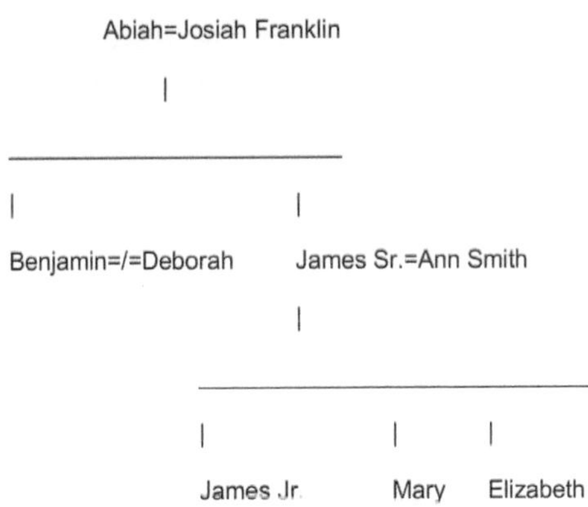


*Sources*

Mays, Dorothy A. *Women in Early America: Struggle, Survival, and Freedom in a New World.* Santa Barbara, CA: ABC-CLIO, 2004: 148–149.

Walker, Gay. "Women Printers in Early American Printing History," *Yale University Library Gazette* 61:3–4 (April 1987): 116–124.

## Mary Spratt Alexander (April 16, 1693–April 18, 1760)

## Maria de Peyster Provoost Spratt (September 5, 1659–May 3, 1701)

## Cornelia Lubberts de Peyster (before 1632–1715)

**Importer, Real Estate Broker**

**New York City**

A prominent trader on a grand scale, Mary Spratt Provoost Alexander learned her skills from the example of a commercial matrilineage.

The daughter of Maria de Peyster Provoost and John "Jack" Spratt, she was descended from Dutch goldsmiths. After Maria's death in 1701 at age forty-one, a maternal grandmother, Cornelia "Neeltje" Lubberts De Peyster, New York's first chamberlain (household manager) and a successful New Amsterdam trader with Virginia Colony, reared Mary on New York's Broad Street. At age eighteen, she wed Samuel Provoost, a wealthy Huguenot-Dutch haberdasher.

In widowhood in her twenties, Mary emulated Cornelia by taking her deceased husband's place and building on his realty and transatlantic dry goods investments. In 1721, Mary married Scots attorney and surveyor James Alexander, a First Ward alderman, and bankrolled his mercantile company, which thrived in the port of Manhattan. The couple's home earned a reputation for merriment and the promotion of London's popular gavottes, bourrees, minuets, marches, jigs, and rigadoons. James rose to state attorney general and New Jersey's surveyor general. At "Mrs. Alexander's Shop," Mary received goods from the Mediterranean, Spain, and the West Indies and conveyed consignments by two-horse coach. As her swatch books indicate, in the 1730s, she specialized in textiles and stocked her store with imported brocades, broadcloths, and tapes for making dresses, slip covers, suits, and liveries. By 1743, her wealth totaled £100,000 (approx. $28,608,435.23).

At a mansion on Beaver and Broad four blocks from Wall Street, Mary reared her ten children to appreciate international marketing. She imported luxury tableware and food items from London suppliers David Barclay and Samuel Storke, who influenced colonial shopping trends. In spring 1745 during the French and Indian War, the siege of Louisburg, Canada, required substantial supplies from her company to ensure control of a strategic site. She saved on shipping overhead by sharing the cost of a sloop to import rations, boats, cannon, canvas, cordage, and tools. To appeal to clients in Albany and New Jersey, she smoothed the approach to her shop and office with the city's first sidewalk. The Alexander–de Peyster clan produced mayors, militiamen, and colonel John Stevens, the pioneer of steam transportation and father of the American railway.

## *Sources*

Keller, Kate Van Winkle. "James Alexander's Collection of Country Dances, New York, 1730," *Libraries, History, Diplomacy, and the Performing Arts*. Stuyvesant, NY: Pendragon Press, 1905, 353–370.

Roberts, William I. "Samuel Storke: An Eighteenth-Century London Merchant Trading to the American Colonies," *Business History Review* 39:2 (Summer 1965): 147–170.

Zabin, Serena. "Women's Trading Networks and Dangerous Economies in Eighteenth-Century New York City," *Early American Studies* 4:2 (Fall 2006): 291–321.

## Grace Mears Levy (1694–October 14, 1740)
**Merchant**
**New York City**

One of Manhattan's merchant widows, Grace Mears Levy earned a living in commerce to support eleven children. The scion of sixteenth-century Roman grandsire Amore DeTorres, seventeenth-century French native Naphtali Franks, Londoners Rabbi David Bloch and Aaron Franks, and Argentine grandmother Mary "Maria" DeTorres Franks, Grace claimed kinship with multinational Jewish refugees. She was born in Spanish Town among Jamaican Ashkenazi Jews to Joy Tabitha Franks and merchant Sampson Mears. Her father died in 1711. Married in London at age twenty-four to a distinguished Hanoverian widower, Moses Raphael Levy, thirty years her senior, she mothered his four children and bore four sons and four daughters. Bilhah Abigail Levy Franks, the London-born daughter Moses had with first wife Richea Asher Michaels, gave her name to Moses's slave vessel *Abigail*.

At the Levy residence on seventy-five acres in Rye, New York, Grace gave birth to Joseph, her last child, within two days of Moses's death on June 14, 1728. His will left her a wealthy woman and inheritor of his fleet of ships—the Jamaican sloop *Caracoa*, the Barbadian pink *Charlotte*, *Four Sisters*, and *Nassau*—to import West Indian slaves and transport goods to London, North Africa, Canada, and the Caribbean. In addition to shopkeeping and land management, she took over Moses's trading clients and marketed grain, furs, hides, and beaver pelts. Grace married a second widower, David Hays, a New Jersey farmer and vinegar seller, who reduced the family to paupers relying on synagogue support.

Abigail set the tone of the Levy-Franks clan, which excelled in the arts and law. She admired her stepmother for surviving a failed second marriage and supporting a large household and the first New York synagogue, Shearith Israel on Mill Street (modern Wall Street). Abigail's son transported the Liberty Bell aboard his ship *Myrtilla*. The clan intermarried with the Harts, Isaacs, Michals, Pues, Seixas, and Thompsons in Philadelphia, Baltimore, and Boston.

### *Source*

Phillips, N. Taylor. "The Levy and Seixas Families of Newport and New York," *Publications of the American Jewish Historical Society* 4 (1896): 189–214.

## Esther Wheelwright (March 31, 1696–November 28, 1780)
### Business Manager
### Wells, Maine

A multilingual frontierswoman, Esther Marie-Joseph Wheelwright turned Abenaki training into a windfall for Ursuline nuns. Reared for seven years at Wells, Maine, on the Kennebec River among ten siblings by English parents Mary Snell and the Rev. John Wheelwright, a taverner and justice of the peace, Esther was the granddaughter of an earlier John Wheelwright, a Protestant minister. She grew up at Wells, Maine, in a pious Puritan home of slave owners and tended younger siblings Jeremiah, Elizabeth, and Mary.

After Esther's capture at the Wheelwright garrison by French Canadians and Catholic Wabanaki during Queen Anne's War, she became a prisoner of war on August 21, 1703, and marched on foot a hundred twenty miles northeast of home. At Narantsouak (modern Norridgewock, Maine), she adapted to a Wabanaki village and adoptive parents. To stave off rampant hunger and scurvy, her captors traded bear, beaver, and otter pelts to the English for cash.

Under the influence of Jacques Bigot and Vincent Bigot, Jesuit missionaries to First Nations in New France, Esther entered Château St. Louis, an aristocratic clifftop residence of the French governor-general Philippe Vaudreuil in Quebec. In January 1709, she enrolled with other native and white prisoners of war at the Ursuline boarding school, which taught her language, music, and embroidery, a major accomplishment for young ladies. In June 1710, she and fellow captives Esther Hayward and Mary Silver, her cousins, requested admittance as nuns.

From 1712–1778, Esther rose from postulant to porter and zelatrix (supervisor) before achieving an administrative position as the only foreign-born Mother Superior. On 12 April 1714, she gave up her white background and pledged herself to God and the committed life. Under the name Sister Esther Marie Joseph de l'Enfant Jésus, she avoided efforts to return her to her Maine family. A teacher, principal, and dean of novices, she once more altered her lifestyle during the 1759 battle of Quebec. She was forced from the convent and nursed combat casualties at the Hôpital Général. As Mother Superior of the Ursuline order, on December 15, 1760, at age sixty-four, she eased relations with the English and French through diplomacy in two languages.

To requite convent debts, Esther instructed nuns in embroidered, quilled, painted, and gilded devotional items, a marketable success to tourists and soldiers. Among the needleworkers, two older nuns, Dorothy Jordan de St. Joseph and Mary Ann Davis de St. Benoit, supplied needlework for altar decoration, boxes, pin cushions, and framing in floss and gold and silver thread. Esther, herself a master needleworker, completed a made-up family coat of arms. The chief Ursuline product, images of saints in native style, incorporated glass and copper beads and bright-toned silk threads and Wabanaki materials—birch bark, deer pelts, dyed moose hair, and porcupine quills—in artificial flowers, cuffs and jewelry, and gilt paintings completed with thrush hair brushes. Active to the mideighties, Esther died in Quebec.

### *Sources*

Baker, Charlotte Alice. *True Stories of New England Captives Carried to Canada During the Old French and Indian Wars*. Cambridge, MA: unknown, 1897.
Little, Ann M. *The Many Captivities of Esther Wheelwright*. New Haven: Yale University Press, 2016.

## Charlotte Hebert (1697–1762)
**Apothecary, Nurse**
**New Orleans, Louisiana**

At New Orleans's Ursuline Convent, Charlotte Hebert (under the name Soeur Saint-François Xavier Hebert or Sister Francis Xavier Hebert), one of the Filles du Charité (Maidens of Charity), set the example for New World altruists with thirty years of dedication to the suffering poor. She was born in Bayeux, France, in 1697 and rose to mistress of novices. For a name, she chose St. Francis Xavier, a sixteenth-century founder of the Society of Jesus (Jesuits), who treated the sick in the West Indies. In medieval style, she took communion frequently, lived on one meal per day of coarse food, and cultivated penitence with self-flagellation, bracelets, horsehair cilices, iron chains, and sackcloth hairshirts.

Products of the Counter-Reformation, nine nuns, two postulants, a novice, and one servant were dispatched by Louis XV to Christianize native Americans. Charlotte departed Rouen on February 22, 1727, aboard the Girondone. Passengers voyaged from Santo Domingo and arrived on pirogues in the Louisiana delta on August 6, 1727. At the king's request, in July 1734, Charlotte directed the French Royal Hospital, a military infirmary at Chartres and Hospital streets.

On May 10, 1736, the progressive gray sisters processed to fife and drum to a next-door teaching facility, the Hôpital des Pauvres de la Charité (Charity Hospital for the Poor). Charlotte, the convent treasurer, kept accounts of social services and, at the end of her workday, tended orphan girl survivors of the 1729 Natchez massacres, who bunked in a six-chamber attic. While the teaching nuns dispensed lessons to boarding students in reading, spelling, writing, arithmetic, and needlework, Charlotte accompanied doctors on their diagnostic rounds. By 1738, the surgeons trusted her curatives and requested a second apothecary to ease the demand for treatment.

A block from the Mississippi River at 1112 Chartres Street, Charlotte grew botanical simples in the courtyard to treat ordinary and mosquito-borne diseases and incurables. She tested French seeds in the coastal climate for survivability and developed one of the South's most varied herb beds. In the laboratory at a wood mortar and distillery she compounded potions and brews that solved problems as common as fever, rash, flux, and broken bones and as complicated as leprosy and yellow fever. She corked dried leaves, blossoms, and seeds in dark bottles to protect them from moisture and insects.

For use by the hospitalieres (medical nuns), pharmacy students, and British and American soldiers, Charlotte, the head nurse, organized stock according to need. She chose dill for sleeplessness, basil and mint for indigestion, cinnamon to lower blood pressure, bay leaf for sprain, marjoram for convulsions and dropsy (heart failure), and oregano for arthritis. Soothing beverages from bay, dandelion, and mint along with liqueur, chervil vinegar, and beer added to liquid reserves. Indian pharmacopoeia treated fever and diarrhea with sassafras leaves, one of the region's most common stew ingredients. An archive preserved pharmacy records and a letter from U.S. President Thomas Jefferson extolling the Ursuline outreach. The annual blessing of the herbs honors Charlotte as America's first female pharmacist.

### *Sources*

Clark, Emily. *Masterless Mistresses: The New Orleans Ursulines and the Development of a New World Society, 1727–1834*. Chapel Hill: University of North Carolina Press, 2007.

Hachard, Marie-Madeleine. *Une Rouennaise à La Nouvelle-Orléans au XVIIIe Siècle: Relation du Voyage des Ursulines (1726–1728)*. Laval, Quebec: Presses de l'Université Laval, 2022.

Thwaites, Reuben Gold, ed. *The Jesuit Relations and Allied Documents: Travels and Explorations of the Jesuit Missionaries in New France, 1610–1791*. Cleveland, OH: Burrows Brothers, 1896.

## Mary Musgrove (ca. 1700–summer 1765)
**Trader, Linguist**
**Savannah, Georgia**

A high-ranking Muskogee speaker and intermediary from the Wind clan, Mary Griffin Musgrove Matthews Bosomworth used bicultural knowledge to further profits and racial harmony. A Lower Creek born on the Oakmulgee River in Coweta (modern Macon, Georgia), she was the daughter of white trader Edward Griffin from Charleston and a Tuckabatchee Creek mother from Alabama. She was named Coosaponakeesa, meaning "Coosa language bearer." The niece of chiefs Brim and Chigelli and cousin of Malatchi, she was motherless by 1703 and reared by her maternal grandmother according to matriarchal custom.

Mary and her younger brother Edward grew up on the Edisto River in Pomponne west of Charleston, South Carolina, and gained a Christian education at Pon Pon Chapel. She returned to Coweta among low country rice plantations on April 14, 1715, at the onset of the Yamasee War. Colonial militias clashed with a coalition of the Catawba, Cherokee, Ochese, Santee, Waxhaw, and Yamasee. At age seventeen, she married Anglo-Creek cattleman John Musgrove, Jr., of Charleston, father of their sons Edward and James, who died in 1735.

## The Retailer

The Musgroves claimed seven hundred acres in Colleton County. At a five hundred-acre land grant on the Savannah River, Mary sold European manufactured goods to Chief Tomochichi, an native influence in the building of Savannah. At a trading nexus at Cowpens on Yamacraw Bluff at Pipemaker's Creek four miles northwest of Savannah, she sold knives, hatchets, hoes, copper cookware, fabric and blankets, bells, beads, rum, and rifles and ammunition. She bartered English stores for Creek goods—skins of white-tailed deer, small animal pelts, beeswax, and bear oil.

At the founding of Georgia Colony in February 1733, General James Oglethorpe engaged Mary as adviser and official interpreter for the English warehouse town of Savannah. With African, Spanish, and Indian bondsmen, she stocked her storehouse with beef, potatoes, corn, and peas and bartered for merchandise at the Savannah commissary. She represented Indians in court, opened her home to dignitaries Malatchi and Chief Chegelli, and, in 1736, taught evangelist John Wesley and missionaries to speak Muskogee. Commerce made her Georgia's wealthiest woman, but debt to Charleston wholesalers forced her to sell land for cash.

Widowed on June 12, 1735, Mary sought a union with indentured servant Jacob Matthews in spring 1737 to preserve her home and business. To simplify water transport, the couple opened a new commercial enterprise and recruiting office on the Altamaha River at Mount Venture near Fort King George, a coastal outpost. While Oglethorpe plotted an invasion of Spanish Florida, Mary advised him on the construction and garrisoning of Fort Frederica on St. Simon's Island as a defense of Georgian settlers. She also served the English as an observer of Indian movement at Tomochichi's village on Yamacraw Bluff. The War of Jenkins's Ear on October 23, 1739, required her authority to muster Creeks in June 1740 to back Oglethorpe's failed attack on St. Augustine.

## The Land Owner

At the loss of Jacob to disease on June 6, 1742, Mary received £100 (approx. $26,250.85) from Oglethope and a promise of annual upkeep in the same amount. In July 1744, she married a Scot, the Rev. Thomas Bosomworth, an unscrupulous Anglican priest, and relocated to St. Catherine's Island. She continued the family business and initiated diplomatic travels to Creek villages. In 1747, she petitioned the British to grant her the deed to Yamacraw Bluff and to pay her £5,700 (approx. $1,644,885.34) for past labors as adviser and translator. The disbanding of Fort Frederica in 1749 gave her fewer bargaining chips.

**Wind Clan-Griffin-Musgrove Genealogy**

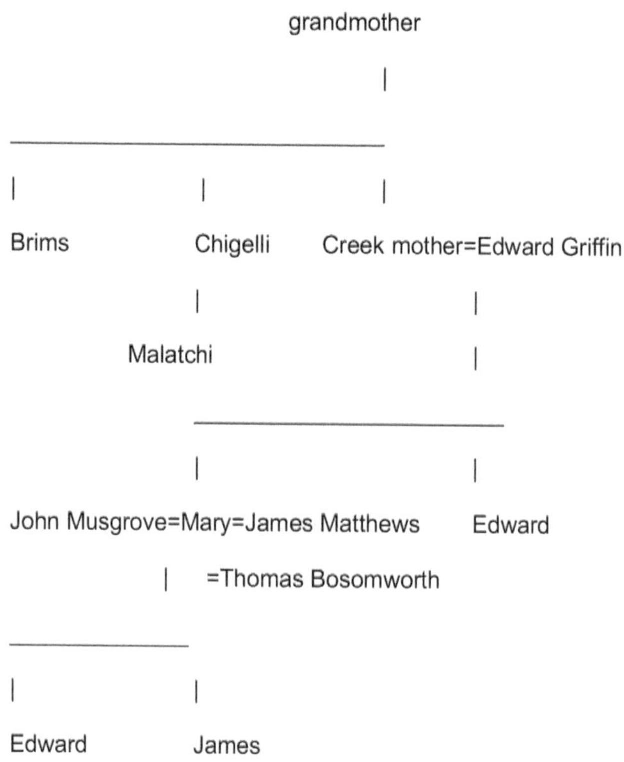

After her cousin Malatchi allotted her Ossabaw, Sapelo and St. Catherines islands, Mary had to establish her claim on the Sea Islands to Georgian officials and to England's board of trade. At her arrest in August 1749 for threatening to incite the Creek against Savannah, court president William Stephens rejected her plea on grounds of insufficient evidence. In 1750, Malatchi, in support of Mary's petition, lowered the English flag and replaced it with a French banner. His death in 1756 stripped her of tribal connections and prestige. At age sixty, she gained a compromise from Governor Henry Ellis: sixty-two hundred acres, the deed to St. Catherines, and £2,100 (approx. $540,979.73) as past salary in exchange for Ossabaw and Sapelo. A retired cattle rancher, she died on her island at age sixty-five.

### *Sources*


Baine, Rodney M. "Myths of Mary Musgrove," *Georgia Historical Quarterly* 76:2 (Summer 1992): 428–435.

Marsh, Ben. *Georgia's Frontier Women*. Athens: University of Georgia Press, 2007.

Perdue, Theda, ed. *Sifters: Native American Women's Lives*. Oxford, UK: Oxford University Press, 2001.


## Abigail Minis (August 11, 1701–October 11, 1794)
**Planter, Merchant, Taverner, Caterer, Cattle Rancher**
**Savannah, Georgia**

Abigail Minis, an able merchant, planter, and widowed matriarch, survived the unpredictable destiny of Savannah, Georgia. In the mid–1720s, she wed Abraham Minis, an Ashkenazic Jew and commercial shipper. With Prussian brother-in-law Simeon Minis and Leah and Esther Minis, the first two of her nine children, she and Abraham emigrated aboard the three-masted cargo ship *William and Sarah*. Funded by three London supporters of the Bevis Marks congregation, forty-two fellow Jews, most of them Sephardic, left London for North America on February 12, 1733.

After a mishap off the North Carolina Outer Banks and an epidemic of dysentery and fever that killed one child, the pioneers reached the New World on July 11, 1733. In that year James Edward Oglethorpe founded the colony and based its settlement on ordinary people rather than aristocrats. The settlement became the world's first Jewish colony that offered equal rights to all faiths. Against the opposition of trustees, in December 1733, Oglethorpe gave the Minis one of the region's first land grants on Market Square (modern Ellis Square).

## Jewish Entrepreneurs

In July 1734, Abigail produced son Philip, Georgia's first white male child and a future Revolutionary War hero. While the couple opened one of the colony's first businesses, they kept faith with their choice of homeland, which other newcomers deserted. In July 1735, the Minis family co-founded Congregation Mickve Israel, which met on rental property. A year later, their four-acre tract on marshland at number four Hucks Ward yielded thirty-six bushels of corn. To increase cash flow, they distributed New York beef, pork, and butter to Georgia's public stores.

At the creation of Fort Frederica ninety miles from Savannah on St. Simon's Island in 1736 and during Oglethorpe's attack on St. Augustine from 1740 to 1743, the Minis supplied the garrison with rations and equipment. Lacking fluent English, Abigail flourished at farming and continued bearing children to age forty-seven, adding to the family line Hannah, Joseph, Judith, Minis, Samuel, and Sarah. She supported her children after her husband's death on January 13, 1757, with a prosperous mercantile and food service. On September 24, 1757, nineteen-year-old son Minis died.

## A Thriving Widow

The widow's commercial savvy secured a fortune from cattle, sheep, and land investments in four Georgia counties. In 1760, she petitioned for a grant of five hundred fifty acres in St. Mary's Parish and acquired lots number three and five in Hucks Ward. With the aid of five unwed daughters and nineteen African slaves, Abigail obtained a license to open a tavern in 1763, where Judith Minis frequently welcomed Oglethorpe. It became a popular gathering place for sixteen years for assemblymen, governor's cabinet, judges, merchants, and General George Washington. Preceding the American Revolution, Abigail bought uniforms and munitions and provisioned the Georgia militia, French mercenaries, and local soldiers in the Continental Army, whom Philip Minis served as paymaster and commissary manager. He aided rebel forces by donating £1,729 (approx. $437,246.52) to the cause and by paying the wages of the North Carolina and Virginia regiments.

During construction of the Tybee lighthouse in 1773, Abigail provisioned workers. Against the disapproval of tories, she maintained her residence after British troops overwhelmed Savannah in December 1778. She visited Colonel Mordecai Sheftall in prison and brought him food. By requesting letters of safe travel to Philip's home in Charleston, South Carolina, from Georgia governor John Wereat, in 1779, she and her daughters avoided charges of treason during the two-month siege of Savannah and sailed north under a flag of truce.

## Post-War Recovery

When the British withdrew, in 1783, Abigail reopened her tavern, bought lots in St. Matthews Parish, and purchased seven farms and five acres of timberland on Sapelo Island. Her estate reached two thousand acres that spanned coastal South Carolina and Georgia. With government reimbursement for wartime loans to the Continental Army, Abigail remained solvent to age ninety-three by catering drinks and meals to the upper class and selling lumber and farm produce. The synagogue reformed on July 7, 1786, and read from the deerskin and cowgut torah they had brought on their voyage.

While living in a town house, managing fifteen slaves, and operating a plantation and shop, Abigail began acquiring real estate in Tyrconnell Ward on Johnston Square. She grieved Philip's death in 1789, the year she bought more land in Moore Ward, Anson Ward, Hucks Ward, and ninety acres of farmland. At the peak of success, she signed a will in 1794 in English and Hebrew that dispersed an estate twice the size of Abraham's. Her descendants maintained the family's high ethical standards as merchants, soldiers, lawyers, and an army surgeon to the Cherokee at New Echota.

### *Sources*

Kole, Kaye. *The Minis Family of Georgia, 1733–1992.* Savannah: Georgia Historical Society, 1992.

"The Minis Family," *Georgia Historical Quarterly* 1:1 (March 1917): 45–49.

# III

# The Treaty of Paris, 1701–1755

In Baltimore in December 1783, Mary Katherine Goddard distributed a supplement to the *Maryland Gazette* announcing the Treaty of Paris, a document concluding the Revolutionary War. Through the labors of Thomas Jefferson, Benjamin Franklin, John Jay, and John Adams, the American colonies achieved peace with Britain and ended conflicts with France, Holland, and Spain. The United States entered the global community with thirteen states east of the Mississippi River—Connecticut, Delaware, Georgia, Maryland, Massachusetts, New Hampshire, New Jersey, New York, North Carolina, Pennsylvania, Rhode Island, South Carolina, and Virginia. The settlement of hostilities enabled female businesswomen to expand their investments and anticipate greater rewards for their ambitions. At Charleston, publisher Ann Timothy distributed the *State Gazette of South Carolina,* which gained a reputation for printing the U.S. Constitution on October 1, 1787, and for covering the 1788 debates on the South Carolina Constitution.

## Sarah Updike Goddard (1701–January 5, 1770)

## Mary Katherine Goddard (June 16, 1738–August 12, 1816)
**Printer, Publisher, Postmaster**
**New London, Connecticut; Providence, Rhode Island; Philadelphia, Pennsylvania**

A descendant of Prussian bureaucrats and the English owners of Davenport Manor in Shropshire, both dating to the twelfth century, Sarah Updike Goddard headed a household of Anglo-Dutch publishers undergirding the colonial American press during the American Revolution. Unfortunately for women's history, her written contributions to the media go unlabeled, unidentified. Outside Wickford, Rhode Island, she, four sisters, and brothers Richard and Daniel, a future colonial attorney general, were born at Smith's Castle, the former trading post of Roger Williams at Cocumscussuc in Narragansett. Her parents, Abigail Newton and Lodowick Updike, ensured her education with the same tutoring in French and Latin that her brothers received.

In December 1735, Sarah married Dr. Giles Goddard, a physician and postmaster at New London, Connecticut. Eight years later, they occupied a residence on Bradley Street between Federal and State streets north of the Block Island Sound, where Sarah promoted her husband's practice. When Giles retired from the onset of gout, she managed the Groton post office on the New Hampshire post road. At the birth of Mary Katherine Goddard in 1738, Sarah homeschooled her in reading and writing and sent her to New London public schools to study math, science, and languages.

## A New Direction

In widowhood at age fifty-six, Sarah inherited £780 (approx. $176,263.87). She and two surviving children, Mary Katherine and William Goddard, the former publisher of the *Maryland Journal and the Baltimore Advertiser,* relocated to Providence, Rhode Island, to launch a printshop. With the aid of master printer and editor John Carter, beginning October 20, 1762, the Goddards published the Saturday *Providence Gazette and Country Journal.* In a building facing the courthouse, John issued transatlantic events, customhouse news and shipping schedules, lost and found, and standard weights for two- and fourpenny loaves and a single biscuit. On their 8" × 14" paper, John and his three journalists, including Benjamin Franklin, promoted independence and acclaimed patriotism.

To satisfy a public need, the company issued astronomer Benjamin West's twenty-four-page *An Almanack, for the Year of Our Lord Christ, 1763,* Rhode Island's first almanac. The compilation received prepublication notices from September into winter. Each contained road and weather advisories, tavern locations, a short colonial history, and wise sayings by colony founder Roger Williams. In authorial commentary, John urged citizens to keep local money in the colony. West's reference annuals remained in production for thirty years at a cost of six cents. The Goddards advertised subsequent editions at a discount for the purchase of one or two dozen. The handy resource also sold in Benjamin Thurber and Daniel Cahoon's import-export shop, the Sign of the Bunch of Grapes.

William's editorial comment on April 26, 1763, complained of outstanding debts. By June 11, 1763, the firm advertised for an apprentice and hired Daniel Bowen the next year. In July, the Goddards moved their equipment near the Great Bridge and continued operations at the sign of Shakespeare's Head, the bookshop of Judge William Jenckes. The company printed three tabulations of the value of ten money denominations, from thirty shillings to three cents; a poetic diatribe on the devaluation of truth; a condemnation of Rhode Island secretary Henry Ward for abuse of powers; and an invitation to a "Petticoat Frisk" at Sarah's house on September 25, 1764. Advertisements offered the paper at seven shillings annually. In December 1764, the Goddards printed Rhode Island founder Stephen Hopkins's *The Right of Colonies Examined,* a stern pamphlet condemning the Stamp Act.

## Making It Pay

Because of William's inability to collect subscription debts, on May 11, 1765, he resigned from the printshop and took his career to a New York printer. Sarah and Mary Katherine renamed themselves S. & W. Goddard and spent four years issuing the annual *West's Almanack,* an epitaph for Obadiah Brown, and politician Samuel Ward's suggestion for a day of thanksgiving. With revolutionary fervor, they broadcast a "Freeman's" call for public support of liberty, Justice Ezekiel Hopkins's 1763 anti-taxation broadside, Stephen Hopkins's opinion of the 1763 Money Bill, and the anonymous, six-page pamphlet "A Discourse Addressed to the Sons of Liberty at a Solemn Assembly near Liberty Tree in Newport, February 14, 1766." A series of handbills publicized William's frustration with debt collection, a universal outcry from noncombatants after soldiers left for war.

The owners' names altered in 1766 to "Sarah Goddard & Company" after they returned the *Providence Gazette* to publication on Market Street near the post office with the aid of Sarah's partner, Samuel Inslee of New York. For fifty-two weekly editions, the family demanded half the annual subscription rate, which could be paid in wool, wood, tallow, or grain. They invested £300 (approx. $62,902.34) in a press that could stamp two hundred finished copies per hour. Their output included sermons and a sixty-page theological manual. Beginning on January 6, 1767, the twenty-five hundred subscribers paid ten shillings per year. Demand for the media encouraged sea captain John Waterman to open a paper mill, which Sarah purchased.

## Sarah's Influence

Sarah's intellectual acumen secured business in binding, day trade in writing supplies and legal forms, and sales of journalist Richard Steele's

*Tatler,* essayist Samuel Johnson's *Rambler,* Henry Fielding's satiric quest fiction *Tom Jones,* and Tobias Smollett's picaresque novel *Roderick Random.* On colonial America's first locally built press, Sarah issued the two-hundred-page Turkish Embassy Letters of Lady Mary Wortley Montagu, an English pioneer of variolation to prevent smallpox. Sarah's issuance of founding father John Dickinson's twelve *Letters from a Farmer in Pennsylvania to the Inhabitants of the British Colonies* in 1767 urged readers to boycott British merchandise and take arms against oppression. On August 1, 1768, the *Chronicle* savaged the British Parliament for passing the Stamp Act on March 22, 1765, taxing newspapers, almanacs, pamphlets, broadsides, legal documents, dice, and playing cards.

After selling business interests to partner John Carter for $550 (approx. $23,705.46) in 1768, Sarah liquidated her Connecticut investments. She and Mary Katherine managed the *Pennsylvania Chronicle and Universal Advertiser,* William's failing enterprise in Philadelphia. The editorial tone favored rebellion against George III. At Sarah's death in 1770, Mary Katherine, an expert compositor at the office on Main Street, continued setting in type the *Chronicle* and an abbreviated almanack called *West's Sheet-Almanack.* In mid–January 1771, the Second Continental Congress chose the *Goddard Broadside* to publish the Declaration of Independence and the names of its signers. Mary Katherine risked arrest for treason by signing her name to the edition.

The *Chronicle* sharpened its support of liberty by praising the Boston Tea Party in 1773, celebrating the repeal of the Stamp Act, honoring the Sons of Liberty, and reprinting Benjamin Franklin's radical views from London papers. In 1774, the Royal Mail drove the company out of business by refusing to deliver colonial newspapers to the *Chronicle.* Identified on the masthead as "M.K. Goddard," Mary Katherine joined William in Baltimore to print the *Maryland Journal* until February 1774. Issuance of competing almanacs spurred a brother-sister feud. The first federally appointed female, Mary Katherine served the city as postmaster from 1775.

On May 11, 1776, after the Battle of Bunker Hill, Massachusetts, Mary Katherine removed the royal coat of arms from the *Journal*'s masthead. She struggled to buy paper and ink, which grew scarce during the Revolutionary War because of the nonimportation agreement. On December 1783, she distributed a supplement announcing the Treaty of Paris, a document ending the war. She continued her postal job until 1789, when political forces fired her. On November 12, some two hundred thirty Marylanders attempted in vain to reinstate her with the post office. Until 1810, she operated a shop selling dry goods, stationery, and books. Her will freed slave Belinda Starling, who inherited Mary Katherine's belongings.

### Sources

Henry, Susan. "Sarah Goddard, Gentlewoman Printer," *Journalism and Mass Communication* 57:1 (Spring 1980): 23–30.
Peterson, Edward. *History of Rhode Island. New York*: John S. Taylor, 1853.
Walker, Gay. "Women Printers in Early American Printing History," *Yale University Library Gazette* 61:3–4 (April 1987): 116–124.

## Elizabeth Timothy (June 20, 1702–late April 1757)
**Editor, Publisher, Journalist, Merchant**

## Ann Timothy (1727–September 11, 1792)
**Printer, Publisher, Editor**
**Charleston, South Carolina**

North America's first female newspaper editor and publisher, Elizabeth Villin Timothy profited from the investment savvy of Boston adviser Benjamin Franklin. Her parents, Claude and Elizabeth Gratiot Vilain of Melun, France, approved female education that included accounting and business management. In Amsterdam on July 23, 1724, she married Louis Timothée, a French printer and translator from Halle, Brussels. Because revocation of the Edict of Nantes ended freedom of worship for French Calvinist Protestants in October 1685, at the age of twenty-nine, she traveled with the first three of their six children and other French Huguenot refugees from Rotterdam, Holland, aboard the three-masted ship *Britannia,* arriving September 21, 1731.

At home on Front Street in Philadelphia, Louis anglicized his name to Lewis Timothy. His short-term employment at the *Pennsylvania Gazette* and the *Philadelphische Zeitung* (the Philadelphia Newspaper), the nation's first German media, preceded replacement of Thomas Whitemarsh (or Whitmarsh), publisher of the weekly *South Carolina Gazette.* Thomas died of yellow fever in summer 1733. His *Gazette* appeared on half sheets of pot paper (colonial newsprint). In partnership with Franklin, Lewis agreed to take over production for one-third share of the profits.

### The Timothys in SC

Elizabeth's arrival at Charles Town in November 1733 coincided with Lewis's opening a post office at his printshop on Church Street. Beginning on February 4, 1734, he printed the twenty-four-page pamphlet *An Essay on Currency,* audits, *The Gentleman's Pocket Farrier,* and news of European royalty and openly supported colonial rebellion against England's George III. Three years later, Lewis served South Carolina as official printer and sought a grant of six hundred acres. At his accidental death at

Christmas 1738, Elizabeth, then pregnant with her seventh child, agreed to honor Lewis's contract while fourteen-year-old son Peter apprenticed in the trade. She concealed under her son's name an intellectual side and the ability to speak Dutch, French, and English.

On January 4, 1739, Elizabeth edited her first issue under her son's name. For copy, she published details of fires and drownings, slave escapes and sales, postal routes, essays, inspirational texts, revival views of the Awakening, and controversy over Calvinist and Wesleyan evangelism. The four-page paper incorporated gleanings from the *Pennsylvania Gazette, Pennsylvania Chronicle, Newport Mercury, New York Journal, Essex Gazette, Providence Gazette, New Hampshire Gazette, Boston News Letter, Massachusetts Spy, Connecticut Journal,* and foreign magazines and newspapers. One news flash on June 13, 1740, reported the failure of General James Edward Oglethorpe's expedition against the Spanish in St. Augustine.

## A Full Printing Service

Elizabeth's business printed laws, religious treatises, pamphlets, and twenty history books and promoted female enterprise, such as Madam Trott's Wharff. Of the religious revival called the Awakening, on June 18, 1741, Elizabeth entered the public debate by warning that unnecessarily graphic sermons terrified women and children. To poems by Alexander Pope and literary reprints of opera, stage farce, and social satire from Joseph Addison's *The Spectator,* she added the sermons, correspondence, and works of Southern writers, acts of the state assembly, and broadsides. During a raging epidemic in the Carolina low country, she posted a rebuttal of blistering as a cure for smallpox and a witty rebuke of swearing and cursing.

By 1746, Elizabeth had bought the *Gazette* for son Peter Timothy and established her stationery and bookshop next door. Her advertisement of English literature illustrated a taste for epic poet John Milton's *Paradise Lost,* novelist Samuel Richardson's *Pamela*, Edward Young's pre–Romantic collection *Night Thoughts,* and Bishop Gilbert Burnet's *History of His Own Times.* The frank editorials blaming Governor James Glen for blue laws in March 1746 held Peter liable for protesting a ban on food sales on the sabbath and for posting guards to prohibit citizens from passing through the city gates on Sunday. Glen chose not to press charges. In May 1746, the Gazette announced purchase of more legible type. In his *Autobiography,* Franklin praised the editor's business acumen and declared it a given for a female trained in the Dutch education system.

Along with mortgage, sales, writ, and shipping forms, Elizabeth sold ink, quills, bibles, readers, and spellers. Her selections veered from English wit and scholarship to piety: Isaac Watts's *Divine Songs*, the first collection of Wesleyan hymns in Watts's *Psalms and Hymns*, and the controversial *Westminster Confession of Faith*, compiled in 1646. She warned readers that subscribers as much as eight years in arrears would face a hired debt collector. After a decade away from Charleston, she returned, signed a will on April 2, 1757, and died two days later, leaving a plot of land, eight slaves, and three residences to Peter and her three surviving daughters.

## The Next Female Printer

Like mother-in-law Elizabeth, Ann Donovan Timothy married into a progressive family of compositors and publishers. She appears to have been the daughter of Ann and Daniel Donovan, Irish immigrants to Charleston in 1687. After the union of Ann and Peter on December 8, 1745, she bore fifteen children, but only five daughters and two sons survived to adulthood.

The Stamp Act of March 22, 1765, spurred the couple into pro-patriot politics and a near monopoly on the Whig media. Throughout the Revolutionary War, they issued governmental statutes while Peter served as library founder and postmaster for the colonial South. In a show of patriotism, the couple promoted a 1765 meeting of the Sons of Liberty under Charleston's Liberty Tree, inveighed against the 1770 Boston Massacre and 1773 closure of Boston harbor, and produced a broadside of the Declaration of Independence in August 1776.

Despite poor eyesight, Peter continued issuing the *Gazette* at the corner of King and Tradd streets and serving as secretary of the Council of Safety until February 1780. A five-month hiatus followed a fire on January 15, 1778, which consumed the office. At the May 12, 1780, siege of Charleston, the British suppressed Ann and Peter's patriot paper for three years. Peter volunteered as a lookout from the steeple of St. Michael's Anglican Church on Broad Street to spy on the approach of Lord Charles Cornwallis, commander of the enemy invasion. Peter's journal recorded tarring and feathering episodes, the British navy maneuvers up the Ashley River, and flatboats entering the marsh at Wappoo Cut, a shallow creek joining the Ashley and Steno rivers. The military arrested him for refusing to pledge loyalty to the crown and exiled him for ten months to a St. Augustine prison until war's end.

## On Her Own

Peter drowned in autumn 1782 off the Delaware shore on the way to Antigua with two daughters and a grandson, leaving Ann to support eleven-year-old Benjamin Franklin Timothy and younger siblings Robert and Sarah by running the printshop. On July 16, 1783, she returned to print the renamed semiweekly *The Gazette of the State of South-Carolina* to press. At a clapboard house at the corner of Broad and Meeting streets, she remained in business for a decade. On March 28, 1785, the masthead changed once more to *State Gazette of South Carolina* and appeared above "A. Timothy" and alongside the state seal and its motto "Dum Spiro Spero" (While I breathe, I hope).

In 1785, Ann's quality typography marked legal forms, leaflets, almanacs, broadsides, and books and won her the position of state printer. She issued a 1785 message from Governor William Moultrie and offered a copy of the works of Horace for $3.00 (approx. $96). A year later, she printed a general assembly ways and means report and Irish compiler Isaac Bickerstaff's *North and South Carolina and Georgia Almanac.* After giving up her location at 89 Broad Street, in May 1787, she posted a notice requesting payment of her late husband's debts. Her paper gained a reputation for endorsing liberty and independence from colonialism and for printing the U.S. Constitution on October 1, 1787, and covering the 1788 debates on the South Carolina Constitution.

At Ann's death on September 11, 1792, at age sixty-five, son Benjamin Franklin Timothy resumed the family's three-generation business begun by Lewis Timothy. His introductory comment requested that Ann's friends and patrons continue to support the paper. He distributed the next edition of the *Gazette* on September 20 under the name "B.F. Timothy" and scheduled triweekly editions for Tuesday, Thursday, and Saturday at the same price as the semiweekly rate. In 1800, he introduced the *Federal Carolina Gazette.*

## Donovan-Timothy Genealogy

Elizabeth Villin Timothy=Lewis Timothy

|

Peter Timothy=Ann Donovan Timothy

|

Benjamin Franklin Timothy

### *Sources*

Cohen, Hennig. *The South Carolina Gazette, 1732–1775.* Columbia: University of South Carolina Press, 1953.

Cook, Elizabeth Christine. *Literary Influences in Colonial Newspapers, 1704–1750*. New York: Columbia University Press, 1912.
King, William L. *The Newspaper Press of Charleston, S.C.* Charleston, SC: Edward Perry, 1872.
Walker, Gay. "Women Printers in Early American Printing History," *Yale University Library Gazette* 61:3–4 (April 1987): 116–124.
Wroth, Lawrence C. *The Colonial Printer*. Portland, ME: Southworth-Anthoensen Press, 1938.

## Anna Catharina Zenger (1704–1751)
### Publisher, Printer, Merchant
### Manhattan, New York

During two stints distributing the *New-York Weekly Journal*, Anna Catharina Maulin Zenger made history as the first female publisher and printer of an American newspaper, which thrived throughout a landmark trial defending liberty. The daughter of Palatinate Germans, she left Rotterdam, Holland, at age six along with Dutch refugees John Peter Zenger, his mother, Johanna M. Wagenaar Saenger, and two siblings, Johannes and Anna Margaretha Zenger. On the 1710 voyage, Peter's father, Nicolaus Eberhardt Saenger, died.

A mass departure of three thousand German Reformed immigrants from the Rhineland traveled under the aegis of Queen Anne, who disapproved of religious persecution. While Anna taught Sunday school in New York, Peter tried his luck printing in Chesterfield, Maryland, where Mary White, his first wife, died. At his return to New York, on September 11, 1722, Anna married the widower in Queens, reared his three-year-old son John and six-year-old Elizabetha Zenger, and bore five children.

### The Printer's Trade

Peter became the business partner of public printer William Bradford before opening an independent printshop in 1725 on Smith Street between Maiden Lane and Pearl. To Bradford's half sheet paper of foolscap, Peter appended his specialty—scholarly and theological essays and sermons in Dutch and English. In 1732, he added controversial anti-government pamphlets to his output. According to Frederich de Peyster's article "John Peter Zenger, and His Persecution for Libel" in an 1888 issue of the *New Amsterdam Gazette*, on November 5, 1733, Peter introduced the *New-York Weekly Journal*, the voice of America's first political party, at three shillings per quarter. His exemplary paper modeled sympathy with a common cause and the constitutional concepts of trial by jury, the right to protest corruption and endorse freedom of speech and freedom of the press.

In May 1734, Peter relocated his shop to Broad Street near Long Bridge and issued the colony's first arithmetic book. To his detriment, he alluded to Governor William Cosby, a despised tyrant suspected of tax theft, stealing land from citizens and Indians, and allowing French ships to anchor in New York harbor. Public outcry resulted in satiric advertisements and popular ballads smearing Cosby. After two failed attempts, on November 2, 1734, the governor ordered the hangman to burn #7, #47, #48, and #49, the four most offensive issues of the *Journal,* before New York's ten thousand citizens. On November 17, the sheriff arrested Peter for libel and sedition and imposed a £400 (approx. $127,909.53) bail and an equal amount in surety. Peter refused to pay £800 bail or to identify the authors and remained behind bars for thirty-five weeks. On November 25, 1734, he summarized his plight to readers and continued with details in a two-phase essay on December 16 and December 23.

During nearly nine months of incarceration at Old City Jail on Wall Street, Peter was denied seeing or speaking with people and the use of pen, ink, and paper. Anna kept before readers the court's selection of a rigged jury and, in April 1735, the disbarring of Peter's attorneys, James Alexander and William Smith. During the two-day trial on August 4, 1735, Peter received an opportunity to address his wife and servants through a hole in the jail door. He advised Anna on continuing the paper and its advertisements every Monday.

## Making a Living

Meanwhile, before a biased judge, Chief Justice De Lancey, noted Philadelphia attorney Andrew Hamilton fended off the death sentence by arguing *pro bono* the cause of liberty vs. arbitrary power. The name "Mrs. Zenger" appeared in one witness statement alleging that she had printed and distributed "two scandalous Libels" (Rutherford, 1904, 240). On August 5, 1735, the jury acquitted Peter of four counts of criminal libel on the basis of factual news. The printshop on Stone Street completed "The Charter of the City of New-York" with a bold heading and a quip at the end thanking God for the publisher's freedom.

When Peter left prison in 1735, he returned to editing and distributing the *Journal* and serving New Jersey and New York as official printer. In 1736, he published "A brief Narrative of the Cafe and Tryal of John Peter Zenger," which circulated in Boston, Philadelphia, and London. At his death on July 28, 1746, Anna again assumed the lead role and, under the name "the Widow Catharine Zenger," often misspelled as "Cathrine Zenger." She published "Nathan's 1747 Almanack" by John Nathan Hutchins, a speech to the New Jersey assembly, and a manual of weights, measures, and interest rates under the title *The Country Man's Help and Traders Friend.* On September 14, 1747, she quashed a rumor that she had quit the printing business.

Under the name of stepson John Zenger, Jr., in 1748, Catharine composed "A Brief VINDICATION OF THE Purchassors Against the PROPRITORS IN a Christian Manner." She admitted to readers that unpaid subscriptions endangered the future of business. Outside of town at Stone Street near Fort George (modern Washington Heights), she relocated her bookshop, marketed stationery and books, and advertised the 1749 almanac under her name. When paid in kind with canary wine, she offered it for sale. In mid–October 1749, she relinquished her career in publishing.

### *Sources*

Cook, Elizabeth Christine. *Literary Influences in Colonial Newspapers, 1704–1750.* New York: Columbia University Press, 1912.
De Peyster, Frederich. "John Peter Zenger, and His Persecution for Libel," *New Amsterdam Gazette* (1 February 1888): 13–15; (17 April 1888): 9–10.
Rutherford, Livingston. *John Peter Zenger, His Press, His Trial, and a Bibliography of Zenger Imprints.* New York: Dodd, Mead, 1904.
Wroth, Lawrence C. *The Colonial Printer.* Portland, ME: Southworth-Anthoensen Press, 1938.

## Jane Mary Camuse (ca. 1710–?)

## Elizabeth Anderson (fl. 1740s)
**Silk Winder**
**Savannah, Georgia**

A defender of her trade, artisan Jane Mary Camuse (or Camuche or Camuso) protected the skill of extracting threads from silk cocoons. After immigrating from Piedmont Italy, she and thirty-five families of indentured servants traveled aboard the *Anne* in November 1732 and reached Yamacraw, a Creek and Yamasee heritage site, on January 14, 1733. Along with silkworm eggs and five hundred white mulberry seedlings raised on fifty acres, the Camuse family were valued as prime laborers for Governor James Oglethorpe's colonial sericulture trust, which awarded £10 (approx. $2,973.84) bonus for their work. The trust offered free passage in five years if employees chose to return to Italy. English investors hoped to save £500,000 (approx. $152,245,257.35) by producing New World silk and to provide employment for twenty-thousand English factory workers.

Mary reached Georgia in April 1733 with mechanic husband Jacques and three sons, who shared a forty-five-acre lot. He received a family salary of £12 (approx. £3,653.89) a year plus upkeep and clothing and the use of horse and cart. As an expert employee of the trust, Mary tended two hundred sixty acres of mulberry trees (*Morus alba*) east of Savannah at Ockstead, Georgia's first plantation established by Thomas Causton, Oglethorpe's bailiff and stores manager. Called Causton's Bluff, it flourished on twenty-five hundred acres of tidewater wetlands along Augustine Creek on the Savannah River.

## The Task

Mary's work required gathering worm eggs in May and warming them in paper-lined boxes. During hatching, she began to feed the larvae on hand-picked white mulberry leaves, the species that produced the best silk. To prevent stain, at the end of the growing season, she killed the chrysalis by dipping cocoons into boiling water. From an ounce of ova, at the end of six weeks, she extruded up to ten pounds of organzine (silk floss). The raw material passed to Thomas Lombe, who established a throwing mill for winding and cleaning fibers. By June 1734, Oglethorpe transported the first eight pounds of silk to English authorities. In April 1735, he loaded a trunkful of fiber on a ship bound for England, where Queen Caroline ordered her seamstress to turn the silk into a party dress. The trust employed English apprentices to learn tree culture and fiber extraction.

Causton proved financially unreliable by 1738, when Mary ruled over the Chatham County project as head winder and maven of the silk reel that riddled the filament from the cocoon. A test batch in July 1739 earned praise for quality and an asking price of twenty shillings per pound. The first shipment of silk thread reached buyers in February 1742 after Mary stripped two hundred thirty pounds of casings. Although she received a £10 (approx. $2,625.08) bonus for instructing two new winders, in November 1743, she rejected a salary offer of £48 (approx. $13,732.05) and tried to blackmail the trust into additional payments. In Italian and French, she lambasted Georgia official William Stephens on March 20, 1744, for "injurious" treatment. By 1745, while company officials worried about Mary's advanced age and possible death, competitors complained of her monopoly.

## Female Competition

Marie lost primacy after her pupil, Elizabeth Anderson, replaced her in August 1747 in exchange for free housing and £20 (approx. $5,771.53). With a more amenable temperament than Mary Camuse, Elizabeth began silk culture lessons in the home of the Rev. Johann Martin Boltzius. She trained three Austrian women from Salzburg, refugees of religious persecution who tended the worm culture with more proficiency than English apprentices. The newcomers surrounded the area with a fence to keep out pigs and destructive wild animals. Despite dysentery and malaria from the swampy environment, their cautious feeding and harvesting earned an extra two shillings per pound of cocoons and, in December 1742, a grant of five hundred trees that yielded three hundred forty-four pounds of cocoons. In March 1746, the larvae filled a hatchery twenty-four feet long.

Mary expressed jealousy of the Salzburgers, who produced half of the colonial silk output, by deliberately concealing crucial steps in fiber processing. The new winders continued to excel, building their own reels and raising the 1750 yield to a ton of cocoons and silk worth £110 (approx. $30,882.56). The Salzburgers exposed filament to sunlight for added sheen, a quality that made Georgia a world silk capital. In 1752, Georgia silk merchants built a filature factory in Savannah as a trade school for silk workers. By 1772, Georgia's wetlands sericulture yielded four hundred thirty-five pounds. The onset of the American Revolution curtailed production, which was supplanted by cotton at war's end.

### *Sources*

Beltucci, Paola. "Spinners' Hands, Imperial Minds," *Technology & Culture* 62:4 (2021): 1003–1031.
"Causton's Bluff, Deptford, Brewton Hill: Three Allied Plantations," *Georgia Historical Quarterly* 23:1 (March 1949): 28–54.
*The Journal of William Stephens*. Athens: University of Georgia Press, 1958.
Stephens, Pauline Tyson. "The Silk Industry in Georgia," *Georgia Review* 7:1 (Spring 1953): 39–49.

## Martha Daniell Logan (December 29, 1704–June 28, 1779)
**Botanist, Seed Merchant, Teacher**

## Elizabeth Pitts Lamboll (1725–October 1770)
**Botanist, Landscaper**
**Charleston, South Carolina**

One of North America's self-trained naturalists, Martha Daniell Logan promoted seed exchange from European plant beds to colonial Carolina gardens. The daughter of Martha Wainwright and Lieutenant Governor Robert Daniell III, a Welsh nurseryman and shipper, she was born one of six on a two-hundred-seventy-acre plantation at Archbell Point northeast of Bath, North Carolina. Her father acquired land in 1678, 1681, 1683, 1694, and 1695 and became wealthy and influential. On the sixty-two-acre Daniel Island at the confluence of the Cooper and Wando rivers, he built

Daniell's Pier with slave labor. His ship the *Daniel of Carolina* exported plantation produce to Bermuda and Barbados.

Until her teens, Martha received tutoring. At age fourteen, her father's will left her forty-eight thousand acres on the Wando River northeast of Mount Pleasant and ten miles from Charleston. At fifteen, she married Colonel George Logan, Jr., and made their home at Charleston's Trott's Point (modern Ansonborough), a thirty-five-acre property between the Cooper River and King Street. Of their eight children, Robert Daniell Logan and Frances Logan died in childhood. Son William Logan, at age fifty-four, was a British captive at the battle of Charleston later imprisoned in Philadelphia.

## From Hobby to Career

The Logans purchased Wando Plantation northwest of modern Mount Pleasant, where the soil proved acceptable to forest plants, berries, and ornamentals. At age thirty-eight, Martha opened a literacy academy for boarding students and advertised classes in the *South Carolina Gazette* until 1754. For financial security, in 1749, she put her property and residence on the market before a necessary move to Meeting Street in Charleston. To increase family income, son Robert advertised her imported flora for sale and may have managed the nursery.

The author of America's first standard horticultural text, Martha earned lasting recognition for the "Gardener's Kalender," an anonymous column in the 1751 *South Carolina Gazette*. Revised and reissued in John Tobler's 1752 *South Carolina Almanack* and the 1796 *Palladium of Knowledge: or, the Carolina and Georgia Almanac*, the practical compendium helped growers regulate their annual labors according to lunar cycles. The manual, signed "Done by a Lady," remained in print for five decades. Key to its popularity, seasonal instructions on cultivating low country soil aided gardeners in accommodating indigenous flora in a humid, sultry climate.

## Instructing Gardeners

Martha's treatise of recommendations for kitchen gardens was precise, yet simple and clear:

| | |
|---|---|
| *January* | transplant orchard stock; sow spinach, parsley, artichoke, and cabbage |
| *February* | prune and graft fruit trees; sow a full range of vegetables and melons |
| *March* | plant peas and kidney beans; water thoroughly |

| | |
|---|---|
| *April* | sow rosemary, thyme, and lavender; shade spinach and lettuce |
| *May* | weed and water |
| *June* | select evergreen and herbal stock for drying; enrich with manure |
| *July* | water at evening; collect seeds for preservation; sow turnips and onions |
| *August* | weed and water; sow a second crop of turnips and peas |
| *September* | ready soil to receive lettuce, spinach, radish, endive, peas, and beans |
| *October* | plant artichoke suckers; trim asparagus; enrich with dung |
| *November* | blanch celery and endive; prune vines and fruit trees |
| *December* | plant and prune fruit trees and roses |

After selling the plantation, Martha experimented with plant hybridizing and marketed rare specimens from the green at Trott's Point. At her home adjacent to the Ashley River on King Street, the deepening of beds with leaf mold absorbed rainwater and saved it from runoff. She immersed herself in the Linnaean classification system and academic horticulture and landscaping. Close to home, she studied Elizabeth Pitts Lamboll's methods of procuring and raising garden specialties—lilies, tulips, aniseed (*Pimpinella anisum*), magnolia, berries, and orange trees. Martha's investigations and networking with fellow enthusiasts helped Charleston become a scientific center of the New World.

## Networking with Naturalists

In her early fifties, Martha, like Elizabeth Lamboll, began corresponding with Quaker devotee John Bartram, the royal botanist. She petitioned for a modest number of plants:

| | |
|---|---|
| anemone (*Anemone ranunculaceae*) | aster (*Astereae*) |
| carnation (*Dianthus caryophyllus*) | cyclans (*Cyclamen primulaceae*) |
| gillyflower (*Matthiola incana*) | hesperis (*Hesperis matronalis*) |
| jessamine (*Gelsemium sempervirens*) | kalmia (*Kalmia latifolia*) |
| peony (*Paeonia*) | purple molly (*Passiflora incarnata*) |
| ranunculus (*Ranunculeae*) | siberian rocket (*Eruca vesicaria*) |
| snowball (*Viburnum macrocephalum*) | sweetpea (*Lathyrus odoratus*) |
| sweet sultan (*Centaurea imperialis*) | wallflower (*Erysimum*) |

By return correspondence, Bartram requested showy varieties:

| | |
|---|---|
| andromeda (*Pieris Japonica*) | Caledonian iris (*Iris Caledonia*) |
| canary shrub (*Rosa xanthina*) | catalpa (*Catalpa speciosa*) |
| crocus (*Crocus sativus*) | feather leaf (*Calathea rufibarba*) |

foxtail (*Hordeum murinum*)
honeysuckle (*Lonicera Caprifoliaceae*)
indigo (*Indigofera tinctoria*)
narcissus (*Amaryllidoideae*)
oleander (*Nerium oleander*)
Persian lilac (*Syringa Persica*)
pomegranate (*Punica granatum*)
rose cassia (*Cassia nodosa*)
scarlet vine (*Thunbergia coccinea*)
snail flower (*Vigna Caracalla*)
sweet shrub (*Calycanthus floridus*)
turkish balm (*Sedum monregalense*)
grape hyacinth (*Muscari armeniacum*)
ice plant (*Delosperma*)
laurel (*Laurus nobilis*)
nutmeg myrtle (*Myristica fragrans*)
olive (*Olea europaea*)
pink (*Dianthus plumarius*)
ragged lily (*Lychnis flos-cuculi*)
Savannah locust (*Ilex attenuata*)
scorpesene (*Faboideae scorpiurus*)
starry hyacinth (*Prospero autumnale*)
tuberose (*Agave amica*)
yellow wood (*Cladrastis kentukea*)

In exchange for shipments from Philadelphia, Martha introduced Bartram to South Carolina exotica:

bouncing bess (*Saponaria officinalis*)
crategus (*Crataegus monogyna*)
horse sugar (*Symplocos tinctoria*)
loblolly bay (*Gordonia lasianthus*)
striped grass (*Miscanthus sinensis*)
cassine holly (*Ilex cassine*)
dwarf plum (*Prunus salicina*)
lychnis (*Lychnis coronaria*)
spung tree (*Tetrameles nudiflora*)
virgin stock (*Malcolmia maritima*)

To wealthy gardeners, Martha marketed edging plants, pods, nuts, and fruit stones from London. She dispatched seeds and slips of the cushion rose (*Silene acaulis*) in a silk pouch and received cuttings, rhizomes, and roots in boxes and tubs that traveled by Captain North's ship from Bartram's home on the Schuylkill River outside Philadelphia.

In 1761, Bartram praised Martha's varied nursery of garden plants and flowering shrubs, some of which he had shared from his collection in Philadelphia. In May 1763, he described her passion for food production and novelties as magnetic enough to lure her through fire and water. In May 1768, she again advertised stock from her own array. Still attached to Charleston terroir and sensitive to its uniqueness, in 1770, Martha, at age sixty-six, bought from sister Sarah Daniel Beresford another parcel of land for £900 (approx. $208,793.50). Historians laud Martha's energy and scientific curiosity as a foundation of American botany.

## Sources

Edwards, Thomas S., and Elizabeth A. De Wolfe, eds. *Such News of the Land: US Women Nature Writers*. Hanover, NH: University Press of New England, 2001.
Hollingsworth, Buckner. *Her Garden Was Her Delight*. New York: Macmillan, 1962.
Logan, Martha, and Mary Barbot Prior. "Letters of Martha Logan to John Bartram, 1760–1763," *South Carolina Historical Magazine* 59:1 (January 1958): 38–46.

Parrish, Susan Scott. "Women's nature: Curiosity, Pastoral, and the New Science in British America," *Early American Literature* 37:2 (2002): 195–238.
Robbins, M.L. "Martha Logan," *Horticultural Science* 10:449 (1975).

## Hannah Breintnall (December 14, 1706–August 27, 1770)
### Optician, Taverner
### Philadelphia, Pennsylvania

A Quaker optician, Hannah Sharp Breintnall operated an upscale spectacle shop in Philadelphia. The wife of a widower, haberdasher and whalebone cutter John Breintnall, she was one of the nine children born in Chesterfield, New Jersey, to planter Hugh and Rachel French Allen Sharp. Her parents and uncles Thomas and William Sharp immigrated to Willingboro, West Jersey, from England in May 1682. They traveled aboard William Penn's fleet in the three-masted ship *Samuel* and arrived on September 18.

Hannah scandalized the Quaker meeting by courting a non-Quaker twelve years her senior and the father of two children. The quandary took months to settle with an apology and plea for forgiveness. They wed in New Jersey on October 29, 1724. While rearing Rebecca and Elizabeth Breintnall next door to John's brother Joseph Breintnall, Hannah went into business by operating the Hen and Chickens Tavern on Chestnut Street, where the sheriff offered property at public auction. After John's death on June 22, 1747, Hannah inherited a £1,282 (approx. $369,954.91) estate.

With adequate cash, Hannah flourished as an optician, her second career. At Black-Horse Alley under the Sign of the Spectacles on Second Street, she served aged, handicapped, and educated colonists with finely ground glasses framed in horn, tortoiseshell, silver, and steel and carried in a wood, shagreen, pasteboard, leather, or shell case. Travelers' glasses folded at center with a hinge over the bridge of the nose. In 1756, she advertised in the *Boston Evening Post* goods imported by Captain Francis Marsden on the scow *Two Brothers*. On March 30, 1758, she touted sophisticated wares: multifaceted multiplying glass, perspective or two-dimensional glasses, and glasses for Davis's quadrants, navigational devices for measuring planetary altitudes.

On December 31, 1758, Hannah placed an end-of-year ad in the *Pennsylvania Gazette* announcing a new shipment of glasses. Relayed from London aboard Captain Richard Budden's cargo ship *Myrtilla,* the transporter of the Liberty Bell, Hannah's stock consisted of Venetian green lenses to strengthen weak or weepy eyes, concave lenses for the myopic, and magnified reader's glasses. She offered spyglasses, bone microscopes, and various sizes of pocket compasses. She seemed most pleased with fine crystal glass lenses in leather or steel frames and temple bars, which could cost up to $200 (approx. $9,263.46).

Hannah's understanding of individual needs and tastes enlarged her customer appeal. On May 16, 1765, she presented ox-eye glasses with large round lenses for examining landscapes. Within two years, her property was worth £30 (approx. $6,290.23). At her death in 1770, she left unsold thimbles, shoemaking hammers, silk watch strings, and ninety-three pairs of glasses, an estate worth £161 (approx. $37,350.84).

### *Sources*


Breintnall, Hannah. "Advertisement of 1756 in the *Boston Evening Post*," *Optical Journal* 54 (10 July 1924): 36.

Dexter, Elisabeth Anthony. *Colonial Women of Affairs*. Boston: Houghton Mifflin, 1924.

Wulf, Karin. *Not All Wives: Women of Colonial Philadelphia*. Ithaca, NY: Cornell University Press, 2000.


## Allice Shannon Hight (1715–October 25, 1780)
**Taverner, Shopkeeper**
**Portsmouth, New Hampshire**

A prosperous saloon keeper in Portsmouth, New Hampshire, Allice Frost Shannon Hight thrived in pre–Revolutionary War New England. She was born to New Castle mariner Samuel Frost. On November 10, 1737, at age twenty-two, she wed a local man, Nathaniel Shannon, a Mason and innkeeper from a moderately prestigious family. The couple's business offered pasturage and stabling for travelers' horses, rental steeds, and food and cider for townspeople. Portsmouth residents relied on the hostelry for news and as a venue for small gatherings and card games.

Allice and Nathaniel kept a dry goods emporium stocked with tobacco, meat, fish, cloth, indigo, and hemlock lumber. Close to their residence, he may have processed leather at the Islington tannery for his inventory of bridles, saddles, and hides. While rearing George, Nathaniel Jr., Abigail, and Margaret, the Quaker family attended South Meeting House. They added to their property in 1746 a plot on the Piscataqua River. At an ideal spot for their tavern, they served meals and drinks to travelers by boat and ferry and to fellow Masons from St. Johns Lodge.

The family relocated to north Portsmouth, New Hampshire, near the North Meeting House and relied on their children and slaves Diana and Prince for spare help to compete with the town's fifty-eight taverns. In widowhood in 1753, Allice obtained a cow, domestic goods, and her own tavern license and continued managing the business. An inheritance of

£1,404.14 made possible the purchase of sixteen acres on Woodbury Avenue, which adjoined grazing space for her cow and customers' horses. A lawsuit by her mother-in-law, Abigail Walker, failed to retrieve from the estate the slave Diana and her daughter Phillis.

Allice's remarriage to local sailmaker Charles Hight, probable owner of the tavern Bunch of Grapes Bow Street, joined five stepchildren to the family. In 1754, Charles, a former constable, took over the pub and sired son Samuel. In addition to supplying dry goods to Portsmouth, Charles ran the ferry to Kittery, raising his taxable worth from £8 (approx. $2,154.70) to £25 (approx. $6,733.45). Legal claims by Abigail Walker and her son Cutts Shannon cost the Hights £27 (approx. $7,272.12) and a year of court investigation.

After Charles's death from pleurisy in 1761, Allice inherited his boat, slaves, and dry goods store. For income, she purchased a half share of her stepson's inheritance for £1,545 (approx. $416,804.87) and found renters for the house and barn, cropland, and a wharf on Church Hill. She managed the tavern and Kittery, Maine, to Portsmouth, New Hampshire, ferry, which earned £7 (approx. $1,888.44) from the city council. In her midforties, she passed ferry operation to Nathaniel Jr. Abigail Walker's death in 1763 entangled Allice in more lawsuits.

### *Source*

Pope, Laura. *Portsmouth Women*. Charleston, SC: Arcadia, 2013.

## Nonhelema Hokolesqua (c. 1718–December 1786)
**Trader, Linguist**
**Chillicothe, Ohio**

A Shawnee chief and negotiator, Nonhelema Hokolesqua chose a peaceful future for the northeastern woodland nomads by accentuating agricultural products and trade with the neighboring Delaware and Iroquois. Born at the commercial center of Chalakatha, Ohio, on the Ohio River, she grew up in Pennsylvania with brothers Cornstalk, Nimwhwa, and Silverheels. From her father Okowellos and mother Bird Whitefish Sunfish, she took the name Nonhelema meaning "not a man," a reference to her unusual height of six feet six inches. With Cornstalk, she lived in alternate seasons in Ohio and Kentucky.

Although proselytized by Moravians and baptized under the name Katy, Nonhelema honored the mythic fertility goddess Corn Woman and the power of corn production. Each year, she celebrated the Bread Dance and Green Corn Dance. Cultural interchange wrought by the French and Indian War encouraged tribal acceptance of English foods and costume, notably matchcoats (togas), leather shoes, linen shirts, and wool blankets. Women sowed cabbage, cucumbers, and turnips among plots of traditional beans, corn, and pumpkins. Hearth cooking shifted to the iron kettle and recipes for English dishes. From the European farming model, Nonhelema built her own cattle herd.

Nonhelema fought as a warrior named "The Grenadier Shaw," but also influenced Shawnee women to produce and trade with the English. At the onset of the American Revolution in 1776, she fostered neutrality, even though the Kentucky militia attacked Shawnee villages on the Ohio and murdered Cornstalk and his son Ellinipsico on November 10, 1777. From Coshocton, Ohio, Nonhelema led French Major General Augustin Mottin de La Balme, the American cavalry inspector, on an expedition to Illinois. While living on Scippo Creek in exile from her people, in 1785, she requested one thousand acres in northeastern Ohio as payment for aiding and translating for the patriots, disguising white spies, and brokering peace. Congress denied her petition for back pay and chose to allot daily food and a yearly gift of clothing and blankets.

In October 1786, Nonhelema and her husband Moluntha were imprisoned at Fort Pitt, Pennsylvania, a tract that the United States claimed. After his murder by tomahawk at the beginning of the Northwest Indian War, she devoted herself to compiling a Shawnee dictionary in the Algonquian language. She died free in December 1786, but her people retained mistrust for Americans. Her Irish Shawnee son Tamanatha supported the British. Her Canadian Shawnee son Thomas McKee served as a major in the Canadian militia during the War of 1812.

### *Source*

McEuen, Melissa A., and Thomas H. Appleton, Jr. *Kentucky Women, Their Lives and Times.* Athens: University of Georgia Press, 2015.

## Sarah Hallam Douglass (ca. 1714–April 1777)
**Actor, Director**
**Williamsburg, Virginia**

## Margaret Cheer (ca. 1740–February 15, 1800)
**Actor**
**Charleston, South Carolina**

The director of North America's first permanent stage company, Sarah Rich Hallam Douglas gained fame as the nation's first leading lady. Nothing remains of her parentage except the possibility that actor John Rich was her father. In childhood, she passed to the care of an aunt. After marrying Anglo-Irish actor Lewis Hallam, Sr., who claimed theatrical ancestry, she gave birth to Helen in 1737, Adam in 1738, Lewis Jr. in 1740, and Isabella Hallam Mattocks in 1746. Adults and children extended the Hallam dynasty of theatrical performers.

Sarah took the Shakespearean parts of historical figures—Lady Anne in *Richard III* and Lady Percy in *Henry IV.* Less classic roles depicted her as Almeria in William Congreve's tragedy *The Mourning Bride* and Hypolita in Colley Cibber's 1702 comedy *She Would & She Would Not.* In John Dryden's tragedy *The Tempest,* she played the innocent Miranda. Bankruptcy in December 1751 of the London Company of Comedians sent the Hallams and Lewis's brother William Hallam to the colonies to recoup financial losses.

## New World Drama

Leaving six-year-old Isabella with aunt Ann and uncle John Barrington at Whitechapel, England, in September 1752, Sarah, sons Lewis Jr. and Adam, daughter Helen, and ten company members joined her husband in Yorktown, Virginia. They advertised their stage season in the *Virginia Gazette.* At age twelve, Lewis Jr. played the roles of Hamlet and Arsaces, protagonist of Thomas Godfrey's tragedy *The Prince of Parthia,* America's first original drama.

At Williamsburg's Waller Street, the troupe paid £150 (approx. $41,341.81) to fit taverner Alexander Finnie's warehouse with box seats, a gallery, balconies, and orchestra pit for the nation's first evening of professional theater. On opening night, September 14, 1752, the playhouse served as the setting for English dramatist George Granville's *The Jew of Venice,* with Sarah starring as Portia and Lewis Jr. as her servant. Set to harpsichord melodies, the production and Ravenscroft's farce *The Anatomist; or Sham Doctor* appealed to the Virginia elite and earned as much as £300 (approx. $82,683.61) per night. On November 9, 1752, visiting Cherokee dignitaries attended a production of *Othello.* The Hallams ended an evening's performance with fireworks on Palace Green Street. On May 19, 1753, they sold the Williamsburg property and traveled north to lengthy bookings in Annapolis, Providence, Charleston, and Philadelphia.

In June 1753, Lewis remodeled Manhattan's two-story Theatre on Nassau Street as a venue for Elizabethan and Restoration plays, satire, and operetta. In ingenue parts and epilogues, the next September 17, Sarah delighted audiences with the role of Indian in Richard Steele's sentimental comedy *The Conscious Lovers* and the lead in Colley Cibber's farce opera *Damon and Phillida.* Sarah played Queen Gertrude in *Hamlet,* the tender daughter Cordelia in Nahum Tate's tragedy *King Lear,* the Trojan widow Andromache in Ambrose Philips's *The Distrest Mother,* the snippy heiress Angelica in William Congreve's *Love for Love,* and corrupter Sarah Milwood in George Lillo's *The London Merchant.*

## More Adaptations

The Hallam company toured among Quakers and Presbyterians in a more censorious region than London and Williamsburg. To escape mounting Whig-Tory antipathies and conservative religious suppression, in June 1752, they journeyed through Charleston and boarded the Rhode Island privateer schooner *Charming Sally.* To the crew's amusement, the company rehearsed on the quarterdeck. On arrival among more sophisticated, less Puritanic patrons in Jamaica, Sarah and Lewis performed in the island's first permanent playhouse. She presented the role of Lady Macbeth.

When Lewis died of yellow fever in 1755, British stage manager David Douglass remained in Jamaica to avoid the French and Indian War. He married Sarah the next year. With son Lewis Jr., in summer 1758, she reformed the original players as the Old American Company and dominated leading roles. On return north, she played the part of Lady Randolph in John Homes' medieval tragedy *Douglas.*

In 1761, Sarah began ceding younger female character parts to a niece, Nancy Hallam. She missed the Virginia Company's ebullient programs of May 1768, which thrived from presentations of *The Constant Couple, The Gamester,* and a reprise of *The Beggar's Opera.* Sarah continued acting into 1770–1771 in the commanding characterization of Mrs. Heidelberg, a wealthy Dutch widow in George Colman and David Garrick's Drury Lane comedy *The Clandestine Marriage,* and the allegorical Lady Wronghead, a meddler in nuptial plans in Colley Cibber's comedy *The Provoked Husband.*

At 1771, female competition tipped the scale. As Mrs. Woodcock in Thomas Arne's ballad pastiche *Love in a Village* in Williamsburg on May 1, 1771, Sarah shared the stage with niece Nancy as the coloratura Rosetta. At Sarah's death in April 1777, Jamaican actor Margaret Cheer replaced the diva temporarily in the company staging of Cleopatra, Cordelia, Imogen, Juliet, Lady Macbeth, Ophelia, and Portia until Nancy took her place as America's "third Juliet." Sarah's children and niece continued the family business, followed by her grandson Mirvan Hallam.

*See also* Nancy Hallam.

## Genealogy of the Hallam Family

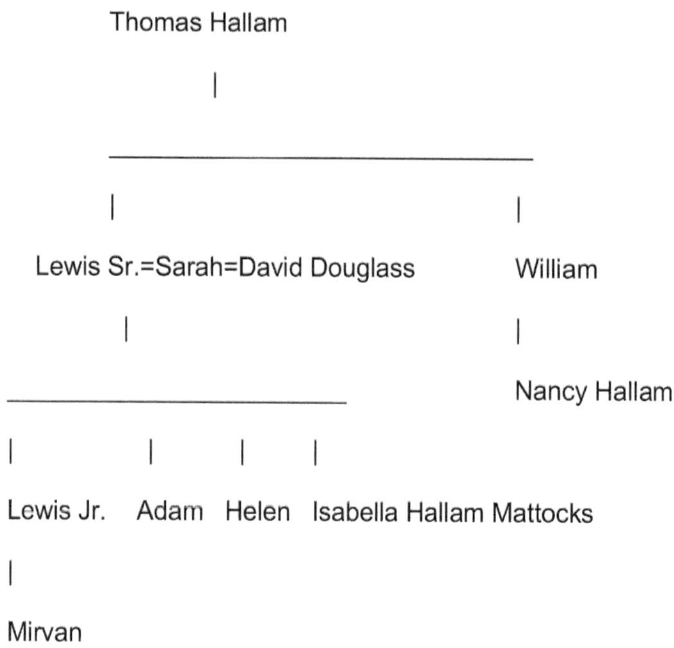


### *Sources*

Brockett, Oscar G. *History of the Theatre.* Boston: Allyn & Bacon, 1968.
Rankin, Hugh F. *The Colonial Theatre: Its History and Operations.* Chapel Hill: University of North Carolina Press, 1965.
Roberts, Vera Lowry. *On Stage: A History of Theatre. New York*: Harper & Row, 1962.

## Margaret Lew (ca. 1720–1750)
**Pianist**
**Groton, Massachusetts**

The first known colonial female keyboardist, Margaret Lew played the piano while serving a white master in Groton, Massachusetts. Born in Cape Verde, in childhood, she was the slave of Samuel Scripture, a white soldier whose family died in late September 1723 during a smallpox outbreak. On December 28, 1741, she married a West African, Primus Lew, a servant of Bostonian militia captain Jonathan Boyden, a fifer during the French and Indian War. Resettled in Dracut on the Massachusetts–New Hampshire border, Primus and Margaret reared two daughters and two sons.

Margaret's oldest, cooper Barzillai Lew, gained a reputation for spirited talent as fifer and drummer. He married Lexington pianist Dinah Bowman. As a member of the 27th Massachusetts Regiment, he taunted the British at the battles of Lexington and Concord and of Bunker Hill with repeats of "Yankee Doodle," a traditional European tune dating to fifteenth-century Holland. In 1777, he performed on fife and fiddle with Ethan Allan and the Green Mountain Boys at Fort Ticonderoga and at General John Burgoyne's surrender on October 17, 1777, at Saratoga, New York. The Lews' thirteen children thrived at string and wind instruments and, with their mother on keyboard, formed a band that entertained in Boston and Portland, Maine.

### *Sources*

Buckley, Gail. *American Patriots: The Story of Blacks in the Military. New York*: Random House, 2002.
Walker-Hill, Helen. *From Spirituals to Symphonies: African-American Women Composers and Their Music*. Urbana: University of Illinois Press, 2007.

## Anne Catharine Green (1720–March 23, 1775)
**Printer, Publisher, Merchant**
**Annapolis, Maryland**

At age forty-seven, Anne Catharine Hoof (or Hoff) Green undertook a massive job as colonial printer and single mother of fourteen children, of whom only five survived her. The daughter of Immetje Tieleman and Jacobus Van Hoof of Leiden, Holland, she migrated with them to Philadelphia. At age eighteen, she married Bostonian printer Jonas Green in Philadelphia. Soon after marriage, the couple relocated to a two-story home on Charles Street in Annapolis, Maryland. The owner remodeled the residence with ten fireplaces to accommodate the Greens' growing household and a backyard printshop.

In 1745, the couple restored to circulation the *Maryland Gazette*, a staunch defender of commercial and personal liberties. In addition to learning the printer's trade, Anne earned a second income by marketing chocolate, coffee, and raisins at the in-house post office. In August 1747, the paper published an advertisement from Daniel Dulany, Sr., concerning the Frederick-Town fair, promising that all sales "ſhall be free and exempt from the Payment of any Toll, Stallage, Piccage, or any other Charge" (Haugh, 2016). The 1756–1757 smallpox epidemic afflicted the family so terribly that subscribers feared contagion from handling the newspaper.

The *Gazette* boldly defied the Stamp Act in March 1765 by publishing idealist Daniel Dulany, Jr.'s protest of Parliament's right to tax New

World colonies. His widely read pamphlet *Considerations on the Propriety of Imposing Taxes in the British Colonies* stirred patriot support for local duty-free merchandise. While rejecting personal attacks, the Greens also championed the Sons of Liberty, a defiant group of activists founded by William Paca and Samuel Chase in early 1766 who met openly under the Liberty Tree.

## Going It Alone

Five days after Jonas's death on April 11, 1767, widowhood obliged Anne to continue publishing the paper and serve as parish registrar to satisfy her husband's twelve hundred i.o.u.s. Under the name "A.C. Green," she finished Jonas's contract to print the acts, votes, and proceedings of the 1767 assembly session and aired patriot John Dickinson's anti–Townshend Acts opinions in *Letters from a Farmer in Pennsylvania, to the Inhabitants of the British Colonies*. With sons William and Frederick Green and son-in-law John Clapham, Anne attained the post of provincial printer, in part by announcing threats by Rector Bennet Allen to destroy her equipment.

For an annual salary of $948.50 (approx. $38,491.25) and forty-eight thousand pounds to tobacco, Anne promoted independence from British rule, which involved greater control of colonies via the four Townshend Acts. Her editorial policy promised to print ads, bail bonds, testamentary letters, shipping bills, legal forms, and bills of exchange. In addition, she produced bills of credit, the annual *Maryland Almanack*, political and satirical treatises, tobacco prices, and a book of notes and manifests for tobacco inspectors.

For convenience, Anne moved the business into her home and broadened the schedule to include political leaflets and more advertisements. Her service informed residents of the Chesapeake Bay of general assembly proceedings, events preceding the American Revolution, and controversy over what type of government should replace the monarchy. She promoted freedoms of speech, religion, and the press, but tempered media tone and theme by rejecting character attacks.

## The Patriot Voice

In 1769, Anne posed for a portrait by Charles Willson Peale. In 1770, she accepted the duty of printing paper notes worth $318,000 (approx. $11,960,561.71) in one-sixth of a dollar, half dollar, four-, six-, and eight-dollar denominations. Each contained the printers' names—A.C. and W. Green—and the warning, "'Tis Death to Counterfeit." She invigorated weekly columns about the Boston Massacre of March 5, 1770, and the buildup of munitions, troops, and funds supporting the British army. Enthusiasm for the latest editorial prompted citizens to crowd the printshop to snatch a copy of the Thursday edition. In 1774, she completed *The Charter & Bye-Laws of the City of Annapolis* and the *Deputy Commissary's Guide,* a tedious manual on inheritance probate and settling estates.

Significant shifts in colonial relations with the mother country received restrained notice in the *Gazette,* beginning with the Boston Tea Party of December 16, 1773. Editorials enlivened support for rebellion after the Boston Port Act of March 31, 1774, closed the harbor to commerce. On September 29, 1774, she applauded pacifist Quakers for boycotting English tea. Her lack of response to the arson on the *Peggy Stewart* in Annapolis harbor in October 1774 for violating the tea boycott indicated a radical redirection away from loyalists toward the patriot cause.

Anne continued covering the political lead-up to the American Revolution. So many contenders sought space in the *Gazette* that she was forced to defy the Intolerable Acts in printed handbills. Her sons Frederick and Samuel Green filled the publishing role after her death on March 23, 1775. They issued local diatribes legitimizing Philadelphia patriot Thomas Paine's *Crisis,* completed on December 23, 1776, condemning turncoat Benedict Arnold for turning Tory in May 1779, and rejoicing over General George Washington's victory at Yorktown, Virginia, on September 18, 1781.

*See also* Clementina Rind.

## *Sources*

Green, Ann Catherine Hoof. "Maryland Gazette: December 1, 1774," https://archive.org/details/mg12011774/page/n21/mode/2up.

Haugh, Chris. "The Forgotten Father of Frederick," *www.historysharkproductions.com/* living-united-for-80-years-part-i-a-community-chest/the-forgotten-father-of-frederick (18 June 2016).

Skaggs, David C. "Editorial Policies of the *Maryland Gazette,* 1765–1783," *Maryland Historical Magazine* 59 (1964), 341–342.

## Alice Greele (ca. 1721–1795)
**Taverner**
**Falmouth, Maine**

A respected innkeeper at Greele's Tavern in Falmouth (modern Portland), Maine, the widow Alice Ross Greele gained esteem for protecting property during the American Revolution. In 1746, she married Thomas Greele and produced John, Mary, and William before Thomas's death in 1758. During an upsurge of smallpox in 1761, she volunteered to nurse the sick. For four decades, the story-and-a-half building at the corner of Congress and Hampshire streets five blocks from the harbor welcomed merrymakers, sailors on shore leave, privateers, and hungry citizens seeking a hot meal of baked beans. She enticed the adventuresome with servings of coffee aged in a barrel.

The Committee of Public Safety, political conventions, and court sessions debated legalities in Alice's spacious rooms. On October 18, 1775, Captain Henry Mowatt jeopardized the gathering spot by demanding surrender of arms, part of his investigation of smuggling and identification of patriots engaged in a boycott of English goods. To the town's refusal, he launched a bombardment on Falmouth Neck from his twenty-gun sloop *Chanceaux* (Lucky). The previous evening, volunteers policed the street to prevent hostilities arising between his men and hotheaded citizens who objected to naval impressment, the force drafting of sailors. The eight-hour assault from 9:40 a.m. to 5:00 p.m. rained grapeshot, cannon balls, bombs, grenades, incendiary carcasses, and mortar shells on the populace, fortunately not killing anyone. In the afternoon, Mowatt's shore patrols from the four-ship flotilla set fires.

With water bucket in hand, Alice, out of stubbornness or patriotism, extinguished flames on her property and near the debris around her chopping block and at the shed and barn. With a dishpan, she corralled a cannon ball and dumped it in the street. Extensive arson incinerated stores, warehouses, and one hundred thirty residences on private property, creating a total loss of £55,000 (approx. $11,430,810.79). Throughout the winter of 1775–1776, city dwellers relied on handouts to stay alive. At the surrender of General John Burgoyne on October 26, 1777, Alice treated patriot celebrants with buckets of punch and wine passed out the tavern window. In competition with John Greenwood's and Marston's saloons, Alice Greele's Tavern hosted town meetings and remained a Falmouth landmark until 1846.

### *Sources*

Goold, Nathan. "Falmouth Neck in the Revolution," https://www.kellscraft.com/FalmouthNeck/FalmouthNeckinTheRevolutionPage.html

"The Wrap: Brea Lu Cafe Finds New Home in Westbrook," *Portland Press Herald*, www.pressherald.com/2023/03/29/the-wrap-brea-lu-cafe-finds-new-home-in-westbrook.

## Jane Eustis (1722–January 21, 1771)
**Merchant, Seamstress**
**Boston, Massachusetts**

A widowed she-merchant for two decades, Jane Eustis circulated an extravagantly scrolled business card listing her wares as green tea, hats, shoes, cotton hose, cap lace, and fabrics from India and England. She was reputedly divorced from a first husband. A single female merchant, she received mentoring and financial backing from Boston shopkeeper Elizabeth Murray Inman. At the townhouse to the north of the court building on King Street, in 1755, Jane's brick shop offered luxury fabrics—worsted, silk, satin, brocade, damask, lawn, and Irish linen, available cheap for cash. In 1756, she ended a partnership with Mary Purcell and ran the business alone.

On April 23, 1764, an ad in the *Boston Gazette,* declared Jane's fashion choices "bloom colour'd." In addition to dressing stylishly, she continued advertising her wares on April 20, 1767, to female gentry who read the local newspaper. Her correspondence with Christopher Champion of Newport, Rhode Island, offered a stock of white thread and lawn from Glasgow, Scotland. On April 17, 1769, she tempted buyers with lace, kid and lamb gloves and mittens, muffs, hoops, stomachers, stays, umbrellas, hair hats, beads, brolios (garlands), and embossed or corded paduasoy (peau de soie) yard goods and ribbon. The colonial boycott of English goods in 1772 forced her to abandon specialties manufactured in England.

The pressure of suiting customer demands cost Jane a livelihood in elegant fabrics used in quilted petticoats, riding habits, mantuas, ducapes, cloaks, capuchines, palances, and gowns in the current fashion. Her hat department featured bonnets, jockeys, chip and beaver hats, and plumes and feathers. She stressed the variety of goods, which included buckles and broaches, earrings and necklaces, leather-mounted fans, turbans, apron materials, clogs, galoshes, mitts, tippets, cambric, tammies, and calimancoes. When profits declined, she again stocked shelves with seasonal fabrics ferried to the colonies by captains Robert Jenkins, John Skillings, and David Stevens and a fresh assortment of enamel and silver frames that made her wealthy. She added copies of novelist Samuel Richardson's newest fiction, *Clarissa* and the 1740 epistolary bestseller *Pamela.*

The *Boston Chronicle,* a patriot newspaper, demanded that shoppers avoid Jane's business because she violated her signed agreement on March 1768 to boycott trade with the British. In 1770, she returned to England. A year of health struggles precipitated madness and despair at age forty-eight. After her death, according to an ad in the *Massachusetts Spy* on June 6, 1771, Boston retailers Benjamin Kent, Johnathan Head, and Joseph Peirce collected her debts and paid an inheritance to daughter Sarah Kent.

*See also* Elizabeth Murray Inman.

## *Source*

Breen, T.H. "'Baubles of Britain': The American and Consumer Revolutions of the Eighteenth Century," *Past and Present* 119 (May 1988): 73–104.

## Eliza Lucas Pinckney (December 28, 1722–May 27, 1793)
## Agronomist
## Wappoo, South Carolina

North America's premiere developer of cash crops, Elizabeth "Eliza" Lucas Pinckney turned a knack for botany into a regional endowment. The oldest of four, she was born on Antigua to a West Indian mother, Mary Anne Milldrum, and Colonel George Lucas, governor of the island. Her paternal grandfather, John Lucas, served the assembly of Antigua and Barbuda while securing colonial rights and buying land for building his fortune. In view of the Shekerley Mountains, she grew up at her family's sugar plantation at Cabbage Tree on Willoughby Bay, an estate valued in 1673 at £8,000 (approx. $2,265,201.23). Her doting father called her his "dear Betsey" and predicted that she would "produce something of real and public utility" (Glover, 2020, 29, 56).

After five years of training in Latin, French, English literature, music, philosophy, and refined penmanship at Mrs. Pearson's girls' academy in London, Eliza made herself "busy in providing for Prosterity" (*Ibid.*, 2). She resolved to base her agricultural career on diversified botany. At age seventeen, she returned to family properties on Charleston's Tradd Street and South Bay (modern White Point) and managed an investment in low country rice, lime, pitch, and tar. The Stono Revolt of September 9, 1739, forced her to return temporarily to Antigua. Escorted by George Jr. to South Carolina, she directed a team of twenty slaves on the fifteen-hundred-acre Garden Hill Plantation on Combahee River, the six-hundred-acre Bluff Plantation on James Island at Wappoo Creek, and Pinckney's Island Plantation, a three-thousand-acre tract on the Waccamaw River.

### From Indigo to Blue Dye

Through experiments along Wappoo Creek in indigo (*Indigofera*) cultivation with seeds from the Leeward Islands, Eliza developed blue dye along with more common ventures in alfalfa, cotton, figs, flax, ginger, hemp, and rice. She transported filament from her silkworms to processors, designers, and tailors and preserved hen eggs in rum to ship to Antigua as experimental refiners of sugar with albumin. By collaborating over three years with James Nicholas Cromwell, a French expert from Montserrat in the West Indies, she adapted the indigo plants to Carolina terroir and tented them with framed glass to survive both frost and worms. In October 1741, she assured her father that, since March, she had made twenty weight (six pounds, five ounces) of blue dye and expected ten more.

By sharing seed and instructions in 1744 with other planters, Eliza more than doubled colonial commercial income and stabilized revenue from rice, which frequently fluctuated. South Carolina became the continent's richest colony. While superintending laborers in harvesting pods, tending foul-smelling vats, and molding indigo into dye bricks, she used medicinal plants to treat fevers and accidents and supervised variolation for smallpox. She taught slaves to read and write and to order seed and equipment and readied two slave girls to train others in literacy. In her free time, she studied law, read Samuel Richardson's popular novels *Pamela* and *Clarissa*, and played the flute and harpsichord under the instruction of Charles Pachelbel.

In 1744, Eliza wed a neighboring widower twenty-two years her senior, attorney Charles Cotesworth Pinckney of Belmont plantation on Charleston Neck. They built a mansion in Charleston at Colleton Square on East Bay Street overlooking the courthouse and Cooper River. At home in Charleston and at Belmont, she perused the media for details of global markets, commodities distribution, and land prices and scheduled bicoastal shipping through overseers, factors, and ship captains. By 1750, South Carolina's indigo exports dominated global trade in blue dye while the colony maintained lucrative rice exports, which later fed the Continental Army and boosted the East Coast economy.

## Lifetime Botanist

In 1753, the Pinckneys repatriated to London. In 1756, she served as her own agent in England and combated cargo weight, loss, and wartime insurance during the French and Indian War. Throughout periods of conflict in the Caribbean, she feared for her father and younger brother, George Lucas, Jr. On return to South Carolina in 1762, Eliza continued managing the Lucas property along with Charles's tract after his death in summer 1758 from malaria. In widowhood for three decades, she researched a cure for breast tumors and encouraged her sons to support the American Revolution after British raiders destroyed her residence, library, furniture, sheep, and poultry at the thousand-acre Auckland Plantation on the Santee River. While residing in Charleston, Eliza corresponded with American botanists and took up cultivating copses of cedar, magnolia, and oak.

By 1775, the output of indigo reached more than one million one hundred thousand pounds. A refugee in 1778, Eliza financed rations, arms, and regiments to relieve the siege of Charleston. At a tenuous period of American history, her laudable children displayed staunch patriotism, particularly Charles Cotesworth Pinckney, a delegate to the 1787 Constitutional

Convention and the U.S. minister to France, and Thomas Pinckney, a ratifier of the U.S. Constitution and governor of South Carolina. During a trip north in 1793 to consult an oncologist, she died of breast cancer on May 26. A matrilineal commitment to her detailed letterbooks passed personal writings to daughter Harriott Pinckney Horry, an organized plantation manager like her mother, and great granddaughter Harriott Horry Rutledge Ravenel, a biographer and historian who wrote *Charleston: The Place and the People.*

## *Sources*

Bellows, Barbara L. "Eliza Lucas Pinckney: The Evolution of an Icon." *South Carolina Historical Magazine* 106:2/3 (2005): 147–165.

Glover, Lorri. *Eliza Lucas Pinckney: An Independent Woman in the Age of Revolution.* New Haven, CT: Yale University Press, 2020.

Pinckney, Eliza Lucas. *The Letterbook of Eliza Lucas Pinckney, 1739–1762.* Chapel Hill: University of North Carolina Press, 1972.

## Christiana Campbell (1722–March 25, 1792)
**Taverner**
**Williamsburg, Virginia**

A high point in female entrepreneurship, Christiana Burdett Campbell's tavern thrived on the political fever that stoked the American Revolution. She grew up in food service and emulated her father, John Burdett, in choosing a spot that supplied the populace with a comfortable retreat for relaxing and talking business and politics. In motherly fashion, Mary Burdett trained her daughter in the domestic end of kitchen and inn work and the accounting of food, drink, and equipment. At John's death in 1746, Christiana settled the estate, which willed her £300 (approx. $83,658) and the bondsmen Shropshire, wife Belle, and two children.

Christiana wed an older man, pharmacist Ebenezer Campbell, in 1747 and made their home on the Appomattox River at Blandford, Virginia. A widowed mother of Mary "Molly" Campbell Russell and Ebenezer Campbell Day, in 1752, Christiana liquidated the pharmacy and returned to the job she knew best. From Carter's Grove and Yorktown, she established a standing order of beef, pork, and wheat supplies. Her genteel dining facilities offered a quality menu to merchants and court authorities who sought comfort and privacy in the club room.

Beginning at Duke of Gloucester Street, Christiana ran her tavern for a quarter century during the uncertainty of rebellion against George III and profited from Masonic balls and the overnight stays of George Washington and Virginia burgesses. From 1771 to 1777, Thomas Jefferson remained a steady customer. Her dependence on black slaves demanded minimal education at the Bray School at the corner of North Boundary and Prince George streets for Aggy, London, Mary, Sally, Shropshire, Sukey, and Young.

In October 1771, Christiana reopened at a new location east of the capitol in Jane Vobe's former tavern. By 1774, Christiana owned the property and refurbished eight rooms, three halls, two porches, and a bar. In November, a thief broke into her house and stole two trunkfuls of clothes. From October 1782 to July 1783, she invested in fresh plaster and whitewashing of rooms, porches, bar, and halls.

When wartime inflation and shortages compromised Christiana's trade, she rented her home as dormitory rooms for students at the College of William and Mary. The move of Virginia's capitol from Williamsburg to Richmond relocated her clientele and forced her to close. After selling her furnishings from the Waller Street site in October 1787, she settled at her daughter Ebenezer's house in Fredericksburg. Cared for by her maid Betty, Christiana lived to age seventy. Her granddaughter, Christiana Day Benson, bore her name.

*See also* Jane Vobe.

### *Source*

Meacham, Sarah Hand. *Every Home a Distillery: Alcohol, Gender, and Technology in the Colonial Chesapeake*. Baltimore, MD: The Johns Hopkins University Press, 2009.

## Jane Colden (March 27, 1724–March 10, 1766)
**Naturalist, Illustrator, Cheesemaker**

## Alice Christy Colden (January 5, 1690–March 1762)
**Accountant**
**New York City**

From a five-year integral analysis of Hudson Valley flora, Jane "Jenny" Colden Farquhar earned the title of first New World female botanist. The daughter of Scots Alice Christy Colden of Kelso and naturalist Cadwallader Colden, the lieutenant governor of New York, she gained a basis in food and plant research at home in New York City, where she made cheese from the family dairy herd and learned Latin translation of binomial classification. The family emigrated in 1718 and, a decade later, moved to a three-thousand-acre wilderness in Orange County (modern Newburgh, New York). Alice set an example of female accountability by managing the farm and its ledgers while Cadwallader studied the colony's accommodation of local Iroquois. During the French and Indian War, Jane developed natural curiosity for Latin nomenclature and common names, beginning with dandelions and hollyhocks.

North of New York in the Hudson Highlands, Jane lived at Coldengham, a stone mansion, and landscaped ornamental gardens and retreats for trees and exotic wildflowers. Because her father's research drew extensive correspondence, he drafted Jane into the job of secretary and field agent to collect seeds or dried specimens. She impressed him with meticulous morphology. By networking with Swedish naturalist Carolus Linnaeus, author of *Systema Naturae* (Systems of Nature), and adding to his genera and orders, she applied taxonomy to the bewildering mass of New World plant life and established a career as a professional scientist of global repute.

## Jane's Specifics

In 1752, Jane's study and drawing of St. John's wort (*Hypericum virginicum*), wild basil (*Clinopodium vulgare*), and hellebore (*Copti groenlandica*) employed Linnaean names of plant parts and grouped them according to their reproductive organs. A manuscript of her three hundred forty ink drawings cataloged American varieties and their herbal uses:

| | | |
|---|---|---|
| *Ambrosia artemisifolia* | ragweed | emetic, astringent, fever |
| *Asclepius tuberosa* | butterfly weed | colic, bronchial inflammation |
| *Clematis virginiana* | clematis | syphilis, joint pain, diuretic |
| *Digitalis purpurea* | foxglove | wounds, heart regulator, epilepsy |
| *Clinopodium vulgare* | wild basil | edema, mastitis, ulcers, diabetes |
| *Erythronium americanum* | yellow trout lily | wounds, edema, contraception |
| *Hypericum virginicum* | St. John's wort | mood elevator, antidepressant |
| *Mertensia virginica* | Virginia bluebells | tuberculosis, venereal disease |
| *Monarda didyma* | bee balm | antiseptic, wounds, flatulence |
| *Pedicularis canadensis* | betony | sterility, digestion, blood flow |
| *Phytolacca decandra* | pokeweed | analgesic, anti-cancer |
| *Polygala senega* | snakeroot | diuretic, expectorant, analgesic |

She violated strictures for refined women by speaking candidly of sexual reproduction, glands, and ovaries.

Jane conducted rigorous field work that embedded botany in Western culture and forced European scientists to broaden formerly closed systems of observation. By interviewing New York farmers and indigenous Lenape, she investigated the practical use of more than three hundred plants in nutrition and curative teas and poultices. During John Bartram and son William Bartram's dinner visit to the Coldens, she invited them outdoors to collect seeds. John stated in autumn 1753 that they had stayed in the field for two hours in the dark to validate her observations.

### The Male View

Jane's father condescended to her botanic interests: "Botany is an Amusement which may be made agreable for the Ladies who are often at a loss to fill up their time if it could be made agreable to them," as though scientific endeavors were safe ways to spend idle time ("National"). In summer 1754, Dr. Alexander Garden of Charleston sent Jane's description of the gardenia to scientists for evaluation. He promised to instruct her on preserving butterflies. In 1756, the Edinburgh philosophical society published her cataloging in *Essays and Observations Physical and Literary*, the first Linnaean categorizing by a woman. Nonetheless, Linnaeus refused to name a plant after her. She modestly asked fellow plant enthusiasts not to make her work public or to aggrandize her discoveries.

Jane's enthusiasm for botany grew in 1757 when her father requested indigo (*Amorphia fruticosa*) seeds from her wanderings. Garden posted Persian seeds from Russia and native South Carolina flora: umbrella tree (*Magnolia tripetala*), fringe tree (*Chionanthus*), yellow jessamy (*Gelsemium sempervirens*), and horse chestnut (*Aesculus pavia*). Jane replied with more seeds and the taxonomy of arbutus (*Arbutus unedo*). Her missive contained some three hundred illustrations stamped with printers' ink and rolled through a press.

In 1759, Jane married Scots widower William Farquhar and retired from floral taxonomy. At age forty-one, she died in childbirth along with the fetus. Until an upsurge in women's history in 1978, her work largely disappeared from scientific annals. Her description of plants in Johann David Schoepf's 1787 *Materia Medica Americana* assigns no credit to Jane.

## *Sources*

*Essays and Observations Physical and Literary*. Edinburgh: Philosophical Society of Edinburgh, 1756.

Gronim, Sara Stidstone. "What Jane Knew: A Woman Botanist in the Eighteenth Century," *Journal of Women's History* 19:3 (2007): 33–59.

"National Gallery of Art," https://heald.nga.gov/mediawiki/index.php/Jane_Colden.

Parrish, Susan Scott. "Women's Nature: Curiosity, Pastoral, and the New Science in British America," *Early American Literature* 37:2 (2002): 195–238.

## Patience Lovell Wright (1725–March 23, 1786)

## Rachel Lovell Wells (1735–1796)
**Sculptor**
**Bordentown, New Jersey; Philadelphia, Pennsylvania**

America's first sculptor, Patience Lovell Wright joined Quaker younger sister Rachel Lovell Wells in the art business and transatlantic spying. Native New Yorkers from Oyster Bay, they were born to farmers John and Patience Townsend Lovell and grew up at 100 Farnsworth Avenue in Bordentown, New Jersey. She and Rachel concocted a malleable bread dough for shaping into figures like putty or clay and tinted the forms with plant juices. One artistic effigy personified literature by drafting childlike figures. Their traveling show of portraits gained local popularity and won new commissions. Rachel also shaped an anatomical anomaly—Siamese twin girls conjoined face to face.

After marrying cooper Joseph Wright in March 1748, Patience made their home in Philadelphia. Widowed at age forty-four during pregnancy with daughter Sarah "Sally" Lovell, Patience joined sister Rachel in creating colored wax likenesses as a lucrative form of popular art. To warm the material, Patience held it under her apron until it was soft enough to shape.

To house some fifty-five life-size busts of living people, Rachel opened galleries in Philadelphia and Staten Island, New York, and sold busts of celebrities for home display. In 1770, she completed a life-size likeness of the Rev. George Whitefield, a founder of Methodism; Thomas Penn, a proprietor of Pennsylvania; and Cadwallader Colden, New York's lieutenant governor. A year later, the sisters received publicity from the *Virginia Gazette* for models of the biblical prodigal son and Philadelphia patriot John Dickinson, which pleased viewers in Charleston, New York, and Philadelphia.

## A New Start

A fire at 100 Queen Street destroyed the Lovells' earliest waxworks in June 1771, costing the sisters hundreds of pounds. While Patience initiated a Boston studio, Rachel started anew in Philadelphia. Patience relocated to Chudleigh Court on St. Alban's Street at London's Pall Mall and cultivated scholarly and military clientele—King George III and Queen Charlotte, Colonel Isaac Barré, Prime Minister William Pitt, Prime Minister Frederick North, historian and pamphleteer Catharine Macaulay, naval officer and poet Edward Thompson, Admiral of the Fleet Richard Howe, actor David Garrick, painter Benjamin West, radical publisher John Wilkes, and Thomas Pownall, governor of Massachusetts. She entertained sitters with spiels of American gossip and spoke familiarly of the royal couple as Charlotte and George. At the death of William Pitt, she sculpted a life-size statue for his monument in Westminster Abbey. Her traveling shows continued with the help of daughter Elizabeth Wright Platt and toured Bristol, England, where she first learned of the Battle of Bunker Hill and the onset of the Revolutionary War.

The Lovell sisters remained fixed on colonial prospects of winning the American Revolution and alerted founding father John Dickinson to preparations of the British army for invasion. While colonial prisoners of war resided in England, Patience distributed cash to them from patriots and recorded data on British military tactics. To transport secrets to George Washington's Continental Army, she hid details in wax figures bound for the colonies. In 1773, a wax head of William Pitt, Lord Chatham, reached Rachel in Philadelphia with hidden dispatches intended for the Continental Congress. She repaired any travel damage before displaying Patience's work.

### End-of-War Aims

When patriot fervor made Patience unpopular among English loyalists, she spent two years in Paris at the Hôtel d'York and shaped a wax image of Benjamin Franklin. On return to London in 1781, she modeled in wax a historical vision of the Paris peace consortium of September 4, 1783. She maintained a New York presence in October 1785 with a showing of Bel and the Dragon, an apocryphal episode from the book of Daniel, and planned to add George Washington to her list of artistic subjects. She suffered a debilitating fall and died before she could return to Pennsylvania.

Rachel, the widow of shipwright James Wells, retired to Bordentown, New Jersey, and displayed thirty-three wax dramas and tableaux, including "The Treachery of Delilah to Samson" and "The Murder of Abel by Cain." She made four formal requests to the New Jersey Legislature and the Continental Congress for refunding of £2,000 (approx. $381,226.33) in war bonds loaned to New Jersey to finance the war effort. Phoebe and Joseph Wright, Jr., her niece and nephew, became artists. Joseph achieved his mother's aim to make a model of George Washington.

### *Source*

Snodgrass, Mary Ellen. *American Colonial Women and Their Art.* Jefferson, NC: McFarland, 2017.

## Elizabeth Hunter Holt (1726–March 6, 1788)

## Elizabeth Holt Oswald (April 19, 1746–June 1748)

**Printer, Publisher**
**Williamsburg, Virginia**

New York's official printer, Elizabeth Hunter Holt belonged to a journalistic family whose work helped unite the American colonies under a common cause. The sister of William Hunter, postmaster general and editor of the *Virginia Gazette,* she was born in Yorktown, Virginia, to Mary Ann and Scottish Irish immigrant William Thomas Sempill Hunter. Her paternal grandsires included twelfth-century Baron Lambinus Loudon and two named Reginald Craufurd, the twelfth-century sheriff of Ayr and the fourteenth-century laird of Auchnames, Ayrshire. When she was sixteen, she lost her father to a Cherokee attack.

In 1744, Elizabeth Hunter Holt united with Williamsburg merchant and printer John Holt, an educated Virginian who served the city as mayor in 1752. The couple produced Elizabeth Holt Oswald, Sarah Holt Brewer, and John Hunter Holt, who died in childhood. Because of a business failure, in 1754, John took the jobs of deputy postmaster of New Haven, Connecticut, and editor of the *Connecticut Gazette*, the colony's first paper, a military record reporting the events of the French and Indian War. William Hunter's death in August 1761 left £1,000 (approx. $269,776.61) to Elizabeth with which the couple founded an independent press championing the Sons of Liberty. Their son John Jr. took the post of Virginia colony's official printer.

## The Media Business

With New Haven printer James Parker, John Holt ran a bookstore and shared responsibility for the *New York Gazette, or The Weekly Postboy* on May 6, 1762. He continued the *Gazette* until October 9, 1766, when he began *The New York Journal, or, General Advertiser,* which ran sporadically for sixteen years with news of British atrocities against Boston patriots. In 1772, his apprentice, Eleazer Oswald, married John's daughter Elizabeth. The *Journal* moved temporarily to Kingston and Poughkeepsie during the British seizure of New York on August 27, 1776. On January 31, 1777, Supreme Court Justice John Jay hired John to serve New York state as official printer throughout the Revolutionary War for an annual salary of £200 (approx. $41,723.64). On February 10, 1783, he resigned and informed the New York Senate that he had not been paid in over six years.

In November 1783, Elizabeth managed the weekly *Independent New York Gazette* as publisher and printer. Benjamin Franklin declared her punctual in sending him copies, which he followed with gifts of London papers. At the same time, she pursued her husband's back pay of more than £2,000 (approx. $381,226.33). Within the year, the weekly appeared under the name *The Independent Gazette, or, the New York Journal Revived* and remained in print until March 11, 1784, a week after John's death. His estate left her a printing press, iron composing stick, letter boards, and sufficient type worth £280.15 (approx. $453,094.78).

## A State Oversight

On March 18, 1784, Elizabeth altered the masthead to read *The New York Journal, and State Gazette*, which maintained its pro-independence stance until she sold it on February 10, 1785. Her paper, the only one to continue publication after the Revolutionary War, summarized the withdrawal of British forces and issued comments on the future of slavery. She reported the opening of the Bank of New York and also completed the 1784 *Journal of the Senate of New York*. In 2024, one folded sheet of her senate journal was valued at $10,000. Her lawsuit reached the New York Assembly, when members granted only one year's pay of £200 (approx. $37,904.54) or only 90.8 percent of its original value.

Elizabeth relocated to Philadelphia to live with her daughter and son-in-law, Colonel Eleazer Oswald, a war veteran and publisher of the *Independent Gazetteer*. Elizabeth gave the *Journal* to Eleazer and pressed John's lawsuit until the expiration of wartime claims. Following her death in 1788, Eleazer continued petitioning for his deceased father-in-law's back pay of £1,383.60 (approx. $273,162.61) covering eleven years and eleven months of work. He also sought £3,200 (approx. $631,772.45) for materials and $20,000 (approx. $43,948,577.83) in damages for a total worth of $44,853,512.89. The state settled the lengthy litigation on February 6, 1795, at $5,315 or approximately $130,903.39 today. At Eleazer's death in September 1795, his wife Elizabeth Holt Oswald continued printing the *Independent Gazette* until her death in 1797.

### *Sources*

Holt, John. "Journal of Occurrences," *New York Journal* (9 November 1768): 2.
Marcus, Maeva, and James R. Perry. *The Documentary History of the Supreme Court of the United States, 1789–1800. New York*: Columbia University Press, 1985.
Paltsits, Victor Huto. *John Holt, Printer and Postmaster. New York*: Public Library, 1920.

## Elizabeth Murray Inman (July 7, 1726–May 25, 1785)
**Milliner, Needlework Teacher**
**Boston, Massachusetts**

A prosperous navigator of the Revolutionary War economy and non-importation agreement, Elizabeth Murray Campbell Smith Inman became an icon of the colonial entrepreneurial female by merchandizing dry goods and buying land. A native Scot from Unthank in Roxburghshire, she was born to Anne Bennet and John Murray of Bowhill and orphaned in 1737. The family claimed roots to the Norman Conquest of 1066 and kinship with King James II of Scotland.

At age twelve, Elizabeth migrated to North Carolina to keep house for older brother James Murray, a merchant and member of the North Carolina general assembly, and his wife and daughter Dorothy "Dolly" Murray Forbes. In 1743, Elizabeth sojourned in London and studied British luxury goods and fashions, which she purchased for her shop. Six years later, with the proceeds of three of James's slaves, she established a needlework school and millinery in Boston opposite the Brazen Head in Cornhill, the city's literary center. She advertised imported goods in the *Boston Evening Post* and the *Boston Gazette*. In addition to boarding pupils on half or full stipend, she taught niece Dolly literacy, stitchery, and business basics and advised milliner and needlework teacher Jannette "Jane" Day Barclay, who advertised as far south as Newport, Rhode Island.

## Managing Matrimony

Elizabeth surrendered independence in 1755 by marrying mariner and trader Thomas Campbell, who managed stock purchases for her shop at the corner of Queen Street. Her ads in the *Boston Gazette* offered vests, hats, clogs, stockings, hoop petticoats, cloaks, bonnets and cardinals, Polanaise, and umbrellas. Her range of fabrics—damask, holland, garlix, taffeta, corduroy, lawn, satin, brocade, lutestrings, minionett, cap and blond lace—carried the restriction of cash sales or short credit.

At Thomas's death four years later, Elizabeth wed widower James Smith, a sugar refiner, and arranged to keep her earnings separate from his. While residing at their Brush Hill farm, she continued educating in trade skills Scots immigrants Ame and Elizabeth "Betsy" Cuming and nieces Anne Murray Powell and Elizabeth "Betsy" Murray. Before James's death, he incurred patriot spite because he housed British soldiers in a sugar warehouse after Royal Fleet's arrival on October 2, 1768. She retired in October 1769.

On a family visit to Scotland and Norwich, England, Elizabeth added her well educated niece Mary "Polly" Murray to the girls she groomed for shopkeeping. Letters in 1770 from trading partners Edward Bridgen and James Waller advised her about apprentices, stocking shelves, and bookkeeping. They exported satin and curtains to her and answered her questions about dyeing Indian damask, insuring the ship *Charriott*, and investing in silver-handled tableware. Her letter from Norwich to brother James on February 26, 1770, scorned the notion of genteel ladyhood for Polly: "Usefull members of sosiety are certainly preferable to all the delicate creatures of the age" (Inman, 1770, 3).

### The Loyalist's Fate

In late April 1771, Elizabeth returned to Boston aboard the East Indiaman *Osterly-Lizard* and married third husband Ralph Inman, a dealer in kersey and broadcloth, osnaburg, duffels, pottery, glass, tobacco pipes, wine, and beer. For political reasons, she lived apart from his three-story mansion, his son George, and his two daughters at Brush Hill, Cambridge (modern Milton, Massachusetts). When George graduated from Harvard, Elizabeth hosted a grand party and ball. To elude Ralph's demand for money, she moved to Boston to aid niece Anne in deciding between business and wedlock.

When Boston's wartime boundaries separated parts of the family, Elizabeth facilitated a prisoner exchange for hero Ethan Allen and offered candles, cheese, hair powder, linen, and rum in the swap. In March 1776, because brother James Murray fled to a loyalist enclave in Nova Scotia, patriot forces arrested Ralph and commandeered his property in retaliation for his loyalist sympathies. The couple reunited at war's end, when Ralph claimed a £5,000 (approx. $1,067,286.34) loss because of the war. At Elizabeth's death on May 25, 1785, she willed most of her money to nieces Anne, Betsy, and Dolly.

*See also* Ame and Elizabeth Cuming; Jane Eustis.

### *Sources*

Cleary, Patricia. *Elizabeth Murray: A Woman's Pursuit of Independence in Eighteenth-Century America*. Amherst, MA: University of Massachusetts Press, 2000.
Inman, Elizabeth Murray. Letter to James Murray (26 February 1770): 1–4.
Lemire, Elise. *Black Walden*. Philadelphia: University of Pennsylvania Press, 2009.

## Margaret Green Draper (May 3, 1727–1804)
**Printer, Journalist**
**Boston, Massachusetts**

A risk-taker in the publishing world and one of the fourteen female printers in the American colonies, Margaret Green Draper defied the Boston majority of patriots and supported the British monarchy. On May 30, 1750, she married her cousin, loyalist Richard Draper of Banbury, England, and joined Boston's West Church. They both named as great-grandfather Samuel Green, printer of the Cambridge Press, and grandsire Bartholomew Green, an immigrant from Devonshire, England, to Cambridge, Massachusetts. During the Great Puritan Migration in September 1633, Bartholomew traveled aboard the *Griffin*.

Richard edited and printed the Monday *Boston News-Letter*, the nation's first printed media and first continuously published colonial paper of Massachusetts. Under the motto "Published by Authority," the paper had a reputation from April 17, 1704, for meticulous reportage, particularly details of combat deaths in Quebec on December 31, 1775, and a 1776 subscription ball and a performance of Nicholas Rowe's tragedy *Tamerlane*. At the small wooden office on Newbury Street, the couple issued documents and speeches from the Massachusetts Governor and Council, the *Ames Almanack* for 1774 by anti-federalist Nathaniel Ames, and the *Academiae Typographus*, a compendium of commencement theses from Harvard College. He died at home on June 5, 1774, at his Boston home on Washington Street. In widowhood during reaction to the Stamp Act, Margaret allied with John Boyle, a convert to patriotism who fled Tory fervor out of fear of retaliation.

Margaret introduced herself to subscribers on August 11, 1774, by promising to maintain quality reportage, such as sale of Lisbon lemons and Cheshire cheese, the governor's call for public fasting and prayer, a speech by John Hancock, and details of the Charleston lottery as a means of paying for a highway to the South Carolina coast. She issued a speech by George III to the House of Commons and commentary from Westminster and Whitehall government offices. By gathering international news of politics and wars, reprints from other media, shipping and piracy, trade, and local information, she continued publication at eight shillings per year as a model of freedom of speech and freedom the press. Ads for books and medicine cost as low as twelve pence.

Margaret published the onset of the American Revolution, particularly the Boston Tea Party, and the Boston Massacre. She pursued the subject of colonial rebellion with broadsides detailing the firefights at Lexington and Concord and Bunker Hill. To earn a living, she fought the *Massachusetts Spy* in an understated struggle for readership and dodged letters denouncing her. Sons of Liberty made public bonfires of the *News-Letter*. During the siege of Boston, while political crisis drove out the *Boston Evening Post, Boston Poe-Boy, Boston Gazette,* and ultimately the *Massachusetts Spy*, her paper became the only survivor.

Margaret based her Tory career on books, leaflets, royal proclamations, and gubernatorial broadsides. In partnership with John Howe beginning September 7, 1775, she continued printing until February 22, 1776, under the name "Draper's." The paper ceased publication at the issuance of the Declaration of Independence. On March 17, 1776, at the evacuation of British forces from Boston, she joined the one thousand fleeing monarchists en route to Halifax, Nova Scotia. Patriots confiscated her home and several properties. After securing her family at Pimlico, England, she relocated to London, where she obtained royal compensation for colonial losses and earned an annual pension.

### Sources

Stark, James Henry. *The Loyalists of Massachusetts and the Other Side of the American Revolution*. Boston: self-published, 1910.
Walker, Gay. "Women Printers in Early American Printing History," *Yale University Library Gazette* 61:3–4 (April 1987): 116–124.

## Penelope Barker (June 17, 1728–1796)
**Planter**
**Edenton, North Carolina**

One of North Carolina's most famous rebels, Penelope Pagett Hodgson Craven Barker knew the planter's work from childhood. Her maternal grandfather, Captain James Blount, managed nine hundred sixty acres in Chowan County. Her uncle, John William Blount, inherited sixteen hundred acres at Mulberry Hill, a rice and silkworm plantation on the Albemarle Sound overlooking the Staunton River, which survived the Yamasee War of 1715. Her parent's, Elizabeth Blount and physician Samuel Pagett, produced Penelope at Blenheim Plantation, a two-thousand-acre land grant made in 1714.

Penelope's brief marriage to Attorney General John Hodgson, manager of Blenheim, left her a pregnant teenaged widow, a single mother of two sons, and guardian of a niece and two nephews. She inherited Hodgson's Edenton acreage, its twenty-five slaves and Padgett's Plantation, the property of her husband, James Craven, on the Great Marsh. The bequest awarded her a handsome house on Macedonia Road, ten slaves, furniture and silver, a library, a liquor cellar, and herds of sheep, pigs, and cattle. During her six years as business manager, the steady return on the sale of sugar, cinnamon, and nutmeg gave her ample cash. In total, her survival of a childless marriage made her North Carolina's richest widow.

Wealth accompanied Penelope's third marriage to widower Thomas Barker. Bequests left her in charge of Barker House and extensive property on South Broad Street facing Edenton Harbor. During his absence to London in 1761 to represent the North Carolina colony, she managed the business dealings for seventeen years. On October 25, 1774, she canvassed door to door and rallied fifty-one Edenton women to oppose the Tea Act of 1773 by boycotting English tea and textiles. Their petition to George III, the first all-female political action in the colonies, generated mockery on January 16, 1775, in the *Morning Chronicle and London Advertiser*. A third widowhood in 1778 left her more duties in conducting business for the Hayes Plantation. Her only surviving child, Elizabeth "Betsy" Barker, also married a planter, Colonel William Tunstall of Pittsylvania, Virginia, father of Penelope's ten grandchildren.

### Source

Smith, Margaret Supplee, and Emily Herring Wilson. *North Carolina Women Making History*. Chapel Hill: University of North Carolina Press, 1999.

## Lucy Harrison Randolph Necks (1728–March 12, 1789)
**Milliner**
**Williamsburg, Virginia**

During the American Revolution Lucy Carter Harrison Randolph Necks, one of the First Families of Virginia, maintained a bicoastal business in hats and women's fashion accessories. Born to the pioneering Harrison clan, who emigrated to Tidewater Virginia in 1632 from Northamptonshire, England, Lucy claimed as grandsire Robert "King" Carter I, the governor of Virginia and developer of Corotoman (modern Weems, Virginia), a Georgian mansion on three hundred thousand acres on the Rappahannock River. Lucy was the first of the eleven children of Anne Carter and Colonel Benjamin Harrison IV of Yorktown. Little brother Henry died when she was a teenager. The family occupied Berkeley Hundred, one of America's first plantations, on the north bank of the James River, where her grandfather opened the first shipyard to transport tobacco to England.

Engaged to sea captain Edward Randolph II of Gloucestershire at age eighteen, Lucy bore a dowry of £800 (approx. $230,861.10) and three slaves. She was married in 1740 at the Harrisons' three-story Georgian brick manse, where she bore daughter Lucy Jett and son Harrison Randolph. A tobacco and pelts merchant, Edward sailed the scow *Harrison* on a cyclical route between Virginia and England. The family suffered a triple loss on July 12, 1745, when lightning struck an upstairs window in their residence and killed Lucy's fifteen-year-old sister Hannah and their father. His will left Lucy $799 (approx. $54,250.71). Tragedy again traumatized her in April 1757, when Edward died at sea, leaving her his only heir. She cohabited with a man named Papley, who sired their invalid daughter Betty Dards.

### The Widow in Commerce

To support the family, in June 1769, Lucy initiated a London-to-Virginia cash-only coat and millinery business. Both by retail and wholesale, she exploited the posh European nexus of specialized fabrics and apparel. Of unique appeal were Dresden needlework, blond lace, muslin, lawn, and flowered gauze. Her ads in the *St. James's Chronicle; Or, The British Evening Post* and the *Virginia Gazette* stressed "lately arrived" from the London shop at Three Angels, No. 9, Long Walk, Cloysters, Smithfield. The stock in June 1770 emphasized children's toys and clothes, Brussels pillow lace, mechlin, dimity, russels, durants, blond and black lace, catgut, crepe, silk purses, mitts and gloves, ferrets, tippets, ostrich and cock feathers, hair rolls and tates, chenille, fans, velvet collars, combs, and costume jewelry. She also marketed psalters and prayer books and subscriptions to *Lady's* and *Universal* magazines, popular monthly British women's media offering fashion advice and entertainment.

The time was fortuitous for genteel milliners like Lucy selling to fashion-conscious Williamsburg colonists west of the capitol and on Duke of Gloucester Street, the city's fashion center. Relatives encouraged elite Virginians to shop at her emporium. For the viewers of the Virginia Comedians Company's May 1768 performances of Irish playwright George Farquhar's *The Constant Couple,* James Shirley's comedy of manners *The Gamester,* and a reprise of John Gay's masterwork *The Beggar's Opera,* Lucy displayed London's latest bonnets, ribbons, cardinals, and caps along with shoes, stays, fans, and handkerchiefs. Demand for seasonal couture and court session outfits and for accessories to mark engagements, nuptials, and mourning required variety of design and materials available only in London.

## Virginia's Economy

Prior to the Revolutionary War, the Harrison shipyard produced eighteen battleships at a time when 80 percent of British immigrants chose residency in urban Virginia and the Carolinas. In June 1770, Lucy wed Virginia tobacco and hemp hauler Robert Necks, the Norfolk sea captain of the merchantmen *Fauquier, Adventure,* and *Lunn and Lloyd,* and the ketch *Good Intent.* In the troubled 1773 economy, he aided his wife's business by posting a newspaper ad demanding payment of debt or threatening legal action for past-due accounts. He died of chronic ills in Norfolk in late September 1774.

Amid clamorous patriots, Lucy stayed true to the mother country. On September 5, 1774, her son Harrison Randolph V was elected to the First Continental Congress and signed the Declaration of Independence, but she remained an enthusiastic loyalist even though the conflict robbed her of cash and inheritances. Her grandson, Benjamin Harrison VI, served the Continental Army as deputy paymaster. In December 1781, she petitioned the British treasury as a wartime refugee to recover £100 (approx. $21,795.11) of the £7,000 (approx. $1,422,699.24) in property seized during the American Revolution. To stay afloat financially, in summer, she liquidated silver and furnishings. The British government rejected her pleas for help.

## Sources

Breen, T.H. *The Marketplace of Revolution: How Consumer Politics Shaped American Independence.* New York: Oxford University Press, 2004.
Cabell, Eleanor Kelley. *Women Merchants and Milliners in Eighteenth Century Williamsburg.* Williamsburg, VA: Colonial Williamsburg Foundation, 1988.
Cowden, Gerald Steffens. "Spared by Lightning: The Story of Lucy (Harrison) Randolph Necks," *Virginia Magazine of History and Biography* 89:3 (July 1981): 294–307.

## Mercy Otis Warren (September 25, 1728–October 19, 1814)
### Lyricist, Poet, Pamphleteer, Satirist, Historian
### Plymouth, Massachusetts

A prominent voice of the anti-colonial movement, Mercy Otis Warren wrote poems, essays, plays, and songs that shaped radical American patriotism. The third of thirteen children born in Barnstable, Massachusetts, to Mary Allyn and farmer, attorney, and judge James Otis, she was a scion of a *Mayflower* immigrant and a supporter of the Sons of Liberty. James Otis, Sr., advocated her training under the mentorship of the tutor of her brothers James "Jemmy" Jr. and Joseph. From reading, she learned geography, literature, and the heroes of world history named in her poem "Simplicity." A faithful friend-maker, she corresponded with Martha Custis Washington, Abigail Smith Adams, and Hannah Fayerweather Winthrop, a Cambridge activist and refugee from the battles of Lexington and Concord.

As wife of sheriff and commissary officer James Warren, in November 1754, after a six-year courtship, Mercy relocated to the Windsor Mansion, a two-and-a-half story clapboard house at the corner of Main and North streets in Plymouth. Simultaneously, she tended Clifford Farms, the family estate two miles out of town on the Eel River, where James experimented with scientific improvements. In the Clifford-Warren house, Mercy reared five sons with her strong sense of "radical redress of grievances." Her son Samuel served the U.S. Senate as secretary for a quarter century.

Mercy's formidable activism was not devoid of loss and setbacks. In 1769, a tax agent's cudgeling on the head of her brother James Otis, Jr., rendered him brain damaged. He died in 1783 from a lightning bolt that struck his Andover residence. Sons George and Henry died in their twenties; Charles succumbed to tuberculosis; James Jr. lost a leg during a sea battle with British sloops. She lost her enthusiasm for Plymouth because of its tolerance for loyalists. The burning of the British revenue schooner HMS *Gaspée* off the Rhode Island shore aroused her spite toward England's indifference to colonial rights. In 1772, she advocated for committees of correspondence to endorse opposition to British tyranny.

## Observations and Letters

While her husband functioned as paymaster of the Continental Army, Mercy traveled to bivouacs to write his military correspondence. She observed patriot leadership in person and extolled Commander George Washington's tactics. The turncoat Benedict Arnold she relegated to the likes of criminals and villains for his ravaging of Virginia. At the capture of General Charles Lee at a Basking Ridge, New Jersey, saloon, she smarted at his carelessness and his scorn of the Continental Army's commander in chief. The British predations on New York in 1777 infuriated her, as did the lack of provisions, tents, ammunition, and uniforms during the winter of 1777–1778 at Valley Forge, Pennsylvania, a source of perplexity and despair. In 1781, the Warren family moved nearer Boston to Milton House, the colonial governor Thomas Hutchinson's former manse. After they returned to Plymouth, Winslow Warren was killed in Ohio in 1791 during combat with Miami chief Little Turtle, leader of the plains Indians.

Mercy's propagandist letters inspired the pantheon of liberty—Thomas Jefferson, John Adams, Sam Adams, Patrick Henry, George Washington, and John Hancock, the one founding father whom she suspected of being more surface than substance. In April 1770, her "Massachusetts Song of Liberty" proclaimed the monarchists "insolent Tyrants." Her sassy verse farce "Squabble of the Sea Nymphs" depicted Tories as pimps and sycophants of George III. The mythic parody, which appeared in the March 21, 1773, issue of the *Boston Gazette*, made high epic fun out of the Boston Tea Party. Her letters reduced the British to cutthroats and mocked General John Burgoyne's self-pity. Correspondence with John Adams in 1776 during his control of the Massachusetts Superior Court took on an acerbic tone as he asserted federalism and she promoted states' rights.

## Political Philosophy

In the thick of war, Mercy issued *The Adulateur* in 1772 in the *Massachusetts Spy* and *The Defeat* in installments the next year in the *Boston Gazette*. The two stage satires demeaned Hutchinson as a semi-comic felon, a monarchist whom mobs attacked for promoting exorbitant colonial taxes. Following closet drama successes with *The Blockheads* in 1776 and *The Group* and *The Motley Assembly* in 1779, she surveyed the formation of a new government in *Observations on the New Constitution* and called for a Bill of Rights. Her ideals of personal integrity and conscience dominated a 1790 compendium, *Poems, Dramatic and Miscellaneous*, which she dedicated to George Washington.

Mercy's unconventional defense of human rights and women's

education set the tone of colonial feminism. "To the Hon. J. Winthrop," the female response to a boycott of British goods, certified the resolve of patriot women to end colonialism. In her late seventies, she suffered eye infection, partial blindness, deafness, and headaches. Nonetheless, she compiled commentary on the American progress toward liberty into a unified history. She became America's premiere female historian in 1805 by completing meticulous research for *History of the Rise, Progress, and Termination of the American Revolution*, a three-volume chronicle of the Revolutionary War. Former U.S. President John Adams blasted her criticism with ten letters while admirers dubbed her the First Lady of the American Revolution and the Muse of the Bill of Rights.

### *Sources*

Brown, Alice. Mercy Warren. New York: Scribner, 1896.
Warren, Mercy Otis. Mercy Otis Warren: Selected Letters. Boston: Larkin, 1805.

## Elizabeth Cuming (ca. 1730–1797)

## Ame Cuming (September 19, 1733–1819)
**Shopkeepers, Needlework Teachers**
**Boston, Massachusetts**

To survive in big city commerce, Ame and Elizabeth "Betsy" Cuming openly violated the Boston mercantile agreement to boycott goods from England. Scots aristocrats from Ardormie, their parents, Helen and Robert Cuming, immigrated to Concord, Massachusetts, where Ame, Elizabeth, and their brother John were born. At their parents' death, the sisters inherited acreage in Rutland, Vermont. They rejected control by John, a member of the Concord Committee of Correspondence, and, in 1765, settled in Boston.

At the intersection of King and Queen streets, the Cuming sisters joined a coterie of female merchants serving refined customers. They rented out funeral clothes and marketed London fashion—velvet masks, French broaches and buckles, hair bags, and fringed Barcelona handkerchiefs. In addition, their October 7, 1765, ad in the *Boston Gazette* listed hair powder, snuff boxes, buckskin and dogskin gloves, horn and tortoiseshell combs, and toothbrushes and tincture for toothache. A week later, their ad mentioned patches and court plaister, faddish markings for the face. On October 21, their adviser, philanthropist Elizabeth Murray Inman, exonerated the two single women for trying to make a living.

On November 11, 1765, the sisters moved their business to a remodeled shop of Anna Adams in Cornell facing the Old Brick Meeting House near the Town House. Their lengthy ads continued to offer millinery and stressed the availability of salvolatile (smelling salts), Stouton's elixir for upset stomach, and eau de Luce, a costly blend of soap with wine and ammonia for treating insect bites and burns. They stocked Hungary water, a brandy-based perfume blended with citrus oil and seven herbs. Ads for canisters of expensive Hyson green tea ignored the fact that the commodity was imported by the British East India Company. They liquidated seven acres and a house and store thirty miles outside Boston and established a replacement for Mrs. Day's School for boarding needlework students of embroidery, coats of arms, and Dresden stitchery, a combination of embroidery and airy backgrounds made by pulling filler stitches.

In the Cumings' fourth year in business, they imported an order of wrought silk and hats worth £300 (approx. $69,306.63). On October 28, 1769, one thousand patriots subjected customs officer John Mein to tar and feathering outside the sisters' door. On November 20, 1769, the Merchants' Committee pressured them with warnings and threats. A denunciation in the *Boston Gazette* declared them sordid "Enemies to their Country" and accused them of "[preferring] their own little private Advantage to the Welfare of America" (*Boston Gazette*, 1769, 3).

Despite the loyalism of Governor Thomas Hutchinson, the media broadcast patriot scorn of a merchants' meeting at Faneuil Hall. Hectored from December 1769 through March 19, 1770, the consortium forced the sisters to return to a Concord farm. Amid the British retreat of March 1776, Ame and Elizabeth joined the throng of loyalists settling in Halifax, Nova Scotia. They resumed business and, by 1780, thrived among endorsers of George III.

*See also* Elizabeth Murray Inman.

### Sources

Archer, Richard. *As If an Enemy's Country: The British Occupation of Boston and the Origins of Revolution*. New York: Oxford University Press, 2012.
*Boston Gazette* (20 November 1769): 3.
Cleary, Patricia. *Elizabeth Murray: A Woman's Pursuit of Independence in Eighteenth-Century America*. Amherst, MA: University of Massachusetts Press, 2000.

## Indian Hannah Freeman (March 1731–March 20, 1802)
**Healer, Basket Maker**
**Chester County, Pennsylvania**

A Delaware or Lenni Lenape farmer and artisan, Indian Hannah Freeman outlived her people in Chester County, Pennsylvania. Born in a log cabin on the William Webb farm at Kennett on Brandywine Creek along the Delaware border, she lived with parents and two younger brothers under the authority of Chief Checochinican, a broom maker. Under the negotiated détente of peacemaker William Penn, she grew up in a tight matrilineage of mother Sarah, grandmother Jane, and aunts Betty and Nanny. Among Quakers at Center in Christiana Hundred on the Delaware River, the family relocated in the 1730s to a cabin on the farm of Swithin Chandler and his wife, the Rev. Ann Wilson Chandler.

The Indian family grew the traditional Iroquois "three sisters"—beans, corn, and squash—and fished for turtles and shad with grapevine nets during the spring run. Hannah's father abandoned his wife and children as a way to avoid white settlers and relocated to the northwest at Shamokin (modern Sunbury, Pennsylvania), seat of the tribal sachem on the Susquehanna River. She took a common-law husband named Andrew Freeman and fished from a small island at Peach Bottom. From female traditions, she learned to weave wood baskets like the slatted splint harvest container displayed by the Chester County Historical Society. In 1949, historian Arthur G. Volkman described her style as one over, one under weaving with rows alternately from three narrow to one wide.

Because of her bilingualism in English and Unami, an Algonquian dialect, Indian Hannah lived a nomadic existence and relied on Quakers for temporary residence. A local law protected Indian vendors from 1730 to 1773. In return for jobs spinning flax into yarn and sewing for three shillings and six pence (approx. 40¢) per week, she bartered native root and herb medicines and prescribed botanical teas to treat patients during an outbreak of dysentery. Along the way, she sold her baskets and brooms while leading her pets—a pig, a cow, and two dogs. To avoid the French and Indian War, she settled with her clan at Thornbury, Pennsylvania, on Chester Creek and devoted herself to weaving and dyeing baskets while she chanted songs and smoked her pipe.

Indian Hannah's relatives fled with her in winter 1764 up the Delaware River south of Philadelphia to Woodbury, New Jersey, to escape murderous raids by the Paxton Boys, a bloodthirsty band of Scottish Irish Presbyterian vigilantes who slew and scalped Conestoga natives at Conestoga Town. Her seasonal itinerant trade took her to a summer hut at Centreville, Delaware. In a decade of loss, her female network declined. By her sixties, rheumatoid arthritis bent her back, reduced her wanderings, and left her dependent on charitable Quakers. From 1773–1775, she spent three years with the Mary Thomson Levis and Samuel Levis family, who operated a paper mill on Darby Creek at Springfield, Delaware.

Beginning on November 12, 1800, Hannah spent her seventieth year at the new Chester County almshouse at West Bradford, Pennsylvania, and the Embreeville State Hospital, an asylum for the insane in Newlin. After sixteen months, she died a pauper at age seventy-one. Burial at the poorhouse cemetery flouted her request to lie among Lenape ancestors in their traditional burying ground. Her name appears on a quartz memorial, baskets at the county history center, the Hannah Freeman pole bean (*Phaseolus vulgaris*), and Indian Hannah Road.

### *Sources*

Futhey, John Smith, and Gilbert Cope. *History of Chester County, Pennsylvania*. Philadelphia: L.H. Everts, 1881.
Volkman, Arthur G. "Lenape Basketry in Delaware," *Archaeological Society of Delaware Bulletin* 4:5 (1949): 15–18.
Weslager, C.A. *Red Men on the Brandywine*. Wilmington, DE: Hambleton Company, 1953.

## Mary Draper Ingles (1732–February 1, 1815)
### Saltmaker, Ferrykeeper, Blacksmith, Taverner
### Ingles Ferry, Virginia

One of the legendary heroines of the colonial era, Mary Draper Ingles survived kidnap by Shawnee and a six-hundred-mile trek home to develop a business career at a traveler's hub of western Virginia. A native Philadelphian, she was the daughter of Elenor Hardin and George Draper, Irish immigrants from Donegal. The family were the first pioneers to cross the Alleghenies. They occupied a 7,500-acre tract. George's disappearance in 1744 left the household to fend for itself.

In 1750, Mary wore a white gown at her marriage to Virginia militiaman and pioneer hero William Ingles of Dublin, Ireland. She gave birth to Thomas, the first white baby born west of the Alleghenies. He set an example of enterprise by constructing Ingles Mill, one of the first in western Virginia, at the corner of Crozier (modern Central Street) and Vine Avenue in old Knoxville. He founded Draper's Meadow (modern Blacksburg, Virginia) and secured some seven hundred acres on the Roanoke River amid limestone springs and swaths of bluegrass.

### The Massacre

At age twenty-three, Mary, in the sixth month of pregnancy, survived a Shawnee raid during the French and Indian War and lived through ten weeks of captivity and self-rescue. On July 30, 1755, at Draper's Meadow at the juncture of the Ohio and Scioto rivers, sixteen warriors armed by the French massacred Elenor Draper, an infant, and two other pioneers. They plundered and burned the Ingles' cabin and abducted five whites to Kentucky. The band separated Mary from sons Thomas and George. In October, she gave birth to a daughter, whom she left behind in a bark cradle.

Mary entered slave labor making salt from sulfur brine at Big Bone

Lick (modern Union, Kentucky). Under the pretext of gathering wild grapes, she and a German woman, wife of Henry Bingamin, fled along the Ohio River, feeding themselves on wild fruit, nuts, pawpaws (*Asimina triloba*), roots, and frogs. Escaping on foot and by raft and canoe along the Kanawha and New River, Mary reached home forty-two days later on December 1, 1755, naked, malnourished, and white-haired. From the rich bottomland, she moved with her family to Bedford County to elude more Indian attacks. Her detailed memories of Lower Shawneetown enabled William to join an expedition of three hundred fifty volunteers into West Virginia seeking vengeance on the kidnappers.

## The Aftermath

The last portion of Mary's life pictures a well-grounded mother, farmer, and businesswoman. At a one-room log cabin on nine hundred acres at Dunkard's Bottom (modern Pulaski, Virginia) in the Allegheny hill country, she bore three daughters and a son while building a ferry business at a crossing of the New River in western Virginia. Operated by mother and son, the transport drew traffic from soldiers during the Anglo-Cherokee War of 1758, motivating the Ingles to purchase more land at what is now Radford. In November 1762, the couple posted charges of three pence (approx. $7.79) for horse or traveler, many of whom continued west through the Cumberland Gap to the prairies and New Orleans. In 1768, the ransom of Thomas Ingles with $150 (approx. $6,506.92) restored the oldest son to the family.

To stave off Cherokee raiders, William built Fort Hope, a defensive blockhouse. Mary suffered depression and withdrew from conversation with visitors. In 1772, the couple opened the two-story, log and frame Ingles Ferry Hill Tavern, store, stables, tannery, and blacksmith forge to serve passengers on their way west. Clientele at their social center included Andrew Jackson and George Rogers Clark, a patriot military officer. While living on the Great Wagon Road linking Philadelphia and the Carolina frontier, the nation's most heavily traveled highway, the couple acquired slaves, horses, and cattle and two thousand acres in West Virginia. From 1797 to 1805, the Ferry Hill Tavern ledger recorded daily details of buying calico and a dairy cow.

William advanced to sheriff, militia colonel, and judge before his death in 1782, when Thomas began managing the ferry. In widowhood, Mary retained one hundred acres while sons Thomas and John divided the rest. She made her home at a 16' × 14.5' cabin and lean-to near a spring a half mile from the landing. Daughter Mary inherited proceeds of the ferry, a National Historic landmark on the Ingles Ferry Road, which remained in operation for two centuries. James Alexander's historical novel *Follow the River*, the Hallmark film version, and memorials retain Mary Ingles' example of frontier fortitude. An outdoor theater hosts Earl Hobson Smith's outdoor drama *The Long Way Home.*

*Sources*

Foote, William Henry. *Sketches of Virginia, Historical and Biographical.* Philadelphia: W.S. Martien, 1850.
Steele, Robert Ingles, and Andrew Lewis Ingles, eds. *The Story of Mary Draper Ingles and Son Thomas Ingles.* Radford, VA: Commonwealth Press, 1969.

## Jane Vobe (1733–late November 1786)
**Taverner, Slave Trader**
**Williamsburg, Virginia; Manchester, Virginia**

A prosperous taverner east of the capitol in Williamsburg, Virginia, Jane Vobe went into business at age nineteen and retained a respectable career for three decades, offering food and drink to Continental soldiers. On January 16, 1748, she was abandoned after the departure of her husband, Williamsburg saloon keeper Thomas Vobe, who left debts for her to pay. She bore son David Miller, sired by Scots immigrant Robert Miller, bursar at the College of William & Mary. Her second husband, widower Matthew Moody, Sr., was a competitor in the saloon business.

At Capital Landing, in 1764, Jane leased acreage for grazing the mounts of her clientele, selling lottery tickets, and posting broadsides and prints of Roman ruins. Perhaps for ethical reasons, she encouraged the religious conversion of four of her slaves at Bruton Parish church. Comments about her refined service in 1765 east of the Capitol on Waller Street preceded her separation from Moody five years later. Because of her location next to the theater, she appealed to the elite in May 1768 by selling tickets to the Virginia Comedians Company's performance of Irish playwright George Farquhar's *The Constant Couple; or A Trip to the Jubilee.* On February 16, 772, she sold her property to competitor Christiana Campbell and relocated the King's Arms Tavern to a two-story house on West Duke of Gloucester Street across from the Raleigh Tavern. In private rooms, George Washington, Thomas Jefferson, Patrick Henry, members of the House of Burgesses, and Baron Friedrich von Steuben, the Prussian inspector general of the Continental Army, met to debate the political climate or talk business with ship captains, businessmen, and attorneys.

At the height of the tavern's appeal, Jane increased the staff from three to thirteen, including Scots barman William Duncan. Matthew's death on June 8, 1775, made her a widow a second time. In 1776, Jane's son served the Continental Army as a lieutenant and gained parole from a prisoner of war camp at Haddrell's Point (modern Mount Pleasant, South Carolina) to take a job with Jane. She sponsored two slave children at the Bray School for freedmen to learn literacy, etiquette, and Anglican catechism. When Virginia's burgesses chose Richmond as its new capital on December 24, 1779, the Williamsburg economy faded. Jane and David relocated operations to Osborne Landing, a public ferry depot on the James River.

In December 1785, Jane spent the last year of her half century of innkeeping at Manchester (modern South Richmond) while David began his own establishment. At her death at age eighty-three, she left her property to David, who, in 1793, manumitted Jane's protégé, Baptist preacher Gowan Pamphlet, the nation's first ordained black minister. David continued in Jane's profession and dealt in slave sales at Water's Storehouse.

*See also* Christiana Campbell.

### *Sources*

Meacham, Sarah Hand. *Every Home a Distillery: Alcohol, Gender, and Technology in the Colonial Chesapeake.* Baltimore, MD: The Johns Hopkins University Press, 2009.

Sturtz, Linda L. *Within Her Power: Propertied Women in Colonial Virginia. New York*: Routledge, 2002.

## Lucy Mouse Tondee (1733–1785)
**Taverner**
**Savannah, Georgia**

Lucy Mouse Tondee, a barkeep in Savannah Georgia, supported the conspiracies of the Council of Safety and the Sons of Liberty against the British. An Englishwoman born the last of five girls to midwife Lucy Mouse and clogmaker Thomas Mouse, Huguenot refugees from Châtillon-sur-Loire, she and sister Mary arrived in Georgia in infancy after setting sail on the *James* on September 28, 1733. At Modena plantation on Skidaway Island south of the Wilmington River, the family cultivated ten acres. They operated a pub and way station for passengers traveling south until Indians burned the residence. The parents moved inland to Savannah to work at midwifery and as custodian of the Bethesda House of Mercy, America's first orphanage, where Lucy lived from age six until her indenturing in September 1745.

In 1751, Lucy married Gallo-Swiss carpenter Peter Tondee, Jr., a fellow orphan and father of their five daughters and two sons. A Mason and master builder, he helped construct the two-story brick Courts of Province on Wright Square, Christ Church Episcopal on Bull Street, and a silk factory on Reynolds Square and served the port as lumber inspector. In 1761 the couple opened Tondee's Tavern at the northwestern corner of Broughton and Whitacker streets and hosted Masonic lodges, Irish Catholics from the Society of St. Patrick, and thirty members of the Sons of Liberty during local furor over the Stamp Act. He repaired the courthouse in 1773 and worked as a messenger of the Georgia Assembly, a job that paid £25 (approx. $4,843.36) annually and placed him in intimate contact with government news.

In July 1774, the closing of Boston harbor motivated a patriot rally at Tondee's Tavern that included George Walton, a founding father and signer of the Declaration of Independence. Nine months after the Boston Tea Party, the pub hosted planners of opposition to the punitive Intolerable Acts. In spite of a ban by Governor James Wright on meetings to air grievances, Peter guarded the entrance from intruders while members elected delegates to the Continental Congress. On August 10, 1774, the Sons claimed citizens' rights and posted their charge to other colonies that Parliament had taxed American subjects illegally. To back Boston patriots, Savannah's Sons sent help. The *Essex Journal* of Newburyport, Massachusetts, reported by way of letters from Georgia on the stout challenge of Savannah's Sons of Liberty to English rule.

On May 11, 1775, Peter abetted theft of a twelve hundred pounds of gunpowder from the royal magazine for transporting to Boston. Patriots used the explosive at the Battle of Bunker Hill. On June 5, 1775, the official birthday of George III, Savannah's liberty boys raised the colony's first liberty pole and flag and fired thirteen guns from the Bay Street battery while raising thirty toasts. The defiers hoisted arms with fixed bayonets and marched from Tondee's Tavern through Savannah. Headquartering at the pub, the Sons captured British weapons, persecuted monarchists, and halted trade in British goods. On July 4, 1775, the rebels voted to break ties with Britain.

At Peter's sudden death from fever in October 1775, Lucy operated the pub. At the height of the American Revolution, she continued serving ale, scheduling weddings, and arranging gatherings of the All Saints Quoits Club, a disguise for the secretive Sons. She accepted £15 (approx. $3,048.64) in payment for the clandestine use of her long room by fomenters of revolt and the creators of Georgia's first state government. At the pub in 1776, Georgians heard a first reading of the Declaration of Independence.

In March–April 1776, the *Connecticut Journal* and the *Massachusetts Spy* reported a clash between four hundred British sailors and the Georgia Sons of Liberty. Fortunately, a thousand Charlestonians intervened for the patriots. On June 6, 1781, Lucy opened the long room for a sale of cashmere, thread, damask tablecloths, toweling, port wine, soap, candles, window panes, and brandy kegs. The provincial congress reconvened to celebrate the Treaty of Paris and continued to meet in Lucy's establishment until her death in 1785. After the tavern burned in the Great Savannah Fire of November 26, 1796, Colonial Dames of America marked the state's "cradle of liberty" with a plaque.

### *Sources*

Colquitt, Dolores Boisfeuillet. "Peter Tondee the Carpenter," *Georgia Historical Quarterly* 10:4 (December 1926): 302–316.

Weeks, Carl. "Peter Tondee," *New Georgia Encyclopedia*, www.georgiaencyclopedia. org/articles/history-archaeology/peter-tondee-ca-1723–1775/, 2018.

## Elizabeth Maxwell Steele (1733–November 22, 1790)
**Taverner, Real Estate Broker**
**Salisbury, North Carolina**

A supporter of the Whig cause, Elizabeth Maxwell Gillespie Steele hosted at her tavern the instigators of rebellion against an English king. A Scot born in Pennsylvania to immigrant parents, she and her brother James moved with them in childhood to Rowan County, North Carolina. She gained an introduction to saloon operation after marrying tavern owner Robert Gillespie of Delaware on November 6, 1753. The job called for relaying mail, stocking a general mercantile, hosting group meetings, and offering rooms for the night to such historical figures as Daniel Boone and the Regulators, Carolina backwoodsmen who challenged colonial authority. She was rearing Robert Jr. and Margaret on February 27, 1760, when Cherokee warriors scalped and murdered her husband at the siege of Fort Dobbs on the Dan River.

As a single mother, Elizabeth continued operating her tavern with the help of son Robert. She wed innkeeper and realty broker William Steele, father of son John, and was again widowed in 1776. In letters to brother-in-law Ephraim Steele in Pennsylvania, Elizabeth filled in the peril of North Carolina from the Revolutionary War. She described the raid of General Charles Cornwallis, which occurred while she was nursing the family through the smallpox that killed her granddaughter. The plundering of her tavern cost her liquor, provisions, forage, and herd animals. The British blockade at Fort Moultrie limited the flow of supplies.

When General Nathanael Greene reached Elizabeth's establishment on February 2, 1781, his need for support won her heart. She retrieved a bag of coins she had saved and led him to a cache of seventeen hundred weapons belonging to the local militia. With adequate cash and guns, Greene made a strong showing on March 15, 1781, at the battle of Guilford Court House that cost the British more killed and wounded than the patriots incurred. Cornwallis swung to the southeast and sought British assistance at Wilmington. At Elizabeth's death in 1791, the Fayetteville *Gazette* extolled her as a friend to the nation.

### *Source*

Smith, Margaret Supplee, and Emily Herring Wilson. *North Carolina Women Making History.* Chapel Hill: University of North Carolina Press, 1999.

## Anne Pogue McGinty (1735–November 11, 1815)
**Taverner, Textile Designer, Miller**
**Harrodsburg, Kentucky**

A vigorous, valiant frontierswoman from Ireland, Anne Kennedy Wilson Pogue Lindsay McGinty introduced business firsts in Harrodsburg, Kentucky. She and her eleven siblings claimed Scots ancestry with the Dunlops and Kennedys from sixteenth-century Glasgow. Her immigrant parents, Elizabeth Moffatt of County Antrim and miller Joseph Langdon Kennedy of Ulster, relocated to the Holston River settlement in Augusta County, Virginia. At age twenty-four, Anne married New Jersey militiaman John Wilson, the first of four husbands, and bore daughter Martha, who died at age three. Left childless and widowed, in Augusta, Virginia, on April 17, 1762, she married William Preston Pogue, father of their two sons and five daughters and maker of the first Kentucky plow.

Four months after the birth of daughter Mary "Polly" Pogue, the household joined Daniel Boone's group expedition over the Wilderness Road, traversing the Cumberland Gap with brothers John and Joseph Kennedy and reaching Boonesborough, Kentucky, in September 1775. They added to the train the area's first pigs and chickens and planted corn two miles away at Gore's Spring. Anne loaded her packhorse with the region's first spinning wheel, which she demonstrated to other women.

In February 1776, Anne moved to Fort Harrod (modern Harrodsburg, Kentucky), where William assembled her loom. Living in a two-story blockhouse in the southwest corner of Kentucky's first fort, Anne enjoyed the security and support of other newcomers. She experimented with local grasses and weeds and replaced eastern-style linsey-woolsey with a coarse blend of buffalo hair and nettles. Production of textiles made Anne the fort's clothing supplier. At the death of William on September 7, 1778, from a firefight with Shawnee chief Blackfish at Danford (modern Danville), she reared five older children and one-month-old Amaziah Pogue alone until her union with army storekeeper Colonel Joseph Lindsay on June 18, 1781. Fourteen months later, along with five family members, he died at the battle of Blue Lick, a severe loss to Daniel Boone's settlement.

Anne saw sixteen-year-old son Robert enlist in the military as scout and spy; in 1781, she built a fulling mill powered by a dam at Fort Harrod Spring. In 1787, she dedicated her Harrodsburg home to use as a tavern and inn, which she operated with the aid of three slaves. Her investment in land elevated the family holdings to some £1,900 (approx. $377,363.78).

Anne once more reorganized her household after marriage to James McGinty, a penniless ne'er-do-well who abused her, dominated her tavern, and spent her money. Over a decade of lawsuits, Anne and son Robert negotiated separation papers with the court, which included alimony to James. Widowed a fourth time in 1806, Anne survived on her own terms to age eighty. In autumn 1812, James joined Colonel Robert Pogue in the building of Fort Amanda, Ohio, a supply depot named for Anne's granddaughter, Hannah Amanda Pogue.

### *Sources*

McEuen, Melissa A., and Thomas H. Appleton, Jr. *Kentucky Women, Their Lives and Times.* Athens: University of Georgia Press, 2015.

Sachs, Honor R. "The Myth of the Abandoned Wife," *Ohio Valley History* 3:4 (Winter 2003): 3–20.

## Martha Moore Ballard (February 8, 1735–June 9, 1812)
**Herbalist, pharmacist, healer, midwife, mortician**
**Hallowell, Maine**

The colonial frontier's most prolific diarist, Martha Moore Ballard, a healer and confidant, sufficed as a weaver and trader until she established a mid-life medical practice at Hallowell in Kennebec County, Maine. In a series of ten thousand journal entries, she documented a twenty-seven-year career in the medical arts, which covered parturition, trauma, acute illness, and contagion. She practiced in central Massachusetts before introducing midwifery on the New England frontier. According to Charlotte G. Borst, a professor of history at Union College, and historian Kathleen W. Jones, on staff at Virginia Polytechnic Institute, like other apprentices, Martha networked with "wives, mothers, friends, and neighbors whose domestic duties put them in charge of most local health care" (Borst and Jones, 2005, 23). Daily recounts in longhand and personal abbreviations for deliveries and remuneration structured house calls along with spiritual professions thanking God, the world's great parent, for assistance.

While her vocation flourished in the female economy, the daybook answered Martha's need for an emotional outlet. At the rate of more than thirty births a year, she delivered eight hundred fourteen babies, reaching a height of fifty-nine in 1796. Of the total cases, forty-six presented delivery complications. Total losses included fourteen fetal deaths, twenty infant mortality, and five maternal deaths within two weeks of parturition. Her literary labors in rural Hallowell, Maine, yielded a survey of communal birthing and the rare cases of hemorrhage, convulsion, stillbirth, and postnatal infant death. Notes stressed Martha's relief of patients' symptoms and disapproval of the obstetrical proficiency of Dr. Benjamin Page, who, in June 1798, dislocated the limbs of a stillborn girl during a violent delivery. Her mortuary care from January 1785 to late May 1812 included the losses of Susanna Clayton and her child, whom Martha delivered on August 20, 1787.

During a New England epidemic of scarlet fever, Martha was born one of the ten children of Dorothy Learned and Elijah Moore. She claimed a heritage of physicians that included an uncle, Abijah Moore, brother-in-law Stephen Barton, and a grandniece, Clara Barton, founder of the American Red Cross. A religious upbringing by an illiterate mother influenced

**Ballard-Moore Genealogy**

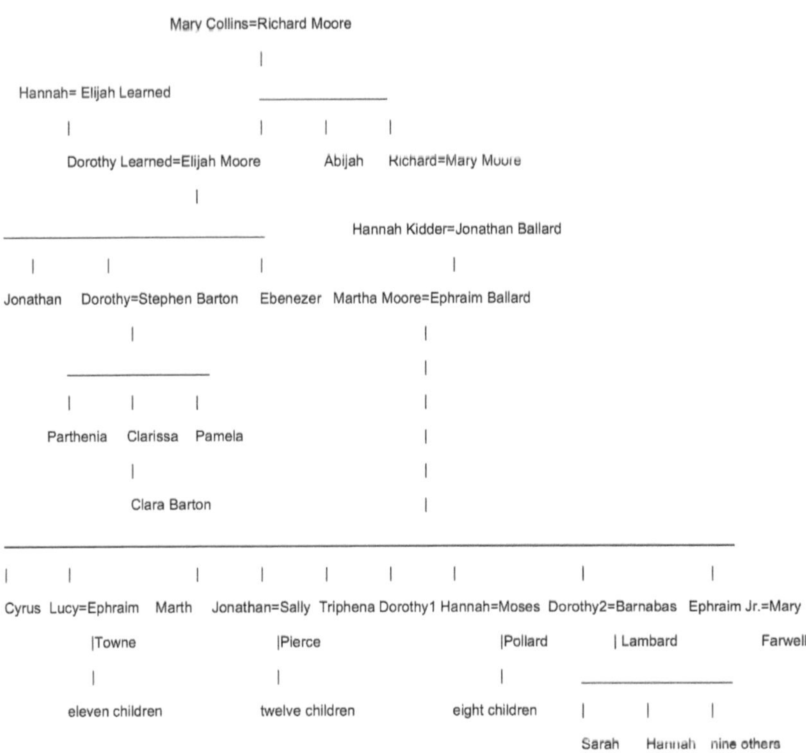

Martha's concerns for the human condition and inspired her to attend church services and pray for the suffering. Her brother Jonathan Moore, a Harvard-trained librarian, entered the ministry.

During the French and Indian War begun in late May 1754, at age nineteen, Martha wed surveyor-cartographer Ephraim Ballard and bore nine children—Cyrus, Lucy, Martha, Jonathan, Triphena, Dorothy1, Hannah, Dorothy2, and Ephraim Jr. In Martha's last trimester of pregnancy with Hannah, three daughters—eight-year-old Martha Jr., four-year-old Triphena, and two-year-old Dorothy1—died during the summer 1769 outbreak of diphtheria. Pestilence killed one hundred forty-four or one out of eight townspeople of Oxford, but spared her sons Jonathan and Cyrus, who recovered.

## The War Years

The March 5, 1770, Boston Massacre heightened fears of a patriot war against the British, whom rebels Samuel Adams and Joseph Warren goaded by initiating the vigilante Sons of Liberty and, in 1772, the Boston Committee of Correspondence. Martha joined her sister, Dorothy Barton, in holding tea parties that violated the house rules of their father, patriot Stephen Barton, who supported the colonial boycott of imported British goods. Within months of the Boston Tea Party in 1773 and assembly of the First Continental Congress the next year, Ephraim inspected land at Fort Halifax in Winslow, Maine, for possible purchase and settlement. He completed the lease in April 1775 and opened a tavern and mill.

When further conflict exacerbated by the battle of Lexington and Concord on April 19, 1775, and the Declaration of Independence on July 4, 1776, the Ballards cut ties with Massachusetts. On October 14, 1777, a week after the colonial victory at Saratoga, New York, the frontier family moved northeast of Portland, Maine, to Kennebec, home to one hundred households. While raising poultry, a cow, and oxen, Martha sowed her garden with beans, carrots, cucumbers, and parsnips and "puked, purged, and bled" the sick (Ibid., 24). In July 1778, she offered her first obstetrical service and curative teas, lotions, and elixirs made with botanicals, fruits, and vegetables from her garden, which she fenced with alder branches from the mill pond. At Jones Mill on Bowman's Brook, while Ephraim served Hallowell's city council, planting and cultivation dominated Martha's efforts from May to July; food harvesting, preservation, and drying herbs required steady labors into October. In between, she traded goods with neighbors.

Before the professionalization of obstetrics and pharmaceuticals, Martha's healthcare career involved birthing white and black babies, hand extraction of placentas, blending medicines, diagnosing such ills as earache and nosebleed, administering treatments, attending and dressing corpses, and court appearances. She identified thirteen fathers of out-of-wedlock babies, a service that saved the district from supporting fatherless children. The August 1787 scarlet fever epidemic placed emotional demands on the healer/mortician. She sat by the dying, wrapped the dead in grave clothes, and witnessed eighty-five autopsies. In whatever weather, she assisted physicians with deliveries, often remaining all night with mother and child. Communal birthing with the aid of relatives and neighbors required bedding on pallets and a celebratory dinner.

As a folk healer, Martha represented women pressing paternity suits and complaints of sexual violence. On July 10–11, 1790, she backed defendant Rebecca Foster in a rape case against a Hallowell dignitary, Colonel Judge Joseph North, and two other men, Elijah Davis and Joshua Burgess. Because of the absence of the Rev. Isaac Foster, Martha wrote in her journal margins that she advised the victim to conceal the triple break-ins and assaults rather than expose herself to scandal about giving birth to a daughter. Martha made the unprecedented river journey to the Pownalborough Courthouse to testify before three male justices. North, facing a possible death sentence, defamed Rebecca's character and hurried out of the district to Boston. Rebecca and her husband suffered vicious public slander and rock throwing before fleeing to New York.

## The Diary

At New Year's 1785, Martha began recording herb growing, home health care, folk veterinary, child deliveries, and postpartum checkups in a 1,400-page diary, two pamphlets of half sheets hand-sewn between linen covers. On April 12, 1788, she reported dipping three hundred thirty-six candles. Problematic spelling by sound—deliriam, closd, enforming, tho, fitts, dilivrd—rather than standard orthography epitomized post–Revolutionary changes, particularly Irish pronunciation. On April 21, 1791, she occupied a new residence on cleared land and faced the reduction of family by four after Jonathan, Dorothy, and Hannah began their own households and Lucy sickened and died.

Work shaped Martha's days while writing gave meaning to her labors on behalf of women. After Mrs. David Pattee (forty-four-year-old Lucy Collins Pattee) succumbed to childbirth on December 8, 1789, Martha noted the twelve children surviving without a mother. A whisper of gossip on June 21, 1792, linked Mrs. Peter Jones with illness caused by spousal abuse. As though confronting the husband, Martha stated in her notes that Peter deserved strict punishment for keeping his barefoot wife in the basement. The collapse of a soap barrel cost her the loss of an essential of nursing tool. In 1799, another move to son Jonathan's Hallowell acreage added miles between sixty-four-year-old Martha and her patients.

Daily domestic chores involved Martha in spinning tow (coarse flax) yarn, combing flax, cleaning wool, making cheese and maple syrup, laundry and ironing, candle-dipping homespun wicks, brewing, bread baking, splitting wood, chinking walls, and wallpapering. Late winter in 1800 found her knitting mitts and seventeen pairs of stockings in twelve weeks. Yard work required planting of plum trees and currant bushes, gathering shelly and string beans and cucumbers, paring apples, and drying squash, red pepper, and peas with help from sons Cyrus and Ephraim. Gardening repeated cycles of planting and harvesting vegetables, saffron, and hops and the extermination of potato bugs. She added to her home-grown stock of homeopathic treatments and stash of pharmaceuticals:

| | |
|---|---|
| agrimony (*Agrimonia eupatoria*) | antiviral, wound care |
| balm (*Melissa officinalis*) | improve sleep and healing of wounds |
| balsam syrup (*Hypericum perforatum*) | soothe sores, burns, mucous membranes |
| basswood (*Tilia americana*) | treat migraine, heartburn, colds, burns |
| buckthorn (*Frangula alnus*) | anti-inflammatory, antimicrobial |
| burdock (*Arctium lappa*) | treat arthritis, diuretic |
| burnet (*Sanguisorba minor*) | coagulant, increase appetite |
| catnip (*Nepeta cataria*) | reduce fever, treat colds |
| chamomile (*Matricaria chamomilla*) | soothe stomach and bowel, insomnia |
| comfrey (*Symphytum officinale*) | treat broken bones and sprains |
| coriander (*Coriandrum sativum*) | treat skin and stomach ills |
| dock root (*Rumex crispus*) | ease swelling and pain in nose and lungs |
| feverfew (*Tanacetum parthenium*) | treat arthritis, headache, fever, toothache |
| hyssop (*Hyssopus officinalis*) | treat indigestion, colds |
| lovage (*Levisticum officinale*) | treat kidney stones, cough, indigestion |
| mandrake (*Mandragora officinarum*) | sedative, emetic |
| mugwort (*Artemisia vulgaris*) | contraception, menstrual irregularity |
| mullein (*Verbascum thapsus*) | soothe lungs, treat asthma and diarrhea |
| mustard (*Brassica nigra*) | treat arthritis, chronic pain, and inflammation |
| parsley (*Petroselinum crispum*) | coagulant, skin and bone health |
| pennyroyal (*Mentha pulegium*) | abortifacient |
| rue (*Ruta graveolens*) | snakebite, abortifacient |
| saffron (*Crocus sativus*) | treat heart disease, depression, anxiety |
| sage (*Salvia officinalis*) | treat menopause and dementia |

| | |
|---|---|
| senna (*Fabaceae caesalpinioideae*) | laxative |
| snakeroot (*Ageratina altissima*) | treat anxiety, malaria, high blood pressure |
| Solomon's seal (*Polygonatum arisanense*) | anti-inflammatory, indigestion |
| sorrel (*Rumex acetosa*) | anti-inflammatory, indigestion, treat ulcers |
| sumac (*Rhus coriaria*) | treat hemorrhoids, wounds, ulcer, stye |
| tansy (*Tanacetum vulgare*) | treat ulcers, migraine, gallbladder |
| wormwood (*Artemisia absinthium*) | treat pain and infection |
| yarrow (*Achillea millefolium*) | treat flatulence and cramps, coagulation |

Herbalists like Martha sorted herbs by leaf and root, seed and flower and dried them in a dark place. She augmented home-grown curatives with additional oils and medicinal compounds from Dr. Daniel Cony and Dr. Samuel Colman, a member of the Massachusetts Medical Society:

| | |
|---|---|
| aloe (*Aloe vera*) | purgative, skin lotion, lip balm |
| anise (*Pimpinella anisum*) | diuretic, carminative |
| camphor (*Ocimum kilimandscharicum*) | lung congestion, muscle pain, fainting |
| castor oil (*Ricinus communis*) | stimulate labor, constipation, chapped skin |
| galbanum (*Ferula gummosa*) | treat flatulence, colds, spasm |
| hartshorn (ammonium carbonate) | treat snakebite and insect stings |
| licorice (*Glycyrrhiza glabra*) | antimicrobial, anti-inflammatory |
| linseed oil (*Linum usitatissimum*) | reduce blood pressure |
| myrrh (*Commiphora myrrha*) | mouthwash, liniment, treat asthma and cough |
| nutmeg (*Myristica fragrans*) | anti-inflammatory |
| paregoric (tinctura *opii camphorata*) | diarrhea, cough |
| spermaceti (*Spermaceti*) | treat colds and gonorrhea, lubricant |
| sweet oil (vegetable oil) | treat ear wax and earache |
| turpentine (*Pinus taeda*) | treat wounds and parasites, inhalant |
| vitriol (caustic) | treat anemia, anesthesia |

Martha's treatments involved blistering, poultices, massage, clisters and emetics, burn ointments, and lancing abscesses. In addition to doctoring dysentery, sore throat, whooping cough, measles, colic, and frostbite, she recorded a separate list of births and her income from deliveries. At a time when male doctors demanded £10 (approx., $1,057.07) per house call, she charged a standard fee of six shillings (approx. $3.17). For payment in kind, she collected a variety of remuneration—store credit, or other forms of remuneration, including shingles, flat irons, yard goods, livestock, snuff, lumber, fish, coffee, sugar, apples, ribbon, a mirror, muslin apron, and silk handkerchief. In one case, she rescinded the fee.

In addition to false labors, in 1793, Martha's practice increased by 29 percent to fifty-three infants, some born within hours of each other. By 1800, she managed two-thirds of the town's deliveries. By 1804, she admitted feeling fatigue and despair from a schedule that could include multiple house calls in one day. For the May 1806, birth of the Chaces' daughter, she received nine shillings, three times her standard fee. "Crysmas Day" brought no rest—only two weeks' worth of laundry. President Thomas Jefferson's December 1807 embargo on European goods caused economic shortfalls in pharmaceuticals. At the lifting of the ban in March 1809, Martha and her neighbors rejoiced in fewer shortages, broader markets, lower prices, and a greater selection of pharmaceuticals.

## On the Road

PBS producer Laurie Kahn-Leavitt surmised that journaling "became a way of sort of shaping an identity, a way of accounting for the worth of one's day, a way for jogging memory" ("Martha Ballard's Diary"). Professional acceptance gave Martha a modicum of independence, a rare pre- and post-revolutionary female life. By candlelight with her quill pen, Martha characterized in elliptical phrasing hard journeys over logs and ruts on foot and by horse, sleigh, carriage, and boat. A canoe took her to the bedside of Old Lady Cony, a stroke victim. The increase in birthing during February and March required day and night travels in waist-deep snow, mud, and floods, causing dunking in water, scrapes, falls, and broken glasses. Ice jams choked the Kennebec River in 1785 and 1789, causing her to break through at Sewall's Eddy and narrowly escape a falling tree. On one night journey, she walked in stocking feet by candlelight. During Ephraim's absence on two surveying missions in 1794, she managed home, garden, and medical career alone. In her seventies, when he received a five-month prison sentence for improper tax collection and her son faced a fraud charge, housework became more burdensome, generating more emotional journal entries as her strength waned. When time allowed, she napped at home.

With the marriage of her youngest, Martha lived alone until her alcoholic son Jonathan brought wife Sally and their brood to reside with her in December 1804. The mass murder of Captain James Purrington's wife and six children in July 1806 and James's suicide required Martha's witnessing the carnage. Only James Jr. survived an axe attack and fled. Her journal stated consternation at "ye most Shocking Scein that was Ever Seen in this part of ye world" (Diary, 9 July 1806). She nursed Martha Purrington after surgery and then washed and wrapped eight bodies for burial in sheets and shifts and remained until nightfall with the corpses in the barn during viewing by one hundred visitors. The next day, she attended the funeral, where Purrington lay alongside the axe and razor he had used to murder his kin. By July 12, the crime had sapped Martha's spirit, but she managed to sell cherries and currants to customers and to prepare and bury Martha Purrington, who died of her wounds.

Martha's semi-literate notes demonstrated the slowing of obstetrical calls, which reached a low of three in 1808. The three-day labor and delivery of daughter Hannah Pollard in May 1809 added an eleven-pound granddaughter to the family. Entries continued until May 7, 1812, six weeks before she died at age seventy-seven. Dorothy "Dolly" Lambard and her daughters Sarah and Hannah continued Martha's journal, which lapsed into loose pages. The writings passed in 1884 to Dr. Mary Fearing Hobart, Martha's great-great-granddaughter, who practiced medicine for thirty years at the New England Hospital for Women and Children of Boston. In 1990, Idaho historian Laurel Thatcher Ulrich popularized Martha's place in women's history with an eight-year project, the documentary *A Midwife's Tale: The Life of Martha Ballard Based on Her Diary, 1785–1812*. Because the text dramatized the hardships faced by single mothers, rape victims, and abused wives and children, it earned a 1991 Pulitzer Prize and filming in 1997 by PBS for the series *The American Experience*.

### *Sources*

Ballard, Martha. *The Diary of Martha Ballard, 1785–1812*. Camden, ME: Picton Press, 1992.
Borst, Charlotte G., and Kathleen W. Jones. "As Patients and Healers: The History of Women and Medicine," *Magazine of History* 19:5 (September 2005): 23–26.
"Martha Ballard's Diary," PBS, www.pbs.org/wgbh/americanexperience/features/midwife-gallery-diary/ (4 March 2023).
Ulrich, Laurel Thatcher. *A Midwife's Tale: The Life of Martha Ballard Based on Her Diary, 1785–1812*. New York: Alfred A. Knopf, 1990.

## Nancy Ward (July 20, 1738–March 30, 1822)
**Innkeeper, Business Planner**
**Benton, Tennessee**

A progressive mediator for the Overhill Cherokee, Nanye'hi "Nancy" Ward guided the Wolf clan toward a peaceful, productive way of life in the Great Smoky Mountains. Her biography is filled with gaps about her maternal grandfather, Moytoy Chota, and her parentage at Chota, Tennessee, by Lame Doe and Fivekiller, a Lenape Delaware. History is sparse about her reliance on a maternal uncle Attakullakulla, a famed bicultural diplomat. She wed Kingfisher at age fourteen and bore Littlefellow Fivekiller and Catherine Ka-Ti Kingfisher.

Combat between the eastern Cherokee and the Muskogee Creek involved Nancy and other native women in preparations for a territorial war. At the 1755 battle of Taliwa at Ball Ground, Georgia, near the Etowah River in north central Georgia, son Kingfisher's death forced her to arm herself with a rifle and take his place in a charge against the enemy. Victory brought her additional tribal esteem for rallying the five hundred Cherokee, who defeated one thousand attackers and seized Creek land.

Nancy's marriage to Irish trader Bryant B. Ward in 1759 increased her value as councilwoman, negotiator, orator, and ambassador to European Americans. After a few years, he reclaimed his white wife, Anna Hawkins Kilgore Ward, at their home in South Carolina, leaving Nancy to rear their daughter Elizabeth "Betsy" Ward. In 1763, British authorities promoted relations with the Cherokee as allies during the French and Indian War. In July 1776, Nancy warned settlers on the Holston River of Attakullakulla and his son, Dragging Canoe, who planned raids on cabins along the Watauga River. The peace treaty of 1777 cost the Cherokee over five million acres of land.

The capture of fifty-year-old Lydia Russell Bean from Richmond, Virginia, in July 1776 introduced Nancy to a white compatriot known as Tennessee's first white settler. Nancy retrieved Lydia from burning at the stake. Lydia taught Nancy dairying, spinning yarn, and loom-weaving, European skills that produced valuable trade items. After serving on a peace commission in July 1781, Nancy demonstrated to native women the agrarian methods of white society, the herding of cattle, and the making of cheese and butter. As a token of respect, Nancy sent Lydia back to Virginia under the protection of her son Fivekiller and her brother Longfellow.

In old age, Nancy retained vigor and strong opinions about Cherokee heritage hunting lands in East Tennessee that whites usurped by the Hiwassee Purchase of February 27, 1819. The treaty left the Indians with only six hundred forty acres. She left Chota, moved south, and settled on the federal route between Georgia and Nashville, Tennessee. Known as Granny Ward, War Woman, and Beloved Woman, she fostered orphans and earned a living at her inn and stockyard at Benton on the Womankiller Ford of the Ocoee River. Together, white and Cherokee admirers raised a stone cairn over her grave.

## *Sources*


McClary, Ben H. "Nancy Ward: The Last Beloved Woman of the Cherokees," *Tennessee Historical Quarterly* 21 (1962): 352–364.

Smith, Margaret Supplee, and Emily Herring Wilson. *North Carolina Women Making History*. Chapel Hill: University of North Carolina Press, 1999.

**Kingfisher Genealogy**

Chief Moytoy Chota

Attakullakulla — Tame Doe=Fivekiller

Dragging Canoe (son of Attakullakulla)

Longfellow — Kingfisher=Nancy=Bryant B. Ward=Anna Hawkins Kilgore (children of Tame Doe=Fivekiller)

Catherine — Littlefellow Fivekiller (children of Kingfisher=Nancy)

Elizabeth (daughter of Nancy=Bryant B. Ward)

## Rebecca Dickinson (July 25, 1738–December 31, 1815)
### Seamstress
### Hatfield, Massachusetts

While working independently as a self-supporting itinerant seamstress, Rebecca "Becca" or "Aunt Beck" Dickinson surveyed in her journal an era of tight social networking from a business perspective. A godly Calvinist and respected artisan from rural Hatfield in western Massachusetts, she claimed a genealogy dating to the tenth-century Norman Bigod dynasty and to Humphrey Barrett, a settler of Concord. She grew up on a fifteen-and-a-half-acre farm within miles of her competitors. Into old age, she occupied the Dickinson house on Main Street, a source of autonomy and security.

In a milieu threatened by multiple Indian attacks, Rebecca anchored her existence among her mother and father, Anna Smith and dairyman Moses Dickinson, younger sisters Anna, Irene, Martha, and Miriam, and clients who welcomed her like family. She claimed as great great grandsire Nathaniel Dickinson, a seventeenth-century pioneer to Hatfield, and bore the name of her paternal grandmother, Rebecca Barrett Wright Dickinson. Her great-grandmother, Martha Leonard Waite of Deerfield, was pregnant with daughter Canada Waite Smith in 1677 when Indians captured her, a birthing story that influenced Rebecca's views on womanhood.

## Learning a Trade

At age twelve, Rebecca and friend Catte Graves of Pittsfield together apprenticed in Deerfield under a mantua maker and learned to make stays. During the French and Indian War, Rebecca guided the apprenticing of niece Rebecca Ballard, Patty Smith of Hadley, Polly Wright of Deerfield, and other Hampshire County girls in cutting, sewing, and refashioning wardrobes and superintended Patty's needlework on a mourning gown. A surviving head cloth and bed hangings completed in 1765 depict Rebecca's imaginative blend of fantasy crewelwork flowers, vines, and leaves.

Still residing with her parents in 1774, Rebecca lived on the Connecticut River in a New England saltbox opposite the town meeting hall and philosophized on the human need for companionship. She rejected a widowed suitor, Charles Phelps, in winter 1777. After reencountering suitor Dr. Moses Gunn of Montague, she remained single while earning a living sewing custom gowns for women as far away as Amherst, Conway, Hadley, and Northampton. She completed a maid of honor dress and the wedding gown of farm wife Elizabeth Porter Phelps, mistress of Forty Acres Estate, and a gown for Betsy Huntington that survived until 1788. From merchant Oliver Smith, she purchased on credit callimanco, a thin worsted wool, and cambleteen, a wool and cotton fabric blended with goat's hair.

Rebecca's struggle with maidenhood paralleled the American Revolution. For repair of her sewing equipment, she made infrequent calls on blacksmith Jesse Billings, a former suitor long married to her cousin Sarah Bardwell. In the presence of a rival, she choked back regret and disappointment. Of the pensive, vulnerable female life, her memorandum compared womanly solitude to a bough shorn of branches, a lonely fish, cat, and sparrow that frightened other townswomen with their austerity. She contrasted a spinsterhood "lonesome as Death" to the busy engagement of housewives with children (Miller, 2013). The deaths of sister Irene Dickinson Fuller, infant niece Ruth Billings, and friends Elizabeth Alver and Lucretia Williams deepened Rebecca's isolation, which she relieved by nurturing nieces Anne Billings and Rebecca Ballard and nephews Charles Dickinson and Moses Billings.

## Telling Her Story

In summer 1787, Rebecca pondered suicide. She burned the original journal and began a new one that replaced youthful materialism with spiritual fervor. Sundays after church from July 22, 1787, to August 1802, she filled a foolscap writing book with five hundred personal meditations about spiritual need and age. In 1789, she remarked on end-of-war shortages of bread and a threatened grain harvest. She often mused on male/female pairings, such as the death of jailbird Chester Williams and the four illicit pregnancies of Vici Quiner, for whom Rebecca made maternity clothes.

Rebecca relied on a small bequest of seventy acres of rental land in Williamsburg worth $840 (approx. $29,478.53). A planned move seventy miles north to the house of sister Martha Dickinson Billings in Bennington, Vermont, on September 10, 1788, ended in late autumn with a return home because of her brother-in-law Silas's illness. During a period of financial instability, Rebecca returned to Bennington in winter 1791 for a short stay. A year later, her mother suffered severe illness and broke Rebecca's glasses, an essential for close needlework. In 1793, debt stalked Martha's family.

## Reduced Circumstance

From age and cyclical colic, Rebecca managed a smaller range of clientele and dwindling credit. For insight, as the nation reformed from colony to independence, she studied the situations of patrons during her home fittings and accepted the mixed blessings of living alone and unencumbered. She concluded in her diary, "Too is better than one for if one fall the other can lift him up but i must act my Part alone" (*Ibid.*). In August 1795, she moved to the home of a sister, Miriam Dickinson, wife of Silas Billings, and anticipated company for meals at Silas's tavern.

Rebecca's last years bore out the predictions in her journal. In 1806, a walk from a home visit in Amherst left her stranded in the rain and dependent on Elizabeth Phelps for an overnight stay. Following Silas's death in June 1808, she relocated to Hannah Dickinson and Roswell Billings's residence on Bennington's Mill Lane. After nine months rehabilitating a hip impaired by a fall, she died of flu at age seventy-seven. She willed to niece Anna Davenport a bed and blue quilt.

### *Sources*

Clark, Christopher. *The Roots of Rural Capitalism*. Ithaca, NY: Cornell University Press, 1990.

Miller, Maria R. *Rebecca Dickinson: Independence for a New England Woman*. Boulder, CO: Westview Press, 2013.

Sprigg, June. *Domestick Beings. New York*: Knopf, 1984.

## Ann Matthews Floyd Jessop (October 10, 1738–September 26, 1822)
**Minister, Missionary, Horticulturist**
**New Garden, North Carolina**

The unusually wealthy Quaker, widow Mary Ann Matthews Floyd Jessop, preached to the Society of Friends in Piedmont North Carolina and built a business in seeds and fruit tree grafts. A Pennsylvanian born at York to Mary E. Mendenhall and Walter Matthews, she wed John Floyd in 1758 and produced daughter Elizabeth. In widowhood, Ann married an immigrant widower, Yorkshireman Thomas Jessop, in 1766 and united their nine children. In a log dwelling on Brush Creek near the Great Salisbury Road, Ann reared daughter Elizabeth Floyd along with stepchildren and four children sired by Thomas.

Ann entered the ministry in 1765. Her selflessness took the form of medic to the eighteen hundred forty wounded at the March 15, 1781, battle of Guilford Courthouse, which was fought on the Jessop farm. General Nathanael Greene's army killed one-quarter of the men under British general Charles Cornwallis. Local Quakers tended one hundred eighty casualties from both sides at their homes and in the emergency hospital at the New Garden Meeting House and dug graves for the dead. At Thomas's death in 1783, Ann inherited his plantation along with a horse named Dick, cattle, and sheep and half of his profits. Her stepdaughter, Sarah Jessop, received only five shillings (approx. $47.61), a comeuppance from Thomas out of disapproval that she loved a British soldier.

Ann drove her family by Conestoga wagon to York, Pennsylvania, and routed an itinerant ministry between York and New Garden, North Carolina. Her travels extended to Virginia, Massachusetts, Ohio, Pennsylvania, New Jersey, Maryland, New York, Indiana, Vermont, and, with Englishwoman Hannah Stephenson, Great Britain. In Glasgow, Scotland, Ann reunited with Sarah and Scots son-in-law James MacQueen. She collected grass and English millet (alfalfa) seeds, grapevine cuttings, vegetable stock, and grafts of pears, grapes, and eighteen apple varieties:

| | | | |
|---|---|---|---|
| Father Abraham | French Pippin | Golden Russet | Jannette (Neverfail) |
| Leathercoat | Limbertwig | Pearwarden | Red Pippin |
| Red Romantic | Red Winter Pearmain | Russet | Speckled Pearmain |
| Striped Horse | Striped Pippin | Vandiver | White Winter Pepper |
| White Winter Permian | Yellow Summer Pippin | | |

She educated buyers on the qualities that suited their needs—Father Abraham for a late medium-sized fruit good for cider, Red Romantic and Jannette for tree disease resistance, Pearwardens for baking, Yellow Summer

Pippin for low acid, and the Dutch Vandiver, a crisp, juicy red or green fruit with yellow flesh. The leathercoat and russet, a greenish-brown dessert fruit with rough patches, offered sweet aroma for sauce, jelly, applejack, and fermented cider that balanced acidity, sweetness, and tannin. One early producer, the Speckled Pearmain, yielded a strawberry flavor that had to be eaten fresh rather than stored; an English heritage fruit, the Yellow Summer Pippin smelled and tasted like pineapple. A variant, the Red Winter Pearmain, stored well after gathering in early fall. Cider makers favored the Golden Russet for its tannic balance. Southern orchardists chose the White Winter Permian, a heritage fruit with creamy flesh that eventually flourished in southern California, and the Limbertwig, a classic Appalachian pie and cobbler apple. For heirloom fruit, the White Winter Permian provided a mild tartness that first delighted the English in 1200 AD. By selecting numerous grafts, orchardists could extend the growing season and add texture, flavor, and fragrance to cooked apples and dried apple pies.

As the American Revolution came to an end on September 3, 1783, Ann employed son-in-law Abidjah Pinson to plant an orchard. Her grafted varieties influenced pioneer planting west of the Mississippi in the Middle Atlantic states and earned her the name Annie Appleseed. In colonial food writer Amelia Simmons's *American Cookery,* text on fruit promoted apple trees for easy grafting of as many as fourteen varieties per tree. Pomology interests passed to son Jonathan, who started a nursery at Springwood Farms in York to propagate the York Imperial apple. In 1817, Ann retired to the home of daughter Hannah Willis in Highland County, Ohio. After planting the last fruit cuttings from her saddlebags, she died at age eighty-four. Jonathan's granddaughters inherited the family flair for horticulture and planted apricot orchards in California.

*See also* Amelia Simmons.

### *Sources*

Humphreys, Hannah. *The Ghost Orchard.* Toronto: HarperCollins, 2017.
Smith, Margaret Supplee, and Emily Herring Wilson. *North Carolina Women Making History.* Chapel Hill: University of North Carolina Press, 1999.

## Rebecca Bryan Boone (January 9, 1739–March 18, 1813)

## Rebecca Boone Goe (May 26, 1768–July 14, 1805)

**Merchant, Cook**
**Farmington, North Carolina; Limestone, Kentucky**

A peripatetic frontierswoman, Rebecca Ann Bryan Boone's industry provided for an extended family during the lengthy hunting and trapping expeditions of husband Daniel. The daughter of Quaker parents Hester Hampton and Joseph H. Bryan, she and sister Martha spent their first decade near Winchester, Virginia. At Hester's death, they lived with their paternal grandparents, Welshman Morgan Bryan and Martha Strode Bryan, until the family's move in autumn 1748 over the Great Wagon Road to Bryan's Settlement in North Carolina's Yadkin River Valley. After a two-year betrothal to Daniel Boone of Berks County, Pennsylvania, she married him on August 14, 1756.

Near Farmington, North Carolina, Rebecca began marketing produce and homemade maple sugar from their log house on Sugartree Creek while Daniel hired out as a teamster and served in the militia. For £50 (approx. $9,652.85), they purchased six hundred forty acres from Squire and Sarah Morgan Boone near Mocksville, North Carolina. With daughter Susanna, sons James and Israel, and nephew Jesse and Jonathan Boone, Rebecca managed a family of eighteen, who relocated with her to Wilkes County.

## The Backcountry

In 1773, the household and settlers under Daniel's leadership made their way through the Kentucky wilderness on the Clinch River. The hardships cost her sixteen-year-old son James to Shawnee attack and newborn William Boone and added to Rebecca's family Uncle James's six children. After the company blazed a trail through the Cumberland Gap, in spring 1775, she occupied a cabin inside Fort Boone, becoming the first female settler of Kentucky. Her domestic life required drying pelts, spinning yarn, dyeing fabric with natural juices, and making clothes. Daniel's captivity from February–June 1778 by Chillicothe Shawnee war chief Blackfish led her to believe her husband was dead.

On return to North Carolina, Rebecca reunited with Daniel and followed him once more to Boone Station (modern Athens), Kentucky, where she bore Nathan, her tenth and last child. A maple grove gave her a source of ready cash from the sale of sugar, a rare frontier luxury that she boiled over an open fire. In 1781, she occupied a double cabin in a household of twenty people. Near the end of the American Revolution, she lost twenty-three-year-old son Israel on August 19, 1782, to the battle of Blue Licks, a victory for loyalists who killed sixty Kentuckians.

## Commercial Ventures

Another move took the clan to Limestone (modern Maysville), Kentucky, where the couple built a ferry and landing for flatboats on the Ohio

River. Rebecca, twenty-four-year-old daughter Rebecca Boone Goe, and seven slaves operated a general store and tavern kitchen on Front Street while Daniel surveyed land and gathered medicinal ginseng (*Panax ginseng*) for export. When he traded by boat, she went along as cook. Government pricing set the cost of whiskey, rum, meals, and stabling per night. More family relocations to Charleston, West Virginia, in 1788 and Point Pleasant the next year to open a general store and fur trading post at the confluence of the Kanawha and Ohio rivers preceded a return to Kentucky.

In 1799, Rebecca and Daniel began a four-year residency at a stone house in Alta Louisiana (currently Missouri) while he served as magistrate in Spanish territory. Because joint pain limited his marksmanship, Rebecca continued to hunt game and sell hundreds of pounds of maple sugar. At age seventy-four, she died at Femme Osage, Missouri, in March 1813, leaving Daniel a widower for seven years. In 1937, a flood on the Ohio River destroyed their tavern.

### *Sources*

Hammon, Neal O. *My Father, Daniel Boone: The Draper Interviews with Nathan Boone.* Lexington: University Press of Kentucky, 2013.
Wall, James W., Flossie Martin, and Howell Boone. *The Squire, Daniel, and John Boone Families in Davie County, North Carolina.* Mocksville, NC: Davie Printing, 1982.

## Duchess Quamino (1739–June 29, 1804)
**Baker, Caterer**
**Newport, Rhode Island**

A Rhode Island cook and caterer, Charity Duchess Channing Quamino earned renown for her frosted plum cake. A native of Senegal or Gold Coast (modern Ghana), she claimed royal West African heritage. As a preteen, she was kidnapped and crossed the Middle Passage aboard the vessel *Elizabeth* to Newport, Rhode Island, a transatlantic slave depot. At a two-story manse on School Street near Newport's Bowen's Wharf, she served as cook and nanny for Lucy Ellery and William Channing, the colony's attorney general.

After converting to Congregationalism, at age thirty, Duchess married John Quamino of Anomabu, Gold Coast, an Akan bondsman of Benjamin Church, a physician and member of the Sons of Liberty. Of Duchess and John's four children, Charles, Cynthia, Katharine, and Violet, only Charles Channing survived. In 1773, John won the town lottery and purchased his freedom. Duchess remained in Rhode Island while John studied at the College of New Jersey (modern Princeton). Until the outbreak of the American Revolution in April 1775, he intended to travel to Guinea (modern Liberia) as a missionary for the Society of London.

To save money to buy his family's freedom, John volunteered as a privateer during the American Revolution and died in a sea battle in August 1779, two months before the birth of daughter Katharine Quamino. Duchess gained her liberty from the Channings in 1780 before Rhode Island abolished bondage four years later. She worked for wages and launched a catering business from their residence. Serving customers required delivering spiced fruit cakes, once to the home of Martha Custis Washington for George's birthday.

By 1792, Duchess had gained respect of a local businesswoman and of the Channings, whom she invited for tea. At William's death in 1793, she took her grandson for a last glimpse of his father. At her death at age sixty-five, the funeral drew a throng of mourners. Unitarian pastor William Ellery Channing, whom she had cared for since his birth in April 1780, credited her for inspiring his abolitionism. He inscribed on her headstone a salute to her affection, industry, and spirituality. Rhode Island's colonial "pastry queen" lies buried at Farewell and Warner streets near the resting place of daughter Violet Channing.

### *Sources*

Channing, George Gibbs. *Early Recollections of Newport, R.I.* Newport, RI: Ward & Hammett, Jr., 1868.

Kass, Amalie M. *Midwifery and Medicine in Boston: Walter Channing, M.D., 1786–1876.* Boston: Northeastern University Press, 2019.

## Nancy Hallam (ca. 1740–after 1773)
**Actor, Singer**
**Annapolis, Maryland; Williamsburg, Virginia**

A pioneer singer and celebrity theater performer in colonial America, Nancy Hallam contributed song, dance, and elocution to the Hallam-Douglass dynasty of stage stars. The daughter of William Hallam, founder Lewis Sr.'s brother, she displayed the stage interests shared by her cousins Adam, Lewis Jr., Isabella, and Helen Hallam. At age twenty, Nancy joined the Old American Company as a child actor.

Hallam's troupe initiated American stagecraft in Williamsburg, Virginia, and toured the colonial East Coast. She returned to her native England to develop an operatic voice with vocal training by English composer Thomas Arne. By 1759, she gained experience in breeches parts, a popular trend toward theatrical cross-dressing. In 1761, she made a breakthrough when she began replacing her aunt, leading lady Sarah Rich Hallam Douglass, in prominent roles.

When producer David Douglass began seeking new talent, in 1765, he chose Nancy, who settled into Shakespearean and popular British parts in colonial theaters. She sang a concert to organ accompaniment on November 13, 1765, at Charleston's St. Philip's Church and made a hit with audiences in New York in May 1769 as Juliet Capulet, Romeo's young wife killed by stabbing. Her libretto enlivened with energy and wit George Colman, Sr.'s farce *The Musical Lady,* which ridicules Italian affectations. On June 16, 1770, she starred as naive Polly Peachum in Philadelphia in John Gay's satiric ballad musical *The Beggar's Opera,* attended by George Washington and Thomas Jefferson. On June 20, 1770, she entertained Williamsburg audiences with the title role in Thomas Arne's pastoral opera *Thomas and Sally; or, the Sailor's Return.*

At the New Theatre in Annapolis, Maryland, in September 1771, Nancy developed her largest following of fans for the breeches role Imogen-Fidele in Shakespeare's *Cymbeline* and as a wronged rural virgin in Robert Dodsley's ballad *The King and the Miller of Mansfield.* The subject of an oil painting in Turkish harem pants, feathered turban, and saber by Philadelphia portraitist Charles Willson Peale, the stage sensation at the West Street Theatre in Annapolis received raves from the *Maryland Gazette.*

In Williamsburg on May 1, 1771, Nancy sang the part of the soubrette Rosetta in Thomas Arne's comic opera *Love in a Village* and the singer Lucinda in Samuel Foote's farce *The Buck: or, The Englishman in Paris,* which contained five demanding arias. On May 28, 1771, at the theater in Fredericksburg, Virginia, she sang the role of the rebel Lady Townly in Colley Cibber's comedy *The Provoked Husband,* a popular work that went through numerous revivals. Her hour as glamour girl waned near the end of the Revolutionary War. In 1798, a schooner bore her name.

*See also* Sarah Hallam Douglass.

## Sources

Brockett, Oscar G. *History of the Theatre.* Boston: Allyn & Bacon, 1968.

Johnson, Odai. *The Colonial American Stage, 1665–1774: A Documentary Calendar.* Cranbury, NJ: Associated University Presses, 2001.

Roberts, Vera Lowry. *On Stage: A History of Theatre. New York*: Harper & Row, 1962.

## Molly Ockett (spring 1740–August 2, 1816)
### Healer, Basket Weaver, Storyteller
### Fryeburg, Maine

A Native American artisan and healer, Molly Ockett earned her living while residing among white settlers of southern Maine. Her people, the Pequawket Abenaki, occupied heritage land on the Maine–New

Hampshire boundary. During an annual tribal migration to Massachusetts Bay, she was born around 1740 in the lumber center of Saco Falls, Maine. Her father may have been Paugus, Saquant, or Weranmanhead, chiefs in the White Mountain wilderness. War with French Canadians and New England Protestants and bounties on scalps forced the Indians west from their longhouses to the Connecticut River and north to the St. Francis mission at Odanak in southern Quebec. The Abenaki chose the English side and learned English and Methodist catechism.

Much of Molly's itinerant life is legendary, beginning with her birth name Singing Bird. After her Catholic baptism under the name Marie Agathe, the Abenaki pronunciation reduced it to Molly Ockett or Occut. She established ritual habits of worship and confession and rewarded the poor with cash. Her family came under government supervision in June 1744. Dressed in long tunic and leggings, she traveled to Fort Richmond on the Kennebec River by sloop in spring 1750. At age nineteen, she survived Major Robert Rogers's raid and arson on the St. Lawrence River Valley by hiding in brush. The onslaught killed her parents.

As English insurgents forced out the French, the Abenaki retreated to bark wigwams at Sudbury (modern Bethel, Maine). They planted corn on fertile coastal plains and traded furs for cash. Molly wed Abenaki hunter Piol Susup and, in 1764, bore daughter Molly Susup. With second husband Jean Baptiste Sabattis of Quebec, she produced daughter Hannah Susup Peirpole and sons Apom, John, and Paseel. She had to fight Jean's first wife, Marie-Cecile Sabattis, on Fish Street in Fryeburg to requite his crime of bigamy. Molly's peripatetic travels gave her name to mountains, rocks, caves, creeks, and brooks.

Molly gained respect for rearing Molly, reciting native history, cursing thieves, dyeing fiber, and crafting baskets, bark boxes, pottery, and leather moccasins. Outside Sudbury, she abandoned Jean and joined Captain Swassin's village on Umbagog Lake. Molly compromised her mother's reputation by bearing a fatherless child, Molly Peol, and marrying a fractious Penobscot who abandoned the family. The mother regained esteem for rescuing a Boston militiaman from a planned Indian assault, New England's last Indian foray. He rewarded her by inviting her to spend several years with his family in Boston to study European medicine.

To treat the sick in Andover, Fryeburg, Paris Hill, Poland, and Sudbury, Molly Ockett gathered healing roots, bark, herbs, and wild bloodroot (*Sanguinaria canadensis*) for poultices, ointment, and potions, including root beer. In spring 1772, to please Chief Swanson, for two months, she treated a knife wound in rum dealer Henry Tufts. With the antiseptic inner bark of spruce (*Picea sitchensis*), she cured children during a dysentery epidemic. One of her infant patients, Hannibal Hamlin, became a U.S. vice president under Abraham Lincoln. In July 1790, she delivered Ezekiel and Sarah Merrill's babe, Susan, the first white child born at Andover. Under care of Andover authorities, in spring 1816, Molly sickened and requested a traditional sequestering camp, where she died on August 2 at age seventy-six.

### *Source*

"Molly Ockett and Her World," https://bethelhistorical.org/catalog/exhibits/show/mollyockett/introduction, 2024.

## Clementina Rind (1740–September 25, 1774)
**Printer, Publisher, Editor**
**Williamsburg, Virginia**

One of the many colonial widows left to support a family, Clementina Jane Grierson Rind mastered the dual role of Virginia's printer and issuer of the weekly *Virginia Gazette*. Tentatively identified as residents of Curzon Street, in March 1756, she and her father, radical Methodist minister John Grierson, were transported from London to Annapolis on the ship *Greyhound* for the minister's denunciation of parliamentary marriage laws at his underground nuptial chapel.

During the nine-week voyage, fever killed John and felled Clementina, weakening her health. She survived and sold her shoes, hats, and toys from a New York address. She wed Scots-American printer William Rind of Annapolis, Maryland, a co-producer of the *Maryland Gazette*. In winter 1765, her third year of marriage, she settled with her husband and first child, William Alexander Rind, at a two-story brick house on Main Street in Williamsburg, where she bore five more children—John Grierson, Charles, Sarah, James, and Maria—while learning the printer's trade.

### Serving the Rebellion

Anti-monarchists, notably George Washington and Thomas Jefferson, promoting their opposition to the Stamp Act of March 22, 1765, chose William to publish a free Williamsburg paper. At a time of rising paper costs, Virginia dissidents defied the tax on newspapers, almanacs, pamphlets and broadsides, legal documents, dice, and playing cards. For seven years, William prospered by issuing government proclamations, laws and resolutions of the House of Burgesses, documents, and non-partisan news, begun on May 16, 1766.

At William's death on August 19, 1773, shortly after the birth of daughter Maria A. Rind, Clementina inherited two presses, four fonts, and printing equipment worth £272 (approx. $52,695.73). With finesse and humility, the new editor introduced herself to readers. She collaborated with mayor John Blair to pay William's debts and demanded cash payment for advertisements at the rate of three shillings for a first run and two shillings (approx. $29.06 and $19.37) for subsequent ads.

At a brick office on Duke of Gloucester Street, Clementina, her brother-in-law John Pinkney, and a slave named Dick began publishing the obituaries, shipping news, opinions, crimes, acrostics, essays, and verse and backed patriots in their demand for independence. She reported educational opportunities at the College of William and Mary and remarked on the Sons of Liberty's tossing of tea from the *Dartmouth* into Boston harbor on December 16, 1773. In February, she reported a lack of mail from the north. By April 1774, she could afford new fonts from London, with which she reported Parliament's closure of Boston harbor and a proposed public day of fasting and prayer in May. As the public storm worsened, her diction isolated England's unwarrantable infringements and infamous despotism in Parliament's "h_____e of c_____s." Within the month, the House of Burgesses acknowledged her government position as public printer.

## An Ambitious Beginning

Clementina petitioned successfully for the government forms concession, which paid £450 (approx. $86,875.62) annually. In June 1774, she announced formation of Maryland's committee of correspondence and, in November, a protest of Britain's assaults on constitutional rights via the tea tax. Out of fairness to the public, her masthead declared, "Open to ALL PARTIES, but influenced by NONE." She rejected anonymous submissions.

Clementina's contract jobs provided extra income, particularly Jefferson's pamphlet *A Summary View of the Rights of British America,* a forerunner of the Declaration of Independence, issued on August 8, 1774. As a prompt to Virginia delegates to the August Continental Congress in Philadelphia, the text was risky to author and publisher for its criticism of George III. As a sideline, she took in a boarder and stocked books, religious tracts, and almanacs.

While revolt continued to seethe at an energetic tempo, Clementina incurred a month-long bout of consumption and died at age thirty-four on September 25, 1774. To support the orphaned Rinds, John Pinkney accepted the role of substitute publisher. William Alexander Rind followed his parents' profession as a printer in Nova Scotia at Charlottesville on Prince Edward Island. He named his first daughter for Clementina.

The family profession passed to youngest son John Rind and grandson Samuel.

## *Sources*

Copeland, David A. *Debating the Issues in Colonial Newspapers. New York*: Bloomsbury, 2000.
Kierner, Cynthia, and Sandra Gioia Treadway, eds. *Virginia Women: Their Lives and Times.* Athens: University of Georgia Press, 2015.
Papenfuse, Edward C. "History from the Bottom Up," www.rememberingbaltimore.net/2020/02/history-from-bottom-up-clementina.html (11 February 2020).

## Mary Wilkinson Crouch (September 15, 1740–March 22, 1818)
**Printer, Editor**
**Charleston, South Carolina**

A native Rhode Islander from Smithfield, Mary Ann Wilkinson Crouch adapted from widow and single mother to pro-patriot editor and South Carolina publisher at the height of the American Revolution. At her marriage in 1763 to journeyman Charles Crouch, a controversial protégé of newspaperman Peter Timothy, the couple settled in Charleston, South Carolina, among aggressive radicals. Their family grew with the births of William; Mary; Abraham, a lawyer like his father; Ann, who died in 1764; and Charles Jr. and Elizabeth Crouch, who both died in late summer 1772.

At the corner of Elliot Street and Gadsden's Alley, Mary coedited and printed a colonial miscellany, the weekly *South Carolina Gazetteer; And Country Journal.* The first issue reached readers on December 17, 1765. Two issues later, the owners altered the name by two letters to *South Carolina Gazette; And Country Journal.* They doubled the font size on December 31 to blazon the essay "OBSERVATIONS ON THE LIBERTY of the PRESS." In competition with printer David Bruce, the paper gave thorough coverage to shipping and naval activity from the bay and extended commercial range with legal documents, books, leaflets, and stationery. When paid in kind with bolts of English duck, she offered it for sale.

### A Partisan Paper

Encouraged by local patriots, the Crouches violated the Stamp Act and marked their masthead with the seditious motto "LIBERTY and PROPERTY, and NO STAMPS." The press reported the lamentation of shipmen by lowering the colors at the arrival of British stamp agents. When imports ceased at the harbor in winter 1765–1766, fourteen hundred unemployed mariners filled saloons. Amid efforts by Liberty Boys to soothe planters and merchants, bitter opinions and rumors kept the publication vibrant among grappling sides of the independence question. Reports of public celebration on June 9, 1766, with flags and cannon fire followed Prime Minister William Pitt's promotion of parliamentary repeal of excessive taxation by a vote of 240 to 133. On December 23, 1766, the editors commented on a currency shortage and resultant bankruptcies.

The October 29, 1767, issue announced Charleston's plans for the construction of Charleston's Exchange and Custom House, a stone bridge, and a militia Watch-house at the corner of Broad and Meeting streets. In next January, the Crouches' stock grew with the addition of William Ball's almanac, a forty-four-page miscellany that served readers' needs from Maryland to eastern Florida. During a backlash against strict economy and public revival of non-importation, on July 10, 1769, the editors printed broadsides that backed a renewed boycott of British goods. A pointed rejection of imported porcelain from China appeared on March 13, 1770.

The Crouches sold copies of a small 1770 almanac, the twenty-four-page Thomas More's "Poor Tom Revived," followed by annual editions in 1771 and 1772. They tendered subscriptions for a compendium of essays on the Catawba, Cherokee, Chickasaw, Choctaw, and Creek. In May 1771, the couple stocked broadsides on the Boston Massacre of the previous March 5 that declared the 29th British regiment guilty of murder. In December 1774, they reprinted the agenda of the Continental Congress, which included the Bill of Rights, protests against George III, and a salute to colonial American dissidents. During a period of tightening budgets, slow wintertime mail, and Charles's poor health, he leased the house to renters and lived in the printshop.

In May 1775, the editors bid "King George the third adieu!" On June 13, 1775, the couple gained a reputation for militant patriotism by circulating the momentous Mecklenburg County resolves two weeks after their passage on May 31. The historic suspension of British rule replaced the king's authorities with a temporary county sovereignty in Charlotte and a manifest of North Carolina's independence. Charles Crouch's departure for Philadelphia on August 24, 1775, produced a mystery—the disappearance of the ship at sea. After a decade of media success, because of his loss, his newspaper ended with number 505.

## A Female Editor

Mary retained Charles's vigor by taking his place. On January 15, 1778, she covered the fire of Moore's bake house on North Union Street, which spread by noon near the printshop in Gadsden's Alley and up Tradd Street and destroyed precious documents in the Charlestown Library Society. A detailed account of a sea battle against a Dutch frigate reported victory in March 1778 and epitomized the paper's constant survey of harbor traffic and boosting of militia morale.

In August 1778, Mary's masthead introduced the *Charlestown Gazette,* which commented on British privateering at Edisto, militia defense along the Congaree River, prisoner exchange, estate and slave sales, taxes on Negroes, and the loss of eight local militiamen at Port Royal Island. Into 1779, she followed movements of enemy invaders from St. Augustine into Georgia and British ships at Tybee, James, and John islands. According to individual reports, General Benjamin Lincoln's attempts to locate from General Prevost the prisoners of war on prison and hospital ships from a skirmish at Bryar Creek discovered a death toll of up to twelve a day.

Mary maintained a journalistic detachment amid questionable data from various sources that lauded the heroics of generals William Moultrie and Casimir Pulaski. Governor John Rutledge's May 1779 call-up of colonists offered pay for arrests of the enemy. Her paper survived until the British seizure of the port city on May 12, 1780. As war encroached, she relocated to Salem, Massachusetts, and joined her sons in Providence in 1781.

### *Sources*

Gould, Christopher. "Scottish Printers and Booksellers in Colonial Charleston, S.C.," *Studies in Scottish Literature* 15:1 (1980): 202–220.

King, William L. *The Newspaper Press of Charleston, S.C.* Charleston, SC: Edward Perry, 1872.

Salley, A.S., Jr. "The First Presses of South Carolina," *Proceedings and Paper of the Bibliographical Society of America* Vol. 2 (1907–1908): 28–69.

## Coincoin (August 22, 1742–February 6, 1816)
### Rancher, Apothecary, Slave Dealer
### Natchitoches, Louisiana

At Natchitoches, Louisiana, west of Red River, freedwoman Marie Thérèse Coincoin Métoyer built wealth by growing tobacco, trapping wild animals, and dealing in slaves. The fourth among seven siblings, she was born to African-born parents François and Marie Françoise and reputedly a scion of the Ewe or Yoruba tribe of Guinea (modern Togo). The bondswoman of elderly soldier and explorer Louis Antoine Juchereau de St. Denis, after an epidemic took both parents in April 1758, Coincoin lived with her godmother Marie des Neiges de St. Denis, Louis's sibling. She and sister Marie "Mariotte" Louise studied nursing and pharmaceuticals.

In youth, Coincoin bore five children fathered by an Indian named Chatto. At age twenty-three, she entered into a lease agreement to keep house for French merchant Claude Thomas Pierre Métoyer. A priest had her lashed for bearing illegitimate children. After Coincoin passed to Louis's daughter, Madame de Soto, in 1778, Claude paid for her freedom. Their intimate relationship produced twelve more children—Nicolas Augustin, Marie Suzanne, Louis, Pierre, Dominique, Eulalie, Antoine Joseph, Marie Françoise, Pierre Toussaint, François, Maria Teresa, and Pierre Victorin—all of whom he manumitted. In 1788, he divorced Coincoin and repatriated to France to marry Marie Bruard.

At Claude's river plantation south of Natchitoches near Caddo ancestral settlements, Coincoin acquired sixty-seven acres on the Grand Coast and built a half-timber and adobe house. With her annual allowance of one hundred twenty Livres, she invested in the apothecary's trade, tobacco, indigo, and rendering bears and turkeys for pelts, meat, and bear grease, which she shipped to New Orleans. In collaboration with her sons, she added a six hundred seventy-acre cattle ranch and bought sixteen slaves related to her clan, of whom she manumitted six.

At the 18,000-acre community of Isle Brevelle, Coincoin supported other planters, investors, and slave dealers who formed the heart of Creole culture. In 1796, her second son Louis Métoyer received nine hundred eleven acres on the Cane River in north central Louisiana. With older brother Nicolas Augustin, on March 11, 1832, Louis constructed Melrose (or Yucca) Plantation and St. Augustine Parish Church. The historic Afro-Gallic style home and Africa House with its umbrella roof mark part of the Louisiana African American Heritage Trail.

### *Sources*

Madden, Annette. *In Her Footsteps: 101 Remarkable Black Women.* Berkeley, CA: Conari Press, 2000.

Mills, Elizabeth Shown. "Marie Therese Coincoin," *KnowLA Encyclopedia of Louisiana*, http://www.www.knowla.org/entry.php?rec=799.

## Abigail Smith Adams (November 11, 1744–October 28, 1818)
**Farmer, Secretary, Trader**
**Braintree (modern Quincy), Massachusetts**

A colonial founding mother and epistolary historian, Abigail Quincy Smith Adams joined the country's subsistence farmers, who made up 96 percent of the populace. She took over the family finances during her husband's attendance at the first and Second Continental Congress in Philadelphia's Carpenters' Hall. From September 5 to October 26, 1774, while he compiled a manifesto to King George III opposing taxation without representation under the Intolerable Acts, she managed the family farm in Braintree. On the advice of her cousin, physician Cotton Tufts, she invested in currency, utilities, and securities. John's diplomatic assignments in France and Holland kept him away from home from 1778 to 1784, making him susceptible to capture and execution for treason by the British. Her farm career set an example of family stability and sacrifice and the need of wives for education and rights to cash and property as sources of independence and empowerment.

The petite daughter of Congregational minister-farmer William Smith, Abigail grew up outside Weymouth on the south side of Massachusetts Bay. Her mother, Elizabeth Quincy Smith, homeschooled Abigail and older brother William and sisters Mary and Betsy, both of whom married slackers and relied on handouts. Self-educated in history, theology, and law at the Smith family's library, Abigail acquired a reputation for intellect. She received the attentions of attorney John Adams, who descended from a line of English farmers dating to Braintree, Essex. In letters, John, ten years her senior, called her "Miss Adorable." They married in a home wedding on October 25, 1764.

For twelve years, the couple occupied nine and a half acres two miles from Massachusetts Bay. They settled in a one-hundred-year-old cottage on Franklin Street at Penn's Hill bequeathed by John's father, the elder John Adams, a farmer, shoemaker, and militiaman. The property included thirty acres of pasture for their four horses, timber, and orchards. They produced son John Quincy and daughters Abigail "Nabby" Amelia and Grace Susanna "Suky" in the first four years of marriage. Son Charles followed in 1770 after Suky's death at age thirteen months from failure to thrive, which Abigail combated with home-grown herbs.

## Farming and Motherhood

When political parties opposed the Stamp Act of 1761, an increase in legal work kept John at his Boston law office. In September 1768, when the British military installed two regiments, the couple rented a house in the city and welcomed a circle of revolutionaries—Samuel Adams, John Hancock, James Otis, and Joseph Warren. After they moved to Brattle Street in Boston, Abigail offered her own funds to buy John more land if he would practice law nearer home. In April 1771, she treated bouts of insomnia and migraines by returning to farm management to support the household. John declared his pride in her ability to plant fields and fruit trees, grow corn and asparagus, breed poultry, and supervise hired hands in brewing beer, reaping hay, and building stone fences. A family friend, Dr. Joseph Warren, believed the farm more prosperous under her governance than John's.

More changes in residency united the family at a brick house on Queen Street, Boston, in August 1772, during the last months of her pregnancy with son Thomas. She departed Boston's political unrest over the British Intolerable Acts, which blockaded the harbor and forced citizens to quarter Redcoats in private homes. The heavy snows of winter 1773–1774 seemed to isolate Abigail and the four children more treacherously in the country, but did not lessen her faith in America's future. After John's purchase of a meadow and arable fields in June 1774, she made the farm her permanent home and business. On September 5, John's election to the First Continental Congress at Carpenters' Hall in Philadelphia to promote a boycott of East India tea and other imported goods left his family without a male head of household. He conferred on Abigail control of livestock, farm, and dairy and urged her to question every expense.

Throughout John's absences on a circuit of county and superior courts, Abigail grew more self-confident as she single-handedly taught son John Quincy to read and battled inflation and shortages. A dearth of firewood reduced operations of bakeries, which turned out undersized biscuits. She sold timber and saved on expenses by squeezing out profits from the dairy and importing marsh mud for fertilizer. Ample milk from pasturing cows on Penn's Hill supplied John with butter and cheese. One of America's first female investors, she awakened at sunrise to manage agricultural income and secure retirement funds. Through government bonds supporting the war effort, she gained a profit of over four hundred percent.

At John's insistence, Abigail turned the four children toward industry and self-sufficiency and raised her income by selling potatoes, cider, and lumber made scarce by the war. Back rent from tenants Belcher, Hayden, Curtis, and Tirrell took the form of labor rather than cash. Meanwhile, twenty-three minutemen met in her home in preparation for traveling north to join the Continental Army. She depended on her childhood nanny, freedwoman Phoebe Abdel, whom she employed as a paid house sitter when the family was absent. In appreciation, Abigail gave Phoebe land and treated her final ills.

## War News

Through regular mail delivery by post riders, Abigail greeted John's letters like saints' relics. Her 1,200 replies enabled her to cope with stress while they recorded a front-row view of the American Revolution from the battle of Lexington and Concord on April 19, 1775, to war's end on September 4, 1783. In collaboration with dramatist Mercy Otis Warren and patriotic letter writer Hannah Fayerweather Winthrop in canvassing Massachusetts females about their loyalty, Abigail maintained Unitarian beliefs and a passion for liberty and the abolition of slavery. She accepted separation from John as a patriotic duty. The distant discharge of cannon kept the Adams family from peaceful meals and sleep. On June 17, 1775, while tending Dr. Joseph Warren's two daughters and two sons, she escorted ten-year-old Abby and seven-year-old John Quincy to Penn Hill overlooking Massachusetts Bay. The trio watched the British onslaught against patriots at Bunker Hill and the burning of Charlestown on the Charles River. Dr. Warren died in the conflict.

Abigail composed strategies for protecting the harbor and supported the militia by melting pewter spoons to mold into bullets. In November, she regretted that heavy rain rotted hundreds of bushels of apples and cost the farm five barrels of cider. During the Second Continental Congress, her letter to John in March 1776 predicted that colonial women would eventually rebel against husbandly tyranny. She wrote Mercy Warren proposing an appeal to the legislature for gender equality. By April, she informed John that most shops were closed and that she was perusing a formula for marketing saltpeter, a valuable chemical in gunpowder.

On a personal note, Abigail regretted that the Boston house was deteriorating from occupancy by a British regimental surgeon and that smallpox had reached epidemic numbers. In July, she arranged with Dr. Thomas Bulfinch for variolation of her children and kin by cutting a small slit and inserting pus from a smallpox cyst. By September 5, 1776, Nabby suffered a serious outbreak of pustules. A pestilence of dysentery left Abigail with an orphaned niece, Susanna Adams. John urged Abigail to fulfill family financial needs with loans, which he promised to repay.

Throughout John's misery with a cold in spring 1777, inflation tripled the price of lamb, sugar, dairy, and labor. He longed to see the farm flourishing under his wife's hand and, in March, worried that a fifth pregnancy affected her health. He referred to her as "Portia," the name of Shakespeare's wise heroine in *The Merchant of Venice*. In his absence, her letter assured him that she "enjoyed as much Health as I ever did in the like situation (pregnancy)" (Baker-Benfield, 2012, 9). June brought a plenteous crop of English grass and asparagus. On July 11, Abigail bore her last child, a stillborn daughter, Elizabeth. At a time when some 12 percent of colonial women died in childbirth, she gratefully reported a return to vigor.

In mid-summer 1777, agrarian concerns occupied Abigail's attention. She simplified dairying chores with new scythes and introduced an updated cider press. In August, she reported gathering a bounty of hay, a hundred fifty bushels of flax, and two hundred bushels of corn. From experience, she summarized a rule of husbandry: put maximum manure on the pasture for livestock rather than on corn acreage. Because of John's diplomatic appointment to Paris from 1777 to 1779, for nine months, she joined

**Adams-Smith Genealogy**

William Smith=Elizabeth Quincy

John Adams=Susannah Boylston Hall

William Mary Betsy Lydia Abigail Quincy Smith=John Adams

William=Nabby Smith | John Quincy=Louisa Johnson | Susanna | Charles=Sarah Smith | Thomas=Ann Harrod | Elizabeth

four children | four children | two children | seven children

him in France and managed a three-story, thirty-room French mansion and servants at Auteuil.

On return to Massachusetts, Abigail began dealing in bows, flowers, feathers, yard goods, and hat trimmings, which John sent from his new assignment to Holland. During a period of drought that raised the price of bread, the goods were worth more than cash. While John negotiated with the Dutch for loans and struggled with intermittent fever, in fall 1782, Abigail reflected that her renewed tenure as a Massachusetts farmer should leave the grandchildren a valuable heritage. In October, she invested in sixteen hundred twenty acres of Vermont farmland. Falling prices deflated her outlook in May 1783, when the war ruined merchants and traders.

Abigail kept a positive attitude toward investments. She continued speculating in real estate by purchasing seven acres of timberland and pasture west of Fresh Brook for $200 (approx. $5,787.66). In addition to investing cash in state promissory notes, on December 7, 1783, she added to their holdings nine acres of woods, which she bought for £60 (approx. $5,166.27). To pay for Charles and Thomas's school tuition, she hoped to reap $7 a cord (approx. $202.57) for firewood sold in Boston. John's reassignment to London in April 1785 required tickets for herself and Nabby on the June 18 departure of the *Active* for Plymouth, England, at a cost of £25 each ($4,935.72). On the trans-Atlantic journey, she continued working and writing. After the month-long voyage, the new post gave her diplomatic duties at nine Grosvenor Square as well as the fostering of Mary "Polly" Jefferson, the seven-year-old daughter of Thomas Jefferson. While absent from the farm, Abigail leased the Braintree and Medford acreage but missed feeding chickens and tending the garden.

Abigail longed for the pleasant rural habitation of her small cottage. Her three years in London ended in late February 1788 with restoration to Peacefield, the sixty-acre farm the couple purchased the previous year for £600 (approx. $115,302.43). A settled soul at heart, she remodeled the two-and-a-half story residence called "Old House" with an L-shaped wing to accommodate a large household. In addition to taming a garden gone to wilderness, she planted a York rose and grape vines along the front porch. Her winter farm chores included skimming milk, churning butter, bottling cider, and inspecting apples and pears for rot before repacking. Her concerns at Christmas turned to seasoning pork for bacon and learning a new method of pumpkin preservation.

In spring, Abigail began remodeling Old House with a library, kitchen, and dairy for six cows. Although a calf died in April from horn sickness and late calving cost her sleep, she boasted in May that she had avoided debt, but had to sell a calf and pig to buy hay for forage. In late fall 1788, she listed malt, turnips, ham, pears, cheese, butter, and russet apples in the staples she intended to stock for winter and settled taxes with the profits from selling lambs and wool. When the market price for eggs reached one shilling six pence a dozen, she intended to preserve thirty dozen in brandy.

## Multi-tasking

As the Second Lady in New York in April 1789, Abigail made a decided influence on her husband by scouring the city and Philadelphia for political trends. After the government reopened in Philadelphia in 1790 to be near Congress, she became overworked and sought rest and recovery in Braintree in 1791. Depressed by the inadequacy of a presidential salary of $5,000 (approx. $154,922.22), in February 1793, John regretted a long separation from home from late winter until June. He reflected on his vegetable garden and potato patch, which yielded ninety bushels the next year. He considered buying a dray horse and reported to Abigail the market price of corn at five shillings, rye at six shillings and eight pence, and hay for seven to nine shillings. He maintained an interest in neighboring property in December, when he pondered the price of $10,000 (approx. $316,715.15 in 2024) for Beale's farm and $18,000 (approx. $570,087.27 in 2024) for Black's land. Abigail was alarmed by the high price of oak and walnut firewood. She planned to import grafts of peach and plum trees and to cover Hancocks Meadow in a warming layer of red algae (*Heterosiphonia japonica*) that she transported by scow from Massachusetts Bay. John praised her use of free seaweed, which he called a marine treasure.

During a December snowstorm, Abigail wrote John her thoughts on separating the cattle business from the dairy and on purchasing her sister Elizabeth's half of the Medford farm and wood clapboard house on Cotting Street two blocks south of Mystic River. Despite wintry weather, she followed the Farmers Calendar by plowing, collecting stones for building walls, and surveying the stock of seaweed and barn manure. With quarterly interest, she bought a hog and bargained for a cow before reporting to John her seasonal expenditures. By February 1794, she considered investing in three cows and listed cattle prices as high as twenty dollars (approx. $557.72). Hard frosts and snow prevented her replenishing the post and rail fence. At the time, she nurtured one cow and nine lambs and was pleased to reap an abundance of salt hay or wild cordgrass (*Sporobolus pumilus*) for mulch and fodder and to finish the "sweetening" of cropland with lime. Her shopping list included cheese tubs, churns, cheese baskets and hoops, milk and cream pails, and cream pots. Because of fluctuating prices, she debated a March purchase of English or cultivated hay, brown sugar, molasses, flour, and a year's supply of loaf sugar and thanked John for buying a yoke of oxen.

On March 31, 1794, John mailed $500 (approx. $13,943) for Abigail's use in replenishing farm tools and livestock. In an auspicious April, she claimed the need for another yoke of oxen for manuring, plowing, and sowing. By year's end, John had sent rye and wheat flour and grass seed for the meadows, which she enriched with seventy loads of seaweed. She replied by return letter that rye flour was scarce, even at seven shillings a bushel, and that she preferred flour from Andrew Baines's water-powered mill at Louth in eastern England, a product of the Industrial Revolution. In 1795, she tarred slugs, fertilized clover, covered a calf shelter with seaweed, and plowed the garden.

In mid–February 1796, Abigail declared farming and letter writing her prime amusements. Expanded plans for the year's cropping began with securing clover seed, enriching cornfields, and paying Burrel sixteen cattle to head a team of workers at the Braintree acreage. She requested John's advice on employing more men. In addition to supervising leases, she budgeted pine logs for the dairy. In early March, she required a cart and sled to move manure and firewood. Looking ahead to receipt of grass seed, she enjoyed optimism and better health than previous winters. In mid–April, she cross-plowed and harrowed cropland and reduced garden-eating slugs and miller moths (*Acronicta leporina*).

## The Second First Lady

John's election to the presidency on March 4, 1797, limited the First Lady's productivity and ended her habit of rising at early morning on the farm. She feared being trussed up and targeted like geese and turkeys for being an independent thinker. In her midfifties, rheumatoid arthritis curtailed her activities, but she nursed John's mother, Susanna Boylston Adams, during a month-long illness that killed her on April 21, 1797. Because presidents had to pay their own entertainment expenses out of a $25,000 salary (approx. $603,830.71), Abigail complained of greater penury than ever before. She considered a bank loan and leasing all lands except for her house and garden. For the purchase of horses, John mailed her $600 (approx. $14,941.65 today) and lamented that he was too busy to visit Peacefield.

With careful budgeting, "Mrs. President" spent four years hosting Federalist dignitaries for dinners and Fourth of July celebrations, extending charity to petitioners, composing op-ed letters to the press, advising the president, and editing his correspondence and speeches. She made a return visit to Braintree to collect $45.60 (approx. $1,137.20) from the renters of Medford farm and for potato digging and picking apples, the source of fifty barrels of cider. In the final four months of John's presidency, responsibilities for thirteen wood-burning hearths in the unfinished White House in Washington, D.C., and the fostering of the six children of brother William, John Quincy's two sons, and profligate son Charles's two daughters caused Abigail's collapse.

John's loss of a second term in March 1797 and the decline and death of Charles from alcoholism at age thirty in fall 1800 weighed heavily on the First Family. Abigail's joy in John Quincy's advancement from U.S. senator to Minister to Prussia and secretary of state relieved some of her anguish. Her surrogacy to grandchildren Susanna, John, and George Washington Adams continued during Nabby's three years of suffering from breast cancer. At age seventy-three, Abigail died of typhoid fever at Peacefield. Her wise husbandry and investments left the family wealthy with cash, bank stock, the Medford farm, and shares of the Haverhill and Weymouth Bridges, which she had purchased in 1794. A will designated to female kin her personal wardrobe of satin and silk clothing, which son Thomas distributed.

*See also* Mercy Otis Warren.

## *Sources*

"Adams Family Papers," https://www.masshist.org/digitaladams/archive/letter/.

Barker-Benfield, G.J. "Stillbirth and Sensibility: The Case of Abigail and John Adams," *Early American Studies* (Winter, 2012): 2–29.

Cullen-DuPont, Kathryn. *Encyclopedia of Women's History in America. New York*: Facts on File, 2000.

Holton, Woody. *Abigail Adams*. New York: Simon and Schuster, 2010.

## Lois Crary Peters (April 10, 1747–November 1, 1836)
## Saddler
## Preston, Connecticut

A lone wife and mother of three during the American Revolution, Louisa "Lois" Crary Peters took over the saddlery of her husband, minuteman Nathan Peters. The great granddaughter of Plymouth immigrant John Gallop of Dorset and Scots judge Peter Crary of Glasgow, Lois was born of Anglo-Scots-Irish lineage in Preston, Connecticut, the fourth of the eight children of Sarah Tracy and Robert Crary. Lois and Nathan married in the First Congregational Church on June 10, 1770, at Preston, Connecticut. Southeast of Hartford, Preston farmers and artisans had reacted immediately against the Stamp Act and denied Parliament's right to levy internal taxes. The controversy influenced Nathan's decision to buy a corner lot in Preston and build a blacksmith shop and barn on sixty-three acres along the Plainfield Road and Norwich Highway.

The family's first two children—Benjamin and Nathan—died in infancy. Separation began with Nathan's enlistment among six thousand Connecticut men after the April 19, 1775, battle of Lexington and Concord, the start of a correspondence that extended for two years. The couple exchanged forty-seven letters. At the time, Lois was pregnant; William S. Peters, the third of her nine children, was one year old. Lois had an order for a woman's saddle, but declared, "Nobody wants Saddels" except for those already on order (Guthman, 1980, 21). Her worries consisted of anxiety for her brother Joseph, concern for the drought, and distress for a post rider's gossip that soldiers billeted near New York prostitutes sought treatment for venereal disease.

### Operating a Saddlery

To infantry captain Peters, Lois faithfully posted thirty letters, remarking on June 20, 1775, on the Battle of Bunker Hill and the mustering of auxiliary Mohegans. In Nathan's absence, she raised a corn crop and operated his saddlery despite a shortage of hog skin to shape to patterns with the professional half-moon blade and stitch with an awl and waxed hempen thread. Repair jobs could involve her in waterproofing and sewing pistol buckets, cartridge cases, dispatch pouches, and water bags. Her daily work included cutting hay, tending a cow, and making cheese and cider while sewing the family's clothing and sending Nathan farm produce, cider, chocolate, shirts, his gown, and hose.

The main object, debt collection, filled Lois with bitterness toward men who joined the army and defaulted on their I.O.U.s. She groused,

"Such Men ought To Pay all Their Just Dets and Then bee hangd" (Ibid., 15). Because of women's difficulty borrowing money, she requested Nathan's mare and £4–5 (approx. $812.97–1,016.21) because "Cannot Carry on The Trade without money" (Grunwald & Adler, 2009, 22). By return letter, Nathan assured her the mare was on the way and that he would send cash immediately. He awaited allotment of £5, his pay from the militia for answering the initial alarm.

Lois intended to spend the money for plush used in saddle padding and for "triming." Without a shipment of leather, her employee, Mr. Button, had nothing to do. After sale of oxen for £10 (approx. $2,032.43), on October 8, 1775, she feared she would be out of business without more cash. Ten days later, Nathan sent her £2, 18 shillings (approx. $589.40). She replied with urgings for a brief furlough so he could "See about your business your Self For I am almost Tird of the fatiegs of it" (Guthman, 1980, 27).

## The War and Its Aftermath

While Lois awaited the birth of daughter Sally, she grew too large to visit relatives on horseback. Budgeting for beef, butter, and cheese for winter presented problems, as did the need for someone to cut firewood. Adding to her worries, William was ill and required holding. After Sally's birth in February 1776, Lois needed flour, tea, and Nathan's old shirts and hose for making children's garments.

In June 1776, Captain Nathan Peters served General George Washington's 3rd Continental Regiment as a staff escort from New York to Philadelphia. Lois worded her patriotic love for home in fall 1776 when Nathan joined Washington's men in fleeing over New Jersey. From mustering out a war hero in 1777, he continued in combat with the Connecticut militia until 1781 against the traitor Benedict Arnold at Fort Griswold in Groton. Nathan later served as a privateer and Indian agent for the coastal Pequot of Groton.

After the death of the infant Hannah in 1780, Lois produced her last three children, Robert Crary, Andrew, and Eliza, born in 1793. She inherited from her father eighty-six acres straddling the Shetucket Turnpike, to which Nathan added thirty-one acres and a seven-acre forested tract along the Pine Swamp. Financial difficulties forced him to mortgage his entire one hundred ten acres. He sold five and a half acres in 1795 and concentrated on lawyering and farming. In 1814, at age sixty-seven, Nathan petitioned the state for back combat pay. At his death in February 1824, Lois lived for thirteen years among her four surviving children. Daughter Mary "Polly" Peters Meech named her second daughter Louisa; daughter Eliza Peters Shipman named her first daughter Lois Peters Shipman.

## Sources

Grunwald, Lisa, and Stephen J. Adler, eds. *Women's Letters*. New York: Dial Press, 2009.
Guthman, William H., ed. *The Correspondence of Captain Nathan and Lois Peters*. Hartford: Connecticut Historical Society, 1980.
Hurd, Duane. *History of New London, Connecticut*. Philadelphia: J.W. Lewis, 1882.
Peters, Edmund Frank, and Eleanor Bradley Peters. *Peters of New England*. New York: Knickerbocker Press's 1903.
Sommers, Richard J. *Vignettes of Military History*. Carlisle, PA: United States Army, 1976.

## Sarah Hood Russell (March 8, 1749–October 18, 1806)
**Printer, Publisher**
**Portsmouth, New Hampshire**

A competent writer and media worker, Sarah Penelope Hood Russell married a gadfly printer whose perverse reputation sullied her career. The daughter of Captain Cumbey and Sarah Nolan Hood, on October 7, 1773, she wed at age twenty-four Bostonian Ezekiel Russell, publisher of the *New Hampshire Mercury and General Advertiser* on King Street in Portsmouth. He dabbled in slave brokerage, stationery sales, sermon leaflets, and money lending at the New Auction Room and Intelligence Office. The paper changed hands to Robert Gerrish on December 24, 1784.

Ezekiel relocated his printshop near the Boston Concert Hall on Marlborough Street and distributed Ames's Almanac, Phillis Wheatley's verse, and the *Friday Censor*, a Tory apologetic sold for two cents (approx. $8.14). His bride balanced his radical opposition to the tea boycott with a pragmatic journalistic style that printed two-column news items from London to appeal to the elite international reader. While the couple followed a lengthy course of relocations to Danvers, Salem, and Boston, she reared two sons and three daughters on the proceeds of an annual subscription rate of six shillings (approx. $60.97).

### A Full Catalog

Beside the Bell Tavern, Ezekiel busied their Salem office with the production of broadsides featuring current events, heroic captivity tales and ballads, religious polemics, prophecies, and wartime ditties. He toned down his Hanoverian leanings and offered strong support of New England patriots. On June 21, 1774, the *Essex Gazette* announced Ezekiel's intent to move the paper to Rucket Street near the State House. Traveling salesmen disseminated his twenty-three issues of the *Salem Gazette* and *Newbury and Marblehead Advertiser* into isolated areas to report the British attack on Charlestown, Massachusetts, on April 19, 1775. The *Connecticut*

*Journal, Massachusetts Spy*, and other papers accused the Gazette of shaping facts to favor the British. Subsequent issues were devoid of the latest news about the Declaration of Independence and General George Washington's crossing the Delaware River from Philadelphia on December 25, 1776, to victory over Hessian mercenaries in Trenton, New Jersey.

A graphic title, "Bloody Butchery," announced losses at the battle of Lexington on April 19, 1775, where three thousand five hundred minutemen overwhelmed seven hundred British soldiers, killing two hundred fifty or 36 percent of Redcoats. Two days later, the paper folded and the family moved to Worcester before another relocation in 1776 to Main Street, Salem. On June 18, 1776, the Russells began the *Tuesday American Gazette or Constitutional Journal*, featuring portrait woodcuts and the Poet's Corner, a letter from John Hancock endorsing the militia, and a public service notice about indentured orphans from Marblehead. Page three warned colonists to avoid torn paper currency pasted together. A later issue requested clean linen rags for the printing office. Among their reprints, Thomas Paine's *Common Sense* courted fervent patriots and boosted competition against Isaiah Thomas's *Massachusetts Spy*. More profitable, Bickerstaff's *Boston Almanac* anticipated a colonial victory against Hanoverian forces.

## A Restless Medium

Another uprooting took the Russells to Danvers in 1777 for the issuance of more almanacs and advice to the neophyte retailer. Their hero worship of patriot General Horatio Lloyd Gates, winner of the battle of Saratoga on October 7, 1777, extolled his triumph and the capture of six thousand Redcoats. Two years later, the paper thrilled readers with a reprise of the Battle of Bunker Hill in the epic ode "America Invincible." Resettled at Boston in 1781 near the Liberty Tree, the Russells published the popular *American Almanac*, featuring a woodcut of rebel John Hancock and war hero Ethan Allan, a fable by Jean de La Fontaine, and a layout of the Massachusetts legislature.

Ezekiel continue to move the family business, printing the *Federal Mirror* at Concord on January 1796. At his death on September 10, 1796, Sarah moved to Boston and began advertising sale of the shop and her horse in Pembroke, Massachusetts, and her need for a post rider. After requiting debts on November 22, she devoted a decade to the printing trade. She specialized in half and whole sheet pamphlets of original ballads, a favorite of traveling salesmen. Observers marveled at her skill in composing directly onto frames with type rather than writing out her comments in longhand.

### Source

Tapley, Harriet Silvester. *History of the First Fifty Years of Printing in Salem, Massachusetts.* Salem, MA: Essex Institute, 1927.

## Elizabeth Johanetta Catherine von Hagen (1750–1809)
### Pianist, Organist, Music Teacher, Composer
### Boston, Massachusetts

A concert composer, pianist, organist, and keyboard educator, Elizabeth Johanetta Catherine Treubel von Hagen performed well with a musician husband and talented children. A native of Amsterdam, she wed German violinist and keyboardist Peter Albrecht von Hagen of Rotterdam, who had studied piano in Paris and London. Church work took her to Belgian organs at Bergen, Middleburg, Namur, and Vlissengen. At age twenty-four, she traveled with Peter to Charleston, South Carolina, and bore two sons and a daughter. On October 24, 1774, Peter advertised their musical prowess in the *South Carolina Gazette.*

The family repatriated to Holland in 1776 at the beginning of the American Revolution, when Peter supported the household until 1789 in Zutphen as a church carilloneur at the world's first tuned bell scale. The *Boston Daily Advertiser* announced concerts in October 1792 featuring Elizabeth and Peter playing concerti. Joining them on stage, Peter Jr. began performing duets with his father at age nine. In 1792, Elizabeth's thirteen-year-old daughter Catharina joined the von Hagen musicales for duets and trios.

### Boston Headquarters

From performing and managing "Old City Concerts" in January and February 1794 at Corre's Hotel on Wall Street in New York City, the von Hagens migrated to Boston to compose. In September 1796, Elizabeth joined the staff of Susanna Rowson's Academy, a school for girls at 62 Newbury Street, Boston. She arranged music for the stage and formed a dealership of opera ballads and patriotic songs. Her pupils came from Boston and Salem. Peter commemorated the death of George Washington with an original dirge and sacred concert and honored the nation's discovery with music for the historical spectacle *Columbus: or, A World Discovered,* which open on February 15, 1800, at the Federal Street Theatre.

The couple had numerous methods of earning money. According to ads in the *Columbian Centinel, Boston Independent Chronicle,* and *Massachusetts Mercury,* while teaching voice and instrumental pieces at an academy, the Musical Magazine, in April and June 1797, they published the federal piece "Hail Columbia." For $1.50 (approx. $36) each or $1.00 (approx. $24.69) for subscribers, they offered the monthly *Lady's Musical Miscellany,* which sold classic duets, overtures, rondos, and songs. In March 1798, they relocated to the Old Brick House at the Boston Mall; in March 1799, their business reopened at 55 Marlborough Street. In June 1799, at 3 Cornhill, Elizabeth taught on Tuesday, Thursday, and Saturday at the rate of $17 (approx. $433.36) per quarter. A house fire on December 15, 1799, did little damage.

### Lifetime Dedication

The couple and Peter Jr. presented concerts while Peter Sr. directed a theater orchestra for the patriotic stage play *The Spirit of the Times* and rented, sold, repaired and tuned instruments imported from London. In Boston, Portland, and Salem, Elizabeth specialized in piano concertos, sonatas, liturgical music, four-hand overtures, organ voluntaries, trios, and marches and issued keyboard variations entitled *The Country Maid; or, L'Amour Est un Enfant Trompeur* (Love Is a Baby Trickster). Her monthly newspaper ads in the *Massachusetts Mercury* specified lessons for young ladies in theory and mastery of harpsichord and piano according to European styles.

After Peter sickened in spring 1801, his advertising took on a more desperate tone. He expanded his warehouse instruments to English guitar, German flute, oboe, clarinet, and barrel organ, which he offered cheap for cash in January 1803 along with used pianos and harpsichords. When he died in October 1803, Elizabeth relocated to Common Street before opening a studio at Essex and Short streets. Residing at 7 Winter Street until her death at age fifty-eight, she succeeded Peter as organist at King's Chapel, America's first Unitarian church at Tremont Street opposite the Boston Common. An ad for her last subscription concert appeared in the Boston *Repertory* on February 35, 1806. Son Peter Jr. also worked in Boston as a composer and organist at Boston's Trinity Church.

### *Sources*

Clark, J. Bunker, ed. *American Keyboard Music Through 1865.* Boston: G.K. Hall, 1990.

Snodgrass, Mary Ellen. *American Colonial Women and Their Art.* Jefferson, NC: McFarland, 2017.

Sonneck, O.G. *Early Concert Life in America.* Storrs, CT: University of Connecticut Libraries, 1906.

## Elizabeth "Betsy" Hager (1750–July 12, 1843)
**Blacksmith, Gunsmith, Immunizer**
**Boston, Massachusetts**

A colonial recycler and handywoman, Elizabeth "Betsy" Hager Pratt rescued abandoned British cannon for use by American patriots. Born in

Framingham, Massachusetts, she was orphaned in 1759 and farmed out as a charity case. From home training in weaving and agriculture, she prospered in Boston on the farm of Samuel Leverett as gunsmith and ammunition maker. On inspecting six brass cannons left at the battle of Concord on April 19, 1775, she chose to retrieve them and repair them at Leverett's smithy. Reconditioning began with removing deliberate spiking and filling holes with screws.

When war overtook Massachusetts, Betsy served the Continental Army as battlefield nurse and herbalist. She volunteered to recondition muskets and old matchlock rifles for the militia and donated scraps off her underclothing for wrapping charges. After marrying farmer and minuteman John Pratt at Newton in July 1787, she relocated to Granville, Pennsylvania, and bore five sons and three daughters, giving birth to her last son in 1808. With training in smallpox variolation, she aided neighbors who sought immunization, a vital aid to the Continental Army. She predeceased John by more than a decade.

### *Source*

Farrington, Eloise. "Incidents in the Lives of Famous Women," Harrisburg (PA) *Evening News* (24 September 1918): 12.

## Margaretta Sully West (ca. 1750–June 6, 1810)
**Actor, Director**

## Ann West Bignall (ca. 1768–January 20, 1805)
**Actor, Stage Manager**
**Richmond, Virginia**

In competition with the nation's pioneering acting company, tragedian Margaretta Sully West, America's first female theater manager, directed the Virginia Comedians or the South Carolina Company, a troupe that claimed the southeastern colonial circuit. Born Margaretta O'Sullivan in Long Crendon, England, she chose her profession at a young age. She married producer and stage engineer Thomas Wade West, and in her teens, gave birth to Ann West Bignall, an eventual star player and stage manager, and sons William and Thomas C. West. Ann's stage triumphs included fresh stage plays: "Betty Blackberry alias Eliza Timbertop" in Irish dramatist John O'Keeffe's two-act comic opera *The Farmer,* the "romping hoyden" Moggy M'Gilpin in O'Keeffe and composer William Shields's three-act comic opera *The Highland Reel,* and Priscilla "Little Pickle" Tomboy, the title figure in Irish librettist Isaac John Bickerstaff's two-act farce *The Spoiled Child* (O'Keeffe, 1790).

By incorporating Margaretta's brother Matthew Sully and his prodigy children Chester, Elizabeth, Julia, Matthew Jr., and Thomas, the Wests' thirty-three players and full orchestra competed with the Old American Company throughout the lower South. She ferried their mechanical devices by boat to permanent playhouses in Alexandria, Fredericksburg, Norfolk, Petersburg, and Richmond, Virginia; and Charleston, South Carolina, and chose travel dates based on city festivals for maximum audience appeal. When Thomas died from a fall from the Alexandria Theatre catwalk in July 1799, she became manager and troupe proprietor as well as builder of the Richmond Theatre in 1806. During her struggles to turn a profit, on January 20, 1805, daughter Ann died.

Still promoting her sons' careers, Margaretta reduced the number of stage roles she played to devote herself to theater operation. She relieved boredom for her casts by adding two American shows, James Workman's comedy of manners *Liberty in Louisiana* celebrating the Louisiana Purchase and James Nelson Barker's *The Indian Princess; or, La Belle Sauvage*, a musical bio of Pocahontas. In one of the catastrophic theater fires of the era, on December 26, 1811, Richmond's brick theater on Broad and Twelfth streets caught fire from a chandelier igniting drapes. Seventy or 12 percent of the six hundred attendees died, including Virginia governor George William Smith.

The widow's investment of £2,000 (approx. $204,245.18) from twenty-five subscribers ended in ashes. The night of the conflagration, the company performed for an elite audience Alexander Reinagle's pantomime *Raymond and Agnes, or the Bleeding Nun*, a two-act melodrama. The blackened property sold at auction for $4,500 (approx. $107,289.62) and served as the foundation of the Monumental Church.

### Sources

Bickerstaff, Isaac. *The Spoil'd Child.* London: Barker & Son, 1792.
O'Keeffe, John. *The Highland Reel.* Dublin: The Booksellers, 1790.
Richards, Jeffrey H. *Drama, Theatre, and Identity in the American New Republic.* Cambridge, UK: Cambridge University Press, 2005.

## Anna Maria Brendel Bonn (before 1750–1815)
**Midwife, Nurse**
**Salem, North Carolina**

A respected midwife, Anna Maria Brendel Bonn treated the women and children at Salem, a Moravian settlement on the Carolina frontier. The only daughter of Eva Catharina Frey and Johann George Brendel of Alsace, France, she was probably born at Muddy Creek in Lancaster,

Pennsylvania. She had two older brothers, John and Heinrich. In her teens on November 1, 1766, she traveled with seventeen single female German Protestants down the Great Philadelphia Wagon Road from eastern Pennsylvania through the Shenandoah Valley and Roanoke.

After thirty days on the road, the women arrived in central North Carolina and the 100,000-acre farming tract of Wachovia. At the newly formed community of Bethabara, she married a thirty-three-year-old physician and surgeon, Jacob Bonn. The stockaded fort defended settlers and supplied the Catawba during the seven-year French and Indian War. Anna aided other Moravians during illnesses and births but left no record of her medical career. Documents in German include godparents, witnesses and baptismal dates. After her husband's death in 1781, she remained in the family home until its sale along with an apothecary shop on July 14, 1784, for £250 (approx. $47,380.68).

### *Source*

Culler, Lola Langdon. "Good Wares and Modest Manners" (thesis), https://libres.uncg.edu/ir/uncg/f/Culler_uncg_0154M_10143.pdf, 2009.

## Phillis Wheatley (1753–1784)
**Poet, Tailor**
**Boston, Massachusetts**

An eighteenth-century celebrity, Phillis Wheatley Peters established a literary career heralded on both sides of the Atlantic. In childhood at Gambia/Senegal, she was influenced by animism, sun worship, and the Muslim faith. Culled from the load of seventy-five refugees as a spindly slave not likely to survive, she later reflected on her destiny in "On Being Brought from Africa to America," the most famous of her one hundred forty-five poems. After two hundred forty-five days at sea, in 1761, she disembarked at Boston from the *Phillis,* a West African slave schooner captained by Timothy Fitch over the Middle Passage.

Phillis survived while some eighteen abductees died in transit from the Windward Coast. In prime slave merchandising season at Boston's Long Wharf on Beach Street and at John Avery's store in South End, owners advertised the arrival on July 13 in the *Boston Gazette,* August 3 in the *Boston Evening Post,* and August 7 in the *Boston Weekly News-Letter.* Sellers demanded cash or a swap with black felons being relocated to the Caribbean. Phillis's dirty, bare body wrapped in carpet passed to purchasers Susannah and John Wheatley, a constable and tailor, to serve their fashionable household on King Street and Mackerel Lane in the financial district.

Phillis took the Wheatley surname and the given name of the slave ship. A neighbor, Presbyterian pastor Scipio Moorhead, drew her likeness. Living like a sibling of John and Susannah Wheeler Wheatley's eighteen-year-old twins Mary and Nathaniel, she attended Sunday services during the New Light revival movement called the Great Awakening. Within sixteen months, she adopted Christianity, read the Bible, and perfected embroidery and a stylish longhand. She greeted and dined with white guests and attended formal entertainments as a family showpiece. Conversation revealed her interests in scripture, astronomy, geography, history, and the English authors Alexander Pope, Thomas Gray, and John Milton.

## An African Prodigy

Over two years, Phillis defied capital punishment for literate slaves: she spoke English and Senegalese and read English as well as Greek and Latin. She advanced to familiarity with the classics of Homer, Virgil, and Terence and described Africa as a dark pagan continent. After publishing her first verse, "On Messrs. Hussey and Coffin," in December 1767 in the Newport *Mercury*, she referred to herself as "an Ethiop" in "To the University of Cambridge" and spoke as an exhorter to sinners in the parallel didactic works "An Address to the Atheist" and "An Address to the Deist." In 1768, "To the King's Most Excellent Majesty" thanked George III for repealing the Stamp Act. The reflective ode "On the Death of the Rev. Dr. Sewall" congratulated the Congregational minister Joseph Sewall for accepting salvation and pursuing an exemplary career at Harvard.

The poet gained international renown by translating Horace's ode "To Maecenas" and "Niobe in Distress for Her Children Slain by Apollo," a narrative in Ovid's *Metamorphosis.* The academic rigor earned her the nickname "African genius." The poem "To S.M. A Young African Painter, On Seeing His Works" drew attention to her portraitist, a fellow creative black. Her verbal skills impressed friends, notably Presbyterian and Anglican ministers. John certified the authenticity of her works by issuing a testimonial in Boston newspapers. In summer 1770, while attending Mary Wheatley on vacation at Newport, Rhode Island, Phillis gained a correspondent in freedwoman Obour Tanner, whom she may have met aboard the *Phillis.* Phillis engaged Obour as literary agent and gained clientele for tailoring, including John Hancock. Under Calvinism, in 1771, the poet sought baptism at Old South Congregational Church despite the members' racism. She commemorated evangelist George Whitefield in 1771 with a famous elegy, "An Elegiac Poem, on the Death of that Celebrated Divine, and Eminent Servant of Jesus Christ, the Reverend and Learned George

Whitefield," issued in broadside and leaflet in Boston, Newport, and Philadelphia. Her 1773 book, *Poems on Various Subjects, Religious and Moral,* pleased bookseller Archibald Bell of Aldgate and fans Dr. Benjamin Rush, Massachusetts governor Thomas Hutchinson, state constitution coauthor James Bowdoin, and printer Benjamin Franklin. The imitative nature of her works dismayed Thomas Jefferson, who overlooked her classic allusions and soaring diction in "On Imagination," "On Virtue," and "A Hymn to Evening."

Shortly after the Boston Tea Party, Phillis traveled with Nathaniel Wheatley on the *Beaver* to sing recitals to impress publishers in London. She returned to care for Susannah during her owner's lethal illness. At her mistress's death on March 3, 1774, Phillis grieved for a loving foster parent. Lacking sponsors, the poet survived as a boarding house domestic. She demanded freedom under the law that denied enslavers' rights after the slave entered free territory in England. She gained manumission on October 18, 1775. During the American Revolution, she wrote to abolitionists in England and the colonies and pondered the disconnect between human bondage and morality. Her poetry extolled the commander in chief of the Boston siege with the verse "To His Excellency George Washington," which she dispatched to Continental Army headquarters at Cambridge in 1775. On February 28, 1776, she accepted an invitation to visit him and hoped to influence him to abolish human bondage.

## Wife and Mother

Following John Wheatley's death in March 1778, at age twenty-five, Phillis wed freedman John Peters, a grocer and freelance attorney on Court Street in Wilmington, Massachusetts, and father of their three children. Because he served a debtor's sentence in the county jail, Phillis took janitorial jobs and continued to lambaste racists who "disgrace/And hold in bondage Afric: blameless race." After her husband abandoned the family, poverty and the rigors of asthma engulfed her. All her children died in their youth.

Phillis continued to write and, in October 1779, sought financing for a poetry volume dedicated to Benjamin Franklin. In a long poem in the leaflet "Liberty and Peace," she celebrated the end of colonialism and the victory of Columbia, her name for America. The encomium "To the Right Honorable William, Earl of Dartmouth" expressed gratitude for a free country. The final works consisted of an elegy for Congregational minister Samuel Cooper in 1784 and a lament for a deceased one-year-old named Avis. While tending a frail son, she died of pneumonia at age thirty-one within hours of her daughter's birth and lies buried with the infant at

Copp's Hill. Critics compared her career to that of poets Anne Dudley Bradstreet and Paul Laurence Dunbar.

### *Source*

Carretta, Vincent. *Phillis Wheatley: Biography of a Genius in Bondage.* Athens: University of Georgia Press, 2014.

## Abigail Foote Brainard (March 13, 1757–January 2, 1852)

## Elizabeth Foote Huntington (May 29, 1750–October 25, 1845)
**Spinner, Weaver, Seamstress**
**Colchester, Connecticut**

Skilled with fiber work as well as verse and letter writing, Elizabeth "Betty" Foote Huntington supported herself by making bed rugs, shirts, gowns, and quilts and by designing quilting patterns for neighbors. The eldest of three children, she was born to Elizabeth Kimberly and Israel Foote of New London County and granddaughter of maternal grandparents from Staffordshire and Warwickshire, England. A paternal grandsire, Nathaniel Foote, immigrated from Colchester, England, and surveyed parts of Connecticut.

At age twenty-five, Elizabeth attended coursework in math, grammar, and composition. She and eighteen-year-old sister Abigail kept diaries that described the intricacies of textile production from carding fiber through warping and weaving. On April 13, 1775, Elizabeth sewed a gown for Lydia Treadway Wells and ended the day spinning flax into linen thread. In earshot of news about the outbreak of the American Revolution on April 21, she continued fiber work with another gown and quilting and baked biscuits and a pudding to feed Bostonians who resisted the British. In April 1766, she taught art in Hebron.

In her forties, Elizabeth married a distant cousin, the Rev. David Huntington. The couple shared November 5, 1778, their special day, with Elizabeth's sister Mary, who requested a double wedding in Marlborough for her union with Nathaniel Otis. Two more couples—Sarah Otis and Israel Foote, Jr., and Hannah Otis and Martin Kellogg—made the occasion a quadruple nuptial. While David served the First Congregational Church at North Lyme and Hamburg, Connecticut, Elizabeth produced knitted and quilted goods and weaving on the spinning wheel and loom. The couple had five children—Betsey Kimberly, David, Anna, Israel Foote, and Louis Huntington. Israel, born in December 1787, attended Yale and Princeton Theological Seminary before taking a pastorate in New Brunswick, New Jersey.

In 1778, in brown, white, and three shades of blue, Elizabeth stitched bed rugs with homespun wool yarn over an undyed wool blanket in traditional Elizabeth blackwork motifs from the 1500s and 1600s. She favored abstract scrollery and stylized leaves and flowers in darning and running stitches, which required counting patterns that passed through the ground fabric. She signed her stitchery with EF. Her niece, Lorrain Collins Gotham Benton of Winsor, emulated Elizabeth by completing a similar rug. Elizabeth survived to age ninety-five, living thirty-three years in widowhood.

### *Sources*

Goodwin, Nathaniel. *The Foote Family*. Hartford, CT: Case, Tiffany & Company, 1849.
Snodgrass, Mary Ellen. *American Colonial Women and Their Art*. Jefferson, NC: McFarland, 2017.

## Elizabeth Griscom Ross (January 1, 1752–January 30, 1836)

## Rebecca Young (November 17, 1739–February 6, 1819)
**Seamstress, Upholsterer**
**Philadelphia, Pennsylvania**

Elizabeth Phoebe "Betsy" Ross receives more acclaim for her legendary flag making than for running a sewing shop. A Quaker great granddaughter of Andrew Griscom, a dissenting English immigrant carpenter, she was born in Gloucester City, New Jersey, on the farm of Welsh newcomer Rebecca James and Samuel B. Griscom, a finish carpenter who labored on the woodwork of Independence Hall, in Philadelphia, and owner of a shipyard between Race and Vine streets. Nine of her sixteen siblings died in infancy or succumbed to smallpox. She obtained a basic education at the Friends' Public School on Fourth Street, studied sewing with her great-aunt Sarah Griscom, and served upholsterer William Webster on Second Street as apprentice before marrying Scots apprentice John Ross in 1773. Elopement with an Episcopalian, which ended with a crossing over the Delaware River at Hugg's Tavern in Gloucester City, cost Betsy her Quaker membership.

The outbreak of the American Revolution widowed Betsy at age twenty-three after John's death in a munitions explosion. A Philadelphia competitor, milliner Margaret Manny, led the way into flag sewing in December 1774 with the creation of the Grand Union Flag, under which men signed the Declaration of Independence. Folk belief credits Betsy with sewing a flag on June 1, 1776, according to the orders of General George Washington, commander of the Continental Army. Completed before witnesses George Ross, Jr., a signer of the Declaration of Independence, and financier Robert Morris, the final design placed thirteen white stars in a circle on a blue rectangle.

In front of her daughters, at her store on Arch Street between Bread and Third, Betsy pressed to reduce Washington's six-pointed star and demonstrated the trick of folding cloth to yield a five-pointed star in one snip. Aiding her in the task, Rebecca Minot Prescott Sherman stitched on three stars and used the method to design Connecticut's flag. To the right and below, alternating red and white stripes symbolized the thirteen colonies. George Ross advanced Betsy £100 (approx. $20,783.29) for cloth and thread. At the urging of the Marine Committee, Congress legitimized the national emblem on June 14, 1777. The design remained unchanged until the admission of Vermont and Kentucky in May 1795 required a fourteenth and fifteenth star.

On October 4, 1777, Betsy volunteered to treat some of the one thousand British and American casualties from the battle of Germantown, Pennsylvania, General William Howe's defeat of the Continental Army. Meanwhile, despite shortages of materials, Rebecca Bibb Flower Young, Betsy's Philadelphia competition, ran a successful blanket and drum case shop in 1780 on Walnut Street and offered custom embroidery for cuffs and frills. Her daughter, Mary Young Pickersgill, claimed to have aided Rebecca in turning four hundred yards of bunting into the national ensign for use by the army and navy. Contradicting the claim, Betsy's daughter Clarissa dictated to nephew William J. Canby the earlier account.

A second marriage to sea captain Joseph Ashburn the next day at Old Swedes' Church resulted in success and multiple tragedies. In winter 1777, the British forced the couple to house soldiers. In 1779, the family's upholstery shop profited from wartime demands of the Continental Army for repairing uniforms, filling paper tubes with musket balls, and sewing tents, ship's mattresses, and blankets. Captured while privateering in the brigantine *Patty,* Joseph served time at Old Mill Prison in Plymouth, England, on charges of treason. In his absence, Betsy lost a first child, nine-month-old Aucilla Zilla Ashburn, and gave birth to Eliza in 1779.

Betsy, like flag maker Rebecca Young, joined other colonial seamstresses in providing banners, ensigns, and flags for regiments and ships. A more successful wedlock at Christ Church in May 1783 to John Claypoole produced five daughters. To house them all, in 1786, the couple moved to Second Street in Philadelphia. Simultaneous with the formation of the national government, yellow fever took Betsy's parents and sister Deborah. Widowed a third time in 1817, Betsy remained employed for another decade before limited vision forced her to leave her sewing shop to daughter Clarissa Sidney Claypoole. Betsy relocated to daughter Susanna Claypoole's home in Abington, Pennsylvania, and daughter Jane Claypoole's home in Philadelphia. Betsy died blind at age eighty-four.

*See also* Rebecca Minot Prescott Sherman.

## *Source*

Balderston, Lloyd. *The Evolution of the American Flag*. Philadelphia, PA; Ferris & Leach, 1917.

## Hephzibah Neal Upham (1754–May 11, 1811)
### Needlework Teacher
### Stratham, New Hampshire

A conscientious stitcher, Hephzibah "Hepsy" Neal Upham taught Mary Wiggam and other local students the arrangement of letters within backdrops of sky, flowers, trees, and food plants. A native New Englander from Deerfield, New Hampshire, she instructed girls in the Stratham school in the intricacies of embroidering linen with silk floss. In 1776, she edged a 19.5"×26" sampler with sawtooth framing to set off bright pink and rose threads linking daisies with strawberries on the stem. Anchoring the more imaginative flora at the bottom panel, whimsical blue clouds contrasted the signature and date. In the fluffy background, she stressed, "goodnefs and Mercy ever follow thofe/Who share their Conduct for God's holy Laws."

In October 1799, Hephzibah wed a widower, the Rev. Timothy Upham, a Harvard-educated minister. He pastored the Deerfield Congregational Church from its founding for an annual salary of £80 (approx. $11,543.06). While she managed his two sons and daughter Hannah, the principal of the Ontario Female Seminary in Canandaigua, New York, she helped establish Timothy's reputation for hospitality. However, most biographies detail his first marriage and illustrious son Timothy Jr., a soldier and Hebrew scholar, to the exclusion of Hephzibah.

Within three months of her husband's death from pneumonia, Hephzibah died at age fifty-seven after lengthy suffering with illness. In December 2015, her sampler brought $15,000 at Quinn's Auction Galleries. It appeared on the cover of the 2016 issue of *Samplings*, Volume 49.

## *Source*

Upham, F.K. *The Descendants of John Upham of Massachusetts*. Albany, NY: Joel Munsell's Sons, 1892.

## Ana Gallum Wiggins (1755–1840)
**Planter, Cattle Rancher, Slave Dealer**
**Palatka, Florida**

The survivor of multiple forms of female suppression, at Rolleston (modern Palatka), Spanish Florida, Ana Gallum "Nansi" Wiggins reared seven children on her income from slave dealing, agriculture, and cattle herding. A Muslim captured by Scots in Senegal, at age twenty-six, she was transported to North America and worked in Georgia for Joseph "Job" Wiggins, an English planter. In 1781, she wed her former owner and bore six children, whom Castilian law classed as maroons. To gain the benefits of Catholicism, she had her children baptized.

Under colonial law, Ana became a Spanish citizen who lived safer and more securely than she had in an English colony. In widowhood in 1797, she inherited the Wiggins estate, which included a manse, fourteen hundred acres, one hundred cattle, and fourteen slaves. During a tedious settlement of Job's estate, Ana suffered impregnation in 1799 by rapist Pedro Cassaly, a customer who came to the estate to buy a horse. Spanish courts denied her compensation for the illegitimate son, Pedro Wiggins, and ended her ownership of a slave named Rosa.

Ana pursued commerce by selling livestock and slaves in St. Augustine. Her free-born children flourished: as a militiaman, Benjamin translated Hitchiti for the local Seminole and free black militia of St. Augustine; Abigail Juana and Beatriz owned land at Fernandina on St. Amelia Island. During native American efforts to create a Muskogee state, Ana followed her children to the growing Indian community on Florida's northeastern coast. Rather than anticipate the benefits of a republican legal system, Juana chose to immigrate to Havana to homestead under Cuba's Spanish law.

Throughout the territorial transition of Spanish Florida to American ownership, on a three-hundred-acre land grant of two lots and two half-lots east of Lake George, Ana capitalized on bilingualism and the Creole's political savvy. She made a living herding cattle under the protection of Benjamin Wiggins III and the militia. Additionally, she profited from the 1808 embargo on transatlantic bondage, which spurred the slave trade in Florida among Georgian and South Carolina buyers. Fernandina's liberal attitudes toward biracial children freed the Wiggins family of fears of physical violence and sexual assault.

### *Sources*

Jaffary, Nora E., and Jane E. Mangan, eds. *Women in Colonial Latin America*, Indianapolis, IN: Hackett Publishing, 2018.

Landers, Jane G. *Atlantic Creoles in the Age of Revolutions.* Cambridge, MA: Harvard University Press, 2011.

______. "Founding Mothers: Female Rebels in Colonial New Granada and Spanish Florida," *Journal of African American History* 98:1 (2013): 7–23.

# IV

# A Constitutional Democracy, 1760–1781

For the ten million citizens of the new country, the old confederation yielded to dramatic transitions as colonies acquiesced into loyal and orderly elements of one United States. The business of building a treasury, supporting an army and navy, and coining currency left to women the tasks of educating girls and grasping the freedoms and ideals once limited to men. At Hartford, Connecticut, Amelia Simmons published *American Cookery*, a historic registry of recipes featuring corn meal, molasses, blueberries, and black-eyed peas. In Philadelphia, druggist Elizabeth Marshall stocked supplies for country doctors and introduced from six to twelve apprentices at a time to pharmacological chemistry. In a letter to her husband on June 17, 1782, Abigail Adams applauded female fortitude: "All History and every age exhibits Instances of patriotic virtue in the female Sex, which considering our situation equals the most Heroick" (Adams Family Papers).

## Anna Gardie (c. 1760–July 21, 1798)
**Dancer, Actor, Singer**
**Philadelphia, Pennsylvania**

A successful performer at Saint Domingue (modern Haiti), Anna Gardie brought her talents north to Philadelphia's Chestnut Street Theater. She trained for the stage her homeland. Because of the Haitian Revolution of August 22, 1791, she and her husband, Monsieur Gardie, fled the West Indies. On American soil, she established a professional career with the Old American Company as chanteuse, ballerina, and mime. With other Caribbean refugees, she imported biracial identity and theatrical uniqueness to the U.S. stage and specialized in Creole drama, mime, melodrama, and racial masking.

At age thirty-four, Anna debuted in French dramatist Alexandre Guiraud's three-act pantomime *La Forêt Noire* (The Black Forest): *or, Maternal Affection*, which had premiered in Paris. An intense episodic tale of forbidden marriage, the action pictures Anna as Lucille, the secret wife of military officer Lauridan. To stop her father from arranging wedlock to the effete L'Abbe, Lucille flees with a robber band and rescues her son with the aid of Lauridan's battalion. A plangent moment revives her from a swoon to menace the robber captain with a dagger.

## The Gallic Trend

Anna's success drew more French choreographers and mimes to post-war America. In New York, the Old American Company advanced from shared ticket sales to a managed troupe on salary. The following year, she partnered with a younger man, ballet master John Durang, the nation's first professional male dancer, in Victor Pelissier's innovative production of *Sophia of Brabant,* a historical drama in which she voiced the protagonist with an unusually elevated tone for pantomime. She continued pairing with John in *Tyranny Suppressed: or, Freedom Triumphant* as Mellamor, *Harlequin's Animation; or, Triumph of Mirth,* and *Poor Jack,* in which Anna played the orange girl. In Boston on April 9, 1793, she vivified a more scenic program at a new playhouse at Federal and Franklin streets. Her interpretation of one of the three witches in *Macbeth* shocked viewer John Adams, then a Boston attorney, for comparing England to Lady Macbeth.

With French performer Alexandre Quesnet, Anna cultivated new respect for the Old American Theatre in productions of Suzanne Douvillier's *The Bird Catcher,* Archibald Duff's "Minuet de la Cour (Court Minuet)," and Alexander Placide's *The Two Philosophers; or, The Merry Girl,* a favorite presentation honoring the birthday of the new president in which Anna danced the lead. For Ranieri de' Calzabigi's *Don Juan,* she starred as Doña Anna, the victim of attempted rape; for *Cooper,* she played Mrs. Brett and led a trio in footwork. Her part as Madame Larouge in Stephen Storace's comedic *No Song No Supper* called for broken English; historic glimpse in *Joan of Arc* assigned her a series of choreographies. Performances at season's end pleased George Washington, who made frequent return visits.

## A Lurid End

Over February to June 1796, Anna contributed to the company's *tour de force* season with her part in *Much Ado about Nothing.* John joined Anna in French style theatricals that varied from heroic pantomime to classic stock, expressive theatrics, and standard narrative pieces. She danced the allegory of "America" opposite Britannia and the Goddess of Liberty in the patriotic spectacle *The Independence of America; or, The Ever Memorable Fourth of July 1776.* She wafted a welcome to Robinson Crusoe in a heroic finale and elevated John's repertoire with a range of material from a sophisticated *Hamlet* to a ridiculous *Tom Thumb.*

At the time of her residence in Philadelphia, Anna and her aristocratic husband, a member of the orchestra from the French seaport of Rochelle, roomed at the Fraunces Tavern at 54 Pearl Street, a renowned inn opened by Stephanus Van Cortland. In March 1798, the *American Mercury* reported her decision to open a dance studio while her husband taught French. An investigation into her violent death on July 21, 1798, charged her husband with a stabbing in her sleep before killing himself. His motivation was her refusal to accompany him to France. Their deaths orphaned a son and contributed to New York ghost stories.

### *Sources*

Brooks, Lynn Matlock. *John Durang, Man of the American Stage.* Amherst, NY: Cambria Press, 2011.
Moore, Lillian. *Echoes of American Ballet.* Brooklyn, NY: Dance Horizons, 1976.
Reed, Peter P. "The Life and Death of Anna Gardie," *Early American Literature* 51:3 (2016): 623–652.

## Rachel Stout Allen (February 28, 1760–December 14, 1840)
**Herbalist, Midwife**
**Snow Camp, North Carolina**

An itinerant medical practitioner, Rachel Abigail Stout Allen recorded recipes for frontier pharmacopia. Born the last of seven children to Quakers Margaretha Cypert and Peter "the Quaker" Stout in Warrington, Pennsylvania, she moved to Piedmont North Carolina in 1762. She married teacher and storekeeper John Allen IV at age nineteen and occupied a log cabin with loft, two porches, smokehouse, and a storage nook. Of her nine sons and three daughters, Rachel Jr. and Samuel Allen died in childhood.

John became a contract teacher of reading, composition, spelling, and arithmetic. The family raised corn and oats along with pigs, cattle, sheep, and herbs. From their homestead on six hundred acres at Cane Creek, North Carolina, the couple sold fabrics, buttons, pins, shoes, and pencils along with Rachel's tooth cleaner, salves, medicines, poultices, emetics, syrups, cordials, and purgatives. In addition to curatives, she operated a loom for weaving wool.

Rachel added to practical experience her readings in *Culpepper's Herbal* and William Buchan's *Domestic Medicine*. To patients between Chapel Hill and Greensboro, North Carolina, she gathered healing plants and mixed them with other curatives for treatment of snakebite and other ailments:

| ***Ailment*** | ***Herb*** | ***Additive*** |
|---|---|---|
| burns | rattlesnake (*Eryngium yuccifolium*) | ointment made from butter |
| cancer | persimmon (*Diospyros kaki*) | a salve of dogwood root |
| | sassafras (*Sassafras albidum*) | boiling water |
| consumption | angelica (Radix angelicae) | malt beer, butter, treacle, horseradish |
| | burdock (*Arctium lappa*) | |
| | lignum vitae (*Guaiacum officinale*) | |
| | nettles (*Urtica dioica*) | |
| | sarsaparilla (*Smilax officinalis*) | |
| | watercress (*Nasturtium officinale*) | |
| cough | licorice (*Glycyrrhiza glabra*) | linseed oil, mucilage |
| earache | wormwood (*Artemisia vulgaris*) | milk, onion juice, garlic, honey |
| kidney stone | agrimony (*Agrimonia gryposepala*) | parsnips, onion poultice, white wine |
| | chamomile (*Matricaria chamomilla*) | |
| quinsey | malt | horse dung, bran, milk |
| ulcer | horsetail (*Equisetum arvense*) | |
| weakness | bittersweet (*Solanum dulcamara*) | |
| | cats foot (*Antennaria dioica*) | |
| | cinquefoil (*Potentilla comarum*) | |
| | harts tongue (*Asplenium scolopendrium*) | |
| | maidenhair fern (*Adiantum raddianum*) | |
| | silverwort (*Argyroxiphium grayanum*) | |
| | yarrow (*Achillea millefolium*) | |
| yaws | shoemake root (*Rhus glabra*) | turpentine, deer manure |

On horseback, she galloped to distant patients. She carried catheter and bougie, scales for weighing small amounts of herbs, and a receipt book describing how to blend treatments. Her brother-in-law, Herman Husband, led disgruntled farmers in the Regulators Movement. After John's death in 1826, Rachel lived as a widow for fourteen years and died at age eighty. She lies buried at Cane Creek Monthly Meeting cemetery in Snow Creek. Her home remained occupied until 1929.

### *Sources*

Moss, Kay K. *Southern Folk Medicine, 1750–1820*. Columbia: University of South Carolina Press, 2021.
Smith, Margaret Supplee, and Emily Herring Wilson. *North Carolina Women Making History*. Chapel Hill: University of North Carolina Press.

## Amelia Simmons (ca. 1766–after 1796)
**Food Writer**
**Hartford, Connecticut**

A mystery contributor to American culinary history, recipe collector Amelia Simmons issued *American Cookery* in 1796 with examples of practical, bountiful platefuls "adapted to this country" (Simmons, 1796). Wisps of information linked her with the Hudson Valley, where she made her way from orphanhood. She worked near Albany as a domestic and had some experience with such British recipe standards as plum cake, trifle, and Shrewsbury cake, a fruitcake featuring dried fruit.

Poorly educated, but keen on the new nation's foodways, Amelia spoke with confidence of such indigenous foods as whortleberry (blueberry), speckled or black-eyed peas, and barberry, a shrub plant introduced as an ornamental. For invalid cookery, she recommended a nutritious sick bed custard. From multiple perspectives, she amassed the first colonial cookbook, which Hudson and Goodwin published in Hartford, Connecticut.

Before summarizing the best meats for catering, Amelia spoke of a time of rapid change. Her facility with kitchen vocabulary such as emptins, chine, pluck, bolted rye, musk, amber, leveret, whitpot, neat's foot, and bullace suggests a lengthy experience satisfying demands for a complete menu of meats, vegetables, breads, berry and stone fruit preserves, and desserts. Her recipes for pumpkin pudding and turkey stuffing became staples of Thanksgiving menus. The most detailed instructions covered dressing a turtle. Her awareness of American tastes embraced Jerusalem artichokes (*Helianthus tuberosus*) but ruled out garlic, a French passion that she relegated to medicine rather than the table.

With the friskiness of an early Martha Stewart, Amelia explained how to keep parsnips through the winter, which cabbage variety to boil for slaw, and how to fill a cask with parsley and store it in the cellar. Her commentary spoke candidly of the unprofitability of black currants and the savings of apple trees, which might "extinguish the public debt and enrich our cookery" (Simmons, 1796). She saluted American-style nationalism with election cake, federal pan cakes, and independence cake, complete with raisins and citron, a quart of brandy, and a quart of wine.

For the first time, an American food writer acknowledged the influence of native American cookery and the inclusion of Indian meal in Indian slapjacks (pancakes) and hoecake as well as molasses in buckwheat, gingerbread, and johnny cakes and in spruce beer as a preventive for scurvy. Two signal leaveners, potash and pearl ash, presaged Amelia's inclusion of baking soda in colonial recipes. She also favored a sweet, frothy dessert, creamy syllabub, which allied cider or wine with curdled or whipped cream flavored with sugar, nutmeg, and lemon juice. For its rejection of British kitchen wisdom, Amelia's compendium was dubbed a "second declaration of American independence" (Wegiel, 2018). The pioneering text returned to press in 1800 in Albany and remained in print until 1831.

### *Sources*

Simmons, Amelia. *American Cookery.* Hartford, CT: Hudson & Goodwin, 1796.
Wegiel, Anna. "The British Origins of the First American Cookbook," *New Horizons in English Studies* 1 (March 2018): 150–162.

## Elizabeth Marshall (January 28, 1768–July 26, 1836)
## Apothecary
## Philadelphia, Pennsylvania

Elizabeth Marshall, America's second female pharmacist, gained respect for refined business sense and expertise in a medical field. The daughter of Philadelphia apothecary and chemist Charles Marshall, she followed the family trade begun at Front and Chestnut streets by paternal grandsire Christopher Marshall of Dublin, Ireland. One of the first druggists to make the connection between physician and pharmacist, he sold chemicals, imported drugs, herbs, tea, and spice and compounded doctors' remedies. Artist Robert Thom depicted him in the act of teaching his sons Charles and Christopher the job of pill making in anticipation of the brothers' partnership. The male trio carried a heavy symbolism about the way in which young men acquire family commercial expectations for their own careers.

Christopher Marshall anchored patriotic efforts for independence from England by furnishing medical kits for Delaware, Maryland, New Jersey, Pennsylvania, and Virginia troops. He signed the non-import act of November 7, 1765, rejecting trade with Britain; escorted the first reading of the Declaration of Independence on July 8, 1776; and backed the Society for Alleviating the Miseries of the Public Prisons. At a wartime exigency, two blocks west of the Delaware River, he served the Continental Army as commissioner of the sick and wounded in Philadelphia hospitals, acquiring the nickname "the fighting Quaker." At the same time, he offered hands-on training to future pharmacists at the city's supply depot.

## The Girl Inheritor

Of the ten children born to Charles and Patience Parrish Marshall, Elizabeth Marshall, the eldest, enjoyed the first granddaughter's special place. As a favored child, she apprenticed at the Marshall Drug Store in Philadelphia, a professional venue across from Strawberry Alley at 56 Chestnut Street that rivaled anything in New York City. The owner advertised his location under a large gold ball and conducted the job of gathering curative plants, drying them, and mixing tinctures. Aiding his work were a twenty-five-gallon marble mortar, alembic, still, press, and copper containers. The business became Elizabeth's inheritance, which she managed and, in 1804, revived from financial failure. She stocked supplies for country doctors and introduced from six to twelve apprentices at a time to pharmacological chemistry.

While Elizabeth's father advanced his career as the first president of the Philadelphia College of Apothecaries, she established a location in the front room at the two-story family residence on Chestnut at Second Street. To accommodate changes and modernization, she hired more staff and added a laboratory, ice house, and wholesale warehouse for storing inventory. At the same time, she supported charities and the incorporation of the Apprentices' Library Company of Philadelphia. Later refurbishment added a four-story brick warehouse at Carter's Alley.

## A Flourishing Business

By May 1822, the shop with its second-floor drying room was deeded in Elizabeth's name. Skill at business management made her an exemplary female in Philadelphia, where people relied on the dispensary for treatments as basic as paregoric, a cure for diarrhea. She was the first apothecary to dispense glycyrrhiza compound, a licorice-flavored cough remedy prepared by Dr. Benjamin Smith Barton. For its success with patients, Barton dubbed it the "brown mixture."

At Charles's demise in 1825, Elizabeth retired, passing the progressive apothecary shop to assistants Charles Ellis and Isaac P. Morris. She died at age sixty-eight, willing her entrepreneurship to youngest sister Mary Ann Marshall. At the Washington headquarters of the American Pharmacists' Association, Elizabeth's likeness appeared on a mural saluting women in pharmacy. Her vision helped boost Philadelphia to the center of pharmaceutical commerce.

## *Sources*

Ellis, Evan Tyson. "The Story of a Very Old Philadelphia Drug Store," *American Journal of Pharmacy* (February 1903): 57.
Wilbert, M.I. "Elizabeth Marshall, the First Woman Pharmacist in America," *American Journal of Pharmacy* (June 1904): 271.

# Eufrosina Hinard (1777–after 1819)
**Slave Trader, Brickmaker**

# Mariana Bonifay (1760–1829)
**Brickmaker**
**Pensacola, Florida**

A Florida brickmaker and slave dealer, Eufrosina Hinard profited from the end-of-war economic upsurge. A biracial freedwoman, she was born in New Orleans to a black mother of the *gens de couleur libre* (free people of color) and a white father named Hinard or Hisnard. At age fourteen, she entered concubinage with a Colombian attorney, Nicolás Vidal, the self-important judge and acting governor of Spanish Louisiana. She bore Carolina Maria Salome and Maria Josefa de las Mercedes plus a son, Nicolas Eustaqui Vidal, who died in infancy.

Eufrosina's investment on July 10, 1798, bought her a slave, Maria Isabel Favre Daunoy. Relocated to Pensacola, in 1806 Eufrosina inherited Vidal's bondsmen and wealth, but had to petition Florida governor Andrew Jackson for her daughters' patrimony. While post-war New England was withdrawing from the business of human bondage, she managed investment in laborers in Florida as rental property and the basis for more purchases. Those who saved enough of their wages to buy their papers she let go.

Brickmaking flourished in Pensacola from the Escambia River effluent, which mingled mud, clay, and humus from Alabama in Pensacola Bay. The opportunity for commerce placed Eufrosina in competition with Mariana Pingrow Bonifay, a French widow from Martinique living at West Intendencia Street opposite Pensacola Bay. In partnership with Charles Lavalle, Mariana issued one thousand forty-five hundred bricks annually stamped M. Bonifay. Her slaves readied blocks for mortaring with ground oyster shells. The profits from Eufrosina's business management enlarged the estate, which she left to her daughters at her death at age forty-one.

## *Sources*

Lindman, Janet Moore, and Michele Lise Tarter, eds. *A Centre of Wonders: The Body in Early America*. Ithaca, NY: Cornell University Press, 2001.

Madden, Annette. *In Her Footsteps: 101 Remarkable Black Women*. Berkeley, CA: Conari Press, 2000.
Wernicke, Carl. "Brickmaking," *Pensacola News* (24 November 1981): 1D.

# Chronology

**1492–1600**—The arrival of Europeans in North America caused the Great Dying, a century that saw reduction of indigenous people by 90 percent.

**July 1609–August 4, 1701**—The Beaver Wars embroiled natives of the St. Lawrence Valley and the Great Lakes, disrupted Algonquian and Iroquoian culture, and ousted the French.

**December 26, 1620**—One hundred two Pilgrims aboard the merchantman *Mayflower* left Leiden, Holland, and landed at Plymouth Rock, Massachusetts. The departure marked the beginning of the Puritan Great Migration, a resettlement of some twenty thousand over two decades to flee persecution under Charles I.

**March 19, 1628**—One hundred English migrants established Massachusetts Bay Colony between the Charles and Merrimack rivers.

**April 8, 1629**—John Winthrop's seventeen-ship fleet sailed from Yarmouth on the Isle of Wight and increased Massachusetts Bay Colony by one thousand newcomers.

**1630**—In the Ottawa Valley between Ontario and Quebec, the Mohawk raided the Algonquin.

**July 1636–September 1638**—The Pequot War pitted the Pequot tribe against the Mohegan, Narragansett, and colonists from Massachusetts Bay, Plymouth, and Saybrook. The clash reduced Indian braves by half and resulted in the execution of the rest and bondage for Pequot women and children.

**September 3, 1651**—The triumph of radical Puritan Oliver Cromwell preceded the execution of Charles I and the flight of British Pilgrims to the New World.

**September 20, 1659–July 15, 1660**—The Esopus War pitted the Lenni Lenape against the Dutch of New Amsterdam and resulted in arson to colonial structures and crops and death to herds.

**August 27, 1664**—The British usurped New Amsterdam, New York, which Governor Peter Stuyvesant surrendered.

**June 20, 1675**—During King Philip's War, British troops seized Wenepoykin, the sagamore of Salem and Charlestown, Massachusetts.

**April 21, 1676**—A serious upheaval among whites and Indians, the battle of Sudbury, Massachusetts, pitted New England settlers against triumphant Narragansett, Nipmuc, and Wampanoag raiders led by Metacomet, Muttawmp, and Matoonas.

**December 1677**—Culpeper's Rebellion raised North Carolina settlers' complaints about the Navigation Acts, the attempt of the British crown to intervene against smugglers and pirates.

**October 18, 1685**—Louis XIV renounced the Edict of Nantes and declared Protestantism illegal in France.

**1688**—The Glorious Revolution unseated England's James II and replaced him with William III and Mary II.

**1689**—Scots pirate William Kidd served the British as a privateer against the French.

**March 8, 1702–July 13, 1713**—Queen Anne's War, a thirteen-year conflict spreading from Maine's Kennebec River to Acadia and Newfoundland, matched the English against French Canadians and a coalition of Wabanaki, Apalachee, Timucua, Natchez, Caughnawaga, Choctaw, and Mohawk for control of New World colonies.

**April 14, 1715–1717**—The Yamasee War threatened the survival of rice planters on the Carolina coast until the Cherokee allied with the British against Creek insurgents.

**August 7, 1721**—James and Ann Smith Franklin begin issuing their satiric biweekly the *New England Courant*, a media experiment in freedom of the press.

**February 1733**—General James Edward Oglethorpe negotiated the founding of Georgia Colony.

**September 9, 1739**—A slave uprising in South Carolina led by Jemmy threatened the colony.

**October 23, 1739–October 1748**—During the War of Jenkins's Ear, Creek fighters aided Oglethorpe in attacking the fort at St. Augustine, Florida.

**July 20, 1740**—General Oglethorpe's expedition against St. Augustine, Spanish Florida, failed on July 20 because of the approach of hurricane season.

**May 12, 1745**—The seizure of Louisbourg on Cape Breton Island gave the English an entrance to Canada and the French fisheries.

**September 1752**—Thomas Godfrey's tragedy *The Prince of Parthia*, America's first original drama, opened at Williamsburg, Virginia.

**September 1, 1752**—Captain Richard Budden's ship *Myrtilla* transported the Liberty Bell from London to the Philadelphia State House.

**1755**—At the battle of Taliwa in Ball Ground, Georgia, war chief Oconostota led five hundred Cherokee warriors in a victory over one thousand Muskogee Creek.

**May 28, 1756**—The French and Indian War tested the French and British against each other with the aid of native tribes.

**September 1756**—The three-year Anglo-Cherokee War involved British forces against native tribes of Tennessee, Virginia, and the Carolinas.

**February 27, 1760**—Cherokees besieged Fort Dobbs, North Carolina, on the Dan River.

**February 6, 1765**—Boston's Sons of Liberty initiated violent acts protesting the Stamp Act.

**March 22, 1765**—The Stamp Act aroused anger among colonists for taxing newspapers, almanacs, pamphlets, broadsides, legal documents, dice, and playing cards.

**June 15–July 2, 1767**—The British Parliament passed the four Townshend Acts, which tightened royal control of the American colonies.

**October 2, 1768**—One thousand Crown troops arrived in Boston on a British fleet to suppress agitation and violence.

**March 5, 1770**—A riot between British occupation forces and citizens initiated the Boston Massacre, in which nine Redcoats shot into a mob of four hundred, killing Crispus Attucks, Samuel Gray, and James Caldwell, the first casualties of the American Revolution.

**1772**—Colonists boycotted imported tea in favor of coffee or herbal drinks.

**November 1772**—Rebel leaders Samuel Adams and Joseph Warren mustered the Boston Committee of Correspondence to raise opposition in outlying towns to British imperialism.

**May 1773**—Parliament's Tea Act limited colonial vendors to the marketing of tea from the East India Company.

**December 16, 1773**—The Sons of Liberty, whom wives disguised as Mohawks, overran the ship *Dartmouth* at the Boston Tea Party and tossed three hundred forty-two chests of tea into Boston harbor in protest of the tea tax.

**March 31, 1774**—The Boston Port Act closed the Massachusetts harbor to commerce.

**June 2, 1774**—The British Parliament passed the Intolerable Acts, blockading Boston Harbor and forcing colonists to house Redcoat troops.

**September 5, 1774**—The First Continental Congress convened delegates from twelve American colonies at Carpenters' Hall in Philadelphia to consider threats of British aggression and the need for a boycott of imported goods.

**October 20, 1774**—The First Continental Congress banned theatrical performances, gaming, and cockfighting.

**October 25, 1774**—The Edenton, North Carolina, Tea Party opposed the Tea Act of 1773 through fifty-one signatures on a petition declaring a boycott of tea and English textiles.

**April 19, 1775**—To protect an arms cache, three thousand five hundred colonial minutemen defeated seven hundred British troops at Lexington and Concord, Massachusetts, killing two hundred fifty Redcoats. The battles began the siege of Boston, which ended March 17, 1776.

**May 31, 1775**—Mecklenburg County, North Carolina, replaced the royal government with colonial sovereignty and issued a manifest of independence.

**June 17, 1775**—From her farm, Abigail Adams and son John Quincy watched the Battle of Bunker Hill and the burning of Charlestown, Massachusetts.

**December 31, 1775**—The battle of Quebec resulted in a British victory and the end of an American crusade to seize Canada.

**May 17, 1776**—The Continental Congress declared a public day of fasting and prayer to solidify colonial unity against rising taxes.

**June 1, 1776**—General George Washington guided Philadelphia upholsterer Elizabeth "Betsy" Ross in making the first union flag.

**July 4, 1776**—The Second Continental Congress issued the Declaration of Independence to King George III stating their grievances against the monarchy.

**August 27, 1776**—Some twenty thousand British and Hessian troops landed at western Long Island, New York, and won a conflict against ten thousand of George Washington's Continental Army.

**December 23, 1776**—Thomas Paine's *Crisis*, a pro-independence treatise completed in Philadelphia, encouraged rebellion in American citizens.

**December 25, 1776**—General George Washington led the Continental Army from Philadelphia across the Delaware River to a nonviolent victory over Hessian mercenaries in Trenton, New Jersey.

**October 4, 1777**—At the battle of Germantown, Pennsylvania, the Continental Army contended with British General William Howe and fled to Valley Forge, Pennsylvania.

**October 7, 1777**—At a turning point in the war, the rebel army defeated the British at the battle of Saratoga, New York, killing four hundred forty and capturing more than six thousand enemy troops.

**November 1778**—John Adams joined Benjamin Franklin in France to negotiate a colonial alliance with the French.

**May 1779**—General Benedict Arnold plotted secretly to offer his military service to the British.

**September 16–October 18, 1779**—The siege of Savannah, Georgia, involved five hundred Haitians in the Franco-American attempt to rid the colony of English invaders.

**December 24, 1779**—The Virginia House of Burgesses relocated the capital from Williamsburg to Richmond.

**May 12, 1780**—General Benjamin Lincoln suffered a defeat at the six-week siege of Charleston, South Carolina, ending in British seizure of the town.

**March 15, 1781**—At the battle of Guilford Court House, in Greensboro, North Carolina, General Nathanael Greene redirected the British general Charles Cornwallis from recruiting men in the South.

**September 28, 1781**—At the siege of Yorktown, Virginia, British troops surrendered to General George Washington and the Continental Army.

**February 13, 1782**—John Adams returned to France to negotiate the Paris peace treaty.

**August 19, 1782**—The battle of Blue Licks, Kentucky, was the last Tory victory of the American Revolution.

**September 4, 1783**—The Treaty of Paris ended the American Revolution.

**August 1784**—John and Abigail Adams resided at Auteuil, France, during his diplomatic residency.

**May 26, 1785**—Until spring 1788, John and Abigail Adams filled a diplomatic post in London.

**April 15, 1786–August 3, 1795**—The Northwest Indian War forced tribes to surrender Illinois, Indiana, Michigan, Ohio, and Wisconsin to the United States

**May 16, 1787**—Fifty-five delegates met at Independence Hall, Philadelphia, for the Constitutional Convention.

**August 22, 1791**—Haitian revolutionaries successfully freed themselves from French colonialism.

**November 26, 1796**—The Great Savannah Fire destroyed two-thirds of the city's buildings.

**March 4, 1797**—President John Adams and Vice President Thomas Jefferson swore the oath of office in Philadelphia. Adams appointed son John Quincy as ambassador to Prussia.

**March 4, 1801**—Thomas Jefferson's election to president cost John Adams a second term.

**March 4, 1804**—John Quincy Adams served as U.S. senator from Massachusetts.

**December 23, 1807**—President Thomas Jefferson issued the Embargo Act banning exports and foreign imports from American harbors.

**March 1, 1809**—President Jefferson lifted the Embargo Act to promote American commerce.

**June 18, 1812–February 18, 1815**—The War of 1812 pressed American outrage at the British navy's impressment of American seamen.

**September 22, 1817**—Under President James Monroe, John Quincy Adams served as Secretary of State.

**February 17, 1819**—The Calhoun Treaty took from the Cherokee the Hiwassee district in southeastern Tennessee, leaving the Indians with only six hundred forty acres.

**March 4, 1825**—John Quincy Adams advanced to sixth U.S. president.

**May 21, 1881**—Social worker Clara Barton founded the U.S. Red Cross in Washington, D.C.

# A Guide to Business and Professional Women by Career

### Accountant
Colden, Alice Christy
Marston, Patience Rogers

### Actor
Bignall, Ann West
Cheer, Margaret
Douglass, Sarah Hallam
Gardie, Anna
Hallam, Nancy
Stagg, Mary
West, Margaretta Sully

### Agronomist
Pinckney, Eliza Lucas

### Apothecary
Coincoin
Greenleaf, Elizabeth Gooking
Hallett, Elizabeth Fones
Hebert, Charlotte
Marshall, Elizabeth

### Attorney
Brent, Margaret
Durant, Ann Marwood

### Baker
Quamino, Duchess

### Basket Maker
Freeman, Indian Hannah
Ockett, Molly

### Beer Distributor
Van Rensselaer, Maria van Cortlandt

### Blacksmith
Hager, Elizabeth "Betsy"
Ingles, Mary Draper

### Bookbinder
Bradford, Cornelia Smith

### Bookkeeper
Starbuck, Mary Coffin

### Botanist
Lamboll, Elizabeth Pitts
Logan, Martha Daniell

### Brewer
Estaugh, Elizabeth Haddon
Penn, Hannah Callowhill

### Brickmaker
Bonifay, Mariana
Hinard, Eufrosina

### Business Manager
Barker, Penelope
Durant, Ann Marwood
Franklin, Deborah Read
Josselyn, Margaret Commack
Livingston, Alida Schuyler
Schuyler, Margaretha Brants van Slichtenhorst
Wheelwright, Esther

### Business Planner
Estaugh, Elizabeth Haddon
Ward, Nancy

### Cartographer
Moody, Deborah Dunch
Shaumpishuh

### Caterer
Minis, Abigail
Penrose, Elizabeth
Quamino, Duchess

### Cattle Rancher
Coincoin
Minis, Abigail
Wiggins, Ana Gallum

### Chandler
Wishart, Ann Battson

### Cheese Maker
Colden, Jane
Smith, Joan Barton

### Composer
von Hagen, Elizabeth Johanetta Catherine

### Cook
Boone, Rebecca Bryan
Goe, Rebecca Boone

### Court Recorder
Knight, Sarah Kemble

### Dancer
Gardie, Anna

### Dance Teacher
De Graffenried, Barbara Needham
Stagg, Mary

### Director
Douglass, Sarah Hallam
West, Margaretta Sully

### Editor
Bradford, Cornelia Smith
Crouch, Mary Wilkinson
Franklin, Ann Smith
Rind, Clementina
Timothy, Ann
Timothy, Elizabeth

### Estate Treasurer
Van Rensselaer, Maria van Cortlandt

### Farmer
Adams, Abigail Smith
Devorix, Ann

### Ferrymaster
Ingles, Mary Draper
Lewis, Alice Jones Mackelfresh

### Financial Manager
Adams, Abigail Smith

### Fish Processor
Devorix, Ann

### Flag Maker
Manny, Margaret
Ross, Elizabeth Griscom

### Food Writer
Coit, Mehetabel Chandler
Simmons, Amelia

### Gunsmith
Hager, Elizabeth "Betsy"

### Healer
Ballard, Martha Moore
Estaugh, Elizabeth Haddon
Freeman, Indian Hannah
Kierstede, Sara Jans
Ockett, Molly

### Herbalist
Allen, Rachel Stout
Ballard, Martha Moore
Coit, Mehetabel Chandler
Dyer, Mary
Hawkins, Jane Angell

### Historian
Warren, Mercy Otis

### Horticulturist
Jessop, Ann Matthews Floyd

### Illustrator
Colden, Jane

### Immunizer
Hager, Elizabeth "Betsy"

### Importer
Alexander, Mary Spratt
Brown, Esther
De Peyster, Cornelia Lubberts
Spratt, Maria de Peyster Provoost

### Innkeeper
Durant, Ann Marwood
Foster, Diana Harris
Knight, Sarah Kemble
Lewis, Alice Jones Mackelfresh
McGinty, Anne Pogue
Ward, Nancy

### Inventor
Masters, Sybilla Righton

### Investor
Adams, Abigail Smith
Alexander, Mary Spratt
Brent, Margaret
Hinard, Eufrosina

### Journalist
Draper, Margaret Green
Timothy, Elizabeth
Zenger, Anna Catharina

### Landscaper
Lamboll, Elizabeth Pitts

### Linguist
Kierstede, Sarah Jans
Musgrove, Mary
Nonhelema Hokolesqua

### Literary Agent
Tanner, Obour

### Lyricist
Warren, Mercy Otis

## Merchant
Boone, Rebecca Bryan
Brown, Esther
Eustis, Jane
Goe, Rebecca Boone
Green, Anne Catharine
Green, Martha Coit Hubbard
Graffort, Bridget Cutt
Minis, Abigail
Noyes, Elizabeth Ann Sanford
Pratt, Elizabeth Woodberry
Schuyler, Margaretha Brants van Slichtenhorst
Timothy, Elizabeth
Zenger, Anna Catharina

## Midwife
Allen, Rachel Stout
Ballard, Martha Moore
Blaikley, Catherine Kaidyee
Bonn, Anna Maria Brendel
Dyer, Mary Barrett
Fuller, Bridget Lee
Hawkins, Jane Angell
Hutchinson, Anne
Jans, Anneke
Jonas, Trijn Catherine
Phillips, Elizabeth

## Miller
McGinty, Anne Pogue

## Milliner
Cuming, Ame
Cuming, Elizabeth
Inman, Elizabeth Murray
Manny, Margaret
Necks, Lucy Harrison Randolph

## Minister
Bowne, Dinah Underhill
Bowne, Hannah Feake
Cooper, Hannah Dent
Jessop, Ann Matthews Floyd

## Missionary
Cooper, Hannah Dent
Jessop, Ann Matthews Floyd

## Mortician
Ballard, Martha Moore

## Music Teacher
Flynt, Margery Hoar
von Hagen, Elizabeth Johanetta Catherine

## Naturalist
Colden, Jane
Williams, Hannah English

## Needlework Teacher
Cuming, Ame
Cuming, Elizabeth
Green, Martha Coit Hubbard
Inman, Elizabeth Murray
Turfrey, Mary Baldwin
Upham, Hephzibah Neal

## Nurse
Bonn, Anna Maria Brendel
Hebert, Charlotte

## Optician
Breintnall, Hannah

## Organist
von Hagen, Elizabeth Johanetta Catherine

## Pamphleteer
Warren, Mercy Otis

## Pharmacist
Ballard, Martha Moore
Estaugh, Elizabeth Haddon

## Philanthropist

Graffort, Bridget Cutt

## Pianist

Bowman, Dinah
Lew, Margaret
von Hagen, Elizabeth Johanetta Catherine

## Planter

Callum, Ana
Pinckney, Eliza Lucas
Minis, Abigail

## Poet

Bradstreet, Anne
Warren, Mercy Otis
Wheatley, Phillis

## Politician

Penn, Hannah Callowhill

## Portraitist

Johnston, Henrietta Dering

## Postmaster

Goddard, Abigail Updike
Goddard, Mary Katherine
Timothy, Elizabeth

## Printer

Aitken, Jane
Bradford, Elizabeth Sowle
Bradford, Cornelia Smith
Crouch, Mary Wilkinson
Draper, Margaret
Franklin, Ann Smith
Glover, Elizabeth Harris
Goddard, Mary Katherine
Goddard, Sarah Updike
Green, Anne Catharine
Holt, Elizabeth Hunter
Nuthead, Dinah
Oswald, Elizabeth Holt
Rind, Clementina
Russell, Sarah Hood
Timothy, Ann
Timothy, Elizabeth
Zenger, Anna Catharina

## Publisher

Bradford, Cornelia Smith
Franklin, Ann Smith
Glover, Elizabeth Harris
Goddard, Mary Katherine
Goddard, Sarah Updike
Green, Anne Catharine
Holt, Elizabeth Hunter
Nuthead, Dinah
Oswald, Elizabeth Holt
Rind, Clementina
Russell, Sarah Hood
Timothy, Elizabeth
Zenger, Anna Catharina

## Real Estate Broker

Alexander, Mary Spratt
Askamapoo of Nantucket
Boot, Anna Hack
Brent, Margaret
Cogenew, Hepsibah of Chappaquiddick
De Peyster, Cornelia Lubberts
Knight, Sarah Kemble
Shaumpishuh
Spratt, Maria de Peyster Provoost
Squaw Sachem
Steele, Elizabeth Maxwell
Wunnatuckquannum of Nunepog

## Saddler

Peters, Lois Crary

## Saltmaker

Ingles, Mary Draper

## Satirist
Warren, Mercy Otis

## Sculptor
Wells, Rachel Lovell
Wright, Patience Lovell

## Seamstress
Brainard, Abigail Foote
Dickinson, Rebecca
Huntington, Elizabeth Foote
Ross, Elizabeth Griscom
Young, Rebecca

## Secretary
Adams, Abigail Smith

## Seed Merchant
Logan, Martha Daniell

## Shipping Agent
Levy, Grace Mears
Philipse, Margaret Hardenbroeck
Pinheiro, Esther
Vetch, Margaret Livingston

## Shopkeeper
Adams, Abigail Smith
Bradford, Cornelia Smith
Cuming, Ame
Cuming, Elizabeth
Franklin, Elizabeth
Knight, Sarah Kemble
Zenger, Anna Catharina

## Silk Winder
Anderson, Elizabeth
Camuse, Jane Mary

## Singer
Gardie, Anna
Hallam, Nancy

## Slave Dealer
Boot, Anna Hack
Coincoin
De Torres, Simja
Gallum, Ana
Hinard, Eufrosina
Livingston, Alida Schuyler
Vobe, Jane

## Stage Manager
Bignall, Ann West

## Storyteller
Ockett, Molly

## Tailor
Wheatley, Phillis
Woolman, Sarah Ellis

## Taverner
Breintnall, Hannah
Campbell, Christiana
Draper, Rachel
Greele, Alice
Harditch, Susannah
Hight, Allice Shannon
Ingles, Mary Draper
McGinty, Anne Pogue
Minis, Abigail
Penrose, Elizabeth
Steele, Elizabeth Maxwell
Tondee, Lucy Mouse
Townsend, Mary Hodges
Vobe, Jane

## Teacher
Anderson, Rebeckah
Fuller, Bridget Lee
Knight, Sarah Kemble
Logan, Martha Daniell

## Textile Designer
McGinty, Anne Pogue

## Town Manager

Moody, Deborah Dunch

## Trader

Brent, Margaret
Jenifer, Anne Toft
Livingston, Alida Schuyler
Musgrove, Mary
Nonhelema Hokolesqua
Penn, Hannah Callowhill
Philipse, Margaret Hardenbroeck
Pinheiro, Esther
Starbuck, Mary Coffin
Vetch, Margaret Livingston

## Upholsterer

Lawrence, Elizabeth
Ross, Elizabeth Griscom
Young, Rebecca

## Weaver

Huntington, Elizabeth Foote

## Yarn Spinner

Huntington, Elizabeth Foote

# A Guide to Business and Professional Women by Place

## Connecticut

Brainard, Abigail Foote
Coit, Mehetabel Chandler
Goddard, Mary Katherine
Goddard, Sarah Updike
Green, Martha Coit Hubbard
Hallet, Elizabeth Fones Winthrop Feake
Huntington, Elizabeth Foote
Knight, Sarah Kemble
Peters, Lois Crary
Simmons, Amelia

## Florida

Bonifay, Mariana
Wiggins, Ana Gallum
Hinard, Eufrosina

## Georgia

Anderson, Elizabeth
Camuse, Jane Mary
Minis, Abigail
Musgrove, Mary
Penrose, Elizabeth
Tondee, Lucy Mouse
Townsend, Mary Hodges

## Kentucky

Boone, Rebecca Bryan
Goe, Rebecca Boone
McGinty, Anne Pogue

## Louisiana

Coincoin
Hebert, Charlotte

## Maine

Ballard, Martha Moore
Greele, Alice
Josselyn, Margaret Commack
Ockett, Molly
Wheelwright, Esther

## Maryland

Brent, Margaret
Goddard, Mary Katherine
Green, Anne Catharine
Hallam, Nancy
Lewis, Alice Jones Mackelfresh
Nuthead, Dinah
Vetch, Margaret Livingston

## Massachusetts

Adams, Abigail Smith
Anderson, Rebeckah

Ballard, Martha Moore
Bowman, Dinah
Bowne, Hannah Feake
Bradstreet, Anne
Cuming, Ame
Cuming, Elizabeth
Devorix, Ann
Dickinson, Rebecca
Draper, Margaret Green
Dyer, Mary Barrett
Eustis, Jane
Flynt, Margery Hoar
Franklin, Ann Smith
Fuller, Bridget Lee
Glover, Elizabeth Harris
Greenleaf, Elizabeth Gooking
Hager, Elizabeth "Betsy"
Hawkins, Jane Angell
Hutchinson, Anne
Inman, Elizabeth Murray
Knight, Sarah Kemble
Lew, Margaret
Marston, Patience Rogers
Phillips, Elizabeth
Pinheiro, Esther
Squaw Sachem
Starbuck, Mary Coffin
Turfrey, Mary Baldwin
Vetch, Margaret Livingston
von Hagen, Elizabeth Johanetta Catherine
Warren, Mercy Otis
Wheatley, Phillis

## New Hampshire

Graffort, Bridget Cutt
Hight, Allice Shannon
Russell, Sarah Hood
Upham, Hephzibah Neal

## New Jersey

Cooper, Hannah Dent
Estaugh, Elizabeth Haddon
Wells, Rachel Lovell
Woolman, Sarah Ellis

## New York

Alexander, Mary Spratt
Bowne, Dinah Underhill
Brown, Esther
Colden, Alice Christy
Colden, Jane
Jans, Anneke
Jonas, Trijn Catherine
Kiersted, Sarah Jans
Levy, Grace Mears
Livingston, Alida Schuyler
Moody, Deborah Dunch
Oswald, Elizabeth Holt
De Peyster, Cornelia Lubberts
Philipse, Margaret Hardenbroeck
Pinheiro, Esther
Schuyler, Margaretha Brants van Slichtenhorst
Spratt, Maria de Peyster Provoost
De Torres, Simja
Van Rensselaer, Maria van Cortlandt
Vetch, Margaret Livingston
Zenger, Anna Catharina

## North Carolina

Allen, Rachel Stout
Barker, Penelope
Bonn, Anna Maria Brendel
Boone, Rebecca Bryan
Durant, Ann Marwood
Foster, Diana Harris
Jessop, Ann Matthews Floyd
Steele, Elizabeth Maxwell

## Ohio

Nonhelema Hokolesqua

## Pennsylvania

Bradford, Cornelia Smith
Bradford, Elizabeth Sowle
Breintnall, Hannah
Draper, Rachel
Franklin, Deborah Read
Freeman, Indian Hannah
Gardie, Anna

Harditch, Susannah
Lawrence, Elizabeth
Manny, Margaret
Marshall, Elizabeth
Masters, Sybilla Righton
Penn, Hannah Callowhill
Ross, Elizabeth Griscom
Wishart, Ann Battson
Wright, Patience Lovell
Young, Rebecca

## Rhode Island

Dyer, Mary
Cooper, Hannah Dent
Franklin, Ann Smith
Goddard, Mary Katherine
Goddard, Sarah Updike
Hawkins, Jane Angell
Hutchinson, Anne
Noyes, Elizabeth Ann Sanford
Pratt, Elizabeth Woodberry
Quamino, Duchess
Smith, Joan Barton

## South Carolina

Cheer, Margaret
Crouch, Mary Wilkinson
Johnston, Henrietta Dering
Lamboll, Elizabeth Pitts
Logan, Martha Daniell
Pinckney, Eliza Lucas
Timothy, Ann
Timothy, Elizabeth
Williams, Hannah English

## Tennessee

Ward, Nancy

## Virginia

Bignall, Ann West
Blaikley, Catherine Kaidyee
Boot, Anna Hack
Brent, Margaret
Campbell, Christiana
De Graffenried, Barbara Needham
Douglass, Sarah Hallam
Hallam, Nancy
Holt, Elizabeth Hunter
Ingles, Mary Draper
Jenifer, Anne Toft
Necks, Lucy Harrison Randolph
Rind, Clementina
Stagg, Mary
Vobe, Jane
West, Margaretta Sully

# Glossary

**Algonquian**—a widespread native American language dominant in New England and the Great Lakes area

**Almanac**—an annual planting guide based on tide tables and star patterns

**amber**—a honey-yellow fossilized resin

**Anabaptist**—a Protestant faith based on detailed theological beliefs

**Awakening**—a series of religious revivals launched in 1730 and 1790

**balm**—a fragrant oil for soothing and healing chapped skin

**barrel organ**—a mechanical device playing coded music and operated by a crank

**beaver hat**—a high-top hat made from silk, wool, and beaver pelt

**blockhouse**—a small defense point to protect residents of an area

**blond lace**—French bobbin lace made from naturally colored silk thread

**bolted rye**—sifted rye flour

**bougie**—a surgical tube for removing blockages

**bourrée**—a French clog dance

**bowery**—farmland

**breeches part**—a female stage role that requires posing as a man

**broadsheet**—a long, vertical newspaper printed on one side

**brolio**—a crown or garland

**bullace**—a damson plum

**bursar**—finance manager

**calamanco**—thin worsted wool

**calivanse**—an edible pulse seed

**cambleteen**—a wool and cotton blend woven with goat's hair

**cambric**—a light, tightly wove cotton or linen fabric used for cuffs, bands, and ruffs

**campuchine**—a Moorish garment featuring a pointed hood or cowl

**cap lace**—a wig foundation into which human hair is inserted

**caracoa**—a large, fast boat usually carrying slaves

**carcass**—incendiary projectiles

**cardinal**—flat-brimmed red hat with low rounded crown

**carilloneur**—a keyboardist of a percussion instrument that plays bells

**catgut**—strong thread made from animal intestines

**chamberlain**—financial manager of a city

**chenille**—fabric woven or tufted from fuzzy cotton yarn

**chine**—animal backbone

**chinoiserie**—a decorative item or furniture that features exotic or whimsical East Asian motifs

**chip hat**—wood or palm leaf split into slips or plaited into a bonnet or sunscreen

**cilice**—a coarse sackcloth shirt worn next to the skin

**clipper ship**—a tall sailing vessel that is designed for speed

**closet drama**—a play or drama intended to be read rather than viewed on stage

**coloratura**—a sparkling, ornamented vocal melody sung by an operatic voice

**comedy of manners**—a stage satire of a society's manners and affectations

**committee of correspondence**—an effort to spread news, establish consensus, and coordinate opposition to British tyranny

**Committee of Safety**—emergency legislators or vigilantes who make laws in the field

**Conestoga**—a heavy wagon covered with canvas and named for the Conestoga Indians of Lancaster County, Pennsylvania

**court-leet**—lower court

**court plaster**—a fabric permeated with adhesive for covering lesions and cuts

**Creole**—an individual claiming black and European bloodlines

**crepe**—a luxury fabric used in upholstery, draperies, suits, and evening gowns

**Davis's quadrants**—navigational devices that measure altitudes of stars and planets

**dimity**—sheer cotton woven with raised checks and stripes

**Dresden work**—a combination of embroidery and airy backgrounds made by pulling filler stitches

**ducal**—a dress made of heavily corded silk

**duffel wool**—coarse wool with a thick nap

**durant**—glazed wool fabric permanently creased

**eau de luce**—a treatment for insect bites and burns

**emptins**—liquid leavening from boiled hops or potatoes

**esquire**—a nobleman and attendant on royalty

**factor**—an agent or representative of a commodity

**farrier**—blacksmith who trims horses' hooves and shoes them

**fathom**—a measure equal to six feet

**ferret**—narrow ribbon woven from silk, cotton, or wool

**filature**—the processing of silk strands for weaving

**fomentation**—application of hot moist poultices to relieve pain

**foolscap**—cheap paper measuring 8" × 13"

**fulling mill**—a water course that rinses natural oils from weaving and produces a smooth, tightly matted textile before dyeing and stretching

**garlic**—off-white linen

**gauze**—thin, firmly woven translucent fabric favored for absorbent wound dressing

**genera**—living things classed by common traits

***gens de couleur libre***—free people of color

**goody**—goodwife

**head sauce**—a fermented gravy made from a fish, pig, or calf head for pouring over meat

**headrights**—the right to claim fifty acres per person in payment for bringing settlers to a colony

**holland**—plain woven cotton or linen

**homily**—a spiritual or moralizing discourse

**hornbook**—an alphabet tablet used as a primer

**Huguenot**—a French Protestant

**Hungary water**—brandy-based perfume blended with citrus oil and seven herbs

**indenture**—a binding contract on a worker or apprentice

**ingenue**—a vulnerable, inexperienced female role in a play

**jig**—a British folk dance enlivened with jumps

**jockey**—a skull cap or equestrian helmet to protect the rider in a fall

**kersey**—coarsely napped ribbed wool

**ketch**—a two-masted sailboat

**laid paper**—paper with a ribbed texture

**lawn**— a silky cotton fabric from India also called batiste and used for bedding

**letterbook**—a copy of a letter writer's correspondence

**leveret**—young rabbit

**libretto**—the words to a musical or opera

**limbeck**—distillery boiler

**Linnaean**—of the classification of living things using the generic and specific designations of Swedish naturalist Carl Linnaeus

**loam**—clay and sand soil enriched with humus or dead plant matter

**long fever**—typhus

**lutestring**—glossy silk

**magazine**—ammunition storage

**mantua**—robe or overcoat

**manumission**—a release from bondage

**mastic**—dried tree resin

**matchlock rifle**—a long gun fired by igniting gunpowder with a slow-burning match or cord

**mechlin**—delicate bobbin lace applied to hats and dresses

**midden**—a dumping place for garbage and food waste

**mignionett**—strips of bobbin lace

**minuet**—a French social dance consisting of short, dainty steps

**minuteman**—a New England militiaman trained in weapons and attack strategy

**mitt**—fingerless gloves

**morphology**—the study of structures in biota

**mourning gown**—a female mourner's black bonnet, gloves, shoes, and dress worn with no decoration

**multiplying glass**—multifaceted lenses like kaleidoscopes that produce many views

**musk**—a strong-smelling animal secretion

**muslin**—high quality cotton fabric known for softness, absorption, breathability, and strength

**myopic**—near-sighted

**naval impressment**—forced drafting of seamen

**neat's foot**—cattle hoof

**nonconformist**—a Protestant who rejected the state Church of England

**osnaburg**—heavy cotton or linen sacking or upholstery cloth

**ox-eye glasses**—large round lenses for surveying landscapes

**paduasoy**—embossed or corded fabric for formal suits and vestments

**palance**—an elegant garment kept simple for effect

**Palatinate**—Germans from the Rhineland

**pastiche**—an imitative artwork

**pastoral**—idealized artwork set in herding country or farmland

**patches**—taffeta, mouse fur, or Spanish leather applied as fake moles

**patent**—the right to claim land

**patroonship**—a land grant to settlers of New Netherland Colony

**perspectives**—two-dimensional glasses that add depth to vision

**picaresque**—episodic fiction featuring a rowdy, dishonest hero

**piccage**—rental fee for booth space at fairs

**pillory**—a wood frame with holes for head and hands to secure a prisoner before public shaming.

**pink**—a square-rigged vessel with a narrow stern

**pinnace**—a small tender that accompanied large ships

**pluck**—animal heart, liver, and lungs

**polanese**—a three-quarter length coat and vest worn over a shift

**pomology**—the science of growing fruit

**postpartum**—a mother's period of recovery after giving birth

**pot paper**—colonial newsprint

**prame**—a shallow draft boat or barge poled through shallow waterways to transport cattle

**progressive**—a liberal who advocates social reform

**psalter**—a collection of scriptural psalms

**quinsey**—an abscess formed on the tonsils

**quit-rent**—fees paid to the land granter

**quoit**—a ring used in ring-toss games

**Regulators**—Carolina backwoodsmen who challenged colonial authority

**rhizome**—a cross between a root and a bulb which creeps horizontally

**riding mask**—a face covering to protect a horsewoman's complexion

**rigadoon**—a sprightly French folk dance consisting of hopping steps

**rusk**—a twice-baked biscuit or bread

**russel**—twilled wool used in shoes and clothes

**sachem**—an Algonquian chief on the American northeastern coast.

**sackposset**—a restorative custard of cream, sugar, eggs, and sherry

**salvolatile**—smelling salts

**scow**—a light coaster or dredge with tapered fore and aft

**Sephardic**—of a Jewish refugee who settled in Iberia

**shagreen**—a naturally patterned rawhide from dogfish, horse, shark, or stingray

**small beer**—low-alcohol ale

**Sons of Liberty**—riotous activists who defied British rule with acts of civil disobedience

**soubrette**—a vigorous, flirty female role in opera or theater

**sousae**—a flowering plant found in Colima and Oaxaca

**squaw**—a racist term for a Native American woman

**stallage**—rent on a stall at a fair

**Star Chamber**—an English court at Westminster Palace that judged civil and criminal cases of the upper class

**stocks**—a wood frame with holes for ankles to hold a prisoner before public shaming

**stomacher**—the central panel of a bodice

**Stoughton's elixir**—a treatment for upset stomach

**sucker**—a shoot growing from the root or base of a plant

**supercargo**—a shipboard title that combined the jobs of purchasing agent and loadmaster

**syllabub**—a creamy dessert made from sweetened cream curdled with cider or wine

**tammie**—a traditional flat bonnet worn of Scotsmen, especially the military

**tate**—a "sheep's head" or "tête de mouton" hairstyle set in tight rows close to the scalp

**taxonomy**—classification

**terroir**—land that imparts identifiable qualities to food plants

**tincture**—a mixture of plant material with ethanol

**tippet**—the extension of a cape, hood, or sleeve

**town hall system**—a public official answers questions from the public

**trammel**—a fish trap

**trifle**—sponge cake layered with cream, custard, and jelly

**Ursuline**—a Catholic member of a teaching order

***usus***—the right to use something without damaging or depleting it

**variolation**—a crude form of introducing microbes into a slit in the arm to create permanent immunity

**wampum**—polished shell beads that make up a belt, sash, or strands that are traded as money

**Whitehall**—a term implying England's government offices.

**whitpot**—a sweet custard bread pudding

**whortleberry**—American blueberry

**wrought silk**—embellished or ornamented fabric

**yaws**—a disfiguring skin infection

# Bibliography

## Primary Sources


Balderston, Lloyd. *The Evolution of the American Flag*. Philadelphia: Ferris & Leach, 1917.

Ballard, Martha. *The Diary of Martha Ballard, 1785–1812*. Camden, ME: Picton Press, 1992.

Bickerstaff, Isaac. *The Spoil'd Child*. London: Barker & Son, 1792.

Bradford, William. *The History of Plymouth Plantation*. Boston: Massachusetts Historical Society, 1856.

Bradstreet, Anne. *The Works of Anne Bradstreet*. Cambridge, MA: Belknap Press, 2010.

Burrage, Henry Sweetser. *The Beginnings of Colonial Maine, 1602–1658*. Portland, ME: Printed for the state, 1914.

Channing, George Gibbs. *Early Recollections of Newport, R.I.* Newport, RI: Ward & Hammett, Jr., 1868.

Clark, J. Bunker, ed. *American Keyboard Music Through 1865*. Boston: G.K. Hall, 1990.

Coffin, Allen. *The Coffin Family: The Life of Tristram Coffyn*. Nantucket, MS: Hussey & Robinson, 1881.

Ditmas, Charles Andrew. *Long Island Bulletin*. Brooklyn, NY: Ditmas, 1913.

Dunn, Richard, and Mary Maples Dunn, Ed. *The Papers of William Penn*. Philadelphia: University of Pennsylvania Press, 1982.

*Early Settlers of New Amsterdam*. New York: Mail & Express, 1903.

*Essays and Observations Physical and Literary*. Edinburgh: Philosophical Society of Edinburgh, 1756.

Folsom, George. *History of Saco and Biddeford*. Saco, ME: self-published, 1830.

Frothingham, R. *History of Charlestown*. Boston: Little & Brown, 1845.

Goodwin, Nathaniel. *The Foote Family*. Hartford, CT: Case, Tiffany & Company, 1849.

Guthman, William H., ed. *The Correspondence of Captain Nathan and Lois Peters*. Hartford: Connecticut Historical Society, 1980.

Hammon, Neal O. *My Father, Daniel Boone: The Draper Interviews with Nathan Boone*. Lexington: University Press of Kentucky, 2013.

*A Handbook of New England*. Boston: Porter E. Sargent, 1916.

Hathaway, J.R.B., ed. *North Carolina Historical and Genealogical Register*. Edenton, NC: Clearfield, 1900.

Haxtun, Annie Arnoux. *Early Settlers of New Amsterdam*. New York: Mail & Express, 1903.

Hodge, Christina J. *Consumerism and the Emergence of the Middle Class in Colonial America*. New York: Cambridge University Press, 2014.

Howard, Cecil. *Genealogy of the Cutts Family in America*. Albany, NY: Joel Munsell's Sons, 1892.

Hudson, Frederic. *Journalism in the United States, from 1690 to 1872*. New York: Harper & Brothers, 1873.

Hurd, Duane Hamilton, ed. *History of Middlesex County, Massachusetts*. Philadelphia: J.W. Lewis & Company, 1890.

______. *History of New London, Connecticut.* Philadelphia: J.W. Lewis, 1882.
Johnston, George. *History of Cecil County, Maryland.* Elkton, MD: self-published, 1881.
Jones, Charles C. *History of Savannah, Ga.* Syracuse, NY: D. Mason & Co., 1890.
Jones, Horatio Gates. *An Address Delivered at the Annual Meeting of the Historical Society of Pennsylvania.* Philadelphia: King & Baird, 1869.
Keith, George, and Peter Boss. *The Trials of Peter Boss, George Keith, Thomas Budd, and William Bradford.* London: Richard Baldwin, 1693.
King, William L. *The Newspaper Press of Charleston, S.C.* Charleston: Edward Perry, 1872.
Lamb, Martha Joanna, and Mrs. Burton Harrison. *History of the City of New York.* New York: A.S. Barnes, 1877.
Livingston, Edwin B. *The Livingstons of Livingston Manor.* New York: Knickerbocker Press, 1910.
Macy, Obed. *The History of Nantucket.* Oxford, UK: Oxford University Press, 1835.
Meacham, Sarah Hand. *Every Home a Distillery: Alcohol, Gender, and Technology in the Colonial Chesapeake.* Baltimore: Johns Hopkins University Press, 2009.
Mead, Spencer Percival, and Daniel M. Mead. *Ye Historie of Ye Town of Greenwich.* New York: Knickerbocker Press, 1911.
*Mehetabel Chandler Coit Her Book, 1714.* Cambridge, MA: Harvard University, 1714.
Morrison, Hugh Alexander. *A Preliminary Check List of American Almanacs 1639–1800.* Washington, DC: Library of Congress, 1907.
O'Keeffe, John. *The Highland Reel.* Dublin: Booksellers, 1790.
Peters, Edmund Frank, and Eleanor Bradley Peters. *Peters of New England.* New York: Knickerbocker Press, 1903.
Peterson, Edward. *History of Rhode Island.* New York: John S. Taylor, 1853.
Pinckney, Eliza Lucas. *The Letterbook of Eliza Lucas Pinckney, 1739–1762.* Chapel Hill: University of North Carolina Press, 1972.
*Proceedings of the Nantucket Historical Association.* Waltham, MA: Waltham Publishing Company, 1908.
Rutherford, Livingston. *John Peter Zenger, His Press, His Trial, and a Bibliography of Zenger Imprints.* New York: Dodd, Mead, 1904.
Schuyler, George W. *Colonial New York: Philip Schuyler and His Family.* New York: Charles Scribner's Sons, 1885.
Shattuck, Lemuel. *History of the Town of Concord.* Boston: Russell, Odiorne & Co., 1835.
Simmons, Amelia. *American Cookery.* Hartford, CT: Hudson & Goodwin, 1796.
Steele, Robert Ingles, and Andrew Lewis Ingles, eds. *The Story of Mary Draper Ingles and Son Thomas Ingles.* Radford, VA: Commonwealth Press, 1969.
Stephens, William. *The Journal of William Stephens.* Athens: University of Georgia Press, 1958.
Sturtz, Linda L. *Within Her Power: Propertied Women in Colonial Virginia.* New York: Routledge, 2002.
Upham, F.K. *The Descendants of John Upham of Massachusetts.* Albany, NY: Joel Munsell's Sons, 1892.
Van Laer, A.J.F. *Correspondence of Maria Van Rensselaer 1669–1689.* Albany: University of New York, 1935.
Warren, Mercy Otis. *Mercy Otis Warren: Selected Letters.* Boston: Larkin, 1805.
Watson, John L. *Memoirs of the Marstons of Salem.* Boston: David Clapp & Son, 1873.
Whitmire, William H. *Notes on the Winthrop Family.* Albany, NY: J. Munsell, 1864.
Wise, Jennings Cropper. *Ye Kingdome of Accawmacke.* Richmond, VA: Bell Book and Stationery, 1911.

## *Articles, Chapters, Theses, Letters*

"The Ancient Brewers of New York," *Scientific American* (25 February 1871): 129.
*Boston Gazette* (20 November 1769): 3.
Breintnall, Hannah. "Advertise of 1756 in the *Boston Evening Post,*" *Optical Journal* 54 (10 July 1924): 36.

De Peyster, Frederich. "John Peter Zenger, and His Persecution for Libel," *New Amsterdam Gazette* (1 February 1888): 13–15; (17 April 1888): 9–10.
"Genealogical Notes," *Rhode Island Historical Magazine* 5 (1884–1885): 63.
Holt, John. "Journal of Occurrences," *New York Journal* (9 November 1768): 2.
Logan, Martha, and Mary Barbot Prior. "Letters of Martha Logan to John Bartram, 1760–1763," *South Carolina Historical Magazine* 59:1 (January 1958): 38–46.
Petiver, James. "An Account of Animals and Shells Sent from Carolina," *Philosophical Transactions* (Royal Society of London) 24:299 (May 1705): 1952–1960.
Phillips, Henry, Jr. "Certain Almanacs Published in Philadelphia Between 1705 and 1744" (speech), *American Philosophical Society* (18 February 1881).
Purple, Samuel S. "Genealogy of the First Printer in the Middle Colonies of British America, William Bradford," *New York Genealogical and Biographical Record* 4:4 (October 1873): 183.
Spooner, W.W. "The Van Rensselaer Family," *American Historical Magazine* 2:10 (January 1907): 1–212.
"Substance of the Address of J.W. Wallace," *Historical Magazine* 7:7 (July 1863): 201–218.

### *Electronic*

"Adams Family Papers," https://www.masshist.org/digitaladams/archive/letter/.
Braccio, Nathan. "Quassaquanch's and Shaumpishuh's 1639 Map of the Connecticut Coast," *web.sas.upenn.edu/earlyamericanstudies/2022/03/13/quassaquanchs-*and-shaumpishuhs-1639-map-of-the-connecticut-coast/ (13 March 2022).
De Armond, Anna Janney. "Andrew Bradford," https://journals.psu.edu, 1983, 463–487.
Fuller, Samuel. "The Last Will & Testament of Samuel Fuller," *Pilgrim Hall Museum*, https://pilgrimhall.org/pdf/Samuel_Fullers_Will_Inventory.pdf.
Green, Ann Catherine Hoof. "Maryland Gazette: December 1, 1774," https:// archive.org/details/mg12011774/page/n21/mode/2up.
Jackson, Charlotte. "A Lost Letter of Hannah (Feake) Bowne (1637–1678)," https:// *www.bownehouse.org/letter-from-hannah-bowne* (24 May 1986).
"Molly Ockett and Her World," https://bethelhistorical.org/catalog/exhibits/show/molly ockett/introduction, 2024.
"National Gallery of Art," https://heald.nga.gov/mediawiki/index.php/Jane_Colden.

## Secondary Sources

Agger, Lee. *Women of Maine*. Portland, ME: Guy Gannett, 1982.
Ammer, Christine. *Unsung: A History of Women in American Music*. Portland: Amadeus, 2001.
Archer, Richard. *As If an Enemy's Country: The British Occupation of Boston and the Origins of Revolution*. New York: Oxford University Press, 2012.
Bacon, Edwin Monroe. *Literary Pilgrimages in New England*. New York: Silver Burdett, 1902.
Baker, Charlotte Alice. *True Stories of New England Captives Carried to Canada During the Old French and Indian Wars*. Cambridge, MA: unknown, 1897.
Bell, Landon C. *The Old Free State*. Richmond, VA: William Byrd Press, 1927.
Biemer, Linda Briggs. *Women and Property in Colonial New York: The Transition from Dutch to English Law, 1643–1727*. Ann Arbor: University of Michigan Research Press, 1983.
Breen, T.H. *The Marketplace of Revolution: How Consumer Politics Shaped American Independence*. New York: Oxford University Press, 2004.
Brewster, Charles W. *Rambles About Portsmouth*. Portsmouth, NH: Lewis W. Brewster, 1859.
Brockett, Oscar G. *History of the Theatre*. Boston: Allyn & Bacon, 1968.
Brooks, Geraldine. *Dames and Daughters of Colonial Days*. New York: Thomas Y. Crowell, 1900.

Brooks, Lynn Matlock. *John Durang, Man of the American Stage*. Amherst, NY: Cambria Press, 2011.
Brown, Alice. *Mercy Warren*. New York: Scribner's, 1896.
Buckley, Gail. *American Patriots: The Story of Blacks in the Military*. New York: Random House, 2002.
Burstyn, Joan N. *Past and Promise: Lives of New Jersey Women*. Syracuse, NY: Syracuse University Press, 1997.
Cabell, Eleanor Kelley. *Women Merchants and Milliners in Eighteenth Century Williamsburg*. Williamsburg, VA: Colonial Williamsburg Foundation, 1988.
Carretta, Vincent. *Phillis Wheatley: Biography of a Genius in Bondage*. Athens: University of Georgia Press, 2014.
Clark, Christopher. *The Roots of Rural Capitalism*. Ithaca, NY: Cornell University Press, 1990.
Clark, Emily. *Masterless Mistresses: The New Orleans Ursulines and the Development of a New World Society, 1727–1834*. Chapel Hill: University of North Carolina Press, 2007.
Cleary, Patricia. *Elizabeth Murray: A Woman's Pursuit of Independence in Eighteenth- Century America*. Amherst: University of Massachusetts Press, 2000.
Cohen, Hennig. *The South Carolina Gazette, 1732–1775*. Columbia: University of South Carolina Press, 1953.
Cook, Elizabeth Christine. *Literary Influences in Colonial Newspapers, 1704–1750*. New York: Columbia University Press, 1912.
Copeland, David A. *Debating the Issues in Colonial Newspapers*. New York: Bloomsbury, 2000.
Cott, Nancy F. *The Bonds of Womanhood*. New Haven, CT: Yale University Press, 1977.
Coughlin, Michelle Marchetti. *One Colonial Woman's World: The Life and Writings of Mehetabel Chandler Coit*. Amherst: University of Massachusetts Press, 2012.
Cullen-DuPont, Kathryn. *Encyclopedia of Women's History in America*. New York: Facts on File, 2000.
Daye, Stephen. *Stephen Daye and His Successors*. Cambridge, MA: Cambridge Press, 1921 (orig. printing 1693).
Dees, Pamela Y. *A Guide to Piano Music by Women Composers*. New York: Bloomsbury, 2002.
de Graffenried, Thomas P. *History of the de Graffenried Family from 1191 A.D. to 1925*. New York: self-published, 1925.
Dexter, Elisabeth Anthony. *Colonial Women of Affairs*. Boston: Houghton Mifflin, 1924.
Dorwart, Jeffery M. *Elizabeth Haddon Estaugh 1680–1762: Building the Quaker Community of Haddonfield, New Jersey, 1701–1762*. Haddonfield, NJ: Historical Society of Haddonfield, 2013.
Edwards, Thomas S., and Elizabeth A. De Wolfe, eds. *Such News of the Land: U.S. Women Nature Writers*. Hanover, NH: University Press of New England, 2001.
Foote, William Henry. *Sketches of Virginia, Historical and Biographical*. Philadelphia: W.S. Martien, 1850.
Futhey, John Smith, and Gilbert Cope. *History of Chester County, Pennsylvania*. Philadelphia: L.H. Everts, 1881.
Glover, Lorri. *Eliza Lucas Pinckney: An Independent Woman in the Age of Revolution*. New Haven, CT: Yale University Press, 2020.
Grant De Pauw, Linda. *Founding Mothers: Women of America in the Revolutionary Era*. Boston: Houghton Mifflin, 1975.
Griffenhagen, George Bernard. *Drug Supplies in the American Revolution*. Boston: Hassell Street Press, 2021.
Grunwald, Lisa, and Stephen J. Adler, eds. *Women's Letters*. New York: Dial Press, 2009.
Hachard, Marie-Madeleine. *Une Rouennaise à La Nouvelle-Orléans au XVIIIe Siècle: Relation du Voyage des Ursulines (1726–1728)*. Laval, Quebec: Presses de l'Université Laval, 2022.
Hall, David D., ed. *Witch-hunting in Seventeenth-Century New England*. Boston: Northeastern University Press, 1991.

Hatfield, April Lee. *From Strangers to Citizens*. London: Sussex Academic Press, 2001.
Hinshaw, William Wade. *Encyclopedia of American Quaker Genealogy*. Washington, DC: n.p., 1938.
Hollingsworth, Buckner. *Her Garden Was Her Delight*. New York: Macmillan, 1962.
Holton, Woody. *Abigail Adams*. New York: Simon & Schuster, 2010.
Hood, Henry G., Jr. *The Public Career of John Archdale, 1642–1717*. Greensboro: North Carolina Friends Historical Society, 1976.
Humphreys, Hannah. *The Ghost Orchard*. Toronto: HarperCollins, 2017.
Huston, Geraldine. *Oratam of the Hackensacks*. Paramus, NJ: Highway Printing, 1950.
Jaffary, Nora E., and Jane E. Mangan, eds. *Women in Colonial Latin America*. Indianapolis: Hackett Publishing, 2018.
Jarvis, Michael J. *In the Eye of All Trade*. Chapel Hill: University of North Carolina Press, 2010.
Johnson, Odai. *The Colonial American Stage, 1665–1774: A Documentary Calendar*. Cranbury, NJ: Associated University Presses, 2001.
Kaplan, Yosef. *The Posen Library of Jewish Culture and Civilization*. New Haven, CT: Yale University Press, 2023.
Kass, Amalie M. *Midwifery and Medicine in Boston: Walter Channing, M.D., 1786–1876*. Boston: Northeastern University Press, 2019.
Kierner, Cynthia, and Sandra Gioia Treadway, eds. *Virginia Women: Their Lives and Times*. Athens: University of Georgia Press, 2015.
Kindstedt, Paul. *Cheese and Culture*. London: Chelsea Green, 2012.
King, William L. *The Newspaper Press of Charleston, S.C.* Charleston: Edward Perry, 1872.
Kole, Kaye. *The Minis Family of Georgia, 1733–1992*. Savannah: Georgia Historical Society, 1992.
Landers, Jane G. *Atlantic Creoles in the Age of Revolutions*. Cambridge, MA: Harvard University Press, 2011.
Lemire, Elise. *Black Walden*. Philadelphia: University of Pennsylvania Press, 2009.
Lindman, Janet Moore, and Michele Lise Tarter, eds. *A Centre of Wonders: The Body in Early America*. Ithaca, NY: Cornell University Press, 2001.
Little, Ann M. *The Many Captivities of Esther Wheelwright*. New Haven: Yale University Press, 2016.
MacMaster, Richard. *Scotch-Irish Merchants in Colonial America*. Belfast, Northern Ireland: Ulster Historical Foundation, 2009.
Madden, Annette. *In Her Footsteps: 101 Remarkable Black Women*. Berkeley, CA: Conari Press, 2000.
Marcus, Jacob R. *The Colonial American Jew, 1492–176*. Detroit: Wayne State University Press, 1970.
Marcus, Maeva, and James R. Perry. *The Documentary History of the Supreme Court of the United States, 1789–1800*. New York: Columbia University Press, 1985.
Marsh, Ben. *Georgia's Frontier Women*. Athens: University of Georgia Press, 2007.
Mays, Dorothy A. *Women in Early America: Struggle, Survival, and Freedom in a New World*. Santa Barbara, CA: ABC-CLIO, 2004, 148–149.
McEuen, Melissa A., and Thomas H. Appleton, Jr. *Kentucky Women, Their Lives and Times*. Athens: University of Georgia Press, 2015.
McIlvenna, Noeleen. *A Very Mutinous People*. Chapel Hill: University of North Carolina Press, 2009.
Middleton, Margaret Simons. *Henrietta Johnston of Charles Town, South Carolina: America's First Pastellist*. Columbia: University of South Carolina Press, 1966.
Miller, Maria R. *Rebecca Dickinson: Independence for a New England Woman*. Boulder, CO: Westview Press, 2013.
Moore, Deborah Dash, ed. *City of Promises: A History of the Jews of New York*. New York: New York University Press, 2012.
Moore, Lillian. *Echoes of American Ballet*. Brooklyn, NY: Dance Horizons, 1976.
Moss, Kay K. *Southern Folk Medicine, 1750–1820*. Columbia: University of South Carolina Press, 2021.

Paltsits, Victor Huto. *John Holt, Printer and Postmaster.* New York: Public Library, 1920.
Perdue, Theda, ed. *Sifters: Native American Women's Lives.* Oxford, UK: Oxford University Press, 2001.
Philbrick, Nathaniel. *Away Off Shore: Nantucket Island and Its People, 1602–1890.* New York: Penguin, 2011.
Pope, Laura. *Portsmouth Women.* Charleston, SC: Arcadia, 2013.
Rankin, Hugh F. *The Colonial Theatre: Its History and Operations.* Chapel Hill: University of North Carolina Press, 1965.
Richards, Jeffrey H. *Drama, Theatre, and Identity in the American New Republic.* Cambridge, UK: Cambridge University Press, 2005.
Roberts, Vera Lowry. *On Stage: A History of Theatre.* New York: Harper & Row, 1962.
Romney, Susanah Shaw. *New Netherland Connections: Intimate Networks and Atlantic Ties in Seventeenth-Century America.* Chapel Hill: University of North Carolina Press, 2014.
Saunders, Richard H., and Ellen Gross Miles. *American Colonial Portraits.* Washington, DC: Smithsonian Institution Press, 1987.
Sawyer, T.T. *Old Charlestown: Historical and Biographical Reminiscences.* Boston: James H. West Company, 1902.
Smith, Margaret Supplee, and Emily Herring Wilson. *North Carolina Women Making History.* Chapel Hill: University of North Carolina Press, 1999.
Snabel, Cor, and Elizabeth Johnson. *The Varlet Family of Amsterdam.* San Mateo, CA: PB Works, 2008.
Snodgrass, Mary Ellen. *American Colonial Women and Their Art.* Jefferson, NC: McFarland, 2017.
Sommers, Richard J. *Vignettes of Military History.* Carlisle, PA: United States Army, 1976.
Sonneck, O.G. *Early Concert Life in America.* Storrs: University of Connecticut Libraries, 1906.
Sprigg, June. *Domestick Beings.* New York: Knopf, 1984.
Stark, James Henry. *The Loyalists of Massachusetts and the Other Side of the American Revolution.* Boston: self-published, 1910.
Sturz, Linda. *Within Her Power: Propertied Women in Colonial Virginia.* New York: Routledge, 2002.
Tapley, Harriet Silvester. *History of the First Fifty Years of Printing in Salem, Massachusetts.* Salem, MA: Essex Institute, 1927.
Thwaites, Reuben Gold, ed. *The Jesuit Relations and Allied Documents: Travels and Explorations of the Jesuit Missionaries in New France, 1610–1791.* Cleveland: Burrows Brothers, 1896.
Ulrich, Laurel Thatcher. *A Midwife's Tale: The Life of Martha Ballard Based on Her Diary, 1785–1812.* New York: Alfred A. Knopf, 1990.
Waldrup, Carole Chandler. *Colonial Women: 23 Europeans Who Helped Build a Nation.* Jefferson, NC: McFarland, 1999.
Walker-Hill, Helen. *From Spirituals to Symphonies: African-American Women Composers and Their Music.* Urbana: University of Illinois Press, 2007.
Wall, James W., Flossie Martin, and Howell Boone. *The Squire, Daniel, and John Boone Families in Davie County, North Carolina.* Mocksville, NC: Davie Printing, 1982.
Weslager, C.A. *Red Men on the Brandywine.* Wilmington, DE: Hambleton Company, 1953.
Wilson, Daniel Munro. *Where American Independence Began.* Boston: Houghton Mifflin, 1902.
Wolfe, Missy. *Insubordinate Spirit.* Guilford, CT: Globe Pequot, 2012.
Wroth, Lawrence C. *The Colonial Printer.* Portland, ME: Southworth-Anthoensen Press, 1938.
______. *A History of Printing in Colonial Maryland, 1686–1776.* Baltimore: Typothetae of Baltimore, 1922.
Wulf, Karin. *Not All Wives: Women of Colonial Philadelphia.* Ithaca, NY: Cornell University Press, 2000.
Zimmerman, Jean. *The Women of the House.* New York: Harcourt, 2006.

## Articles, Chapters, Theses, Letters


Andes, Laurie. "Literacy's Role in Revolution and Independence," *Information, Medium and Society* 6:3 (2009): 9–16.

Baine, Rodney M. "Myths of Mary Musgrove," *Georgia Historical Quarterly* 76:2 (Summer 1992): 428–435.

Barker-Benfield, G.J. "Stillbirth and Sensibility: The Case of Abigail and John Adams," *Early American Studies* (Winter, 2012): 2–29.

Barnstone, Willis. "Misalliance of Theory and Practice or Parable of the Bay Psalm Book," *Translation Review* 32:1 (1990): 22–26.

Beal, Jane. "Bridget Lee Fuller," *Midwifery Today* (Autumn 2015): 50–52.

______. "'The Sainted Anne Hutchinson': Midwife of Grace (1591–1643)" *Midwifery Today* 122 (Summer 2017): 29–31.

Bellows, Barbara L. "Eliza Lucas Pinckney: The Evolution of an Icon." *South Carolina Historical Magazine* 106:2/3 (2005): 147–165.

Beltucci, Paola. "Spinners' Hands, Imperial Minds," *Technology & Culture* 62:4 (2021): 1003–1031.

Borst, Charlotte G., and Kathleen W. Jones. "As Patients and Healers: The History of Women and Medicine," *Magazine of History* 19:5 (September, 2005): 23–26.

Breen, T.H. "'Baubles of Britain': The American and Consumer Revolutions of the Eighteenth Century," *Past and Present* 119 (May 1988): 73–104.

Brown, Andrew Benson. "Domestic Arts Inventor: Sybilla Masters," *Epoch Times* (24 November 2023).

"Causton's Bluff, Deptford, Brewton Hill: Three Allied Plantations," *Georgia Historical Quarterly* 23:1 (March 1949): 28–54.

Chilton, W.B. "The Brents in Maryland and Virginia," *Virginia Magazine of History and Biography* 15:3 (January 1908): 324–329.

Colquitt, Dolores Boisfeuillet. "Peter Tondee the Carpenter," *Georgia Historical Quarterly* 10:4 (December 1926): 302–316.

"A Corner in Ancestors," *Washington Progress* (11 February 1915): 4.

Cowden, Gerald Steffens. "Spared by Lightning: The Story of Lucy (Harrison) Randolph Necks," *Virginia Magazine of History and Biography* 89:3 (July 1981): 294–307.

Dorenkamp, J.H. "The Bay Psalm Book and the Ainsworth Psalter," *Early American Literature* 7:1 (1972): 3–16.

Ellis, Evan Tyson. "The Story of a Very Old Philadelphia Drug Store," *American Journal of Pharmacy* (February 1903): 57.

Farrington, Eloise. "Incidents in the Lives of Famous Women," *Harrisburg (PA) Evening News* (24 September 1918): 12.

Gould, Christopher. "Scottish Printers and Booksellers in Colonial Charleston, S.C.," *Studies in Scottish Literature* 15:1 (1980): 202–220.

Gribble, T. Graham. "Fossil Patents," *Scientific American* 65:5 (1 August 1891): 71–72.

Gronim, Sara Stidstone. "What Jane Knew: A Woman Botanist in the Eighteenth Century," *Journal of Women's History* 19:3 (2007): 33–59.

Henry, Susan. "Sarah Goddard, Gentlewoman Printer," *Journalism and Mass Communication* 57:1 (Spring 1980): 23–30.

Hirsch, Alison Duncan. "A Tale of Two Wives," *Pennsylvania History* 61:4 (1994): 429–456.

Hunt, Rachel McMasters Miller. "William Penn and Pennsbury Manor," *Western Pennsylvania Historical Magazine* 28:1–2 (spring-summer, 1955): 5–20.

Inman, Elizabeth Murray. *Letter to James Murray* (26 February 1770): 1–4.

Keller, Kate Van Winkle. "James Alexander's Collection of Country Dances, New York, 1730," *Libraries, History, Diplomacy, and the Performing Arts*. Stuyvesant, New York: Pendragon Press, 1905, 353–370.

Kim, Sung Bok. "A New Look at the Great Landlords of Eighteenth-Century New York," *William and Mary Quarterly* 27:4 (1970): 581–614.

Kolp, John G. "'Mrs. Ann' and 'The Colonel,'" *Virginia Magazine of History and Biography* 130:3 (2022): 218–252.

Landers, Jane. "Founding Mothers: Female Rebels in Colonial New Granada and Spanish Florida," *Journal of African American History* 98:1 (2013): 7–23.
Marzolf, Marion. "The Woman Journalist: Colonial Printer to City Desk," *Journalism History* 1:4 (1974): 100–146.
Mawer, Randall R. "'Farewel Dear Babe': Bradstreet's Elegy for Elizabeth," *Early American Literature* 15:1 (Spring 1980): 29–41.
McClary, Ben H. "Nancy Ward: The Last Beloved Woman of the Cherokees," *Tennessee Historical Quarterly* 21 (1962): 352–364.
McGuire, John P. "William Bradford: Printer to Their Majesties," *American Bar Association Journal* 42:4 (April 1956): 344–347.
Menta, John. "Shaumpishuh, 'Squaw Sachem' of the Quinnipiac Indians," *Artifacts. Journal of the American Indian Archaeological Institute* 16 (1988): 3–4.
"The Minis Family," *Georgia Historical Quarterly* 1:1 (March 1917): 45–49.
Morris, Amy. "The Art of Purifying: The Bay Psalm Book and Colonial Puritanism," *Early American Literature* 4:1 (2007): 107–130.
Muldrew, Craig. "Credit and the Courts: Debt Litigation in a Seventeenth Century Urban Community," *Economic History Review* 46:1 (1993): 23–38.
Needles, Samuel H. "The Governor's Mill, and the Globe Mills, Philadelphia," *Pennsylvania Magazine of History and Biography* 8:3 (October 1884): 279–299.
Parrish, Susan Scott. "Women's Nature: Curiosity, Pastoral, and the New Science in British America," *Early American Literature* 37:2 (2002): 195–238.
Phillips, N. Taylor. "The Levy and Seixas Families of Newport and New York," *Publications of the American Jewish Historical Society* 4 (1896): 189–214.
Reed, Peter P. "The Life and Death of Anna Gardie," *Early American Literature* 51:3 (2016): 623–652.
Reese, William S. "Works of George Keith Printed in America," *Princeton University Library Chronicle* 39:2 (Winter 1978): 98–124.
Robbins, M.L. "Martha Logan," *Horticultural Science* 10:449 (1975).
Roberts, William I. "Samuel Storke: An Eighteenth-Century London Merchant Trading to the American Colonies," *Business History Review* 39:2 (Summer 1965): 147–170.
Rust, Marion. "Personal History: Martha Ballard, Laurel Thatcher Ulrich, and the Scholarly Guise in Early American Women's Studies," *Legacy* 32:2 (2015): 147:166.
Rutz-Robbins, Kristi. "'Divers Debts': Women's Participation in the Local Economy," *Early American Studies* 4:2 (2006): 425–441.
Sachs, Honor R. "The Myth of the Abandoned Wife," *Ohio Valley History* 3:4 (Winter 2003): 3–20.
Salley, A.S., Jr. "The First Presses of South Carolina," *Proceedings and Paper of the Bibliographical Society of America* 2 (1907–1908): 28–69.
Skaggs, David C. "Editorial Policies of the *Maryland Gazette*, 1765–1783," *Maryland Historical Magazine* 59 (1964), 341–342.
Smith, Beatrice Scheer. "Hannah English Williams: America's First Woman Natural History Collector," *South Carolina Historical Magazine* 87 (April 1986): 83–92.
Stephens, Pauline Tyson. "The Silk Industry in Georgia," *Georgia Review* 7:1 (Spring 1953): 39–49.
Stern, Julia. "To Relish and to Spew: Disgust as Cultural Critique in the Journal of Madam Knight," *Legacy* 14:4 (1997): 1–12.
Traister, Bryce. "Anne Hutchinson's 'Monstrous Birth' and the Feminization of Antinomianism," *Canadian Review of American Studies* 27:2 (1997): 133–158.
Volkman, Arthur G. "Lenape Basketry in Delaware," *Archaeological Society of Delaware Bulletin* 4:5 (1949): 15–18.
Walker, Gay. "Women Printers in Early American Printing History," *Yale University Library Gazette* 61:3–4 (April 1987): 116–124.
Wegiel, Anna. "The British Origins of the First American Cookbook," *New Horizons in English Studies* 1 (March 2018): 150–162.
Wernicke, Carl. "Brickmaking," *Pensacola News* (24 November 1981): 1D.
Wilbert, M I. "Elizabeth Marshall, the First Woman Pharmacist in America," *American Journal of Pharmacy* (June 1904): 271.

Yarnall, Charles. "John Bowne of Flushing, 1627–1695," *Bulletin of Friends' Historical Society of Philadelphia* 2:2 (June 1908): 44–67.

Zabin, Serena. "Women's Trading Networks and Dangerous Economies in Eighteenth-Century New York City," *Early American Studies* 4:2 (Fall 2006): 291–321.

## Electronic

Coleman, Kennedy, ed. Colonial Records of the State of Georgia. https://ugapress.manifoldapp.org/projects/colonial-records-of-the-state-of- georgia-07b79a80–769c-4b38-aa48-d967dd62b00b.

Culler, Lola Langdon. "Good Wares and Modest Manners" (thesis), https://libres.uncg.edu/ir/uncg/f/Culler_uncg_0154M_10143.pdf, 2009.

Goold, Nathan. "Falmouth Neck in the Revolution," https://www.kellscraft.com/FalmouthNeck/FalmouthNeckinTheRevolutionPage.html, (2009).

Haugh, Chris. "The Forgotten Father of Frederick," www.historysharkproductions.com/living-united-for-80-years-part-i-a-community-chest/the-forgotten-father-of- frederick (18 June 2016).

Hershkowitz, Leo. "Colonial Entrepreneurs: A Quartet of Jewish Women," https://jwa.org/encyclopedia/article/colonial-entrepreneurs-quartet-of-jewish-women.

Jeffares, Neil. Dictionary of Pastellists before 1800. http://www.pastellists.com/Articles/Johnston.pdf.

Levine, Yitzchok. "Glimpses Into American Jewish History," https://personal.stevens.edu/~llevine/colonial_jewish_bussinesswomen.pdf.

"London Town and Gardens Collection," Digital Maryland, https://collections.digitalmaryland.org/digital/collection/p17340coll24.

"Martha Ballard's Diary," PBS, www.pbs.org/wgbh/americanexperience/features/midwife-gallery-diary/ (4 March 2023).

Mills, Elizabeth Shown. "Marie Therese Coincoin," KnowLA Digital Encyclopedia of Louisiana, https://web.archive.org/web/20110612024433/http://www.knowla.org/entry.php?rec=799.

Nietering, Kristen, and Jordan Sorensen. "Historic and Architectural Resources Inventory for the Town of Guilford, Connecticut," *guilfordpreservation.org/wp*-content/uploads/2016/02/GPA-Context-Statement-Final.pdf (December 2015).

Papenfuse, Edward C. "History from the Bottom Up," www.rememberingbaltimore.net/2020/02/history-from-bottom-up-clementina.html (11 February 2020).

Perley, Sidney. "Marblehead in the Year 1700. No. 3," https://marbleheadmuseum.org/wp-content/uploads/2014/03/Perley-Final-1.pdf.

Quick, Sarah. "The Lady of Gravesend," https://www.bklynlibrary.org/blog/2022/10/25/lady-gravesend-0.

"Treasures of New York: Bowne House" (film), www.treasures-of-new-york/treasures-of-new-york-bowne-house-z4qsbw/ (29 November 2023).

Vickers, Daniel Frederick. "Maritime Labor in Colonial Massachusetts," www.proquest.com/openview/d44a0d4271fd1a658356e6efa8338563/1?pq-origsite=gscholar &cbl=18750&diss=y, 1981.

Weeks, Carl. "Peter Tondee," New Georgia Encyclopedia, www.georgiaencyclopedia.org/articles/history-archaeology/peter-tondee-ca-1723-1775/, 2018.

"The Wrap: Brea Lu Cafe Finds New Home in Westbrook," Portland Press Herald, www.pressherald.com/2023/03/29/the-wrap-brea-lu-cafe-finds-new-home-in-westbrook.

# Index

Numbers in ***bold italics*** indicate pages with illustrations


Abdel, Phoebe 192
Abenaki 4, 15, 57, 102–103, 183–185
Accomack 48
accountant 5, 53, 55, 64, 79–81, 92, 103, 114, 140–143, 153, 172; *see also* bookkeeping
acting 129–132, 231; *see also* theater
Adams, Abigail Smith 1–2, 8, 72, 154, ***190–197***, 215, 228–229, 233, 236, 238
Adams, John 2, 8, 110, 155–156, 190–197, 215–216, 228–229
Adams, John Quincy 192–193, 197, 228–230
Adams, Samuel 155, 168, 191, 227
agronomist 1, 138–140, 231
Alabama 105, 222
Albemarle Sound 42, 46, 49, 151
alcohol 38–40, 68, 82, 89–91, 197, 246
Alexander, Mary Spratt 6, ***99–100***, 233, 235, 239
Algonquin 12, 15, 33, 54, 59, 158, 225, 241, 246
Algonquin-Mohawk Wars 54
Allan, Ethan 133, 149, 201
Allen, Rachel Stout 8, ***217–219***, 233, 234, 239
almanacs 23, 65, 97, 111–113, 117, 119–120, 123, 134, 150, 186, 188, 200–201, 227, 241
*American* Cookery 8, 179, 215, 219–220
*American Magazine* 67
*American Mercury* 66, 217
American Red Cross 167
American Revolution 1, 5, 7–8, 55, 85–87, 108, 110–114, 116, 122, 134, 136–137, 144–150, 152–154, 156, 163–164, 176, 179–183, 187–200, 202–203, 208–209, 227, 229
*American Weekly Mercury* 4, 66, 85, 93, 95
Amish 73
ammunition 8, 53, 59, 105, 155, 203–204, 242, 244
Anabaptist 12, 241
Anderson, Elizabeth ***120–122***, 236–238
Anderson, Rebeckah 88, 237–238
Andros, Edmund 59
Anglicans 66, 78, 106, 116, 162; *see also* Church of England
Anglo-Cherokee War 160, 227
Angola 40, 89
Anne, Queen 65, 118
Antigua 86, 116, 138
apothecary 44, 82–87, 103–104, 189–190, 206, 231; *see also* healing
Arnold, Benedict 2, 77, 135, 155, 199, 228
Askamapoo 6, 235
Attucks, Crispus 2, 227

baker 59–61, 78, 136, 178, 181–182, 192, 209, 220, 231, 246
Ballard, Martha Moore 2, 7, ***166–173***, 233–234, 238, 239
Barbados 16, 19, 39–40, 42, 45, 66, 79, 83, 86, 89, 92, 123
Barclay, Jannette “Jane” Day 148
barges 73, 245–246
Barker, Penelope ***151–152***, 232, 239
Barton, Clara 2, 167
Bartram, John 124–125, 142
basketry 1, 71, 90, 157–159, 183–185, 196, 231
Bay Psalm Book 23–24
beans 55, 123–124, 129, 136, 158, 168, 170
Beaver War 32, 225
beer 26, 72–73, 53–54, 58–61, 77, 82–83, 104, 149, 185, 191, 218, 220, 231–232, 246
beeswax 93, 105, 144–145, 199
Bermuda 16, 48, 54, 71, 86, 123
Bible 23–24, 30, 65–66, 92–93, 115–116,

207, 246; Geneva Bible 28; King James Bible 24; Psalms 23–24
Bignall, Ann West ***204–205***, 236, 240
Bill of Rights 155–156, 188
blacksmith 8, 159–161, 176, 198, 203–204, 231, 243
Blaikley, Catherine Kaidyee ***96***, 234, 240
blankets 53, 59, 105, 129, 211
Bonifay, Mariana 8, ***222–223***, 232, 238
Bonn, Anna Maria Brendel ***205–206***, 234, 239
Book of Common Prayer 66, 96
bookbinder 1, 88, 92–95, 112, 231
bookkeeping 56, 72, 74, 79–80, 86, 92, 113–118, 141, 231
bookseller 44, 66, 93, 95, 112, 114–115, 120, 146, 153, 186–187
Boone, Daniel 164–165, 179–181
Boone, Rebecca Bryan 1, 6, ***179–181***, 233, 238–239
Boot, Anna Hack ***35–36***, 235–236, 240
*Boston Chronicle* 137
*Boston Daily Advertiser* 202
*Boston Evening Post* 126, 148, 150, 206
*Boston Gazette* 137, 148, 150, 155–157, 206
*Boston Independent Chronicle* 202
Boston Massacre 116, 135, 150, 168, 188, 227
*Boston News Letter* 115, 149
*Boston Poe-Boy* 150
Boston Port Act 116, 135, 163, 186, 227
Boston Tea Party 113, 135, 150, 155, 163, 168, 186, 208, 227
*Boston Weekly News-Letter* 206
botanist 4, 82, 104, 122, 124–125, 138–143, 158, 168, 231
Bowman, Dinah 133, 235, 239
Bowne, Dinah Underhill ***44–46***, 234, 239
Bowne, Hannah Feake ***44–46***, 234, 239
boycotts 8, 113, 135–137, 151, 156, 163, 168, 188, 192, 200, 220, 227
Bradford, Cornelia Smith 85, ***92–95***, 235, 239
Bradford, Elizabeth Sowle ***64–66***, 235, 239
Bradford, William 18, 118
Bradstreet, Anne 1–2, 5, ***27–30***, 209, 235, 239
Brainard, Abigail Foote ***209–210***, 236–238
Breintnall, Hannah 92, ***126–127***, 236, 239
Brent, Margaret 2, ***20–21***, 231, 233, 235, 237–238, 240
brewing 26, 53–54, 58–59, 61, 72–73, 82–83, 191, 232, 246
brickmaker 222–223, 232
British East India Company 157, 192, 227
Brown, Esther ***68–69***, 234, 239
Burgoyne, John 133, 136, 155
business management 7, 58–62, 74–76, 79–84, 89–90, 92, 96, 102–103, 114–118, 222, 232, 239
business planner 12, 82–84, 173–175, 232
butter 19, 40, 75, 108, 174, 192, 195, 199, 218
Byrd, William 90–91

Cacao 41
California 179
Calvert, Leonard 20–21
Calvinism 4, 114–115, 175, 208
Cambridge Press 22, 149
Campbell, Christiana 7, ***140–141***, 236, 240
Camuse, Jane Mary ***120–122***, 236, 238
Canada 100–102, 150, 226, 228; *see also* Quebec
Canarsie 12, 27
candles 53, 55, 85, 91–92, 149, 163, 169–170, 172
Caroline, Queen 121
cartographer 2, 12, 31–32, 66, 98, 232
Catawba 105, 188, 206
caterer 1, 89, 107–109, 182, 219, 232; *see also* innkeeper; taverner
Catholicism 20–21, 24, 28, 73, 94, 102, 163, 184, 213, 247
cattle rancher 6, 89–90, 107–109, 181–182, 232
Cayuga 61
ceramics 39, 75, 149, 188
chandler 76, 85, 91–92, 97, 232
Charles I 28, 33, 225
Charles II 2, 12, 21, 42, 56, 63
*Charlestown Gazette* 189
Cheer, Margaret ***129–132***, 231, 240
cheese 75, 141, 149–150, 170, 192, 199
cheesemaking 19–20, 174, 196, 198, 232
Cherokee 101, 109, 130, 146, 160, 164, 173–175, 188, 226–227, 230
Chesapeake Bay 20, 35, 42, 47–48, 62, 69, 134, 184
Chickasaw 188
childbirth 14, 18, 27–28, 30, 39, 73, 77, 83, 88, 143, 166–173, 245; *see also* midwife
chocolate 75, 89, 133, 198; *see also* cacao
Choctaw 188, 226
Church, Benjamin 86
Church of England 22, 245
cider 8, 42, 53, 127, 178–179, 192–193, 195, 197–198, 220, 247
city planning 11–13
clothing 40, 59, 156, 180, 198, 244, 246–247; clogs 148; coats 16, 26–27, 32, 59, 129, 152, 245; girdles 75; gloves 53, 61, 69, 89, 137, 156, 244; hats 53, 71–72,

136–137, 148, 153, 185, 194, 241–242, 244, 247; petticoats 148; shirts 75, 129, 198, 242; shoes 16, 46, 53, 129, 137, 153, 185, 217, 244; stockings 16, 59, 61, 69, 137, 148, 170, 198
coffee 74–75, 89, 133, 136, 172, 227; coffee shop 73, 93
coffin designer 41–42
Cogenew, Hepsibah of Chappaquiddick 6, 235
Coincoin 7, ***189–191***, 236, 238
Coit, Mehetabel Chandler ***76–78***, 233, 238
Colden, Alice Christy ***141–143***, 231–234, 239
Colden, Jane 2, ***141–143***, 234, 239
*Columbian Centinel* 202
Committee of Safety 4, 136, 242
Common Sense 201
composer 154–157, 202–203, 232
Conestoga 158
Congregationalism 18, 31, 67–68, 75, 87–88, 181, 191, 198, 207–209, 212
Connecticut 26, 31, 44, 66–67, 76, 88, 110, 198–200, 209–211, 215, 219–220, 238; Groton 67, 86, 111, 199; Hartford 8, 198, 215, 219–220; New London 3, 18, 28, 67–68, 76–77, 110–111
*Connecticut Gazette* 146
*Connecticut Journal* 115, 163, 200–201
Constitutional Convention 49, 139–140
Continental Army 5–6, 13, 85–87, 108–109, 139, 153, 155, 161–162, 192, 204, 208, 210–211, 228–229
Continental Congress 145, 153, 168, 186, 188, 190, 192, 227–228; Second Continental Congress 113, 190, 193, 228
cook 8, 179–182, 215, 219–220, 232, 246–247
Cooper, Hannah Dent 83, 234, 239–240
Cornwallis, Charles 164–165, 178, 229
Cotton, John 14, 24
*The Country Man's Help and Traders Friend* 119–120
court recorder 67–68, 232
courthouse 46, 60, 242, 246
Creek (Indians) 2, 104–107, 120, 174, 188, 226
crisis 135, 228
Crouch, Mary Wilkinson ***187–189***, 232, 235, 240
Culpeper, Thomas 63
Culpeper's Rebellion 42, 226
Cuming, Ame 6, 148, ***156–157***, 234, 236, 239
Cuming, Elizabeth 6, 148, ***156–157***, 234, 236, 239
Curaçao 39, 61, 68–69
currency 17, 61, 63, 66, 94, 97–98, 112, 114, 134, 188, 191, 201, 215

dairy 18, 73, 174, 192–193, 195–196; *see also* butter; cheese
dance 90–91, 100, 140, 149, 182–183, 214–217, 232, 241, 244, 246; teacher 90–91, 217, 232
Declaration of Independence 113, 116, 150, 153, 163, 168, 186, 201, 210–211, 220, 228
De Graffenried, Barbara Needham ***90–91***, 232, 240
Delaware 40, 83, 85, 95, 116, 110, 157, 164, 220
Delaware (Indians) 128, 157, 173–175
De Peyster, Cornelia Lubberts 6, ***99–100***, 233, 235, 239
De Torres, Simja ***81–82***, 236, 239
Devorix, Ann ***33–35***, 232–233, 239
diarist 3, 67, 76–77, 83, 166–173, 175–177
Dickinson, John 113, 134, 144–145
Dickinson, Rebecca ***175–177***, 236, 239
dictionary 129
diphtheria 168
director 8, 204–205, 232
Douglass, Sarah Hallam ***129–132***, 183, 231–232, 240
Draper, Margaret Green 92, ***149–151***, 233, 235, 239
Draper, Rachel 92, 236, 239
dry goods 6, 75, 100, 114, 127–128, 147
duffels 32, 59, 149, 243
Durant, Ann Marwood ***41–43***, 232–233, 239
Dutch Reformism 37
Dutch West India Company 12, 34, 37, 40–45, 54
dyeing 55, 138–139, 148, 158, 180
Dyer, Mary Barrett 1, 14, 28, 233–234, 239–240
dysentery 26, 34, 38, 77, 82, 108, 122, 158, 171, 184, 193

East River 26, 32, 40, 44
editor 5, 7, 24, 66, 92, 95–99, 111, 113–117, 119, 134–135, 146, 149, 184–189, 197, 232
eggs 138, 195
Elizabeth I 11, 29–30, 139
Embargo Act 172, 229
Endecott, John 12
England 24, 27–28, 30, 40, 44–45, 56, 71, 73, 79, 107, 121, 139, 145, 151, 154, 156, 183, 186, 194–195, 216, 229, 247
English Civil War 20, 33, 42, 56
Episcopalians 78–79, 162, 210
Esopus War 27, 37, 225

*Essays and Observations Physical and Literary* 143
*Essex Gazette* 115
*Essex Journal* 163
estate treasurer 3, 6, 53–56, 73, 232
Estaugh, Elizabeth Haddon ***82–84***, 234, 239
Eustis, Jane 6, ***136–137***, 149, 234, 239
exporter 19, 35, 54, 111, 123, 139, 149, 181, 229

farming 33–35, 108, 138–141, 158, 160, 162, 174–175, 190–197, 203–204, 213–214, 232
*Federal Carolina Gazette* 117
feminism 1–2, 5, 8, 11, 29, 53, 156, 193
ferries 1, 3, 11, 17, 38, 53, 67, 69–70, 87, 127–128, 159–162, 180, 232
fever 28–29, 138, 163, 185, 194
financial manager 1–2, 8, 72, 154, 190–197, 215, 228–229, 233
firewood 37, 58, 112, 170, 192, 194–197, 199
fish 32–36, 43, 48, 53, 55, 57, 60, 127, 172, 226, 233, 247; shellfish 50–51, 55, 222
fish processor 33–35, 233
fishing gear 53, 57, 59
flag maker 5, 210–212, 228, 233
flint 53
Florida 188, 213–214, 222–223, 226, 238; St. Augustine 108, 115–116, 189, 213, 226
flour 17, 43, 59, 60–61, 196, 199, 241
Flynt, Margery Hoar ***30–31***, 234, 239
food writer 8, 77, 179, 215, 219–220, 233
Foster, Diana Harris ***46–47***, 233, 239
*The Frame of the Government of the Province of Pennsilvania in America* 65
France 110, 140, 191, 194, 217, 226, 228–229; *see also* Louis XV
Franklin, Ann Smith ***96–99***, 226, 235, 239–240
Franklin, Benjamin 4, 69, 92–94, 97, 110–111, 114–115, 147, 208
Franklin, Deborah Read 92, 232, 239
Freedom of Religion 107, 114, 134
Freedom of Speech 134, 150
Freedom of the Press 65, 92, 97, 116, 119, 134, 150, 187, 226
Freeman, Indian Hannah ***157–159***, 231, 233, 239
French and Indian War 1–2, 5, 59, 75, 100, 128–129, 131–132, 139, 141, 146, 159–161, 168, 174, 176, 206, 227
fruit 7, 73, 89, 123–125, 133, 138, 150, 219, 245; apples 73, 172, 178–179, 193, 195, 197, 219; cherry 1, 26, 73–74, 82, 173; grapes 73, 83, 158, 160, 178, 195; oranges 124; peaches 83, 195; pears 178, 195; plums 1, 73, 78, 125, 170, 181, 195, 219, 241; quince 73; *see also* cider
Fuller, Bridget Lee ***17–19***, 234, 236, 239
fur trader 32, 35, 37, 39–40, 42, 54–55, 58–60, 101–102, 105, 152, 180–181, 184, 190
furniture 35–36, 139, 151, 153, 242

gardener 37, 74, 122–126, 142–143, 169–172, 195–197, 244, 246–247
"Gardener's Kalender" 123, 196
Gardie, Anna 8, ***215–217***, 231–232, 236, 239
*Gazette of the State of South-Carol*ina 117
*Gazophylacium Naturae et Artis* 51
*gens de couleur libre* 4
George I 65, 71
George II 65, 79, 90
George III 2, 41, 85, 113–114, 140, 144, 151, 155, 157, 163–164, 186, 188, 190, 200, 207, 228
Georgia 6, 105, 109, 110, 122, 163, 174, 189, 213, 226, 238; St. Catherine's Island 106–107; Savannah 89–90, 105, 107, 120–122, 162–164, 229; Sea Islands 107
glassware 32, 39, 75, 103, 126–127, 149, 244–245
Glorious Revolution of 1688 72, 226
Glover, Elizabeth Harris ***22–25***, 235, 239
Goddard, Mary Katherine ***110–114***, 235, 238, 240
Goddard, Sarah Updike ***110–114***, 235, 238, 240
*Goddard Broadside* 113
Goe, Rebecca Boone ***179–181***, 232, 234, 238
Gold Coast 181
governor 74
Graffort, Bridget Cutt ***56–58***, 235–239
grafting 7, 124, 178–179, 195
grain 35, 39–40, 42, 46, 53–55, 60, 69, 71, 101, 112, 138, 140, 165, 178, 184, 194–195, 198, 217
Great Dismal Swamp 42
Great Dying 32
Great Puritan Migration 2, 4, 12–13, 28, 33, 149
Great Savannah Fire 4, 229
Great Wagon Road 4, 161, 180, 206
Greele, Alice ***135–136***, 236, 238
Green, Anne Catharine ***133–135***, 234–235, 238
Green Mountain Boys 133
Greene, Martha Coit Hubbard ***76–78***, 234, 238
Greene, Nathanael 164, 178, 228
Greenleaf, Elizabeth Gooking ***85–87***, 231, 239
Guilford Courthouse 91, 164, 178

Guinea (country) 57, 181, 189
guns 3, 5, 7–8, 16, 40, 47, 92, 100, 105, 136, 163, 174, 188, 203–204, 244–245
gunsmith 7–8, 203–204, 233

Hager, Elizabeth "Betsy" 7–8, ***203–204***, 231, 233, 239
Hallam, Nancy 131, ***182–183***, 236, 238, 240
Hallet, Elizabeth Fones Winthrop Feake 7, ***25–27***, 231, 238
*Hamlet* 130
Hancock, John 150, 155, 191, 201, 207
Harditch, Susannah 92, 236, 240
Harvard University 7, 16, 22, 24, 28–29, 31, 78–80, 86, 149–150, 168, 207, 212
Harvard University Press 24
Hawkins, Jane Angell ***13–14***, 234, 239–240
headrights 47–48, 243
healing 2, 7, 13–14, 18, 26, 36–38, 61, 74, 77, 82–84, 139, 142, 157–159, 166–173, 178–179, 183–185, 233, 243, 246–247; *see also* apothecary
Hebert, Charlotte ***103–104***, 231, 234, 238
Henry, Patrick 155, 161
Henry IV 130
herbalist 2, 7–8, 76–78, 166–173, 217–219, 233, 234, 239
herbs 2, 7–8, 76–78, 82, 104, 142, 157–158, 166–173, 181, 184, 191, 204, 217–219, 221, 233, 234, 239
Hessians 13, 201, 228
hides 40, 60–61, 101, 103, 105, 128, 246
Hight, Allice Shannon ***127–128***, 236, 239
Hinard, Eufrosina 8, ***222–223***, 233, 236, 238
historian 1, 7, 140, 144, 154–156, 159, 173, 184, 190–197, 233
*History of the Rise, Progress, and Termination of the American Revolution* 156
Hiwassee Purchase 174
Holt, Elizabeth Hunter ***145–147***, 235, 240
hops 61, 243
horticulturist 7, 178–179, 233
Hudson River Valley 2, 4, 6, 37–40, 54–55, 60, 65, 142, 219
Huguenots 3, 78–79, 100, 114, 162, 243
hunger 18, 28, 102, 136
Huntington, Elizabeth "Betty" Foote 8, 176, ***209–210***, 235–238
hurricane 43, 78, 226
Hutchinson, Anne 1–2, 12, 14, 28, 234, 239–240
Hutchinson, Thomas 155, 157, 208

Illinois 229
illustrator 141–143, 233
immigration 21, 28, 36, 47, 49, 52, 54, 56, 59–60, 62, 64, 83, 107, 114, 116, 120–122, 126, 148–149, 153–154, 156, 159, 164–165, 225, 245
immunizer 7, 97, 113, 139, 193, 204, 233, 247
importer 6, 98–100, 111, 148, 233, 235, 239
indenturing 4, 20, 22, 35–36, 42, 67, 70, 91, 95, 105, 120, 162, 201, 243
*Independent Gazetteer* 146
*Independent New York Gazette* 146
Indiana 178, 229
indigo 48, 75, 89, 125, 127, 138–140, 143, 190
Ingles, Mary Draper ***159–161***, 231–232, 235–236, 240
Inman, Elizabeth Murray 6, 137, ***147–149***, 156–157, 234, 239
innkeeping 1, 19, 41–43, 46–47, 67–70, 73, 82–84, 90, 96, 127–128, 140, 159–162, 164–166, 173–174, 217, 233; *see also* caterer; taverner
Intolerable Acts 135, 163, 190, 192, 227
inventor 1, 41–43, 70–72, 233
investor 6, 20–21, 64, 67–68, 99–100, 190–197, 222–223, 233
iron 41, 76, 103, 129, 147, 170, 172
Iroquois 59, 141, 225

Jackson, Andrew 161, 222
Jamaica 4, 39, 48–49, 61, 68, 81, 86, 101, 131
Jans, Anneke ***36–37***, 233–234, 239
Jay, John 110, 146
Jefferson, Thomas 2, 7, 104, 110, 140, 155, 161, 172, 183, 185–186, 194, 208, 229
Jenifer, Anne Toft ***47–49***, 237, 240
Jessop, Ann Matthews Floyd 7, ***178–179***, 234, 239
Jesuits 20, 86, 102–103
Jews 43, 68–69, 73, 81, 101; Ashkenazi 101, 107; Sephardic 3, 43, 107, 246
Johnston, Henrietta Dering 6, ***78–79***, 235, 240
Jonas, Trijn Catherine ***36–37***, 234, 239
Josselyn, Margaret Commack ***16–17***, 232, 238
journalist 1, 5, 92, 110, 114–120, 149–151, 233; *see also* editor; newspaper

Kentucky 6, 128–129, 159–160, 165–166, 179–181, 211, 229, 238
keyboardist 6–7, 132–133, 139, 202–203, 234, 242
Kidd, Capt. William 58–60, 226
Kiersted, Sarah Jans ***36–38***, 233–234, 239
King Philip's War 2, 5, 16–17, 33, 76, 88, 225

kitchenware 53, 59, 75, 89, 105
Kittamaquund, Mary 2, 20
Knight, Sarah Kemble 2, ***67–68***, 232–233, 235–236, 238–239; *The Journal of Mme Knight* 67
knitter 8, 53, 170, 209
knives 59, 105

labor 5–6, 8, 11, 23, 27, 34, 40, 53, 55, 120, 123, 139, 169–170, 192–193, 210, 222; *see also* indenturing; slavery
lace 60, 137, 148, 152–153, 244
Lamboll, Elizabeth Pitts ***122–126***, 233, 240
land grants 20, 36, 47, 105, 108, 114, 151, 213, 245–246
landscaper 122–127, 142, 233, 245
law 20, 34, 41, 48, 54, 66, 68, 97, 109, 113, 115, 134, 136, 139, 185, 187, 191, 213, 231, 247; blue laws 115; lawsuits 35, 41, 46–47, 65, 70–71, 75, 105, 128, 146, 153, 166, 168–169, 191–192, 246
Lawrence, Elizabeth 92, 237, 240
Lawrence, Mary Pratt 75
Lawrence, Thomas 63
Lenape 27, 35, 37, 73, 83, 142, 157, 173–175, 225
leprosy 104
letter writing 3, 5, 29, 45, 53–55, 60, 64, 73–74, 77, 113, 134, 140, 148, 150, 164, 190–200, 209–210, 215, 244
*Letters from a Farmer in Pennsylvania to the Inhabitants of the British Colonies* 113, 134
Levy, Grace Mears ***101***, 236, 239
Lew, Margaret ***132–133***, 235, 239
Lewis, Alice Jones Mackelfresh ***69–70***, 232–233, 238
Liberty Bell 101, 127, 226
linguist 36–38, 104–107, 128–129, 233, 235, 237; *see also* translator
Linnaeus, Carolus 3, 124, 141–142, 243–244, 247
literary agent 128–129, 233
livestock 35, 42, 46–47, 55, 58–59, 61, 88, 107–108, 127–128, 139, 151, 160, 165, 168, 172, 174, 178, 189–197, 213, 217
Livingston, Alida Schuyler ***58–59***, 236, 237, 239
Logan, Martha Daniell ***122–126***, 236, 240
Louis XV 103
Louisiana 7, 103–104, 181, 189–190, 205, 222, 238; New Orleans 103, 160, 190, 222
Loyalists 11, 29, 63, 85, 108, 134, 145, 149–151, 153–155, 157, 163, 180, 186, 228
lumber 39–40, 42–43, 53, 55, 60, 109, 127, 162, 172, 191–192, 194
Lutherans 73
lyricist 1–2, 154–156, 192–193, 233

Madagascar 40
magazines 3–4, 21, 49, 51, 56, 66, 72, 74, 89, 92–93, 153
Mahican 55, 59
Maine 16–17, 52, 79, 102, 133, 135–136, 166–173, 183–185, 226, 238
malaria 26, 78, 122, 139, 171
Manny, Margaret 210, 233–234, 240
manumission 162, 190, 208, 244
Marshall, Elizabeth 8, 215, ***220–222***, 231, 240
Marston, Patience Rogers ***79–81***, 136, 231, 239
Martha, Daughter of Mehetabel Chandler Coit, ***1706–1784*** 78
Maryland 20–21, 35, 45, 47, 49, 62–64, 66, 74, 90, 110, 113, 118, 178, 188, 220, 238; Annapolis 58, 64, 130, 133–135, 183, 185; Baltimore 20, 101, 110, 113
*Maryland Gazette* 110, 133–135, 183, 185
*Maryland Journal and the Baltimore Advertiser* 111, 113
Massachusetts 52, 60, 67, 76, 86, 110, 132–133, 149, 163, 175–178, 203–204, 238–239; Boston 22, 31, 51–52, 54, 58, 61, 67–69, 79, 85–88, 101, 114, 119, 133, 136–137, 144, 146–151, 156–157, 163, 184, 191, 194, 200–202, 227; Braintree 8, 28, 30–31, 190–197; Bunker Hill 86, 113, 144, 163, 193, 198, 201, 228; Cambridge 22, 28, 85, 87, 149, 208; Charlestown 2, 15–16, 18, 29, 43, 49, 87–88, 188–189, 193, 200, 225, 228; Concord 85–86, 133, 154, 156–157, 168, 175, 192, 198, 204, 228; Lexington 8, 85–86, 133, 154, 168, 192, 198, 201, 228; Massachusetts Bay 6, 18, 31, 34, 43, 88, 191, 193, 195; Nantucket 3, 6, 52–53, 235; Plymouth 15, 18–19, 24, 154–155, 225; Salem 2, 12, 15–16, 18, 27–28, 33–34, 77, 79–81, 189, 200–202, 225
Massachusetts (Indians) 1, 28
Massachusetts Bay Colony 14, 18, 22–23, 25, 28, 30, 33–34, 79, 88, 225
*Massachusetts Mercury* 202–203
*Massachusetts Spy* 115, 137, 150, 155, 201
Masters, Sybilla Righton ***70–72***, 233, 240
Mather, Cotton 97
Mather, Richard 24
Mather, Samuel 68
*Mayflower* 17–18
McGinty, Anne Pogue ***165–166***, 234, 236
meal 59, 61, 71, 215, 219
meat 41, 46, 53, 59, 61, 75, 77, 89, 108, 127, 140, 190, 193, 195, 199, 219, 241, 243–245

medicines 38, 50, 54, 74, 82, 86, 91, 104, 150, 157–158, 181, 217–219; *see also* healing; pharmaceuticals
*Mehetabel Chandler Coit: Her Book, 1714* 77
Menape 42
Mennonites 73
merchants 1, 6–7, 16–17, 56–58, 68–69, 74–78, 88–89, 107–109, 114–118, 133–137, 179–181, 232–236, 238
Metacomet 33, 76, 226
Methodism 106, 115–116, 144, 184–185
Miami (Indians) 155
Michigan 229
midwife 1–2, 7–8, 12–14, 17–18, 28, 36–37, 87–88, 96, 162, 166–173, 205–206, 217–219, 233–234, 239–240
*A Midwife's Tale: The Life of Martha Ballard* 173
militia 5, 12, 15, 20, 26, 38, 49, 66, 70, 76, 85, 88, 100, 105, 108, 129, 132, 160, 164, 180, 184, 189, 191–193, 199, 201, 204, 213, 228, 244
milliner 6–7, 137, 147–149, 152–154, 156–158, 7, 210, 234, 239–240
milling 17, 28, 34, 40, 43, 52, 55, 58–61, 65, 71–72, 79–80, 86, 92, 96, 112, 120–122, 159, 165–166, 168, 196, 234, 236
miniaturist 6, 78–79, 235, 240
Minis, Abigail 6, ***107–109***, 232, 234–236, 238
minister 1, 7, 44–46, 53, 83, 178–179, 234
missionary 7, 83, 105, 178–179, 234
Missouri 181
Mohawk 54–55, 60, 225–227
Mohegan 4, 33, 77, 88, 198
Mohican 59
molasses 19, 41, 43, 53, 57, 61, 196, 215, 220
Montagu, Mary Wortley 113
Moody, Deborah Dunch 2, ***11–13***, 232, 237, 239
Moravians 95, 128, 205–206
mortician 2, 7, 41–42, 166–173, 178, 234
Mott, Lucretia Coffin 53
Munsee 37–38
Musgrove, Mary ***104–107***, 233, 235, 237, 238
music teacher 6–7, 30–31, 202–203, 234, 239
musicians 6–7, 30–31, 132–133, 139, 202–203, 234–235, 239–239, 242
Muskogee Creek (Indians) 2, 104–107, 174, 213, 226

Nahant 1, 15
nails 42, 53, 59
Narragansett (Indians) 2, 19, 31, 33, 76, 225
Nashaway 2
naturalist 4, 49–51, 82, 104, 122, 124–125, 138–143, 158, 168, 231, 234
Naumkeag 2, 33–32
naval impressment 3, 136, 229, 245
Navigation Act 43, 226
Necks, Lucy Harrison Randolph 7, ***152–154***, 234, 240
needlework 29, 75, 102–103, 212, 176–177, 243, 234, 243; teacher 6, 51–52, 76–78,102, 104, 137, 147–149, 156–157, 212, 234, 239
Nevis 43, 48–49
*New England Courant* 97, 226
New Hampshire 16, 56, 110, 115, 127–128, 132, 183–184, 212, 239; Portsmouth 127–128, 200
*New Hampshire Gazette* 115
*New Hampshire Mercury and General Advertiser* 200
New Jersey 65–66, 71, 82, 85, 91, 95, 100–101, 110, 119, 143, 145, 155, 158, 178, 181, 199, 220, 239; Haddonfield 82–84; Trenton 201, 228
*New York Gazette, or the Weekly Postboy* 146
*New York Journal* 115, 146
*New-York Weekly Journal* 118–119
*Newbury and Marblehead Advertiser* 200
Newfoundland 80, 226
*Newport Mercury* 97–98, 207
newspapers 4, 5, 50, 62–64, 66, 91–95, 97, 110–114, 116, 133, 137, 165, 185, 227, 241; *see also* printer; publisher
New York 2, 13, 32, 40, 58, 67, 69, 73, 89, 92, 101, 110, 119, 142, 144, 169, 178, 199, 239; Albany 37, 53–55, 58–59, 78, 100; Coney Island 12–13; Gravesend 11–13; Long Island 12–13, 19, 27, 32, 37, 44–45, 228; Manhattan Island 26, 37, 69, 100–101, 118–120, 130; New York City 54, 58, 61, 65–66, 78, 95, 100, 195, 202; Saratoga 59, 61, 133, 168, 201, 228; Ticonderoga 87, 133
Nicholson, Francis 64
Nipmuck 2, 76, 226
Nonhelema Hokolesqua ***128–129***, 233, 237, 239
North Carolina 7–8, 38, 41–44, 46–47, 89, 107, 110, 122, 148, 151–153, 160, 164, 178–181, 217–219, 226–229, 239
Northwest Indian War 129, 229
Nova Scotia 6, 149, 186; Halifax 79, 150, 157
novels 93, 97, 113, 115, 138–139, 161
Noyes, Elizabeth Ann Sanford ***88–89***, 234, 240

nuns 102–103
nurse 37, 77, 86, 88, 102–104, 135–136, 173, 189, 204–206, 211, 234
Nuthead, Dinah ***62–64***, 235, 238
Nyack (Indians) 27

Ockett, Molly 2, ***183–185***, 231–233, 236, 238
Oglethorpe, James Edward 2, 105–106, 108, 115, 120–121, 226
Ohio 128–129, 155, 159–160, 166, 178–179, 181, 229, 239
Old American Company 131, 182–183, 105, 215–217
optician 92, 126–127, 234, 244–245
Oratam 38
orchardist 79, 123, 178–179, 191; *see also* fruit
organist 6–7, 202–203, 234
Oswald, Elizabeth Holt ***145–147***, 235, 239
Othello 98, 130
Otis, James 154, 191

Paine, Thomas 2, 136, 201, 228
paint 6, 59, 78–79, 98, 102–103, 144, 183, 245
pamphleteer 44, 50, 65, 95, 97, 112–115, 118, 133, 144, 154–157, 186, 201, 227, 234
paper 24, 32, 40, 50, 63, 68, 65, 68, 75, 78, 92–93, 112, 114, 118–119, 121, 133, 158, 185, 201, 211, 227, 241, 243–245
patriots 87, 134, 136–137, 145–146, 149–150, 153, 157, 160, 163–165, 168, 186–188, 192, 199–200, 202–203, 215, 219, 220
patroons 4, 6, 12, 54, 58, 245
Pawtucket Confederation 15
Paxton Boys 158
Penn, Hannah Callowhill 4, ***72–74***, 235, 237, 240
Penn, Letitia 73
Penn, William 65, 71–72, 82, 93, 126, 158
Pennsylvania 65, 72, 74, 92, 110, 129, 157–159, 164, 178, 205–206, 239; Bristol 26, 52, 56, 72–75, 144; Germantown 71, 94, 211, 228; Philadelphia 65–66, 69, 71, 73, 82, 85, 90–92, 95, 101, 110, 113, 119, 125, 130, 133, 143–145, 159–161, 188, 195, 199, 201, 210–212, 215–217, 221–223, 226, 228; Valley Forge 155, 228
*Pennsylvania Chronicle and Universal Advertiser* 113, 115
*Pennsylvania Gazette* 114, 115, 126
*Pennsylvania Journal* 66
Pennsylvania Land Company 82
Penobscot 184
Penrose, Elizabeth ***89–90***, 232, 236, 238
pepper 75, 89
Pequot 32, 225
Pequot War 32, 225
Peters, Lois Crary 5, ***198–200***, 235, 238
pewterware 75
pharmaceuticals 25–27, 82–85, 140, 166–173, 189, 215; *see also* medicines
pharmacist 2, 7, 82–83, 87, 104, 140, 166–173, 220–221, 234
*Die Philadelphische Zeitung* 114
philanthropy 58, 156, 235
Philipse, Margaret Hardenbroeck 6, ***39–40***, 236, 239
Philipse Manor 39–41
Phillips, Elizabeth ***87–88***, 234, 239
pianist 6–7, 132–133, 202–203, 234–235, 238
pilgrims 2, 4, 18, 28, 225
Pinckney, Eliza Lucas 1, 73, ***138–140***, 231, 235, 240
Pinheiro, Esther 2, ***43–44***, 236–237, 239
piracy 2, 13, 40, 42, 59–60, 68, 72, 78, 80, 150, 226
pitch 42, 138
Pitt, William 144–145, 188
plague 11, 18, 22, 32
planter 1, 6, 73, 107–109, 138–140, 151–152, 226, 232, 234–236, 238
poet 1–2, 5, 27–30, 64, 98, 154–157, 192–193, 197, 200, 206–210, 233–235, 239
politician 4, 72–74, 235, 245
Ponduck 2
portraitist 6, 78–79, 235
Portuguese 60, 81
postmaster 110–118, 234–235
potatoes 192, 195, 197
pottery 39, 188
Pratt, Elizabeth Woodberry 7, ***74–76***, 88, 234, 240
Presbyterians 73, 131, 158, 207
primers 97, 115
*The Prince of Parthia* 130, 226
printer 7, 22, 62–65, 85, 92–99, 110–120, 133–135, 143–147, 149–151, 185–189, 200–202, 226, 232–233, 235, 239–240
prisoners of war 5, 42, 57, 102, 108, 116, 119, 123, 129, 145, 149, 162, 172, 189, 211, 220, 245–247
privateering 2, 35, 75, 80, 85–87, 136, 182, 189, 211, 226
prostitution 89, 198
Protestants 63, 206, 226, 245
*Providence Gazette and Country Journal* 111–112, 115
publisher 62–65, 92–95, 110–120, 133, 135, 143–145, 185–189, 200–202, 235
Purcell, Mary 137
Puritans 4, 14, 23–24, 27–28, 30, 44–45, 76, 97, 102, 131

Quakers 4, 13–14, 27, 44–45, 52–53, 63–66, 70, 72–75, 83, 92, 124, 126–127, 131, 143, 158, 178–181, 210, 220
Quamino, Duchess ***181–182***, 231–232, 240
quartering 192, 211
Quebec 102–103, 150, 184, 225, 228
Queen Anne's War 52, 102, 226
quilting 75, 209
Quinnipiac 31–33

railroads 100
real estate broker 2, 5–6, 15–16, 20–21, 31–33, 35–36, 39, 47–49, 54–55, 58, 67–68, 70, 73, 79, 82, 99–100, 105, 108–109, 139, 147–149, 164–165, 231–233, 235–240, 246
Reformed Church 39; German Reformed 73, 118
Regulators 164, 246
Rensselaerswyck 6, 37, 54–55, 58, 60
Rhode Island 14, 19, 32, 66, 83, 85, 95, 97, 110–111, 154, 187, 240; Narragansett Bay 14, 88, 111; Newport 75, 88–89, 97, 148, 181–182, 207; Providence 75, 98–99, 110–112, 130, 189
*Rhode Island Gazette* 97
Rice 138–139, 151, 226
Richard III 130
Rind, Clementina 7, ***185–187***, 235, 240
Ross, Elizabeth "Betsy" Griscom 5, ***210–212***, 228, 233, 236–237, 240
Royal African Company 81
Royal Society 50
rum 41, 57, 59, 61, 69, 89, 105, 181, 184
Russell, Sarah Hood ***200–202***, 235, 239

Saco (Indians) 17
saddler 127, 198–200, 235
St. Thomas 69
*Salem Gazette* 200–201
Salem witch trials 77
salt 43, 57, 159–161
saltmaker 159–161, 231–232, 235
sand 61, 244
sandstone 21
Santee 139
Sasacacha 53
satire 1–2, 154–156, 192–193, 197, 233–236, 239
Scarburgh, Edmund 47–48
scarlet fever 167, 169
school 18, 52, 68, 102–103, 115, 123, 140–141, 148, 157, 162, 202, 243, 247
Schuyler, Margaretha Brants van Slichtenhorst ***58–62***, 232, 234, 239
sculptor 143–145, 236
scurvy 18, 28, 220
seamstress 5, 8, 41–42, 75, 136–137, 158, 175–177, 198–200, 206, 209–212, 228, 235–238
seaweed 195–196
secretary 1–2, 8, 72, 154, 190–197, 215, 228–229, 236
seed merchant 122–126, 139, 142, 178–179, 236
Seminole 4
Seneca 61
Senegal 181–182, 206, 213
sermons 24, 44, 64, 112, 115, 119, 200, 243
Sewall, Samuel 52
sewing notions 53, 89, 194, 217
Shaumpishuh ***31–33***, 232, 235
Shawnee 128–129, 159–161, 165, 180
Sherman, Rebecca 211–212
ship owner 35, 49
shipping agent 2, 6, 11, 17, 28, 32, 35, 39–43, 47–48, 55, 57–61, 79, 85, 87, 95, 98, 100–101, 107, 111, 115, 122, 134, 139, 150, 186–187, 190, 232, 236–237, 239, 243, 245–246
shipwreck 48, 80
shopkeeper 1–2, 5, 8, 67–68, 72, 85, 92–95, 118–120, 148, 154, 156–157, 190–197, 215, 228–229, 232–236, 238–239
silk 75, 89, 120–122, 137, 151, 153, 157, 162, 172, 197
silk winder 120–122, 236–238
silverware 53–54, 75, 148, 151, 153
Simmons, Amelia 8, 179, 215, ***219–220***, 233, 238
singer 8, 131, 182–183, 215–217, 231–232, 236, 240, 242, 244
Sintsink (Indians) 40
Siwanoy 12, 14, 26
slave dealer 7–8, 35–36, 58–59, 81–82, 140, 161–162, 189–191, 222–223, 235–236
slavery 32, 35, 38–41, 43, 45, 48, 58, 60–61, 69, 74–75, 77, 81–82, 89, 96, 101–102, 108–109, 115–116, 122–123, 128, 132–133, 138, 140–141, 148, 151–152, 159–162, 166, 181–182, 186, 189–190, 193, 200, 206–209, 213–214, 222–223, 226, 242, 244
smallpox 7, 15, 18, 22, 28, 32, 49, 52, 54, 77, 80, 83, 86, 88, 97, 113, 115, 132–133, 135, 139, 164, 193, 210
Smith, Joan Barton ***19–20***, 233, 240
smuggling 2, 42, 54, 81, 98, 136, 226
soap 43, 53, 61, 85, 91, 163, 170
Sons of Liberty 2, 7, 112–113, 116, 134, 146, 150, 154, 162–163, 181, 186–187, 227, 246
South Carolina 49–51, 73, 109–110, 122–126, 138–140, 143, 150, 162, 174, 213, 226–227, 229, 240; Charleston 6, 11, 49–51, 69, 78–79, 89–90, 105, 108, 110,

114–118, 129–132, 138–139, 144, 163, 187, 202, 205, 229
South Carolina Constitution 110, 117
*South Carolina Gazette* 114, 123, 202
*South Carolina Gazetteer; and Country Journal* 187
spice 40, 61, 75, 77, 89, 138, 220
spinning 53, 73, 158, 170, 174, 180, 209–210
Spratt, Maria de Peyster Provoost 6, ***99–100***, 235, 239
spying 143–145
Squam 53
squaw 246
Squaw Sachem ***15–16***, 235, 239
stage manager 204–205, 236
Stagg, Mary ***90–91***, 231–232, 240
Stamp Act 2, 74, 112–113, 133, 149, 163, 185, 187, 191, 198, 207, 227
*Star Gazette of South Carolina* 110
Starbuck, Mary Coffin ***52–53***, 237, 239
*State Gazette of South Carolina* 117
stationer 93, 112, 115, 120, 187, 200
Steele, Elizabeth Maxwell ***164–165***, 235–236, 239
Stone, William 21
Stono Revolt 138
storyteller 2, 183–185, 231–233, 236, 238
Stuyvesant, Peter 13, 37, 40, 45, 54, 225
suffrage 20, 53
sugar 41, 43, 48, 57, 61, 75, 88–89, 98, 138, 148, 172, 193, 196; maple 180–181
*A Summary View of the Rights of British America* 186
swords 40

tailor 1, 98, 200, 206–209, 235–236
*Tales of a Wayside Inn* 83–84
tanning 36, 48, 57, 127, 160
Tappan 40
tar 42, 61, 138
taverner 6–7, 46–47, 53, 64, 68–70, 89–90, 92, 102, 107–109, 126–128, 135–136, 140–141, 159–166, 168, 181, 231–232, 234–236, 238–240
taxation 2, 13, 18, 29, 55, 69, 71, 81, 92, 99, 112–113, 119, 128, 133–134, 154–155, 163, 172, 185–186, 188–190, 195, 198, 227–228
tea 14, 26, 75, 82, 89, 136–137, 142, 157, 168, 192, 227
Tea Act 151, 227
teacher 2, 6–7, 17–19, 30–31, 51–52, 2, 67–68, 76–78, 88, 90–91, 102, 104, 122–126, 137, 147–149, 156–157, 202–203, 212, 217, 232–239
Tennessee 173–175, 227, 240
*The Tenth Muse* 29–30
textiles 35, 39–40, 53, 57, 60, 69, 75, 89, 100, 105, 127, 137, 149, 151, 160, 163, 176, 199, 209–210, 217, 227, 241–247; designer 165–166, 234, 236
theater 8, 91, 129–132, 144, 153, 161, 182–183, 203–205, 215–217, 236, 241–242, 244, 246
Timothy, Ann 110, ***114–118***, 235, 240
Timothy, Elizabeth ***114–118***, 234–235, 240
tobacco 35, 39–40, 47–48, 50, 59, 61, 63, 67, 69–70, 81, 127, 134, 152–153, 190; pipes 53, 59, 149
Tondee, Lucy Mouse 7, ***162–164***, 236, 238
tools 40, 57, 59, 75, 89, 105, 194, 196
town manager 2, 11–13, 232, 237, 239
Townsend, Mary Hodges ***89–90***, 236, 238
Townshend Acts 134, 227
trader 2, 4, 6, 20–21, 32, 37, 39–41, 43, 47–49, 52–53, 58–61, 69, 72–74, 76, 79–81, 86, 88, 99–100, 104–107, 128–129, 150, 166–173, 194, 231–233, 235–240, 247
translation 37–38, 106, 128–129, 141, 158, 213
Treaty of Paris 110, 113, 115, 117, 119, 121, 164, 229
Triangle Trade 89
tuberculosis 71, 142, 154
Tunix 33
Turfrey, Mary Baldwin ***51–52***, 234, 239
typhoid fever 197
typhus 77, 244

Unitarianism 182, 192, 203
U.S. Constitution 110, 117, 140, 155
Upham, Hephzibah Neal ***212***, 234, 239
upholstery 5, 100, 210–212, 228, 237
Ursulines 3, 102–104, 247
usury 20

Van Rensselaer, Maria van Cortlandt 3, 6, ***53–56***, 73, 231–232, 239
variolation 7, 97, 113, 139, 193, 204, 247
venereal disease 198
Vermont 86, 156, 177–178, 194, 211
Vetch, Margaret Livingston ***58–61***, 232, 237–239
veterinarian 169
vinegar 26, 39, 42, 101, 104
Virginia 20–21, 35–36, 47, 85, 90, 100, 108, 110, 130, 146, 152–154, 159–162, 165, 178, 180, 227, 240; Jamestown 62–63; Richmond 162, 174, 204–205, 228; Williamsburg 69, 90, 96, 129–132, 140–141, 143–144, 152–154, 161, 182, 226, 228; Yorktown 135, 146, 229
*Virginia Gazette* 91, 130, 144, 146, 185–187

Vobe, Jane 7, 140, ***161–162***, 236, 240
von Hagen, Elizabeth Johanetta Catherine 6–7, ***202–203***, 234, 239
von Steuben, Friedrich 161

Wabanaki 102–103, 226
Wampage 14
Wampanoag 2, 4–6, 53, 76, 226
Ward, Nancy 1, ***173–175***, 232–233, 240
Warehouses 40, 53, 57, 79, 81, 88, 130, 203, 221
War of 1812 129, 229
War of Jenkins's Ear 106, 226
warrants 26, 63
Warren, Joseph 86, 168, 191, 193, 227
Warren, Mercy Otis 1–2, ***154–156***, 192–193, 197, 233–236, 239
Washington, George 5, 13, 41, 85–86, 108, 135, 145, 155, 161, 183, 185, 199, 201–202, 208, 210, 216, 228–229
Washington, Martha Custis 36, 154, 182
Waxhaw (Indians) 105
weaving 8, 73, 157–158, 165, 174, 176, 183–185, 196, 203, 209–210, 217, 231, 235–238, 243
Wells, Rachel Lovell ***143–145***, 236, 239
Wenuchus 16
Wesleyanism 115
West, Margaretta Sully 8, ***204–205***, 231–232, 240
West India Company 55
West Virginia 160, 181
whalebone stays 89, 126, 137, 153, 176
wharf 40, 57, 79, 88–89, 97, 115, 128, 181, 206
Wheatley, Phillis 1, 98, 200, ***206–209***, 235, 239
Wheelwright, Esther ***102–103***, 232, 238
Wicocombe 42–43
Wiechquaeskeck 40
Wiggins, Ana Gallum "Nansi" 8, ***213–214***, 232, 238, 248
Will Probate 17, 20, 35, 43, 46, 64, 67, 69, 74, 81, 88, 91–92, 96, 101, 109, 113, 116, 127, 135, 140, 146, 152, 177, 185–186, 197, 213, 222
William III and Mary II 63, 65, 73, 226
Williams, Hannah English ***49–51***, 234, 240
Williams, Roger 4, 111
wine 41, 53, 73–74, 77, 136, 163, 220
Winthrop, John 14, 16, 22, 26, 28, 33, 48, 67
Winthrop Fleet 4, 28
Wisconsin 229
Wishart, Ann Battson 85, ***91–92***, 232, 240
wool 32, 40, 52–53, 88, 112, 170, 195, 217
Woolman, Sarah Ellis 83, 236, 239
Wright, Patience Lovell ***143–145***, 236, 240
Wunnatuckquannum 5–6, 235

Yamasee War 105, 120, 151, 226
"Yankee Doodle" 133
yarn spinner 8, 176, 209–210, 235–238
Yellow Fever 104, 114, 131, 211
Young, Rebecca ***210–212***, 236–237, 240

Zenger, Anna Catharina 1, 5, ***118–120***, 234–236, 239
Zenger, Peter 114–118

www.ingramcontent.com/pod-product-compliance
Ingram Content Group UK Ltd.
Pitfield, Milton Keynes, MK11 3LW, UK
UKHW041835100926
8556IPUK00018B/980

9 781476 697734